Contents

Discover Santa Fe, Taos &
Albuquerque.................. **6**
  10 Top Experiences 10
  Planning Your Trip 18
  The Best of Santa Fe, Taos &
    Albuquerque.................. 21
  • Life Imitates Art................ 22
  • High Desert Adventure 24
  Weekend Getaways............... 24
  American Indian Heritage 27
  • New Mexico's Cultural Mix....... 28
  Hiking and Mountain Biking 28
  • The Best of Southwest Cuisine.... 30

Santa Fe........................ **31**
  Sights 36
  Entertainment and Events......... 52
  Shopping 58
  Sports and Recreation............ 61
  Food 68
  Accommodations 76
  Outside Santa Fe................ 79
  Information and Services 105
  Getting There and Around 107

Taos **108**
  Sights 113
  Entertainment and Events......... 128
  Shopping 131
  Sports and Recreation............ 132
  Food 137
  Accommodations 142
  The Road to Chama.............. 146
  The Enchanted Circle 152
  Information and Services 159
  Getting There and Around 160

Albuquerque.................... **161**
  Sights 166
  Entertainment and Events......... 181
  Shopping 186
  Sports and Recreation............ 188
  Food 191
  Accommodations 197
  Outside Albuquerque............. 200
  Information and Services 214
  Getting There and Around 215

Background **217**
  The Landscape 218
  Plants and Animals 220
  History......................... 224
  Government and Economy........ 228
  Local Culture................... 229
  The Arts........................ 232

Essentials **236**
  Transportation.................. 237
  Food and Accommodations 239
  Travel Tips 242
  Health and Safety 246

Resources **248**
  Glossary........................ 248
  Suggested Reading.............. 250
  Internet Resources 254

Index **256**

List of Maps.................... **263**

Santa Fe, Taos & Albuquerque

Breathtakingly beautiful, culturally rich, and heaving with history, this landscape holds an unmistakable cinematic quality. It's easy to feel as if you're stepping onto a grand stage, about to be swept up into a timeless epic—a feeling not lost on New Mexico's burgeoning film industry. There are good reasons for this, of course, not the least of which are the numerous Native American pueblos, cliff dwellings, and petroglyphs that speak to an unbroken heritage that dates back hundreds of years.

With its signature adobe buildings and dusty lanes set against the imposing backdrop of the Sangre de Cristo Mountains, Santa Fe looks every bit the country's oldest state capital. Its identity, like much of New Mexico, is shaped in equal measure by centuries' long Spanish American and Native American influences, yet this is also a city that has been forged by the artists who continue to be drawn to and inspired by its elemental and otherworldly beauty. Taos, too, is a mecca for creative types, yet its greater isolation makes it feel off the grid; its free-spirited residents proudly self-reliant. Far to the south, the old Route 66 slices through the physical heart of Albuquerque, in some ways a literal reminder

Clockwise from top left: water tower in Santa Fe's Railyard district; iconography on Santa Fe's Canyon Road; San Francisco de Asis Church in Taos; Kasha-Katuwe Tent Rocks National Monument; flowers near Red River; Santa Fe Plaza at Christmas.

of the city's strong connection to its past as its forward-thinking efforts to attract tech startups gain traction.

Make no mistake: This is the high desert, and forgiveness is not in its nature. That said, come prepared for outdoor adventures and you'll be rewarded. From Class IV rafting trips buoyed by snowmelt in the spring to perspective-shifting balloon rides in the fall, and hair-raising black diamond ski runs in the winter, the choices before you could occupy a lifetime.

It's this boundlessness—be it in terms of time, vistas, or options—that is perhaps this region's greatest appeal. It's not a place easily contained or defined and it's all the better for it. So, settle back and sample what you can at your own pace. Chances are you will be back for more.

Clockwise from top left: truck outside Taos; votive candles at the Santuario de Chimayó; Rancho de las Golondrinas; dried chile *ristra*.

10 TOP
EXPERIENCES

1 Taos Pueblo: Seemingly rising organically from the earth, these stepped adobe buildings make up the oldest continually inhabited community in the United States (page 122).

2 **Art in Santa Fe:** Art is life in Santa Fe—and **Canyon Road** is its beating heart (page 44).

3 **Ghost Ranch:** See the house where **Georgia O'Keeffe** created her art—and the surrounding landscape that inspired it (page 96).

>>>

4 **Southwest Cuisine:** In New Mexico, the food is as creative as the art and as distinctive as the landscape (page 30).

5 **Rafting the Rio Grande Gorge:** Experience massive scale on an intimate level from the water (page 134).

>>>

6 **Hiking:** Pull on a pairs of hiking boots and you can have this natural splendor all to yourself (page 28).

>>>

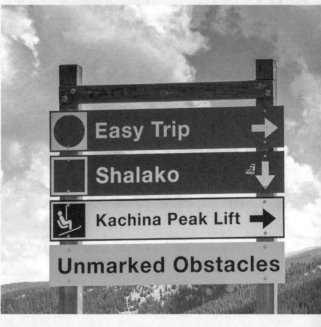

7 **Acoma Pueblo:** Built atop a windswept mesa, the Sky City has persevered for centuries (page 200).

8 **Native American Culture:** The historic culture of the pueblos can be awe inspiring, but the living culture is just as memorable (pages 27, 83, 131, and 185).

9 Ballooning: Take a colorful trip into New Mexico's endless blue sky (page 188).

10 Mountain Biking: Adventure begins with a set of wheels (page 28).

17

Planning Your Trip

Where to Go

Santa Fe

Marked by winding streets and thick-walled adobe homes, New Mexico's picturesque capital is intimate in scale and exudes a golden glow. Scores of **galleries**—including those lining fabled Canyon Road—are a major draw, as are **museums** for state history, Native American and folk art, and more. Scenic **hiking** trails are just a few minutes' drive— not far beyond are the cliff dwellings at **Bandelier National Monument,** as well as the landscape that inspired painter Georgia O'Keeffe at **Abiquiu,** and the birthplace of the atomic bomb at **Los Alamos.**

Taos

A small town of about 6,000, Taos is home to **artists,** trust-fund **hippies, spiritual seekers,** and ski bums—in addition to the Spanish

the view south from Los Alamos

and American Indian families who've called the place home for centuries. There's some sightseeing, at the ancient **Taos Pueblo,** an iconic church, and a handful of small museums, while the **Taos Ski Valley** continues to cement its world-class status. But its atmosphere, cultivated in mellow coffee shops and **hidden hot springs,** is the real attraction. Make a day drive around the **Enchanted Circle,** a loop of two-lane roads through high valleys.

Albuquerque

A modern Western city, and the state's biggest, Albuquerque sprawls at the base of the **Sandia Mountains.** It's proud of its **Route 66** heritage, but it's also preserving **farmland** along the **Rio Grande** and redesigning its downtown core. To the west, the breathtaking **Acoma Pueblo** sits

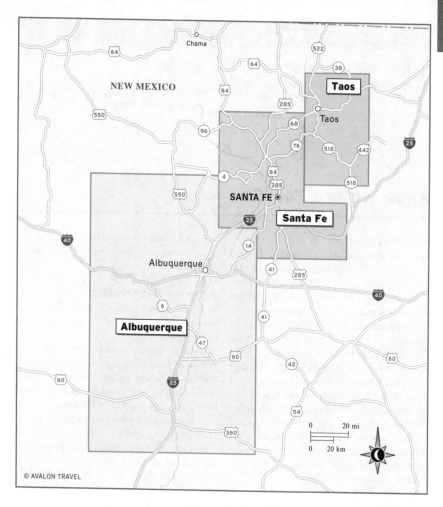

© AVALON TRAVEL

atop a monolithic mesa, while the wetlands of the **Bosque del Apache National Wildlife Refuge** to the south attract thousands of birds.

Head north to Santa Fe through the former ghost towns of the **Turquoise Trail** or alongside the red rocks of the **Jemez Mountains.**

If You Have . . .

- **THREE DAYS:** Pick one city to explore.

- **FIVE DAYS:** Visit Santa Fe, with a night in Taos; or do Albuquerque, with a night in Santa Fe.

- **ONE WEEK:** From Santa Fe, add a day in Abiquiu and Bandelier; from Albuquerque, visit Acoma.

- **TWO WEEKS:** Do it all, including the Jemez Mountains and the Bosque.

Know Before You Go

High Seasons

About 300 days of sunshine annually mean just about anytime is the right time to visit. **High season** for tourism is mid-May to mid-September, but the early summer can be hot, windy, and dry, with a risk of forest fires. The weather is far more pleasant from **July** on, when the day's heat is usually tamed with a strong, brief rainstorm in the afternoon, and the landscape is shrouded in green hues. **Summer** is the only time to hike at higher elevations, as many trails are still snow covered as late as May. If you want to go **rafting,** plan on late May-early June, when the snowmelt makes the rivers run high and wild. **Winter** sees a surge of visitors heading straight to the slopes, and traditional celebrations preceding Christmas are wonderful; many sights are closed or have limited hours, however.

The **shoulder seasons** have their own appeal and can be cheaper, particularly in **April,** when ski season has wound down, and in **November,** when it hasn't gotten started. Note that **Taos Pueblo closes** to visitors for about 10 weeks February-April. **Spring** weather brings the most variables, with chances of snowfall or ceaseless hot winds—and roads can be bogged down with mud. In the **fall,** the crowds disperse, leaving crisp temperatures and generally clear skies through late October—great **hiking** weather, especially among the aspen trees, which turn a brilliant yellow.

Advance Reservations

New Mexico is a just-show-up kind of place, but a few special events and activities require some forethought.

If you're planning a visit between **Christmas** and **New Year's,** during Santa Fe's **Spanish Market** (July) and **Indian Market** (August), or for Albuquerque's **Balloon Fiesta** (October), book a hotel **6-8 months in advance.**

Attending a **ceremonial dance** is worth planning a trip around. They occur several times a year at every pueblo, on village feast days, Catholic holidays, and around seasonal turning points. Check the schedules for **Taos Pueblo** (page 131), as well as pueblos around **Santa Fe** (page 83) and **Albuquerque** (page 185).

The **Georgia O'Keeffe Home** (page 94) in Abiquiu is open to guided tours mid-March through November; book at least a month in advance.

Online ticket sales for the **Santa Fe Opera** (page 54) start in October for the July and August summer season. Book in the winter for the best seat selection.

The Best of Santa Fe, Taos & Albuquerque

While you could conceivably explore Santa Fe, Taos, and Albuquerque for weeks on end, seeking out ever more remote hiking trails and sweeping vistas, six days gives just enough time to appreciate the distinct character of each community.

Day 1

Arrive at Albuquerque's Sunport airport; make your way directly to **Santa Fe.** For old-school style, stay at La Fonda—it's a short stroll to **The Shed** for dinner, and you can cap the evening with a margarita in the lively hotel lobby bar.

Day 2

Start with a breakfast burrito at **Tia Sophia's,** then stroll around the plaza. Depending on your interests, visit the history museum at the **Palace of the Governors** or the **New Mexico Museum of Art.** Pop in to see the winding staircase at the **Loretto Chapel,** then cruise the galleries on Canyon Road, finishing up with drinks and tapas, and maybe even dancing at **El Farol.**

Day 3

Get an early start to **Bandelier National Monument,** followed by lunch at **El Parasol** in Española. In midafternoon, return to Santa Fe to explore the **House of Eternal Return,** followed by happy hour drinks in the **Railyard** at **Cowgirl BBQ.** Settle in for dinner at **Joseph's** or **Bouche.**

Day 4

Drive to **Taos** via the low road, detouring to the pilgrimage site of **Chimayó.** Stop for lunch at **Zuly's** in Dixon. In Taos, head straight to **Taos Pueblo.** Admire the sunset at the **Rio Grande Gorge,** then stop at the **Adobe Bar** at the **Taos Inn** for a margarita and head up the road for dinner at **The Love Apple** or **Orlando's.**

the House of Eternal Return in the Meow Wolf Art Complex

Life Imitates Art

Mabel Dodge Luhan House

Santa Fe and Taos have long histories of fostering creative output, much of it inspired by the surrounding landscape. Tour northern New Mexico with a creative eye, and soon you'll be recognizing locations from paintings and maybe find yourself ready to buy . . . or to dive into some work of your own.

SANTA FE

Art lovers need not spend all their time in museums (though there are some great ones). It can be just as rewarding to visit studios, talk with artists, and see how objects are made. Drive the **High Road to Taos** (page 100) to see woodworkers' studios and weavers' workshops.

Northwest of Santa Fe lies Abiquiu, turf that painter Georgia O'Keeffe called her own, even if she had only a small house in town and a studio at **Ghost Ranch** (page 96). But everything under the sway of flat-topped Pedernal Peak, so often depicted in her work, was grist for her creativity.

Just north of Santa Fe, **Tesuque Glassworks** (page 58) has an open glassblowing studio, where you'll usually find some craftspeople at work. It's remarkable to see such heavy technology creating what are often very delicate pieces.

TAOS

Taos is the best place to see where and how local artists lived: At the **Mabel Dodge Luhan House** (page 119), now an inn, Mabel's own bed is still in place in her sunlit room with views of Taos Mountain. Elsewhere in town, the **E. L. Blumenschein Home** (page 115) and **Taos Art Museum at Fechin House** (page 118) both show how artists adapted their residences to their personal styles.

Perhaps the most illuminating spot is Dorothy Brett's miniscule cabin at the **D. H. Lawrence Ranch** (page 158), barely big enough for a bed and a woodstove. Across the yard, in front of Lawrence's only slightly larger home, is the towering pine depicted in Georgia O'Keeffe's *The Lawrence Tree*. Get her perspective, and the curving lines of the painting come into focus: "There was a long weathered carpenter's bench under the tall tree in front of the little old house that Lawrence had lived in there. I often lay on that bench looking up into the tree . . . past the trunk and up into the branches. It was particularly fine at night with the stars above the tree."

Tinkertown Museum

Day 5

In the morning, have breakfast at **Gutiz** or **Michael's Kitchen**, and, on your way out of town, stop by **San Francisco de Asis Church.** Drive back to **Albuquerque** via the high road past Truchas and Las Trampas, then along the **Turquoise Trail**, stopping for lunch in **Cerrillos** or **Madrid** before visiting the **Tinkertown Museum.** In Albuquerque, take a sunset ride up the **Sandia Peak Tramway.** Enjoy dinner and drinks downtown.

Day 6

Have a big breakfast at **The Frontier** and, if time allows, stroll around **Nob Hill** before catching your plane out of the Albuquerque airport.

Stark, unforgiving, rugged—all words used to describe the high desert, though they fall short of capturing its essence. Marked by jagged mountains, endless and impossibly blue skies, and flora that endures against all odds, this landscape has a primal beauty that can impact you to your core. The sheer vastness is intoxicating; the adventures that await are suitably epic.

- **Valles Caldera National Preserve:** With mountain streams, thick alpine forests, and herds of elk grazing seemingly endless lush meadows, this pristine 13-mile-wide preserve beckons backcountry **hikers, mountain bikers,** and **cross-country skiers** (page 90).

- **Taos Box:** Steep canyon walls loom alongside the 16 miles of surging waters of the Taos Box; the only way out is **rafting** the increasingly wild rapids that provide thrills and gasps in equal measure (page 134).

- **Taos Ski Valley: Skiers** and **snow-boarders** take to the slopes at this world-class resort that has it all—including stunning scenery and a German beer garden (page 135).

- **Hot-Air Ballooning:** As you drift silently over Albuquerque, unmatched views open up

Valles Caldera National Preserve

in all directions—there's simply no better way to take in the Sandia Mountains and the Rio Grande than from a balloon (page 188).

Weekend Getaways

Just an hour from the Albuquerque airport, Santa Fe lends itself perfectly to a romantic weekend. Settle in at one of the many remarkable hotels and make reservations at a couple of the city's best restaurants (those mentioned here are just a few possibilities). With planning, you could also spend an evening at the Santa Fe Opera in the summer. Isolated, countercultural Taos is worth the extra 90-minute drive if you're really looking to get off the map and off the grid, while Albuquerque offers a fun and funky city break, along with great outdoor activities.

Santa Fe

DAY 1

Fly in to Albuquerque. Head to Santa Fe via the scenic **Turquoise Trail** and check in to your hotel: **La Fonda** for a touch of history or **Inn of the Governors.** If it's summertime, head to **Canyon Road** for the gallery crawl, which gets started around 5pm. In winter, have a cocktail at **Secreto Lounge,** then walk over to dinner at **Joseph's.**

DAY 2

Grab breakfast in a booth at the **Plaza Café.**

Traditionalists can spend the morning at the **New Mexico Museum of Art** and **Georgia O'Keeffe Museum.** Quirkier tastes? Head for the **House of Eternal Return** and **Museum of International Folk Art.** In the afternoon, soak in a private hot tub at **Ten Thousand Waves,** followed by a massage then dinner at the spa's restaurant, **Izanami.** Hit the late-night movie at **Violet Crown.**

DAY 3

Take an early morning hike on the **Dale Ball Trails** or a less strenuous stroll around the **Santa Fe Canyon Preserve.** Treat yourself to brunch at **Harry's Roadhouse** or **Café Fina,** a little south of town, for high-end diner-style goodies and one last great view, then drive back down I-25 to catch your flight out.

Taos
DAY 1

Fly in to Albuquerque. Head to Taos via I-25 and the **low road.** Pick a prime plaza-view room at **Hotel La Fonda de Taos** or luxuriate in a suite at **Palacio de Marquesa.** Stroll the **plaza** and

Taos Pueblo

visit the **E. L. Blumenschein Home** and the galleries on Ledoux Street. Have a gourmet burger for dinner at **The Burger Stand,** then check out **The Alley Cantina.**

DAY 2

Visit **Taos Pueblo** in the morning. In the afternoon, tour the **Taos Art Museum** and the **Millicent Rogers Museum.** If you'd rather hike, head for **Williams Lake** in the **Taos Ski Valley**—it's a steep hike, but fairly short. Be dazzled by dinner at **El Meze.**

DAY 3

Drop by **San Francisco de Asis Church** in the morning, then prepare for the drive back south with breakfast at **Old Martina's Hall.** Head out along the **high road** to Santa Fe and then I-25 to the airport, which takes about four hours without much dawdling; a straight shot back down the low road will shave about 40 minutes off the trip.

Albuquerque
DAY 1

Arrive at **Albuquerque airport** and transfer

a balloon ride over Albuquerque

The Grove in Albuquerque

to your hotel: Try **Los Poblanos Historic Inn** for rural quiet, or the **Hotel Andaluz** downtown if you want to be in the middle of the action. Stroll around downtown and peek in the **KiMo Theatre,** then have sunset drinks at the **Apothecary Lounge,** followed by dinner down the street at **Farina Pizzeria.**

DAY 2
Stroll around Old Town and take the **ABQ Trolley Co.** tour. Have lunch at **Duran Central Pharmacy,** then check out the **Indian Pueblo Cultural Center.** Spend the evening in **Nob Hill** with dinner at **Frenchish.**

DAY 3
Get up early (again) for a **hot-air balloon ride,** overlooking the city from the Rio Grande to the mountains. Head to **The Grove** for a late breakfast, then cruise Route 66 and up to the East Mountains to see the **Tinkertown Museum** and **Madrid.** Optional: Cut west on dirt roads to **Kasha-Katuwe Tent Rocks National Monument** and get a last dose of chile at the **Pueblo Restaurant.**

handmade pottery at the Santa Fe Indian Market

Bandelier National Monument

American Indian Heritage

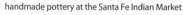

The culture that developed before the Spanish conquest in the 16th century is visible in the pueblos (both ruined and inhabited) and in excellent museums that hold some of the region's finest works. Even if you're visiting only one city on your trip, there's a lot of Native history to see in and around each place—but definitely try to schedule a visit around a dance ceremony, as this will give you the most memorable impression of the living culture.

If you're serious about buying art and jewelry, you could time your visit with the **Santa Fe Indian Market** in August, which showcases more than 1,200 Native American artisans. Otherwise, visit the gift shops at the Museum of Contemporary Native Arts in Santa Fe or the Indian Pueblo Cultural Center in Albuquerque to get an idea of prices and quality; you can also buy directly from craftspeople at the pueblos.

Santa Fe

On **Museum Hill,** visit the **Wheelwright Museum of the American Indian** and the **Museum of Indian Arts & Culture,** two fascinating exhibitions of arts and crafts. Then see what current work is on display at the **Museum of Contemporary Native Arts,** perhaps picking up some craftwork at the gift shop or from the vendors at the **Palace of the Governors.** Even **Hotel Santa Fe,** co-owned by Picurís Pueblo, showcases tribal art.

The pueblos north of the city offer more in the way of casinos than they do in traditional sightseeing, but the **Poeh Museum** at Pojoaque is worth a stop, and collectors will want to make the drive to **San Ildefonso Pueblo** for its stunning black-on-black pottery. Finally, visit the **Puyé Cliff Dwellings** or **Bandelier National Monument** to see the homes inhabited by the ancestors of today's Pueblo people.

New Mexicans have particular ways of identifying themselves and the elements of the state's unique cultural mix. The people who have lived in the highlands and along the Rio Grande for millennia usually refer to themselves as "Indians," or "American Indians" in formal situations; or they will call themselves by their pueblo's specific name—Jemez or Santa Clara, for instance. The term "Native American" appears occasionally, but most New Mexican Indians see it as just another inaccurate label.

Those who trace their roots to the conquistadors call themselves "Spanish" or "Hispano." The latter is not to be confused with "Hispanic," which refers to Spanish speakers regardless of background. "Hispano" is also distinct from "Mexican" and "Latino."

The third category is the catchall term "Anglo," which really just means "none of the above"— whether you're white, Asian, or even African American, you could be considered Anglo, a relative latecomer to the state of New Mexico.

Taos

Head straight to **Taos Pueblo**—one of the most beautiful spots in the state, the organic adobe structures seemingly untouched by time (only *seemingly*—in fact, they get a fresh coat of mud nearly every year). Have a meal at **Tiwa Kitchen,** or at least sample the fry bread and chokecherry syrup. Don't miss the excellent weaving and pottery collections at the **Millicent Rogers Museum.**

Albuquerque

Start with a visit to the **Indian Pueblo Cultural Center,** with its excellent museum and café. Then head to the edge of town: to the West Mesa, where **Petroglyph National Monument** has trails past hundreds of ancient rock carvings, and to Bernalillo, north of the city, where you can climb down into a ceremonial kiva at **Coronado State Monument.**

Mesa-top **Acoma Pueblo** is well worth the drive west of the city—along with Taos Pueblo, it's the most scenic (and oldest) in New Mexico. You can break up the trip with a stop at **Laguna Pueblo** to see its mission church. South and east through the Manzano Mountains are the **Salinas Pueblo Missions,** ruined villages that didn't survive the Spanish conquest. North of the city, the **Jemez Mountain Trail** runs through **Jemez Pueblo**—the red-rock scenery is beautiful, and don't miss the **fry bread** from the vendors set up in front of the **Walatowa Visitor Center.**

Rest up from your road trips at the **Hyatt Regency Tamaya** resort, owned by Santa Ana Pueblo.

Hiking and Mountain Biking

TOP EXPERIENCE

Not only is New Mexico's mountain scenery stunning, but the population is sparse, so it's easy to get out of town and have the natural splendor all to yourself. This route, which takes six days, caters to mountain bikers and hikers who want to spend as much time as possible outside of the cities. When you see the scenery, it's tempting to put on your boots and head straight out, but unless you're coming from a comparable elevation, stick to foothill hikes and scenic drives for the first couple of days. Drink plenty of liquids, and head to bed early.

Don't try this itinerary any earlier than **mid-May;** even then you will still encounter snowpack at higher elevations. Visiting in the fall may be colder, but the glowing yellow aspen groves that stud the mountains are a major attraction.

Aspen Vista Trail

looking down on the Rio Grande Gorge

Day 1

Arrive at Albuquerque's Sunport; pick up your rental car and head north to your hotel in **Santa Fe.** If you arrive on an early flight, take a detour to **Kasha-Katuwe Tent Rocks National Monument** for an easy hour-long hike—but don't push yourself too hard.

Day 2

Rent a mountain bike and get oriented downtown, then head down the **Santa Fe Rail Trail** to Lamy or cruise around **La Tierra Trails** in the rolling hills west of the city. Return to Santa Fe for a hearty dinner at **Cowgirl BBQ.**

Day 3

Take your pick of several hikes in the Santa Fe area: The **Rio en Medio** trail north of Tesuque is a good one, or make the trek along **Aspen Vista** up by the ski basin if the leaves are turning. At

night, relax in the hot tubs at **Ten Thousand Waves,** then have a late dinner at **Izanami.**

Day 4

Drive to **Taos** via the **high road,** spending the afternoon hiking the **West Rim Trail** along the **Rio Grande Gorge.** Relive the views over a pint at the nearby **Taos Mesa Brewing.** Bunk back in town at the **Inn on the Rio.**

Day 5

Drive back south via the **low road** before veering west to take a hike in **Valles Caldera National Preserve;** stay the night in **Jemez Springs,** where you can soak tired muscles in the healing waters.

Day 6

Return to Albuquerque via the **Jemez Mountain Trail.** Grab a last bite of green-chile stew at **The Frontier** if you have time before your flight.

The Best of Southwest Cuisine

Given the region's distinctive cuisine—from only-in-New-Mexico hot chile to gourmet creativity—it would be easy to plan a vacation entirely around eating.

BEST TRADITIONAL NEW MEXICAN

"Red or green?" is the official state question, the dilemma diners face when they order anything that can be drowned in an earthy red-chile sauce or a chunky, vegetal green one (Hint: if you can't decide, choose "Christmas").

- **Tia Sophia's:** History was made in this old-school spot near the Santa Fe Plaza: It's allegedly where the breakfast burrito was invented (page 69).

- **Rancho de Chimayó:** An essential stop after visiting the nearby Santuario, this inviting inn has a menu full of immensely satisfying dishes such as *sopaipilla relleno* (page 102).

- **Orlando's:** The Taos favorite is known for its green-chile sauce, deceptively smooth and velvety, considering the heat it packs (page 137).

- **Mary & Tito's Café:** This family restaurant was named a James Beard American Classic in 2010, thanks to its *carne adovada* (page 195).

BEST GREEN-CHILE CHEESEBURGERS

This greasy treat is so genius, it has been immortalized in the official **New Mexico Green Chile Cheeseburger Trail** (www.newmexico.org). A few GCCB options:

- **Santa Fe Bite:** This casual restaurant grinds its own meat and shapes the enormous patties by hand (page 69).

- **Bang Bite:** The signature roasted five-chile-blend burger at this orange food truck draws long lines. The wait is more than worth it (page 70).

- **Sugar's:** If you're taking the low road, don't miss out on a juicy green-chile cheeseburger at this beloved Embudo institution (page 98).

- **The Frontier:** With a pot of green-chile stew at the condiment counter, you can ladle on as much heat as you want (page 193).

Breakfast burritos with green and red chile are a staple of New Mexican cuisine.

BEST LOCAL AND ORGANIC

New Mexico's extreme climate makes farming difficult—locally grown produce is justifiably treasured.

- **Café Pasqual's:** At this Santa Fe legend, open since 1979, Chef Katharine Kagel went organic before organic was cool (page 68).

- **Joseph's:** Chef Joseph Wrede, formerly a Taos icon, moved to Santa Fe to teach this glitzy town what New Mexican *terroir* really is—and even elevates the GCCB (page 70).

- **Vinaigrette:** This "salad bistro" in Santa Fe grows its own greens on a nearby farm and can vouch for every ingredient on its menu (page 71).

- **The Love Apple:** This candlelit bistro proudly lists the source of all of its fresh ingredients, from its beef to its cornmeal (page 138).

- **Campo:** Guests at Los Poblanos Historic Inn in Los Ranchos de Albuquerque enjoy fresh eggs for breakfast and sublime salads and charcuterie at dinner (page 195).

Santa Fe

Sights 36
Entertainment and Events 52
Shopping. 58
Sports and Recreation 61
Food 68

Accommodations. 76
Outside Santa Fe 79
Information and Services 105
Getting There and Around. 107

Look for ★ to find recommended
sights, activities, dining, and lodging.

Highlights

★ **Canyon Road Galleries:** The heart of Santa Fe's art scene is a visual smorgasbord, no more so than when it's packed with potential collectors, window-shoppers, and party hoppers on summer Friday nights (page 44).

★ **Museum of International Folk Art:** In the main exhibition hall, all the world's crafts, from Appalachian quilts to Zulu masks, are jumbled together in an inspiring display of human creativity (page 48).

★ **Meow Wolf Art Complex:** Meow Wolf's immersive House of Eternal Return expands the mind—and the definition of art—in Santa Fe. Appropriate for anyone ages 6-106, it is an immense amount of fun (page 50).

★ **Violet Crown:** It's more than just a movie theater. With the dinner and drinks you can savor while catching the latest blockbuster, smart homages to cinema's heyday, and a sun-kissed, railroad-themed space, Violet Crown can infuse moviegoers with a sense of giddiness not typically seen outside puberty (page 54).

★ **Santa Fe Indian Market:** The amount and quality of Native American artwork on display during this late-summer celebration is staggering, but it's the opportunity to interact with some of the Southwest's most seminal artists that makes this event truly special (page 56).

★ **Ten Thousand Waves:** As much a part of Santa Fe's identity as a centuries-old adobe, this Japanese-styled spa is the ultimate mountain getaway—and a great place to pamper yourself (page 66).

★ **Bandelier National Monument:** Spend a day exploring the once-hidden valley of Frijoles Canyon, where ancestors of today's Pueblo people constructed an elaborate city complex with cliffside cave homes (page 88).

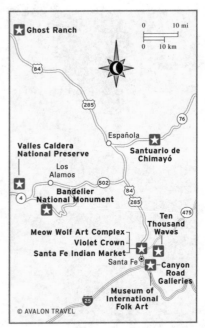

© AVALON TRAVEL

★ **Valles Caldera National Preserve:** You're more likely to spot elk herds in the lush meadows of this crater, where you can also mountain bike (page 90).

★ **Ghost Ranch:** The spread where Georgia O'Keeffe kept a house has dramatic red cliffs and windblown pinnacles. Set out on horseback for a better feel for what inspired her or hike to Chimney Rock for a sweeping view that takes in Abiquiu and the Pedernal (page 96).

★ **Santuario de Chimayó:** Faith is palpable in this village church north of Santa Fe, known as "the Lourdes of America," thanks to the healing powers attributed to the holy dirt found here (page 101).

O ver 400 years since its founding as a remote Spanish outpost, Santa Fe remains proudly and blissfully quite unlike anywhere else in the country.

Indeed, this small cluster of mud-colored buildings in the mountains of northern New Mexico seems to subsist on dreams alone, as this city of 70,000 has a larger proportion of writers and artists than any other community in the United States. Art galleries are ubiquitous—one famous half-mile stretch of road has over 80 alone—and lots packed with film crews are increasingly common sights. In all, nearly half the city is employed in the larger arts industry. (Cynics would lump the state legislature, which convenes in the capitol here, into this category as well.)

The city fabric itself is a by-product of this creativity—many of the "adobe" buildings in the distinctive downtown area are in fact plaster and stucco, built in the early 20th century to satisfy an official vision of how Santa Fe should present itself to tourists. And the mix of old-guard Spanish, Pueblo Indians, groovy Anglos, and international jet-setters of all stripes has even developed a soft but distinct accent—a vaguely continental intonation, with a vocabulary drawn

from the 1960s counterculture and alternative healing.

What keeps Santa Fe grounded is its location, tucked in the foothills of the Sangre de Cristos. The mountains are never far, even if you're just admiring the view from your massage table at a Japanese-style spa or dining at an elegant restaurant on mushrooms sourced from secret high meadows. You can be out of town and at a trailhead in 10 minutes, skiing down a precipitous slope in 30, or wandering among the ochre-colored hills you've seen in Georgia O'Keeffe's paintings of Abiquiu in 60. East of the city is the Pecos Wilderness Area, a couple hundred thousand acres studded with summits such as Santa Fe Baldy and Truchas Peak.

Santa Fe's history is intrinsic to that of the Southwest; what took place here echoed across the region and farther east too. It's the second-oldest city in the United States (after St. Augustine, Florida), and it's surrounded by pueblos that have been inhabited since well before the Spanish arrived, alongside

Previous: Meow Wolf Art Complex; street scene in Santa Fe's Eastside. **Above:** Bandelier National Monument.

Santa Fe

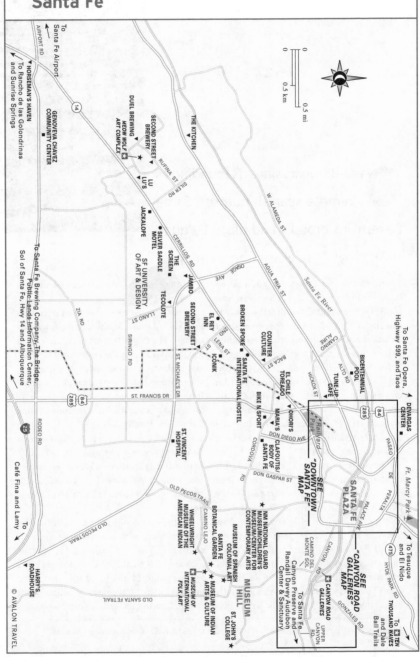

SANTA FE PLAZA

SEE "DOWNTOWN SANTA FE" MAP

SEE "CANYON ROAD GALLERIES" MAP

© AVALON TRAVEL

remnants of older settlements, such as the cliff dwellings in Bandelier National Monument. As the capital of the Spanish territory of Nuevo México, Santa Fe was a far-flung outpost, a gateway to the wilder, emptier lands to the north. And it still is, with two scenic routes running north to Taos: The high road winds along mountain ridges, while the low road follows the Rio Grande.

PLANNING YOUR TIME

Santa Fe is an ideal destination for a **three-day weekend.** Add another day or two to take a day hike outside of town or make the drive to Taos, Los Alamos, or Abiquiu. **Summer** is high season, no more so than during Spanish Market and Indian Market, in July and August, respectively. This is also when the gallery scene is in full swing; plan to be in the city on a Friday night, when the Canyon Road galleries have their convivial openings.

In **fall,** the city is much calmer and offers beautiful hiking; the hills are greener and dense groves of aspen trees on the Sangre de Cristo Mountains turn bright yellow. As in the rest of New Mexico, **spring** and **early summer** can be hot and windy, but the city is still pleasant, as lilacs bloom in May, tumbling over adobe walls and filling the air with scent. **Winter** is cold and occasionally snowy, but cloudy days are few. Late December in Santa Fe is a special time, as houses and hotels are decked with *farolitos* (paper-bag lanterns) and Canyon Road is alight with bonfires on Christmas Eve. After this, in January and February, hotel prices tend to drop dramatically, as the few tourists in town are here only to ski.

HISTORY

Around 1609, La Villa Real de la Santa Fé (The Royal City of the Holy Faith) was established as the capital of Spain's northernmost territory in the New World. The Camino Real, the route that connected the outpost with Mexico, ended in the newly built plaza. Mexico's independence from Spain in 1821 marked a shift in the city's fortunes, as the new government opened up its northernmost territory to outside trade, via the Santa Fe Trail, from Missouri.

When the railroad arrived in nearby Lamy in 1880, it spurred what's still Santa Fe's lifeblood: tourism. Loads of curious Easterners flocked in. In 1912, a council of city planners decided to promote Santa Fe as a tourist destination and preserve its distinctive

Snow falls occasionally in Santa Fe.

New Mexico Culture Pass

A **museum pass** ($30) good for 12 months grants onetime access to all 15 state-run museums and historic sites. This includes four Santa Fe institutions—the New Mexico Museum of Art, the New Mexico History Museum, the Museum of Indian Arts & Culture, and the Museum of International Folk Art—as well as two in Albuquerque (the National Hispanic Cultural Center and the Museum of Natural History and Science), and the Coronado and Jemez historic sites. It also covers attractions farther afield, in Las Cruces, Alamogordo, and more—great if you're a state resident or you're already planning a longer return visit within the year.

architecture. By 1917, the Museum of Fine Arts (now the New Mexico Museum of Art) had opened, and the first Indian Market was held in 1922, in response to the trend of Anglos collecting local arts and crafts.

Decades later, Santa Fe played a minor part in events that would shape the future of humanity. In 1943, the building at 109 East Palace Avenue became the "front office" and only known address for Los Alamos, where the country's greatest scientists were developing the atomic bomb under a cloud of confidentiality. But the rational scientists left little mark. Right-brain thinking has continued to flourish, and the city is a modern, evolving version of its old self, an outpost of melding cultures still drawing artists and an increasing number of adventurers looking to explore the mountainous landscape.

ORIENTATION

Santa Fe is compact, with most of its major sights within walking distance from the central plaza. You're likely to spend much of your time within the oval formed by **Paseo de Peralta,** the main road that almost completely encircles the city's core. On its southwest side it connects with **Cerrillos Road,** a wide avenue lined with motel courts, shopping plazas, and chain restaurants. Compared with the central historic district, it's unsightly, but there are some great local places to eat here, as well as the few inexpensive hotels in town.

Sights

DOWNTOWN
Santa Fe Plaza

When Santa Fe was established around 1609, its layout was based on Spanish laws governing town planning in the colonies—hence the central plaza fronted by the Casas Reales (Palace of the Governors) on its north side. The **Santa Fe Plaza** is still the city's social hub, and the blocks surrounding it are rich with history. In the center of the plaza is the **Soldiers' Monument,** now also a monument to how history gets rewritten. On the original panel, dedicated in 1867 to those who died in "battles with [. . .] Indians in the

territory of New Mexico," the word "savage" was excised in the 1970s, following a debate about the word. One activist took it upon himself to chisel out the word himself, even as some Pueblo leaders thought the word should stand, on the logic that it could accurately describe the way in which Native people fought the Spanish at the time. Another, later panel has been modified too, as "rebel," referring to Southern forces in the Civil War, has been cut away. Then next to it all is yet another plaque, apologizing for the whole mess.

Along the north side, under the portal of the **Palace of the Governors,** is one of the more iconic sights of Santa Fe: American Indians from all over New Mexico selling their craft work as they've been doing since the 1930s. More than 500 vendors are licensed to sell here after going through a strict application process that evaluates their technical skills. Every morning the 69 spots, each 12 bricks wide, are doled out by lottery. Expect anything from silver bracelets to pottery to *heishi* (shell bead) necklaces to freshly harvested piñon nuts. It's a great opportunity to buy directly from a skilled artisan and learn about the work that went into a piece.

New Mexico History Museum and Palace of the Governors

Opened in 2009, the **New Mexico History Museum** (113 Lincoln Ave., 505/476-5200, www.nmhistorymuseum.org, 10am-5pm daily May-Oct., 10am-5pm Tues.-Sun. Nov.-Apr., $12) was intended to give a little breathing room for a collection that had been in storage for decades. Oddly, though, it feels like few actual objects are on display. The permanent exhibits give a good overview, but if you're already familiar with the state's storied past, you might not find much new here.

Your ticket also admits you to the adjacent **Palace of the Governors,** the former seat of Santa Fe's government, and a generally more compelling display. An unimposing building constructed in 1610, it's been the site of several city-defining events. Diego de Vargas fought the Indian rebels here room by room when he retook the city in 1693; ill-fated Mexican governor Albino Pérez was beheaded in his office in 1837; and Governor Lew Wallace penned *Ben Hur* here in the late 1870s. The exhibits showcase some of the most beautiful items in the state's collection: trinkets and photos from the 19th century, as well as the beautiful 18th-century Segesser hide paintings, two wall-size panels of buffalo skin. These works, along with the room they're in (trimmed with 1909 murals of the Puyé cliffs) are worth the price of admission. In a couple of the restored furnished rooms, you can compare the living conditions of the Mexican leadership circa 1845 to the relative comfort the U.S. governor enjoyed in 1893.

The museum has **free admission** every Friday (5pm-8pm) May-October, and the first Friday of the month in winter. **Walking tours** depart from the blue gate on the Lincoln Avenue side of the New Mexico History Museum at 10:15am (Mon.-Sat. mid-Apr.-mid-Oct., $10), covering all the plaza-area highlights in about two hours.

New Mexico Museum of Art

Downtown Santa Fe

To
Hwy 599

N. GUADALUPE ST

JEFFERSON ST

STAAB ST

PASEO DE PERALTA

SAN FRANCISCO ST

To
Santa Fe Opera,
Española, and Taos

BUMBLE BEE'S
BAJA GRILL

MCKENZIE ST

W ALAMEDA ST

Santa Fe River

Santa Fe River State Park

W WATER ST

BOUCHE
BISTRO

DE FOURI ST

SANTUARIO DE
GUADALUPE

W DE VARGAS ST

IRVINE ST

CLOSSON ST

JOSEPH'S

COWGIRL BBQ

AZTEC ST

DOUBLE
TAKE

AGUA FRIA ST

JEAN COCTEAU
CINEMA

MONTEZUMA AVE

0   200 yds

RAIL RUNNER/
SANTA FE CVB

BEE HIVE

0   200 m

S GUADALUPE ST

GARFIELD ST

ROMERO ST

MARKET ST

REI

READ ST

LANNAN
FOUNDATION
GALLERY

SANDOVAL ST

W MANHATTAN AVE

CAMINO DE LA FAMILIA

SANTA FE
SPIRITS

VIOLET CROWN

ALCALDESA ST

W MANHATTAN AVE

HIGH
DESERT ANGLER

SECOND STREET
BREWERY

SANTA FE
MOTEL & INN

EL MUSEO CULTURAL
DE SANTA FE

TAI MODERN

OHORI'S

LEWALLEN

FARMERS
MARKET

HOTEL
SANTA FE

SAGE
BAKEHOUSE

ALARID ST

WAREHOUSE 21

SITE
SANTA FE

PASEO DE PERALTA

GALISTEO ST

NINITA ST

*Railyard
Park*

CERRILLOS RD

SHAKE FOUNDATION

VINAIGRETTE/
MODERN GENERAL

Rail Runner

CAMINO
SIERRA VISTA

SANTA FE
SAGE INN

DON DIEGO AVE

LA CHOZA

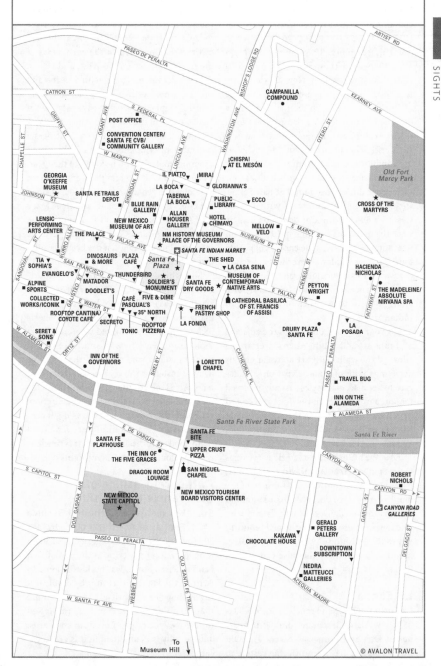

ARTIST RD

PASEO DE PERALTA

CATRON ST

GRIFFIN ST

CHAPELLE ST

BISHOP'S LODGE RD

CAMPANILLA
COMPOUND

KEARNEY AVE

S FEDERAL PL

POST OFFICE

CONVENTION CENTER/
SANTA FE CVB/
COMMUNITY GALLERY

W MARCY ST

GEORGIA
O'KEEFFE
MUSEUM

JOHNSON ST

SANTA FE TRAILS
DEPOT

SHERIDAN ST

LINCOLN AVE

WASHINGTON AVE

OTERO ST

Old Fort
Marcy Park

IL PIATTO

LA BOCA

¡CHISPA!
AT EL MESÓN

¡MIRA!

GLORIANNA'S

Old Fort
Marcy Park

LENSIC
PERFORMING
ARTS CENTER

THE PALACE

BLUE RAIN
GALLERY

NEW MEXICO
MUSEUM OF ART

TABERNA
LA BOCA

ALLAN
HOUSER
GALLERY

PUBLIC
LIBRARY

ECCO

E MARCY ST

CROSS OF THE
MARTYRS

W PALACE AVE

NM HISTORY MUSEUM/
PALACE OF THE GOVERNORS

HOTEL
CHIMAYO

MELLOW
VELO

NUSBAUM ST

SANTA FE INDIAN MARKET

TIA
SOPHIA'S

EVANGELO'S

ALPINE
SPORTS

COLLECTED
WORKS/ICONIK

ROOFTOP CANTINA/
COYOTE CAFÉ

SANDOVAL ST

BURRO ALLEY

SAN FRANCISCO ST

DINOSAURS
& MORE

MATADOR

DOODLET'S

PLAZA
CAFÉ

THUNDERBIRD

CAFÉ
PASQUAL'S

Santa Fe
Plaza

SOLDIER'S
MONUMENT

FIVE & DIME

THE SHED

LA CASA SENA

SANTA FE
DRY GOODS

MUSEUM OF
CONTEMPORARY
NATIVE ARTS

E PALACE AVE

CIENEGA ST

OTERO ST

PEYTON
WRIGHT

HACIENDA
NICHOLAS

FAITHWAY ST

THE MADELEINE/
ABSOLUTE
NIRVANA SPA

SERET &
SONS

SECRETO

35° NORTH

TONIC

ROOFTOP
PIZZERIA

FRENCH
PASTRY SHOP

LA FONDA

CATHEDRAL BASILICA
OF ST. FRANCIS
OF ASSISI

DRURY PLAZA
SANTA FE

LA
POSADA

ORTIZ ST

GALISTEO ST

E WATER ST

SHELBY ST

W ALAMEDA ST

INN OF THE
GOVERNORS

LORETTO
CHAPEL

CATHEDRAL PL

PASEO DE PERALTA

TRAVEL BUG

INN ON THE
ALAMEDA

E ALAMEDA ST

Santa Fe River State Park

Santa Fe River

E DE VARGAS ST

SANTA FE
PLAYHOUSE

THE INN OF
THE FIVE GRACES

DRAGON ROOM
LOUNGE

SANTA FE
BITE

UPPER CRUST
PIZZA

SAN MIGUEL
CHAPEL

CANYON RD

ROBERT
NICHOLS

CANYON RD

S CAPITOL ST

DON GASPAR AVE

NEW MEXICO
STATE CAPITOL

NEW MEXICO TOURISM
BOARD VISITORS CENTER

GARCIA ST

CANYON ROAD
GALLERIES

PASEO DE PERALTA

KAKAWA
CHOCOLATE HOUSE

GERALD
PETERS
GALLERY

DOWNTOWN
SUBSCRIPTION

DELGADO ST

WEBBER ST

OLD SANTA FE TRAIL

NEDRA
MATTEUCCI
GALLERIES

ACEQUIA MADRE

W SANTA FE AVE

To
Museum Hill

© AVALON TRAVEL

New Mexico Museum of Art

Famed as much for its facade as for what it contains, the **New Mexico Museum of Art** (107 W. Palace Ave., 505/476-5072, www. nmartmuseum.org, 10am-5pm daily May-Oct., 10am-5pm Tues.-Sun. Nov.-Apr., $12) is dedicated to work by New Mexican artists. Built in 1917, it is a beautiful example of Pueblo Revival architecture, originally designed as the New Mexico pavilion for a world expo in San Diego, California, two years prior. The curvaceous stucco-clad building combines elements from the most iconic pueblo mission churches—the bell towers, for instance, mimic those found at San Felipe. Inside, the collection starts with Gerald Cassidy's oil painting *Cui Bono?*, on display since the museum's opening in 1917 and still relevant, as it questions the benefits of pueblo tourism. Look out for an excellent collection of Awa Tsireh's meticulous watercolors of ceremonial dances at **San Ildefonso Pueblo,** alongside works by other local American Indian artists.

On your way out, don't miss the adjacent St. Francis Auditorium, where three artists adorned the walls with art nouveau murals depicting the life of Santa Fe's patron saint. It's rare to see a secular style—usually reserved for languorous ladies in flowing togas—used to render such scenes as the apotheosis of Saint Francis and Santa Clara's renunciation, and the effect is beautiful.

As at the history museum, Friday evenings (5pm-8pm) are **free admission** in summer; November-April, only the first Friday of the month is free. Free docent-led **tours** around the museum run daily; call for the latest times. The museum also runs art-themed **walking tours** ($10) around the city center at 10am Monday; June-August, they also run at 10am Friday.

La Fonda

La Fonda (100 E. San Francisco St., 505/982-5511, www.lafondasantafe.com), at the corner of East San Francisco Street and Old Santa Fe Trail, has been offering respite to travelers in some form or another since 1607, and it still hums with history—even though the stacked Pueblo Revival place you see today dates from 1920. "The Inn at the End of the Trail" boomed in the early years of the trade route across the West, and also in the later gold-digging era, with a casino and saloon. It hosted the victory ball following General Stephen Watts Kearny's takeover of New Mexico in the Mexican-American War. During the Civil War it housed Confederate general Henry Hopkins Sibley. Lynchings and shootings took place in the lobby. In the 1920s, La Fonda got a bit safer for the average tourist, as it joined the chain of Harvey Houses along the country's railways, and architect Mary Jane Colter (best known for designing the hotels at the Grand Canyon) redesigned the interior. Since the 1960s, it has been a family-owned hotel.

Something about the waxed tile floors, painted glass, and heavy furniture convey the pleasant clamor of hotel life the way many more modern lobbies do not. Guests pick up their keys at an old wood reception desk, drop their letters in an Indian-drum-turned-mailbox, and chat with the concierge below a poster for Harvey's Indian Detour car trips. Also look around—including up on the mezzanine level—at the great art collection. **La Plazuela** restaurant, in the skylight center courtyard, is a beautiful place for a meal (with good brunches), and the bar is timeless, with live country music many nights.

Cathedral Basilica of St. Francis of Assisi

Santa Fe's showpiece **Cathedral Basilica of St. Francis of Assisi** (131 Cathedral Pl., 505/982-5619, www.cbsfa.org, 9:30am-4:30pm Mon.-Sat., free), towering at the end of East San Francisco Street, was built over some 15 years in the late 19th century by domineering Bishop Jean-Baptiste Lamy. For more than three decades, the Frenchman struggled to "elevate" the city to European standards, and his folly is exemplified in this grandiose cathedral.

Lamy looked down on the locals' religious practices, as the cult of the Virgin of Guadalupe was already well established, and the Penitente brotherhood was performing public self-flagellation. He also disliked their aesthetics. How could a person possibly reach heaven while praying on a dirt floor inside a building made of mud? Lamy assessed the tiny adobe church dedicated to St. Francis of Assisi, which had stood for 170 years, and decided he could do better. Construction on his Romanesque revival St. Francis Cathedral began in 1869, under the direction of architects and craftsmen from Europe. They used the old church as a frame for the new stone structure, then demolished all of the adobe, save for a small side chapel. Lamy ran short of cash, however—hence the stumpy aspect of the cathedral's facade, which should be topped with domed towers.

Inside is all Gothic-inspired light and space and glowing stained-glass windows, with a gilt altar screen installed in 1987, for the centennial of the building's dedication. It features primarily New World saints, such as Kateri Tekakwitha, a 17th-century Mohawk woman beatified in 1980 and canonized in 2012 (her statue also stands outside the cathedral). She is depicted with a turtle, representing her membership in the Turtle Clan.

The salvaged adobe chapel is to the left of the altar. It is dedicated to the figure of La Conquistadora, a statue brought to Santa Fe from Mexico in 1625, carried away by the retreating Spanish during the Pueblo Revolt, then proudly reinstated in 1693 and honored ever since. She glows in her shimmering robes, under a heavy viga ceiling. Lamy, who died in 1888, probably shudders in his crypt in front of the main altar.

On your way out, check the great cast-bronze doors—they're usually propped open, so you'll have to peer behind to see the images depicting the history of Catholicism in New Mexico. One plaque shows the Italian stoneworkers constructing the cathedral, and another shows families fleeing from attack in 1680—a rare depiction of the Pueblo Revolt that's sympathetic to the Spanish.

Museum of Contemporary Native Arts

Occupying two floors in the city's former post office, the **Museum of Contemporary Native Arts** (108 Cathedral Pl., 505/983-8900, www.iaia.edu, 10am-5pm Mon. and Wed.-Sat., noon-5pm Sun., $10) is the showcase for

Cathedral Basilica of St. Francis of Assisi

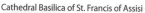

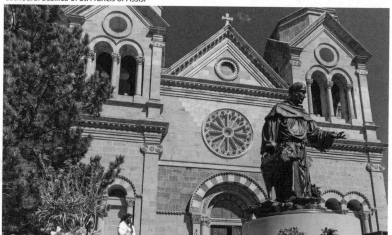

students, professors, and alumni of the prestigious Institute of American Indian Arts. The shows can be hit or miss; if your time is limited, the **Museum of Indian Arts & Culture** is a better bet. The gift shop stocks items with a good blend of modern and traditional styles.

Loretto Chapel

Initiated by Bishop Lamy in 1873, the **Loretto Chapel** (207 Old Santa Fe Tr., 505/982-0092, www.lorettochapel.com 9:30am-4:30pm Mon.-Sat., 10:30am-4:30pm Sun., $3) was the first Gothic structure built west of the Mississippi. Its beautiful interior has a great story to match, although the recording broadcast inside (the place was desanctified in 1971) explaining all this on an endless loop is slightly maddening.

The chapel's decorative elements reflect Lamy's fondness for all things European: the stations of the cross rendered by Italian masons, the harmonium and stained glass windows imported from France. Even the stone from which it was built was hauled at great expense from quarries 200 miles south.

What draws the eye is the elegant spiral staircase leading to the choir loft. Made entirely of wood, it makes two complete turns without a central support pole. It was built in 1878 by a mysterious carpenter who appeared seemingly at the spiritual behest of the resident Sisters of Loretto. The carpenter toiled in silence for six months, the story goes, then disappeared, without taking any payment. He was never heard from again—though some historians claim to have tracked him down to Las Cruces, where he met his end in a bar fight.

San Miguel Chapel

The **San Miguel Chapel** (401 Old Santa Fe Tr., 505/983-3974, www.sanmiguelchapel.com, 10am-4pm Mon.-Sat., $1, free silent worship 5pm-7pm Thurs.) is a sturdy adobe building where Mass is still said in Latin at 2pm on Sunday. It is the oldest church structure in the United States, and it's set in Barrio de Analco, the city's oldest residential neighborhood, at

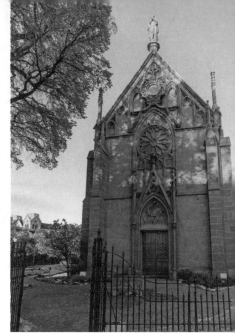

Loretto Chapel

the head of De Vargas, the oldest street. The church was built starting in 1610, then partially reconstructed a century later, after it was set aflame in the Pueblo Revolt. Its stone buttresses are the product of a desperate attempt to shore up the sagging walls in the late 19th century.

The interior is snug and whitewashed, with a restored altar screen that had been covered over in house paint for decades. The late 18th-century work is attributed to the anonymous Laguna Santero, a Mexican artist who earned his name from the intricately carved and painted screen at the Laguna Pueblo church, near Albuquerque. The screen functions as an enormous picture frame, with both oil paintings and *bultos* (painted wood statues of saints) inserted in the openings. In front of the altar, cutouts in the floor reveal the building's original foundations.

The old church bell, set at the back of the church, is said to have been cast in Spain in 1356. It was brought to the New World and installed at San Miguel in the early 19th century, and it hums beautifully even when tapped.

New Mexico State Capitol

A round building with an entrance at each of the cardinal points, the 1966 **New Mexico State Capitol** (491 Old Santa Fe Tr.) mimics the zia sun symbol used on the state flag. In the center of the rotunda is a mosaic rendition of the state seal: the Mexican brown eagle grasping a snake and shielded by the American bald eagle. Don't forget to look up at the stained glass skylight, with its intricate Indian basket-weave pattern.

But the real attraction of the Roundhouse, as the building is commonly known, is its excellent but often overlooked **art collection** (505/986-4589, www.nmcapitolart.org, 8am-5:30pm Mon.-Fri., also Sat. June-Aug., free), with works by the state's best-known creatives. You'll find paintings and photographs in the halls on every floor, in the upstairs balcony area of the senate, and in the 4th-floor Governor's Gallery.

Oh, and the building is used for legislating—though not particularly often (beginning on the third Tuesday in January, for 30 days in even-numbered years, and 60 days in odd). When house and senate meetings are in session, visitors are welcome to sit in the galleries and watch the proceedings.

Georgia O'Keeffe Museum

Opened in 1997, the **Georgia O'Keeffe Museum** (217 Johnson St., 505/946-1000, www.okeeffemuseum.org, 10am-5pm Sat.-Thurs., 10am-7pm Fri., $13), northwest of the plaza, honors the artist whose name is inextricably bound with New Mexico. The contrarian member of the New York avant-garde ("Nothing is less real than realism," she famously said) started making regular visits to the state in the 1920s, then moved to Abiquiu full-time in 1949, a few years after the death of her husband, photographer Alfred Stieglitz.

Many of O'Keeffe's finest works—her signature sensuous, near-abstract flower blossoms, for instance—have already been ensconced in other famous museums, so it's best to temper expectations accordingly. That said, the exhibits provide an intimate look at the artist's life not easily seen elsewhere, as they draw on the work that she kept, plus ephemera and other work her foundation has amassed since her death in 1986. Often the space is given over to exhibitions on her contemporaries or those whose work she influenced or admired.

New Mexico State Capitol

The museum offers a variety of **walking tours**, most notably a Walk & Talk tour of the museum daily at 3pm ($40) and an in-depth look at O'Keeffe's home and studio at Ghost Ranch in Abiquiu ($35-45).

Cross of the Martyrs and Old Fort Marcy Park

Sitting at the top of a hill overlooking downtown Santa Fe, the white **Cross of the Martyrs** is a memorial to the Spanish settlers who were killed in the Pueblo Revolt. It's not a strenuous walk, and the bird's-eye view from the hilltop is excellent.

Behind the cross is **Old Fort Marcy Park,** site of the first American fort in the Southwest, though today there are no signs of it remaining. Built in 1846 by General Kearny, the fort was then abandoned in 1894, and the land was disused for several decades. The path up to the cross begins on Paseo de Peralta just east of Otero Street.

CANYON ROAD AND THE EASTSIDE

This narrow mostly one-way street southeast of the plaza epitomizes "Santa Fe style," or at least the ritzy side of it. The galleries are the primary draw, but it's worth heading a bit off the main drag too. There's a city **parking** lot at the east (upper) end of the road and public parking near the bottom just north off **Canyon Road** on Delgado Street. Public **restrooms** (9:30am-5:30pm daily) are near the west end, in the complex at 225 Canyon Road, behind Expressions gallery.

★ Canyon Road Galleries

The intersection of Paseo de Peralta and Canyon Road is ground zero for the city's **art market.** This is the beginning of a 0.5-mile strip that contains more than 80 galleries. In the summer, Canyon Road is a solid mass of strolling art lovers—pro collectors and amateurs alike. It's especially thronged on summer Fridays, when most galleries have an open house or an exhibition opening, from around 5pm until 7pm or 8pm.

Hard to believe, but the street wasn't always chockablock with thousand-dollar canvases. Long ago, it was farmland, irrigated by the "Mother Ditch," Acequia Madre, which still runs parallel one block to the south. Starting in the 1920s, transplant artists settled on this muddy dirt road, and the area gradually came to be associated with creative exploits.

The view from the Cross of the Martyrs is among the city's best.

Canyon Road and the Eastside

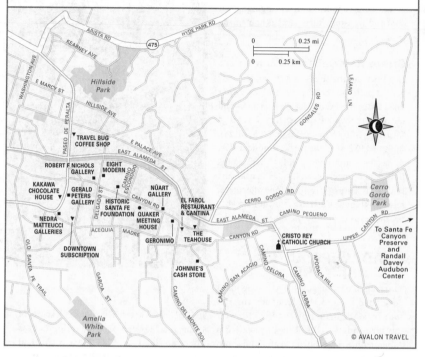

© AVALON TRAVEL

Eventually the art market really boomed in the 1980s. While those days have long since passed and many of the road's galleries seem to be in the throes of a never-ending game of musical chairs, it remains an enthralling stretch with some real gems.

In addition to the galleries and a few of the city's best restaurants, you'll also pass the mid-19th-century house **El Zaguán,** which contains the offices of the **Historic Santa Fe Foundation** (545 Canyon Rd., 505/983-2567, www.historicsantafe.org, 9am-noon and 1:30pm-3pm Mon.-Fri., free). Named for its long internal hallway (*zaguán*), the building was the home of a local merchant, James L. Johnson, from 1854, and then occupied by several other city bigwigs after he lost his fortune in 1881. Its **garden** (9am-5pm Mon.-Sat.), laid out in the late 19th century, is a lovely place to rest in the summer.

Camino del Monte Sol

To get some sense of what the neighborhood was like before the gallery era, walk south on **Camino del Monte Sol,** which is still residential—though decidedly tonier now than in centuries past. Turning off Canyon Road, you'll cross Acequia Madre, shaded by cottonwoods and channeling water through the city. Farther up the road, starting at No. 558, is a clutch of homes first inhabited in the 1920s by Los Cinco Pintores, the band of young realist painters who called themselves the "five little nuts in five mud huts." (Will Shuster is the best known of the five today, in part because he started the Zozobra tradition; Walter Mruk, Fremont Ellis, Joseph Bakos, and Willard Nash were the other four.)

Cut east on Camino Santander, then north on Camino San Acacio and northwest on Camino Don Miguel to find **Johnnie's Cash**

Store (420 Camino Don Miguel, 505/982-9506, 8:30am-5pm Mon.-Sat.), a little relic of a corner store, complete with a swinging screen door and a steamer full of famous homemade tamales.

Cristo Rey Catholic Church

Head beyond the shops and through a residential stretch to the far north end of Canyon Road to see John Gaw Meem's enormous and recently renovated **Cristo Rey Catholic Church** (1120 Canyon Rd., 505/983-8528). Built of 180,000 adobe bricks around a steel frame, the church opened in 1940 but looks as if it could be much older. Inside is a dramatic mid-18th-century baroque stone altarpiece, salvaged from La Castrense, the military chapel that used to occupy the south side of the plaza.

GUADALUPE AND THE RAILYARD

This neighborhood southwest of the plaza developed around the depot for the rail spur from the main line at Lamy. Now it's the terminus for the Rail Runner from Albuquerque. The clutch of cafés and shops here are more casual and local, and generally lighter on the adobe look, as **Guadalupe Street** is just outside the most stringently policed historic zone.

South of the train depot, the focus of much of the city's efforts at enlivening its downtown core is the **Railyard** (www.railyardsantafe.com), a mixed-use district where former warehouses and workshops have been adapted to new business. As well as holding the city's excellent farmers market, it's also home to the best theater in the state. The south side of this area is the green space of **Railyard Park,** nicely landscaped with local grasses and fruit trees.

Santuario de Guadalupe

Built 1776-1796, the **Santuario de Guadalupe** (417 Agua Fria St., 505/983-8868, 9am-noon and 1pm-4pm Mon.-Sat., free) is the oldest shrine to the Virgin of Guadalupe

Canyon Road

in the United States. The interior is spare, in front of a Mexican baroque oil-on-canvas altar painting from 1783. Mass is still said regularly, and a museum in the small anteroom displays relics from earlier incarnations of the building, such as Greek-style columns carved in wood. In winter, the church is closed on Saturday.

SITE Santa Fe

Fronted by a striking, angular facade, the modern exhibition space of **SITE Santa Fe** (1606 Paseo de Peralta, 505/989-1199, www.sitesantafe.org, 10am-5pm Thurs. and Sat., 10am-7pm Fri., noon-5pm Sun., $10) shows edgy art year-round, with installations often taking over the whole interior (and sometimes exterior). In July and August, it's also open on Wednesday, and entrance is free on Friday and Saturday till noon, when the farmers market is on, kitty-corner across the train tracks. A recent renovation and expansion dramatically increased its footprint and its visual impact, as well as adding a 200-seat auditorium and a coffee bar.

El Museo Cultural de Santa Fe

Dedicated to Hispanic culture in New Mexico and beyond, **El Museo Cultural de Santa Fe** (555 Camino de la Familia, 505/992-0591, www.elmuseocultural.org, 1pm-5pm Tues.-Sat., donation) is a grassroots effort in a surprisingly massive warehouse space that has room for installations, live theater, and more. It often hosts special events outside of normal museum hours.

Lannan Foundation Gallery

The influential Lannan Foundation, which funds art projects in Marfa, Texas, and an excellent speaker series in Santa Fe, among many other creative endeavors, operates the **Lannan Foundation Gallery** (309 Read St., 505/954-5149, noon-5pm Sat.-Sun.). In two adjacent houses, it displays selections from the family's ever-expanding trove of contemporary art, usually with an eye toward social justice.

MUSEUM HILL

These museums on the southeast side merit the trip from the plaza area. It's a short drive,

or you can take the "M" route bus or the free Santa Fe Pick-Up shuttle, optionally strolling back downhill to the center, about a 30-minute walk.

Museum of Spanish Colonial Art

The museum of the **Spanish Colonial Arts Society** (750 Camino Lejo, 505/982-2226, www.spanishcolonial.org, 10am-5pm daily June-Aug., 10am-5pm Tues.-Sun. Sept.-May, $8) exhibits a strong collection of folk art and historical objects dating from the earliest Spanish contact. One-of-a-kind treasures—such as the only signed *retablo* by the 19th-century *santero* Rafael Aragón—are shown alongside more utilitarian items from the colonial past, such as silk mantas, wool rugs, and decorative tin. New work by contemporary artisans is also on display—don't miss Luis Tapia's meta-*bulto, The Folk-Art Collectors.*

Museum of Indian Arts & Culture

The excellent **Museum of Indian Arts & Culture** (710 Camino Lejo, 505/476-1250, www.miaclab.org, 10am-5pm daily May-Oct., 10am-5pm Tues.-Sun. Nov.-Apr., $12) is devoted to Native American culture from

Santuario de Guadalupe

across the country. Cornerstone exhibit *Here, Now and Always* traces the New Mexican Indians from their ancestors on the mesas and plains up to their present-day efforts at preserving their culture. It displays inventive spaces (looking into a Housing and Urban Development-house kitchen on the reservation, or sitting at desks in a public schoolroom), sound clips, and stories. Another wing is devoted to contemporary art, while the halls of craft work display gorgeous beaded moccasins, elaborate headdresses, and more. The gift shop has beautiful jewelry and other tidbits from local artisans.

★ Museum of International Folk Art

A marvelous hodgepodge, the **Museum of International Folk Art** (708 Camino Lejo, 505/476-1200, www.internationalfolkart.org, 10am-5pm daily May-Oct., 10am-5pm Tues.-Sun. Nov.-Apr., $12) is one of Santa Fe's biggest treats—if you can handle visual overload. In the main exhibition space, some 10,000 folk-art pieces from more than 100 countries are on permanent display, hung on walls, set in cases, even dangling from the ceiling, juxtaposed to show off similar themes, colors, and materials. The approach initially seems

jumbled but in fact underscores the universality of certain concepts and preoccupations. Join a guided **tour** (10:30am, 11:30am, and 2pm) to learn all the details.

A separate wing is dedicated to northern New Mexican Hispano crafts (a good complement to the Museum of Spanish Colonial Art) and a lab area where you can see how pieces are preserved. Temporary exhibits take up the rest of the space, usually with colorful interactive shows. Don't skip the gift shop, which stocks some smaller versions of the items in the galleries.

Wheelwright Museum of the American Indian

In the early 1920s, Mary Cabot Wheelwright, an adventurous East Coast heiress, made her way to New Mexico, where she met a Navajo medicine man named Hastiin Klah. Together they devised the **Wheelwright Museum of the American Indian** (704 Camino Lejo, 505/982-4636, www.wheelwright.org, 10am-5pm daily, $8), which opened in 1937 as the House of Navajo Religion. The mission has since incorporated all Native American cultures, with exhibits of new work by individual artists rotating every few months. The building is modeled after a traditional

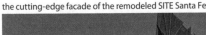
the cutting-edge facade of the remodeled SITE Santa Fe

It's Not *All* Adobe

Santa Fe's distinctive look is the product of stringent building codes that define and maintain "old Santa Fe style," from the thickness of walls (at least eight inches) to the shade of stucco finish, in only "brown, tan, or local earth tones." But look closely, and you'll see some variations.

Colonial is the term applied to adobe (or adobe-look) buildings, usually one story, with their typical rounded edges and flat roofs supported by vigas, the long crossbeams made of single tree trunks. The style mimics one developed by the Spanish colonists in the 16th, 17th, and 18th centuries, based on their previous experience with adobe architecture and forms they saw in the pueblos.

In the 19th century, when New Mexico became a U.S. territory and the railroad could carry new building materials, timber-frame houses came into fashion. These so-called **territorial** buildings were often two stories tall, with balconies, and trimmed with brick cornices and Greek revival details, such as fluted wood columns and pediments above windows. The Catron Building, on the northeast corner of the plaza, is a fine example of the style developed in this period.

In the early part of the 20th century, the **Pueblo Revival** style was the product of architects like John Gaw Meem and Isaac Rapp, who admired the pueblo mission churches and Spanish colonial adobes for their clean-lined minimalism. Because they used frame construction, Pueblo Revival buildings could be taller: Rapp's New Mexico Museum of Art towers on the northwest corner of the plaza, and Meem's additions to the La Fonda hotel make it five stories. The trend coincided with an aggressive tourism campaign and the development of a comprehensive look for the city, and in the process many territorial houses were simply covered over in a thick layer of faux-adobe plaster. The result is not really true to history, but the city planners achieved their goal: Santa Fe looks like no other city in the United States.

Navajo hogan, with huge timbers supporting the eight-sided structure, and a new wing (added in 2015) is dedicated to Southwestern jewelry. The basement gift shop is a re-creation of a 19th-century trading post, which would feel like a tourist trap if it weren't for the authentically creaky wood floors and the beautiful antique crafts on display. The museum offers guided **tours** (10:30am, 11:30am, and 2pm).

Santa Fe Botanical Garden

Opened in 2013, the 14-acre **Santa Fe Botanical Garden** (715 Camino Lejo, 505/471-9103, www.santafebotanicalgarden. com, 9am-5pm daily Apr.-Oct. $10, 11am-3pm Thurs.-Sun. Nov.-Mar., $7) is still growing, and until all three of its planned areas are open and flourishing, only really curious gardeners are likely to consider it worth the price of admission. The plantings emphasize drought-tolerant plants, including a garden

thriving on zero irrigation and an orchard containing peach, apple, and cherry trees. To get the most out of your visit, take a guided tour at 10am or 2pm.

The gardens also maintain a wetland preserve near Rancho de las Golondrinas, just outside of the city, with free walking tours (by appointment) on weekends, May through October.

SANTA FE METRO AREA
New Mexico National Guard Museum

One of three small museums in a single complex a bit out of the center, the **New Mexico National Guard Museum** (1050 Old Pecos Tr., 505/474-1670, www.bataanmuseum.com, 10am-4pm Tues.-Fri., free) began as a home-grown memorial for soldiers in the Bataan Death March of World War II. It was a particular tragedy in New Mexico because most of the state's national guardsmen, drafted as the 200th Coast Artillery, were among the more than 70,000 U.S. and Filipino soldiers subject to torture, malnourishment, random execution, and three years' imprisonment. Of the 1,800 who started in the regiment, fewer than 900 came home, and a full one-third of those men died in the first year back. The troops' experience is recalled with newspaper clippings, maps, and testimonials. The museum also contains Civil War memorabilia and exhibits on Native American contributions in U.S. wars, such as the Choctaw and Navajo code talkers of World War I.

Santa Fe Children's Museum

Kids can have tons of hands-on fun at the **Santa Fe Children's Museum** (1050 Old Pecos Tr., 505/989-8359, 10am-6pm Tues.-Wed., Fri.-Sat., 10am-6:30pm Thurs., noon-5pm Sun., www.santafechildrensmuseum.org, $7.50 adults, $5 children). Fitting for New Mexico, pint-size looms give kids a chance to learn to weave. Then there are the globally appealing bits: a giant soap-bubble pool, face painting, fun-house mirrors, and a dazzling collection of bugs. On Thursdays after 4pm, admission is free.

Center for Contemporary Arts

Behind the Children's Museum, the long-established **Center for Contemporary Arts** (1050 Old Pecos Tr., 505/982-1338, www.ccasantafe.org, noon-5pm Thurs.-Sun., free) has been mounting multimedia art shows and screening films since 1979. (An early James Turrell Skyspace is on the grounds here; unfortunately, it is now in disrepair and not open to visitors, though the center aspires to restore it.) The center is a nice alternative to the slicker gallery spaces and usually a good spot to check the pulse of younger resident artists.

★ Meow Wolf Art Complex

The anchor of the emerging Siler-Rufina neighborhood, the **Meow Wolf Art Complex** (1352 Rufina Circle, 505/395-6369, meowwolf.com, 10am-8pm Sun.-Thurs., 10-10pm Fri.-Sat., $20) features an ethereal permanent exhibition dreamed up by a Santa Fe-based art collective. Giving life

the House of Eternal Return in the Meow Wolf Art Complex

to a massive and long-shuttered space once occupied by a bowling alley, the 20,000-foot multilevel **House of Eternal Return** consists of a bewildering mix of kaleidoscopic rooms and nooks, each loosely building on an evolving narrative of the melding of real and otherworldly dimensions. Equally immersive and ambitious, the Victorian house holds the kinds of unexpected and multilayered surprises that reward multiple visits. It's great for both kids and adults, and you'll want to block out at least two hours, if not four.

In addition to the permanent exhibit, the complex also contains the **David Loughridge Learning Center,** used by Meow Wolf's nonprofit educational outreach program, a gallery space that features the works of local artists, and a music venue that quickly established itself as one of the best spots in town to catch live acts.

Rancho de las Golondrinas

About a 15-minute drive southeast, **Rancho de las Golondrinas** (334 Los Pinos Rd.,

505/471-2261, www.golondrinas.org, 10am-4pm Wed.-Sun. June-Sept., $6), the "Ranch of the Swallows," is Santa Fe's equivalent of Colonial Williamsburg, a 200-acre museum where staff members in period costumes demonstrate crafts and other aspects of early New Mexican history. The core of it is a restored Spanish colonial *paraje*, a way station on the Camino Real, and outbuildings contain a blacksmith shop, a schoolhouse, mills, and even a rebuilt Penitente *morada* (the docent who works here is a Penitente himself and may sing some of the group's hymns).

The ranch hosts big to-dos (entrance fees typically $10-15), including a wine festival in early July, a celebration of Mexican culture in late July, a lively renaissance fair in September, among other things. It's a good idea to pack your own picnic; there's a basic café at the ranch, but it's open only on weekends. Allow a few hours to see the whole place. In April, May, and October, the museum is open on weekdays for guided tours by appointment; call 505/471-2261 to make arrangements. In these shoulder months, the ranch is also occasionally open for special theme weekends.

Lamy

Probably worth the drive only if you're a rail fan, this village is little more than a depot with an attached restaurant, though it is a mighty fine place to step off Amtrak's Southwest Chief. Across the road, the **Lamy Railroad & History Museum** (151 Old Lamy Tr., 505/466-1650, www.lamymuseum.org, noon-4pm Sat.) is a sprawling Old West saloon and dining room (known as Legal Tender) that doubles as a treasure trove of old railroading days; there's even a model train set. The place has a spotty record of opening, so call ahead if you plan to make the trip.

Take Old Las Vegas Highway (or I-25) southeast out of Santa Fe; six miles out of town, turn south on U.S. 285. After six miles, turn left for the last bumpy mile to Lamy.

historic Rancho de las Golondrinas

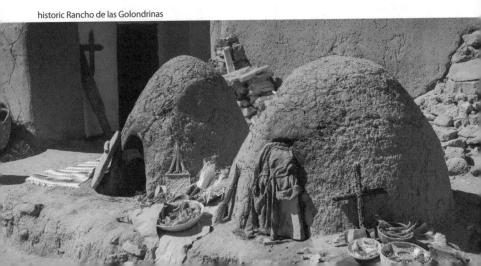

Entertainment and Events

NIGHTLIFE

With breezy summer evenings and a populace that always seems to be able to knock off work a little early, Santa Fe typically favors happy hour over late-night carousing.

Bars and Clubs

Longtime city haunt the **Dragon Room Lounge** (406 Old Santa Fe Tr., 505/983-7712, 4pm-midnight Tues.-Sun.) is so dim you might not notice at first the huge tree growing up from the left side of the bar. Guys in cowboy hats chat with mountain bikers and dressed-up cocktail drinkers. There's live music Tuesday, Thursday, and Saturday.

South of the city center, **Maria's** (555 W. Cordova Rd., 505/983-7929, 11am-10pm daily) has gained a devoted following by serving impeccably balanced margaritas, with fresh lime and nearly any brand of tequila you can imagine.

The grungier side of Santa Fe is on display at **Evangelo's** (200 W. San Francisco St., 505/982-9014, 11am-1am daily), where soul and blues bands take the small stage at the back. When there's no band, there's room at the pool tables, plus no shortage of crusty characters. Its basement space, **The Underground,** hosts all kinds of bands. On the opposite corner, those who descend the stairs to the basement-level **Matador** (116 W. San Francisco St., entrance on Galisteo St., 505/984-5050, 5pm-2am daily) will find a good cross section of Santa Fe's younger artists, among other renowned drinkers. If there's not a live band, there's punk rock on the stereo to match the concert posters on the walls.

A few downtown restaurants have standout bars and merit a visit alone even if you're not looking for a meal. The upscale **Rooftop Cantina** (132 Water St., 505/983-1615, 11:30am-11pm daily, May-Oct.) of the **Coyote Café** has one of the liveliest scenes around the plaza, while the snug bar at **Geronimo** (724 Canyon Rd., 505/982-1500, 5:30pm-9:30pm daily) is a good place to put your feet up after a Canyon Road cruise. **La Casa Sena** (125 E. Palace Ave., 505/988-9232, 11am-10pm daily) is set in a truly dreamy garden courtyard; order a cocktail and an appetizer and enjoy the eye candy.

Breweries

Local operation **Second Street Brewery** brews stouts, bitters, IPAs, and other beers on tap in a chummy, semi-industrial atmosphere, sometimes backed up by a band. There are multiple locations: the original site that gave it its name (1814 2nd St., 505/982-3030, 11am-10pm Mon.-Thurs., 11am-11pm Fri.-Sat., noon-9pm Sun.), the more central branch in the Railyard (1607 Paseo de Peralta, 505/989-3278, 11am-10pm Mon.-Thurs., 11am-11pm Fri.-Sat., noon-9pm Sun.) with a patio area, and another in the heart of the Siler-Rufina neighborhood (2920 Rufina St., 505/954-1068, 11am-midnight Mon.-Sat., noon-midnight Sun.). Happy hour is 4pm-6:30pm daily.

Cozy **Duel Brewing** (1228 Parkway Dr., 505/474-5301, noon-midnight Mon.-Sat., 1pm-8pm Sun.) focuses mainly on Belgian-style beers—Duel's potent saison is a standout—with a few other options on tap as well. An eclectic selection of live acts performs regularly on the small stage, and the menu features items filling sandwiches and tasty finger food.

On the southern outskirts of the city, venerable **Santa Fe Brewing Company** (35 Fire Pl., 505/424-3333, 11am-10pm Mon.-Fri., Sat 11am-9pm 2pm-8pm Sun.) is the oldest brewery in New Mexico. The small taproom has over a dozen crafted beers, including its popular Happy Camper IPA and Santa Fe Gold lager as well as seasonal varieties. Saturday **tours** (noon) provide an excellent glimpse behind the scenes of the onsite brewery.

Open-Air Bars

For a perfectly perched sunset drink, get to the **Bell Tower Bar** (100 E. San Francisco St., 505/982-5511, 11am-sunset daily May-Oct.) early if you can, as this spot on the rooftop at La Fonda fills up fast. It's usually packed with tourists, but the view—from the 5th floor, the highest in the center of town—is inspiring.

If there's no room at the Bell Tower, the next best spot is **Thunderbird** (50 Lincoln Ave., 505/490-6550, 11:30am-9pm, 11:30am-10pm Fri.-Sat.), which has a 2nd-floor porch with views onto the plaza. At happy hour (4pm-6pm), margaritas are $6.

The mellow patio scene at **Cowgirl BBQ** (319 S. Guadalupe St., 505/982-2565, 11:30am-midnight Mon.-Thurs., 11am-1am Fri.-Sat., 11am-11:30pm Sun.) gets started early, with happy hour kicking off at 3pm and lasting till 6pm, with two-for-one apps and $4 margaritas. It's good later too, with live music many nights.

On Canyon Road, stalwart **El Farol** (808 Canyon Rd., 505/983-9912, 11am-10pm Sun.-Thurs., 11am-11pm Fri.-Sat.) is the gallerists' after work hangout, with outside seating on a creaky wooden portal and a back patio.

A strong selection of over 30 craft ales is on tap at the **Violet Crown** (1606 Alcaldesa St., 505/216-5678, 10:30am-11pm daily) which offers one of the more scenic views in the Railyard and a great starting point to a night out in the district.

Cocktail Lounges

While most Santa Fe bars stick to margaritas, **Secreto Lounge** (210 Don Gaspar Ave., 505/983-5700, 4pm-midnight Mon.-Thurs., noon-midnight Fri.-Sat., noon-10pm Sun.) is up on the cutting edge of cocktail culture. Its "garden to glass" menu uses only fresh herbs and other seasonal ingredients in such drinks as the Ginny Juice, a lemonade, orange juice, and vodka concoction with a serious kick. Of course, it still does a margarita or two: Its Agave Way is a pseudo-margarita that's spicy and sweet, with black grapes. Happy hour (4pm-7pm Mon.-Fri.) is worth planning around, as it knocks the price down to $7 or so, and you can sit out in the loggia of the Hotel St. Francis and watch the passing parade.

Intimate and ornately designed, **Tonic** (103 E. Water St., 505/982-1189, www.tonicsantafe.com, 5pm-3am Mon.-Sat.) unabashedly evokes a bygone era. Sip on sophisticated cocktails—several of which are fairly elaborate—and enjoy the art deco flourishes steps from a jazz quartet.

Boozehounds will also want to drop by the tasting room of **Santa Fe Spirits** (308 Read St., 505/780-5906, 3pm-8:30pm Mon.-Thurs., 3pm-9pm Fri.-Sat.), a relaxed place to sample all the local distiller's products. Order a full flight, or enjoy a showcase drink such as the Whiskeyrita, which features the distiller's un-aged Silver Coyote whiskey, or a simple gin and tonic with its aromatic, sage-infused gin.

Live Music

El Mesón (213 Washington St., 505/983-6756, 5pm-11pm Tues.-Sat.) has live music five nights a week, with a particularly devoted crew of regulars for tango on Tuesdays. You can order traditional tapas or bigger dishes from El Mesón's excellent dinner menu, or just join in the dancing on the small wood floor.

The Bridge (37 Fire Pl., 505/557-6182), Santa Fe Brewing Company's indoor and larger outdoor performance spaces, hosts touring bands and local acts across the lot from the taproom.

THE ARTS
Performing Arts

Set in a 1931 Moorish curlicue palace, the **Lensic Performing Arts Center** (211 W. San Francisco St., 505/988-1234, www.

lensic.com) is Santa Fe's showpiece venue, with 820 seats and an eclectic wide-ranging schedule. The six-week-long summer **Santa Fe Chamber Music Festival** (www.sfcmf.org) holds events here, with performances nearly every day July-August. The chamber orchestra **Santa Fe Pro Musica** (505/988-4640, www.santafepromusica.com) also performs at the Lensic, fall-spring, as well as in Loretto Chapel and other intimate venues.

If you think opera is all about tuxes, plush seats, and too-long arias, give the **Santa Fe Opera** (U.S. 84/285, 505/986-5900, www.santafeopera.org) a chance. Half the fun is arriving early to "tailgate" in the parking lot, which involves gourmet goodies, lots of champagne, and time to mill around and check out other attendees' bolo ties. Then there's the show itself, featuring the country's best singers, who treat this as their "summer camp" July-August. The elegant 2,000-plus-seat open amphitheater is beautiful at sunset; pack blankets to ward off the chill later on. If you have kids to entertain, time your visit for bargain-priced "family nights" or a special dress rehearsal with extra info to introduce young ones to the art form.

Cinema

★ VIOLET CROWN

Santa Fe's take on the Austin, Texas, beloved cinema and the Railyard's biggest draw, the **Violet Crown** (1606 Alcaldesa St., 505/216-5678, www.violetcrownsantafe.com) offers the most well-rounded and enjoyable movie-watching experience around. Select from a full snack and dinner menu and an extensive beer and wine list and settle into cushy seats to watch the latest blockbusters, handpicked indies, and one-night-only showings of film classics.

OTHER CINEMAS

The delightful **Jean Cocteau Cinema** (418 Montezuma Ave., 505/466-5528, www.jean-cocteaucinema.com, 2pm-10pm daily) gets press because of its owner, resident author George R. R. Martin, but it's a real treat on its own. The 120-seat theater oozes art-house charm and shows eclectic offerings and hosts readings for an appreciative local audience. It also holds a small bar area where you can order a pint and admire signed *Game of Thrones* merchandise.

Santa Fe University of Art and Design also has an excellent theater, **The Screen** (1600 St. Michaels Dr., 505/473-6494, www.thescreensf.com). The curator brings in

Grab a beer and catch the latest blockbuster at the Violet Crown.

George R. R. Martin in Santa Fe

Eclectic films await at the Jean Cocteau Cinema.

Santa Fe has been home to the wildly celebrated author **George R. R. Martin** since long before readers and HBO viewers were devouring his epic tales of warring nobles, zombie armies, and dragons in a land called Westeros. The author is quick to profess his love for the city—and green chile—and that affection is writ large around town. He restored and reopened the **Jean Cocteau Cinema,** giving Santa Fe its most eclectic theater—the kind of place where obscure 1970s horror movies can be seen on the big screen alongside Italian film classics. Part of the impetus behind the theater was to provide "The City Different" with something different—a compelling late-night diversion unlike anything else in town. That desire was likely also a contributing factor in his decision to back the **Meow Wolf Art Complex.** Now a runaway success, the complex was anything but a surefire hit when the idea to fund it was presented to Martin by its directors. It's hard to imagine the project getting off the ground without his support.

Though Martin is busy writing the latest book in his *A Song of Ice and Fire* series and helping HBO to create *Game of Thrones* spinoffs, he continues to give back to Santa Fe. His latest venture is **The Stagecoach Foundation** (stagecoachfdn.org), a nonprofit formed in 2017 to support Santa Fe's growing presence in the film industry as well as in the fields of education and technology. Its headquarters include space for film productions. Perhaps the White Walkers will someday come to the high desert . . .

quality first-run independent films along with repertory gems. Additionally, the **CCA Cinematheque** (1050 Old Pecos Tr., 505/982-1338, www.ccasantafe.org) has a film program with an emphasis on international titles and music documentaries.

Lectures

The **Lannan Foundation Lecture Series** (www.lannan.org, 505/986-8160) is run by a Santa Fe-based organization funding international writers and socially active artists. The program brings major writers and intellectuals to the Lensic for fascinating interviews and conversation. Events usually sell out quickly—check the schedule a couple of months before your visit.

The **Southwest Seminars Series** (www. southwestseminars.org, 505/466-2775) runs weekly year-round. Speakers are anthropologists, archaeologists, and other researchers with a special interest in the history and people of the region. Talks take place nearly every Monday (50 weeks a year) at 6pm at the Hotel Santa Fe (1501 Paseo de Peralta).

FESTIVALS AND EVENTS

★ Santa Fe Indian Market

Approaching its centennial mark, the city's biggest annual event is held in late August, when 100,000 visitors come for the **Santa Fe Indian Market** (505/983-5220, www.swaia.org). Centered on the plaza, the massive showcase of Native American art features over 1,200 artisans selling jewelry, pottery, weaving, and more. The biggest crowds wander amongst the numerous stalls over the weekend, though there are celebratory events leading up to it.

Other Events

The **Outside Bike & Brew** (www.outsidesantafe.com) kicks off Santa Fe's festival season in mid- to late May with an inviting blend of fat tires of craft ales in the Railyard. As befitting its name, the weekend festival features a full slate of events centered around bikes or beer—and occasionally both—starting with Friday's kick-off event in the Farmer's Market Pavilion. After a weekend of area rides, short films, clinics, and concerts, the festival draws to a close with the Santa Fe Century, held separately (see page 65).

One weekend in mid-July, the **International Folk Art Market** (505/992-7600, www.folkartalliance.org) showcases traditional crafts from all over the globe, often from the artists in person. It's set up on Museum Hill so that the center of the city is not disrupted. On Sunday, tickets are cheaper than Friday and Saturday, and vendors are ready to make deals.

In late July, **Spanish Market** (505/982-2226, www.spanishcolonial.org) takes over the plaza with traditional New Mexican woodwork (especially santos), weaving, and furniture.

Alongside, the upstart **Indigenous Fine Art Market** (www.indigefam.org), based at

Artisan Jolene Bird exhibits turquoise jewelry at the Santa Fe Indian Market.

Railyard Park, emphasizes more contemporary work. It's all a bit of a frenzy, but festive, due to free music and dance performances in the week leading up to the market itself.

After the bustle of summer tourism, locals celebrate the arrival of fall with the weeklong **Fiesta de Santa Fe** (505/204-1598, www.santafefiesta.org), which has been celebrated in some form since 1712. It begins with a reenactment of Diego de Vargas's *entrada* into the city, then a whole slew of balls and parades, including the Historical/Hysterical Parade and a children's pet parade—eccentric Santa Fe at its finest. The kickoff event is usually the **Burning of Zozobra** (855/969-6272, www.burnzozobra.com), a neo-pagan bonfire; the schedule has fluctuated a bit but typically falls on the Friday before Labor Day. Some downtown businesses close for some fiestas, particularly on Zozobra day.

Held in early September in the Farmers Market Pavilion, relative newcomer **Green Chile Cheeseburger Smackdown** (ediblesmackdown.com) is the definitive showcase for

The Burning of Zozobra

Every fall a raucous chant fills the air in Santa Fe's Fort Marcy Park: "Burn him! Burn him! Burn him!" It's the ritual torching of Zozobra, a 50-foot-tall marionette with long, grasping arms, glowering eyes, and a moaning voice. In the weeks before the event, Old Man Gloom, as he's commonly known, is stuffed with divorce papers, pictures of his ex, hospital gowns, and other anxiety-inducing scraps. Setting Old Man Gloom aflame is intended to purge these troubles, clearing the way for a fresh start.

This Santa Fe tradition sounds like a medieval rite, but it dates only from the 1920s, when artist Will Shuster—a bit of a local legend who's also credited with inventing piñon-juniper incense and starting the tradition of citywide bonfires on Christmas Eve—wanted to lighten up the heavily Catholic Fiesta de Santa Fe. Shuster, who had moved to Santa Fe in 1920 to treat his tuberculosis, was inspired by the Mummers Parade from his native Philadelphia, as well as the Yaqui Indians in Tucson, Arizona, who burn Judas in effigy in the week before Easter. A 1926 *Santa Fe New Mexican* article describes the spectacle Shuster developed, with the help of the Kiwanis Club:

the ritual torching of Old Man Gloom

Zozobra . . . stood in ghastly silence illuminated by weird green fires. While the band played a funeral march, a group of Kiwanians in black robes and hoods stole around the figure. . . . [Then] red fires blazed at the foot . . . and leaped into a column of many colored flames. . . . And throwing off their black robes the spectators emerged in gala costume, joining an invading army of bright-hued harlequins with torches in a dance around the fires as the band struck up "La Cucaracha."

Shuster oversaw Zozobra nearly every year until 1964. In the late 1930s, actor Errol Flynn, in town with Olivia de Havilland and Ronald Reagan to film *The Santa Fe Trail,* set Zozobra aflame. A few years later, during World War II, the puppet was dubbed Hirohitlomus, a stringing together of abbreviated names of the enemy leaders. In 1950, Zozobra appeared on the New Mexico state float in the New Year's Day Rose Bowl parade and won the national trophy.

Although Zozobra now has a Twitter account and accepts worries-to-burn online, the spectacle is roughly unchanged, with dozens of white-clad children playing "glooms," followed by a "fire dancer" who taunts Zozo until he bursts into flame; fireworks cap off the event. It's a raucous spectacle, attended by a great cross section of New Mexicans. But anyone leery of crowds may prefer to watch from outside the perimeter of the ball field; the streets above and to the east of Fort Marcy Park provide a great vantage point and less intense experience.

all things green-chile cheeseburger. Judges and the public take on the tough task of tasting and choosing the best green-chile cheeseburger around—perhaps not surprisingly, it's a hugely popular event.

In late September, foodies flock to the city for the **Santa Fe Wine and Chile Festival** (505/438-8060, www.santafewineandchile. org), five days of tastings and special dinners at various venues around town.

Shopping

Even people who clutch their purse strings tight may be a little undone by the treasures for sale in Santa Fe. The rational approach would be to consider the most expensive shops more as free museums. (The cheapest, on the other hand, are stocked with made-in-China junk and are eternally on the brink of "going out of business" and should be avoided.) Several souvenir shops and a few influential galleries are clustered around the plaza. Canyon Road is lined with a bewildering number of galleries, though there can be a certain sameness to many of them. South Guadalupe Street and surrounding blocks have more funky and fun boutiques. If you buy too much to carry, **Pak Mail** (369 Montezuma Ave., 505/989-7380) can ship your treasures home safely; it even offers free pickup from hotels.

ART GALLERIES

The densest concentration of artwork is on Canyon Road, though it can seem a bit crowded with Southwestern kitsch. Summer hours are given here; in the winter, most galleries are closed at least Monday and Tuesday.

Local Artists

At the top end of Canyon Road, **Red Dot Gallery** (826 Canyon Rd., 505/820-7338, 10am-5pm Thurs.-Sun.) is the exhibition space for Santa Fe Community College students and alumni, a nice antidote to the high-toned vibe on the rest of the street. In the convention center, the **Community Gallery** (201 W. Marcy St., 505/955-6705, 10am-5pm Tues.-Fri., 9:30am-4pm Sat.) is run by the Santa Fe Arts Commission and always has a wide mix of work on display.

Contemporary

Santa Fe's contemporary scene isn't always easy to find, with the notable exception being **LewAllen** (1613 Paseo de Peralta, 505/988-3250, 10am-6pm Mon.-Fri., 10am-5pm Sat.), fittingly across the street from SITE Santa Fe. One of the Railyard's longtime draws, the vast industrial space holds a strong collection of well-conceived exhibitions. **TAI Modern** (1601 Paseo de Peralta, 505/984-1387, 9:30am-5:30pm Mon.-Sat., 11am-4pm Sun.) focuses on colorful, abstract, and pop art.

A rare spot for abstraction on Canyon Road, **Nüart Gallery** (670 Canyon Rd., 505/988-3888, 10am-5pm daily) also showcases a wide variety of international artists, with a focus on magic realism.

North of Santa Fe, in the village of Tesuque, the bronze foundry **Shidoni** (1508 Bishops Lodge Rd., 505/988-8001, 9am-5pm Mon.-Sat.) has two large gardens full of metalwork sculpture, open from sunrise to sunset every day; its foundry, which ran for over 25 years, is now closed. Immediately adjacent, **Tesuque Glassworks** (1510 Bishops Lodge Rd., 505/988-2165, 9am-5pm daily) functions as a co-op with a range of glass artists using the furnace and displaying their work. To get to Tesuque, head north out of Santa Fe on Washington Avenue, which becomes Bishops Lodge Road; Shidoni is on the left side of the road.

Native American and Southwestern

Near Canyon Road, **Gerald Peters Gallery** (1011 Paseo de Peralta, 505/954-5700, 10am-5pm Mon.-Sat.) and **Nedra**

Matteucci Galleries (1075 Paseo de Peralta, 505/982-4631, 9am-5pm Mon.-Sat.) are the biggies when it comes to Taos Society of Artists and other Western art, though both have contemporary artists too. Even if nothing inside hits the spot, the one-acre sculpture garden and ponds in back of Nedra Matteucci are a treat. Smaller **Robert Nichols Gallery** (419 Canyon Rd., 505/982-2145, 10am-5pm Mon.-Sat., 11am-5pm Sun.) specializes in Native American pottery, including some with whimsical, boundary-pushing sensibilities.

Near the plaza, **Allan Houser Gallery** (125 Lincoln Ave., 505/982-4705, 10am-5pm Mon.-Sat.) showcases the work of the Southwest's best-known Native sculptor; it also maintains a sculpture garden south of the city near Cerrillos, with visits by appointment. In the Railyard, **Blue Rain Gallery** (544 S. Guadalupe St., 505/954-9902, 10am-6pm Mon.-Sat.) showcases work from many pueblo residents, such as Tammy Garcia's modern takes on traditional Santa Clara pottery forms—she sometimes renders bowls in blown glass or applies the geometric decoration to jewelry.

CLOTHING AND JEWELRY

On the plaza, **Santa Fe Dry Goods** (53 Old Santa Fe Trail, 505/983-8142, 10am-6pm Mon.-Sat. 11am-5pm Sun) has a wide-ranging collection of high-end women's clothing and accessories, including jewelry, bags, and shawls; it also sells stylish home decor items. Nearby ¡Mira! (101 W. Marcy St., 505/988-3585, 10:30am-5:30pm Mon.-Sat.) has a hip mix of clothes and housewares, with T-shirts by local designers ("Fanta Se" in the old Santa Fe Railroad logo, say) as well as cool imports from far flung locales such as Ghana. Just down the block, **Glorianna's** (55 W. Marcy St., 505/982-0353, 10am-4:30pm Mon.-Tues. and Thurs.-Sat., often closed for lunch 1pm-2pm) is a treasure trove of beads, packed to bursting with veritable eggs of raw turquoise, trays of glittering Czech glass, and ropes of African trade beads.

The city's best consignment shop is **Double Take** (321 S. Guadalupe St., 505/989-8886, 10am-6pm Mon.-Sat.), a sprawling two-story space with an excellent selection of boots, as well as cool clothing, rodeo-themed 1950s sofas, Fiestaware, and plenty more.

Double Take

Santa Fe for Kids

Doodlet's

In addition to the **Santa Fe Children's Museum** (1050 Old Pecos Tr., 505/989-8359, 9am-5pm Wed., 10am-6:30pm Thurs., 10am-5pm Fri.-Sat., noon-5pm Sun., www.santafechildrensmuseum.org, $7.50), the following are fun options, all open 10am-5pm Monday-Saturday, except where noted.

- **Bee Hive** (328 Montezuma Ave., 505/780-8051, also open noon-4pm Sun.): A lovingly curated kids' bookstore, often with story time on Saturdays.

- **Dinosaurs & More** (137 W. San Francisco St., 505/988-3299, also open Sun.): The owner can tell a story about nearly every meteorite, fossil, and geode in the place.

- **Doodlet's** (120 Don Gaspar St., 505/983-3771, 10am-5:30pm Mon.-Sat., 10am-5pm Sun.): A totally absorbing corner shop filled with bits and bobs for kids and adults, from toy accordions to kitchen tchotchkes.

GIFT AND HOME

Santa Fe icon **Seret & Sons** (224 Galisteo St., 505/988-9151, 9am-5pm Mon.-Fri., 9am-6pm Sat., 9:30am-5pm Sun.) deals in finely woven rugs, antique doors, and large-scale wooden creations from its cavernous warehouse just south of the plaza.

For funky folk art that won't break the bank, head for the equally gigantic **Jackalope** (2820 Cerrillos Rd., 505/471-8539, 9am-6pm Mon.-Sat., 10am-6pm Sun.), crammed with mosaic-topped tables, wooden chickens, Mexican pottery vases, and inexpensive souvenirs. Sharing the space is a community of prairie dogs—a good distraction for children while adults cruise the breakables.

OPEN-AIR MARKETS

As much a quirky fashion show and social scene as a shopping event, the **Santa Fe Flea** (505/982-2671, www.santafetraditionalflea.com) convenes vintage aficionados, fine artists, crafty folks, and "tailgate traders" of miscellaneous oddities. Late May-mid-October, it takes place at the **Santa Fe Downs** (27475 West Frontage Rd., just off Hwy. 599, north of I-25, 8am-3pm Fri.-Sun.). In winter, many of the vendors move indoors to **El Museo Cultural** (555 Camino de la Familia, 8am-3pm Sat.-Sun. late Nov.-Apr.) at the Railyard complex.

In the Santa Fe Farmer's Market Pavilion, the **Railyard Artisan Market** (1607 Paseo de Peralta, www.artmarketsantafe.com, 10am-4pm Sun.) showcases locally crafted goods, such as blown glass, ceramics, blankets, jewelry, and clothing. The selection is better in the shoulder seasons, when fewer competing craft fairs siphon off vendors.

SWEET TREATS

Todos Santos (125 E. Palace Ave., 505/982-3855, 10am-5pm Mon.-Sat.) adds the sweet smell of chocolate to the air in Sena Plaza. The closet-size shop has the perfect (if short-lived) Santa Fe souvenir: *milagros*, the traditional Mexican Catholic prayer charms shaped like body parts, rendered in Valrhona chocolate and covered in a delicate layer of gold or silver leaf. If you prefer nuts and chews, head to longtime candy vendor **Señor Murphy** (100 E. San Francisco St., 505/982-0461, 10am-5:30pm daily) for some "caramales" (chewy balls of caramel and piñon nuts wrapped up in little corn husks) and other New Mexico-inspired sweets.

Sports and Recreation

It's no accident *Outside* magazine has its offices here. After work and on weekends, Santa Feans leave the town to the tourists and scatter into the surrounding mountains on foot and bike—and in winter, on skis and snowboards. You'll find something to do all four seasons, though hikes above the foothills shouldn't be attempted till mid-May at least (and not until you're acclimated to the altitude). If you're in town in the fall, don't miss the aspen leaves turning, usually in mid-October. The access route for activities in the Sangre de Cristos is winding Highway 475—it starts out from the north side of Santa Fe as Artists Road, then the name changes to Hyde Park Road, and farther north it's Ski Basin Road.

Information, Guides, and Gear
Just off Highway 14, immediately south of I-25, the **Public Lands Information Center** (301 Dinosaur Tr., 505/954-2002, www.publiclands.org, 8am-4:30pm Mon.-Fri.) is the best starting point for any planning. The staff will also know the latest status on areas affected by wildfires or floods. **Outspire!** (505/660-0394, www.

outspire.com) runs guided full- and half-day outings—hiking in summer, snowshoeing in winter. **Santa Fe Mountain Adventures** (505/988-4000, www.santafemountainadventures.com) offers guided mountain biking trips of varying difficulty levels between 4-6 hours in and around Santa Fe; they also lead guided hikes and 4x4 outings.

For gear, visit **REI** (500 Market St., 505/982-3557, 10am-8pm Mon.-Fri., 10am-7pm Sat., 11am-6pm Sun.) in the Railyard district.

HIKING
Some of the best hiking trails in the state can be reached by just a short drive or bike ride from the center of Santa Fe. Even in the height of summer, none of them feels particularly overcrowded, meaning you can enjoy some seriously gorgeous scenery in relative solitude. The trails in this section are ordered based on their distance from downtown.

Santa Fe Canyon Preserve
For an easy saunter in town, head for **Santa Fe Canyon Preserve,** a 190-acre patch

Scenic Drive: Fall Foliage

With its evergreens and scrub trees, New Mexico doesn't seem a likely spot for a vivid display of fall colors. But the deciduous trees that flourish here—aspen, maple, cottonwood—are wild pockets of color against the rocky landscape, often bright gold against red rocks. You don't have to drive far to see the colors, which are usually at their peak in mid-October.

From Santa Fe, just drive up **Highway 475** (the road to the ski basin), where pull-outs are positioned for the best vistas of the many colorful aspen stands; the pullout at the aptly named Aspen Vista trailhead is one of the best. Abiquiu's dramatic rock formations are also a good backdrop for cottonwoods.

From Albuquerque, head to the east face of the **Sandia Mountains** and up the road to the peak, stopping off at Cienega Picnic Area and Las Huertas Picnic Area, about midway up the mountain. Or head southeast to the Manzano Mountains, where **Fourth of July Canyon,** with maple leaves turning shades of pink and crimson, is a beautiful color show. The area around Jemez is especially nice, with the cottonwoods contrasting with red canyon walls, though when you get close to Valles Caldera National Preserve, you hit wildfire damage.

From Taos, the entire **Enchanted Circle** drive passes through various patches of color.

Aspen Vista Trail in fall

of the foothills managed by **The Nature Conservancy** (505/988-3867). The preserve covers the canyon formed by the now-diverted Santa Fe River. An easy interpretive loop trail leads around the marshy area for 1.5 miles, passing the remnants of the dam and winding through dense stands of cottonwoods and willows. The trailhead is on Cerro Gordo Road, just north of its intersection with Upper Canyon Road. The area is open only to people on foot—no mountain bikes and no pets.

Randall Davey Audubon Center & Sanctuary

Birders of course will want to start a hike here, but even general visitors will be intrigued by the house of artist **Randall Davey** (1800

Upper Canyon Rd., 505/983-4609, 8am-4pm Mon.-Sat., $2 suggested donation) and two pretty trails that lead into the forest and canyons behind. The beautifully painted back rooms of the house are open for a guided **tour** ($5) at 2pm every Friday, and a free guided bird walk departs from the parking lot at 8am every Saturday.

Sun Mountain

The two-mile round-trip trail up solitary **Sun Mountain** (elev. 7,920 feet) sets off from a small roadside parking area 2.2 miles southeast of Paseo de Peralta on Old Santa Fe Trail. The start of the hike is fairly flat, passing through shaded woods, before beginning a sharp ascent. After 0.25 mile, the trail emerges on Sun Mountain's exposed western flank, where a series of switchbacks pass by yucca, cholla, and prickly pear. From the top, a little over 900 feet from the trailhead, sweeping panoramas take in the city's orderly grid below and an arc of jagged Sangre de Cristo summits to the east.

Atalaya Mountain

One of the most accessible trails in the Santa Fe area (you can take the M city bus to the trailhead on the campus of St. John's College) is also one of the more challenging. The mostly-shaded hike heads up to a **9,121-foot peak,** starting out as a gentle stroll along the city's edge, then becoming increasingly steep, for a round-trip of approximately six miles. Allow about four hours for the full up-and-back.

Aspen Vista

The most popular trail in the Sangre de Cristos is probably **Aspen Vista.** It is well traveled in fall, as the promised views of golden aspen groves are spectacular. In the densest spots, when the sun is shining through the leaves, the air itself feels yellow. Though at a high elevation, the hike is reasonably easy, on a service road with a gradual slope. The full length is 11.5 miles, but it's the first 2.5 miles that are the most aspen-intense. A little under 4 miles in, you get a great view of Santa Fe below; this makes a good turnaround point for a two-hour hike. Look for the parking area on the right of Ski Basin Road (Hwy. 475), just under 13 miles up the road from town.

Raven's Ridge

This is another local favorite, though not too heavily traveled, with great views of Santa Fe Baldy (elev. 12,622 feet)—while you're busy slogging up and over several peaks yourself. The trail starts at the Winsor trailhead (no. 254) in the Santa Fe ski area parking lot, but when you reach the wilderness boundary fence, the **Raven's Ridge Trail** heads to the right along the outside of the fence. The trail shows up on only one local map (Drake

Mountain Maps' *Map of the Mountains of Santa Fe*), but it's easy to follow once you're up there. When in doubt, just head uphill: You'll bag Deception, Lake, and Tesuque peaks in a total of seven miles and with a top elevation of 12,409 feet, returning to the ski area parking lot by walking down along the Tesuque chairlift. But this final stretch isn't particularly scenic, so you may want to take in only one or two of the peaks (**Lake Peak,** the second you reach, is the highest) and then retrace your steps.

Rio en Medio

The serene **Rio en Medio Trail** (no. 163) begins north of Tesuque and parallels a clear stream to a series of waterfalls and then up some rather strenuous switchbacks to a large meadow that's filled with wildflowers in springtime. From the trailhead to the first cascade is 1.7 miles. The meadow is at the 3.5-mile mark, where you'll probably want to turn around, for a hike that will take a total of four or five hours.

To reach the trailhead, drive north out of Santa Fe on Washington Avenue, which becomes Bishops Lodge Road (Highway 590). Drive straight through the village of Tesuque and then turn right in less than a mile onto Highway 592, passing the Four Seasons along the way and following signs for the village of Rio en Medio. In the village, which you reach after 6.5 miles, the road turns into County Road 78-D, an unpromising-looking dirt track that winds through front yards for 0.8 mile before ending in a small parking area. A forest road carries on from there for a short stretch, and then the trail proper heads off to the right and down along a stream. As parking is limited, hiking the trail in off-peak hours is advisable.

BIKING

Mountain bikers have fantastic outlets close to Santa Fe, while those who prefer the open road will love the challenges in the winding highways through the mountains north of the city. There are several reliable bike shops in and around town. Two of the best are **Broken Spoke** (1426 Cerrillos Rd., 505/992-3102, 10am-6pm Mon.-Fri., 10-5pm Sat.) and **Bike N Sport** (524 W. Cordova Rd., 505/820-0809, 10am-6pm Mon.-Fri., 10-5pm Sat.). Both provide a full range of bike services, including tune-ups and repairs.

For bike rentals, **Mellow Velo** (132 E. Marcy St., 505/995-8356, 9am-6pm Mon.-Fri., 9am-5pm Sat., 9am-3pm Sun., from $20/day), just off the plaza, stocks cruisers for around town as well as deluxe mountain and road bikes. It's also an excellent resource of area rides.

Mountain Biking

A local classic and the gentlest introduction to mountain biking around Santa Fe, the **Santa Fe Rail Trail** starts as a paved path in the Railyard Park, then turns to dirt outside the city limits, following a relatively easy route along the railroad tracks to Lamy. The trail is about 12.5 miles one-way; except for a grade near I-25, it's fairly level.

The **Dale Ball Trails** are the heart of the city's mountain biking scene: 22 miles of single-track routes for both hikers and mountain bikers, winding through stands of piñon and juniper in the Sangre de Cristo foothills.

Two trailheads give access to the North, Central, and South Sections of the trail. From the northern trailhead, on Sierra del Norte (immediately off Highway 475 after mile marker 3), the North Section trails vary a bit in elevation, but the Central Section (south from the parking area) is more fun because it's a longer chunk of trails. The southern trailhead, on Cerro Gordo just north of its intersection with Canyon Road, gives access to the Central Section and the South Section, which is for advanced riders only. Note that the trail that starts at the southern trailhead lot, part of the Santa Fe Canyon Preserve, is for foot traffic only—ride your bike 0.1 mile down Cerro Gordo to the start of the Dale Ball system.

In the rolling hills west of the city, **La Tierra Trails** are for biking, hiking, and horseback riding—though it's the two-wheel crew who makes the most use of them, especially after work, when the day is cooler (there's not much shade out here). There are three trailheads, all interconnected by various loops. Look for the turn west (not at a light) off Highway 599, the bypass road around the city.

A bit farther out of town is the immensely popular **Winsor Trail** (no. 254), a catchall that covers a great range of scenery and

Santa Fe Rail Trail

terrain and presents a few challenges, too. Heading up, there are few deadly steep ascents, so it's tiring but not impossible, and you'll rarely have to hike-a-bike; you're rewarded with a long, joyful downhill run. The trailhead is in Tesuque: Take Washington Avenue north out of the center of Santa Fe, continuing as it becomes Bishops Lodge Road (Highway 590). After not quite four miles, turn right onto County Road 72-A, also signed as Big Tesuque Canyon. There are two small pullout areas for parallel parking, and the trail starts about 0.1 mile up the road from the second parking area—the first 0.5 mile is through private land.

Road Biking

Make sure you're acclimated to the altitude before you set out on any lengthy trip and stay hydrated—road biking typically means little shade and long distances in between resupply points. Shoulders aren't a given; it's especially important to ride single file. The area's best tour, along the **High Road to Taos,** will take you through some of the area's highest elevations. Starting in Chimayó shaves some not-so-scenic miles off the ride and gives you a reasonable 45-mile jaunt to Taos.

A less taxing ride can be had by taking Washington Avenue north from downtown. After .25 miles it becomes Bishops Lodge Road (Highway 590) and descends into the shady village of **Tesuque.** Past Tesuque the road continues as Highway 591 before turning into Frontage Road, just past the Highway 285 overpass. The stretch along Frontage Road before it ends near the Buffalo Thunder Casino is not as scenic as the earlier portion, but it is generally blissfully free of traffic.

The annual **Santa Fe Century** (www.santafecentury.com) is the biggest organized riding event in the state, taking place every May. The course runs a 104-mile loop south down the Turquoise Trail and back north via the old farm towns in the Galisteo Basin, southeast of Santa Fe; there's even a Gran Fondo version that pits you against the clock and other riders.

ROCK CLIMBING

To polish your **rock climbing** skills or get tips on nearby routes, talk to the experts at **Santa Fe Climbing Center** (3008 Cielo Court, 505/986-8944, www.climbsantafe.com, noon-9pm Mon., 9am-9pm Tues., Thurs., and Fri., noon-10pm Wed., noon-8pm Sat., 10am-6pm Sun.). You can play around on the walls at the gym ($16 for a day pass) or sign up for a guided group trip to a nearby climbing site (starting at $70 for half a day).

RAFTING

With the **Rio Grande** within easy reach of Santa Fe, some of the best rafting opportunities in the country are close at hand. Snowmelt runoff determines the peak spring times for many of the runs—including the challenging 17-mile-long **Taos Box**—though it has much less of an impact throughout the summer months, when the water levels are more constant. One of the more popular trips is the **Racecourse,** an adrenaline-packed half-day adventure near Pilar. A succession of Class III rapids with names such as The Maze and The Narrows provide plenty of white-knuckle moments. There are more mellow trips too, particularly in the Lower Gorge, where it's easy to float carefree.

The **Rio Chama** offers mostly gentle outings through the heart of O'Keeffe Country, with some Class III rapids as well. Half-day and full-day trips on both rivers are offered by longtime outfitters **Kokopelli Rafting Adventures** (1401 Maclavia St., 505/983-3734, kokopelliraft.com, from $60).

FISHING

Trout teem in the Rio Chama, northwest of Santa Fe, in the streams of **Valles Caldera National Preserve,** and in pockets of a few lesser-known rivers north of the city. The fly shops the **High Desert Angler** (460 Cerrillos Rd., 505/988-7688, 10am-6pm Mon.-Sat., 11am-4pm Sun.) and **The Reel Life** (526 N. Guadalupe St., 505/995-8114, 8am-7pm Mon.-Fri., 8am-6pm Sat., 8am-5pm Sun.), in the DeVargas Center, sell gear and can also arrange guided day-trips to nearby waters (from $350 for two).

GOLF

Marty Sanchez Links de Santa Fe (205 Caja del Rio Rd., 505/955-4400, www.links-desanta fe.com) is a "water-aware" course that uses indigenous grasses and other plants to minimize water use. It offers great views of the mountains as you tour the 18 holes designed by Baxter Spann; there's also "The Great 28," an additional par-3 nine-holer that's exceptionally challenging. With five sets of tees, the course is good for both beginners and experts. Greens fees start at $21 for nine holes, and there are discounts after 2pm.

WINTER SPORTS

Sixteen miles northeast of town in the Santa Fe National Forest, **Ski Santa Fe** (Hwy. 475, 505/982-4429, www.skisantafe.com, $75 full-day lift ticket) is a well-used day area with over 80 trails of varying difficulty, including quite a few challenging runs. Along with its impressive cross-section of trails, another major selling point is that there are virtually no lift lines.

Exclusively for cross-country skiers, the groomed **Norski Trail** (also known as Trail #255) starts about 0.25 mile before the Ski Santa Fe parking lot, off the west side of the road. The standard route is about 2 miles, winding through the trees and along a ridgeline, and you can shorten or lengthen the tour by taking various loops and shortcuts, as long as you follow the directional arrows counterclockwise.

Just seven miles out of town along the road to the ski basin, **Hyde Memorial State Park** (740 Hyde Park Rd., 505/983-7175, www.emnrd.state.nm.us) has an ice rink, a couple of nicely maintained sledding runs, and some shorter cross-country ski routes.

For gear, **Cottam's Ski Shop** (740 Hyde Park Rd., 505/982-0495, from 7:30am daily in ski season) is the biggest rental operation in the area, handily located at the entrance to Hyde Memorial State Park.

In town, the knowledgeable **Alpine Sports** (121 Sandoval St., 505/983-5155, 10am-8pm Mon.-Fri., 10am-6pm Sat.-Sun.) specializes in winter apparel and equipment.

SPAS
★ Ten Thousand Waves

A Santa Fe institution, **Ten Thousand Waves** (3451 Hyde Park Rd., 505/982-9304, www.tenthousandwaves.com, 9am-10:30pm

Ten Thousand Waves

Wed.-Mon., noon-10:30pm Tues. July-Oct.) is a traditional Japanese-style bathhouse that melds seamlessly into the mountainside just outside of town. Featuring two big communal pools, it also has five smaller private ones tucked among the trees; many have adjoining cold plunges and saunas. The place also offers full day-spa services, with intense massages and luxe facials and body scrubs. Prices are relatively reasonable, starting at $24 for unlimited time in the public baths and $117 for 50-minute massages. In the winter (Nov.-June), the baths open at 10:30am (at 2pm Tues.) and close earlier on weeknights.

Other Spas

The relaxed and welcoming atmosphere of **Body of Santa Fe** (333 W. Cordova Rd., 505/986-0362, www.bodyofsantafe.com, 9am-9pm Mon.-Sat., 9am-3pm Sun.) has helped it earn a devoted following—and its affordable treatments (massages from $85/hour) help, too. There's also an on-site studio offering yoga classes daily.

In town, **Absolute Nirvana Spa** (106 Faithway St., 505/983-7942, www.absolutenirvana.com, 10am-6pm Sun.-Thurs., 10am-8pm Fri.-Sat.) runs a "green" operation with a Balinese inspiration for many of its treatments and massages (from $115). Afterward, you can relax in the gardens with a cup of tea and some organic sweets from the adjacent tearoom.

South of the city and down the road from Rancho de Las Golondrinas, **Sunrise Springs** (242 Los Pinos Rd, 505/780-8145, www.sunrisesprings.ojospa.com, 10am-8pm daily) is suited for those looking to truly get away. Spread over 70 idyllic acres, the spa includes yoga and fitness studios, outdoor pools, soaking tubs, hot tubs, and an art studio. A comprehensive list of services and packages is offered, including hot stone massages ($125 for 50 minutes) and various forms of bodywork.

SPECTATOR SPORTS

The **Santa Fe Fuego** (www.santafefuego. com), a baseball team that puts the minor in minor league, plays at Fort Marcy Park, just north of the plaza area, mid-May-early August. It's part of the incredibly scrappy Pecos League (www.pecosleague.com), established in 2011 and fielding 12 teams from around New Mexico, Arizona, California, and west Texas, and Kansas.

SPORTS FACILITIES

For bargain yoga classes, swimming in a 25-yard indoor pool, and other activities close to the plaza, stop in at the **Fort Marcy Recreation Complex** (490 Bishops Lodge Rd., 505/955-2500, www.santafenm.gov, 6am-8:30pm Mon.-Fri., 8am-4pm Sat., $5).

Genoveva Chavez Community Center (3221 Rodeo Rd., 505/955-4000, www.chavezcenter.com, 5:30am-9:45pm Mon.-Thurs., 5:30am-7:45pm Fri., 8am-7:45pm Sat., 9am-5:45pm Sun., $7) is the city's biggest recreational facility. It has a large swimming pool with a slide and a separate lap pool (both are indoors); basketball and racquetball courts; a gym; and a year-round ice rink.

The city's only outdoor pool is **Bicentennial Pool** (1121 Alto St., 505/955-4779, www.santafenm.gov, $3), open late May-early September.

Food

Dining is one of Santa Fe's great pleasures. For its size, the city supports a dazzling range of excellent restaurants, some nationally recognized and others simply revered by locals. Sure, you can get a cheese-smothered, crazy-hot plate of green-chile-and-chicken enchiladas, but most locals eat more globally than that. Top-notch Southwestern, Italian, French, Mediterranean, and—of course—New Mexican fare can all be had within walking distance of the plaza; drive a little farther out and the options open up exponentially.

DOWNTOWN

The ring formed by Alameda Street and Paseo de Peralta contains some classic Santa Fe spots, plus a few hidden treats. On the plaza itself, the carnitas cart and the fajitas cart are classics too—and the Chicago hot dog stand, when it's set up, gets strong votes for authenticity.

New Mexican

The Shed (113½ E. Palace Ave., 505/982-9030, 11am-2:30pm and 5pm-9pm daily, $17) has been serving up platters of enchiladas since 1953—bizarrely, with a side of garlic bread. But that's just part of the tradition at this colorful, comfortable, marginally fancy place that's as popular with tourists as it is with longtime residents. There are perfectly decent distractions like lemon-garlic shrimp and fish tacos on the menu, but it's the red chile you should focus on. Reservations are essential throughout the summer.

Mexican

The specialty at **Bumble Bee's Baja Grill** (301 Jefferson St., 505/820-2862, 11am-8:30pm Sun.-Wed., 11am-9pm Thurs.-Sat., $5) is Baja-style shrimp tacos, garnished with shredded cabbage and a creamy sauce, plus a spritz of lime and your choice of house-made salsas. The seafood stew is also delicious, as are the fried-fresh tortilla chips and that Tijuana classic, Caesar salad. Don't leave without indulging in the churros dipped in chocolate sauce.

Fresh and Local

Open since the late 1970s, ★ **Café Pasqual's** (121 Don Gaspar St., 505/983-9340, 8am-3pm and 5:30pm-9:30pm daily, $29) has defined its own culinary category, relying almost entirely on organic ingredients. Its breakfasts are legendary, but the food is delicious any time of day. Expect nearly anything on the menu, such as smoked-trout hash or Yucatán-style *huevos motuleños* for breakfast and grilled filet mignon with Portobello mushrooms or mole enchiladas for dinner. Call ahead for a reservation or brace yourself for the inevitable line, as the brightly painted dining room seats only 50.

Cafés

Adorned with handsome maps denoting international coffee trade routes, **35° North** (60 E. San Francisco St., 505/983-6138, 7am-6pm daily), on the second floor of The Arcade and overlooking Water Street, serves up some of the best espressos around the plaza as well as a filling and energizing "Latitude Adjustment"—coffee blended with grass-fed butter, coconut oil, and MCT oil.

Ecco (128 E. Marcy St., 505/986-9778, 7am-9pm Mon.-Thurs., 7am-9:30pm Fri., 8am-9:30pm Sat., 8am-6pm Sun.; $3) is packed with coffee junkies in the mornings, giving way to gelato lovers later in the day; choose from nearly 100 flavors of the cold treat.

The **French Pastry Shop** (100 E. San Francisco St., 505/983-6697, 6:30am-5pm daily, $5) has been doling out sweet crepes, buttery pastries, croques monsieurs, and chewy baguette sandwiches for more than 40 years. Early mornings attract a fascinating crew of Santa Fe regulars.

Diners

Longtime burger connoisseurs may remember Bobcat Bite, just outside the city. It closed in 2013, becoming ★ **Santa Fe Bite** (311 Old Santa Fe Tr., 505/982-0544, 11am-8pm Tues.-Thurs., 11am-9pm Fri., 8am-9pm Sat., 8am-8pm Sun., $13)—an even better incarnation, close to the plaza and in much more comfortable digs. The 10-ounce green-chile cheeseburgers, made from beef ground fresh every day and served on a home-baked bun, remain worthy of a pilgrimage. There's plenty more now too, including a bulging patty melt, big salads, and, on Friday, fish-and-chips.

★ **Tia Sophia's** (210 W. San Francisco St., 505/983-9880, 7am-2pm Mon.-Sat., 8am-1pm Sun., $9) is one of the last places around the plaza that feels untouched by time and tourists, serving no nonsense New Mexican plates to a slew of regulars without a touch of fuss or fusion—so authentic, in fact, the kitchen claims to have invented the breakfast burrito decades back.

Plaza Café (54 Lincoln Ave., 505/982-1664, 7am-9pm daily, $11) may look shiny and new, but it's a city institution where residents have long come to read the paper and load up on coffee and great renditions of New Mexican and American diner favorites. This is no greasy spoon, though—the piñon blue-corn pancakes are fluffy and fresh, the posole is perfectly toothsome, and the chicken fried steak is a plateful of comforting goodness. There's another, far larger and livelier outpost on the **southside** (3466 Zafarano Dr., 505/424-0755, 8am-9pm Sun.-Thurs., 8am-10pm Fri.-Sat.).

For just about the most casual lunch around, stop in at the **Five & Dime General Store** (58 E. San Francisco St., 505/992-1800, 8am-10pm daily, $5), on the plaza. In this former Woolworth's where, allegedly, the Frito pie was invented (Frito-Lay historians beg to differ), the knickknack shop has maintained its lunch counter and still serves the deadly combo of corn chips, homemade red chile, onions, and shredded cheese, all composed directly in the Fritos bag. Eat in, or, better still, lounge on the plaza grass—and don't forget the napkins.

Spanish

Cozy, creative-tapas joint **La Boca** (72 W. Marcy St., 505/982-3433, 11:30am-10pm daily, little plates $7-16) tempts with a strong selection of Spanish staples, such as olives stuffed with jamón serrano, gilled octopus, and bruschetta. The little plates can add up fast, unless you're at La Boca 3pm-5pm weekdays, when there's a selection for half price. Reserve, ideally, and go early if you're sensitive to noise.

Italian

Off the plaza, next to Mission San Miguel, **Upper Crust Pizza** (329 Old Santa Fe Tr., 505/982-0000, 11am-10pm Sun.-Thurs. and Sat., 11am-11pm Fri., $14) is a slice of old-school Santa Fe, with a nice, creaky front porch, often with a live country crooner. Choose from regular, whole-wheat, or gluten-free crust and several specialty pizzas, or build your own. Piping-hot calzones and big super-fresh salads round out the menu.

Locals head to amber-lit and intimate **Il Piatto** (95 W. Marcy St., 505/984-1091, 4:30pm-10:30pm Sun.-Tues., 11:30am-10:30pm Wed.-Sat., $25) for understated Italian and a neighborly welcome from the staff, who seem to be on a first-name basis with everyone in the place. Hearty pastas such as pappardelle with duck are served in generous portions—a half order will more than satisfy lighter eaters. This is a great central spot to take a breather from enchiladas and burritos, without breaking the bank. As well as a standard afternoon happy hour, its bar offers a pleasant later happy hour, 9pm-10:30pm every night.

GUADALUPE AND THE RAILYARD

An easy walk from the plaza, the Railyard and a few surrounding blocks hold some of the better, quirkier dining options in town.

Food Trucks

Gorge on burgers and sammies at Bang Bite.

Slowly but surely, Santa Fe's food truck scene is gaining traction, and these days not only are there are several to choose from, but they can be counted on for some of the tastiest meals in the city. Food trucks are now fixtures at major events around town, though many pull up at the same spot throughout the week. The greatest concentration can be found parked in front of Meow Wolf, particularly in summer. These include **Taqueria Gracias Madre** (505/795-6397), which serves chicken and beef tacos; **Kebab Caravan** (505/577-9987), which specializes in Mediterranean kebabs; and **Trinity Kitchen** (505/395-6369), which doles out plates of spicy Cajun and Southern cuisine such as fried chicken with waffles. For mouthwateringly good burgers, including one with sharp cheddar, bacon, and maple bacon jam, stop by ★ **Bang Bite** (411 Water St., 505/469-2345), a few blocks west of the plaza. **Bambini's** (905 S. St. Francis Dr., 505/699-2243) prepares authentic and immensely satisfying Philly cheesesteaks and hoagies. One of the city's longest-running food trucks remains one of its best: **Santa Fe Barbecue** (600 Old Santa Fe Tr., 505/573-4816), where you'll need a bib and a big appetite to handle pulled pork, beef brisket, and baby back pork ribs slathered with a barbecue sauce not soon forgotten. Of course, as food trucks are mobile by nature, it's good to call ahead to find out current locations.

New Mexican

The cousin of downtown's The Shed, **La Choza** (905 Alarid St., 505/982-0909, 11am-2:30pm and 5pm-9pm Mon.-Sat., $17) has a similar creative New Mexican menu but is more of a local's hangout and has a livelier atmosphere; in the summer months, it's especially packed after the workday ends. Count on well-executed New Mexican fare, such as a posole stew and a filling chile relleno. The location in the Railyard district makes it a handy destination if you're coming to Santa Fe by train—just walk back along the tracks a few blocks.

Fine Dining

The understated exterior of Chef Charles Dale's ★ **Bouche Bistro** (451 W. Alameda St., 505/982-6297, www.bouchebistro.com, 5:30pm-9:30pm Tues.-Sat. $26) belies one of Santa Fe's most sumptuous dining experiences. Rich earth tones, warm lighting, and elegant decor complement a menu filled with French classics, such as sautéed sweetbreads, black mussels in white wine, and hanger steak with *pomme frites*. For dessert, choose from a slew of decadent offerings, including tiramisu and crème brûlée.

Whether you want hearty bar food or an ethereal creation that will take your taste buds in new directions, Chef Joseph Wrede delivers at his lovely, candlelit space ★ **Joseph's** (428 Agua Fria St., 505/982-1272, www.josephsofsantafe.com, 5:30pm-10pm Sun.-Thurs., 5:30pm-11pm Fri.-Sat., $16-44). Wrede's best dishes are vegetable-centric, though not necessarily vegetarian, such as an organic chicken, kale, and mushroom roulade. But he's also into local meats, so carnivores will find a beef tenderloin, green chile, and potato stew, and a seemingly simple lamb patty that may be the state's best green-chile cheeseburger. Book ahead if you can, or try for a seat at the bar. And whatever happens, don't miss the duck-fat ice cream.

Fresh and Local

If you're on green-chile-and-cheese overload, head to ★ **Vinaigrette** (709 Don Cubero Alley, 505/820-9205, 11am-9pm Mon.-Sat., $14) and dig into a big pile of fresh greens. The so-called salad bistro uses largely organic ingredients from its farm in Nambé,

in imaginative combos, like a highbrow taco salad with chorizo and honey-lime dressing. The setting is pure homey Santa Fe, with tea towels for napkins, iced tea served in canning jars, and local art on the whitewashed walls. There's a shaded patio too. Next door, you'll first see the same owner's faux farm shop and café, **Modern General** (637 Cerrillos Rd., 505/930-5462, 8am-5pm Mon.-Sat., 10am-5pm Sun., $7), which is also good, with its simple menu of juices, avocado toast, a few other breakfasts all day, and exquisite Czech kolaches—pastries with all manner of sweet fillings. Vinaigrette is in the building behind that.

Just outside the Paseo de Peralta loop, the ★ **Tune-Up Café** (1115 Hickox St., 505/983-7060, 7am-10pm Mon.-Fri., 8am-10pm Sat.-Sun., $9) is a homey two-room joint that locals love, whether for fish tacos or a suitably Santa Fe-ish brown-rice-and-nut burger. The place is especially packed during weekend brunches, when early morning outdoor adventures are recapped over heaping plates of fruit compote-stuffed French toast and steak and eggs.

The popular ★ **Santa Fe Farmers Market** (1607 Paseo de Peralta, 505/983-4098, www.santafefarmersmarket.com, 7am-1pm

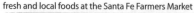
fresh and local foods at the Santa Fe Farmers Market

Tues. and Sat. late May-Nov., 8am-1pm Sat. Dec.-mid-May) is a buzzing social scene and a great place to pick up fresh local produce and treats as well as souvenir chile *ristras*. It's in a market hall in the Railyard complex, off Paseo de Peralta near Guadalupe Street.

Burgers and Barbecue

All things Texan are the specialty at **Cowgirl BBQ** (319 S. Guadalupe St., 505/982-2565, 11:30am-11:30pm Mon.-Thurs., 11:30am-12:30am Fri., 11am-12:30am Sat., 11am-11pm Sun., $11-18)—think mesquite-smoked baby back ribs, chile with cheese and jalapeño cornbread, and barbecued chicken. It's a kitsch-filled spot that's as friendly to kids as it is to margarita-guzzling, barbecued-rib-gnawing adults. Non-meat-eaters won't feel left out: An ooey-gooey butternut squash casserole comes with a salad on the side. Both carnivores and veggies can agree on the flourless chocolate cake with red chile and the ice cream "baked potato."

An outdoor burger joint that's so good people flock to it even in winter, **Shake Foundation** (631 Cerrillos Rd., 505/988-8992, 11am-7pm Mon.-Thurs., 11am-8pm Fri. and Sat., 11am-6pm Sun., $3.95-7.50), serves undersized beef, lamb, and turkey burgers (order a double if in doubt) on lavishly buttered buns; there's also a melt-in-your-mouth fried oyster sandwich with red-chile mayo. The eatery's dense, namesake drinks come in "adobe mud shakes," with ice cream made from New Mexico dairy. Seats in the shade are in short supply; plan accordingly in the heat of a summer afternoon.

Cafés

Make room in your morning for an almond croissant from ★ **Sage Bakehouse** (535 Cerrillos Rd., 505/820-7243, 7:30am-2:30pm Mon.-Sat., $5). Washed down with a mug of coffee, these butter-soaked pastries will have you set for hours. Before you leave, pick up some sandwiches for later—classics such as egg salad on sourdough and smoked turkey and cheddar on the bakery's excellent

Geronimo

homemade whole wheat crust. And maybe a pecan-raisin wreath. And a cookie too.

A few steps away, **Ohori's Coffee, Tea & Chocolate** (505 Cerrillos Rd., 505/988-9692, 7am-6pm Mon.-Fri., 8am-6pm Sat., 9am-2pm Sun.), is Santa Fe's small-batch coffee epicure; its dark-as-night brew makes Starbucks seem weak. With few seats, it's not so much a place to linger long but rather one at which to appreciate a clear attention to detail. There's a second shop just out of the center, at 1098 South St. Francis Drive (7am-6pm Mon.-Fri., 8am-6pm Sat.).

CANYON ROAD AND THE EASTSIDE

Gallery hopping can make you hungry—but there are only a handful of places to eat on Canyon Road, and most are more dedicated to getting caffeine into your system.

Fine Dining

Elegant **Geronimo** (724 Canyon Rd., 505/982-1500, 5:45pm-9pm daily, $27-52) is

The Teahouse

Subscription (376 Garcia St., 505/983-3085, 7am-6pm daily), an airy coffee shop buzzing with locals and stocked with a bewildering selection of magazines.

Chocolate devotees should consider ★ **Kakawa Chocolate House** (1050 E. Paseo de Peralta, 505/982-0388, 10am-6pm Mon.-Sat., noon-6pm Sun., $4) an essential—and educational—stop. It elevates hot chocolate to an art form, specializing in historically accurate drinks based on Mesoamerican and medieval European recipes. Kakawa also has decadent bite-size chocolates as well as dense dark-chocolate brownies. It's in a tiny adobe house with a kiva fireplace; when the temperature drops in winter, there's no place better to settle in.

Located at the top end of Canyon Road, **The Teahouse** (821 Canyon Rd., 505/992-0972, 9am-9pm daily, $12) is the ideal place to put your feet up after a long art crawl. Choose from an incredibly long list of teas from around the world, many of which are prepared in a variety of ways. There are also vittles such as mixed greens with cranberries, pecans, and feta and a deliciously hearty bowl of oats, black rice, buckwheat groats, and maple cream for breakfast. The service could be euphemistically described as "very Santa Fe" (i.e., forget about a quick meal), but the teas and food are unquestionably worth it.

CERRILLOS ROAD

This commercial strip isn't Santa Fe's most scenic stretch, but you'll find some great culinary gems out this way.

New Mexican

When the original and much-loved ★ **Tecolote** (1616 St Michael's Drive, 7am-2pm Sun. and Tues.-Sat., $10) closed its doors in 2014, the consternation among its longtime customers was understandable and fortunately short-lived. The restaurant reopened its doors at its new location a little over a year later in much nicer environs and with a welcomed expanded menu to boot. Old favorites such as bacon breakfast burritos stuffed with

consistently rated one of Santa Fe's best restaurants, and it's easy to see why. Standouts on the menu include an elk tenderloin, grilled rack of lamb and a blackened Pacific snapper; the service is impeccable, too.

Spanish

One of the oldest restaurants in the country, **El Farol** (808 Canyon Rd., 505/983-9912, 11:30am-11pm daily, $7-36) is Canyon Road's liveliest nightspot. There's usually lots of action in the bar area, including frequent live flamenco, but it's the outside seating, under a creaky wooden portal and on a back patio, that really makes this historic adobe one of the better places in town to settle in for an evening. Pair drinks with numerous hot and cold tapas, such as *patatas bravas* and Spanish olives with anchovies and roasted peppers or opt for larger plates, including its popular house paella.

Cafés

For a morning brew, stroll over to **Downtown**

posole remain alongside healthier options such as homemade roasted piñon pecan-maple granola with vanilla yogurt.

Long appreciated for its dazzling list of margaritas, **Maria's** (555 W. Cordova Rd., 505/983-7929, 11am-10pm daily, $10) is well worth settling into for a meal of hearty New Mexican classics, starting with a genuinely hot table salsa and chips. Both red and green are sold here, and the tamales are exceptionally rich and creamy (even the vegetarian ones!).

A nice no-frills family diner, **The Pantry** (1820 Cerrillos Rd., 505/986-0022, 6:30am-8:30pm Mon.-Sat., 7am-8:30pm Sun., $9) has been slinging eggs, pancakes, and chile since 1948. There's a lunch counter up front, but regulars request the back room.

The decision of which chile to slather your breakfast burrito with is not one to be taken lightly at the ★ **Horseman's Haven** (4354 Cerrillos Rd., 505/471-5420, 8am-8pm Mon.-Sat., 8:30am-2pm Sun., $8), home to some of the hottest green chile in Santa Fe. It picks and mixes chile varieties to offer a couple of consistent grades to go with filling plates of old-school New Mexican fare. Like all good chile purveyors, the café is in an unassuming box of a building next to a gas station, and it takes cash only.

Mexican

El Chile Toreado (950 W. Cordova Rd., 505/800-0033, 8:15am-3pm Mon.-Fri., 8:15am-2pm Sat., $7), a nondescript hut in a parking lot on Cordova Road, just east of Cerrillos, delivers a cilantro-tinged green salsa that is a near-mystical experience. Its carnitas may be the best in town; it also serves excellent breakfast burritos—get one with Mexican chorizo.

French

In a new location somewhat incongruously inside Body of Santa Fe, ★ **Clafoutis** (333 W. Cordova St., 505/988-1809, 7am-4pm Tues.-Sun., $5-12.50) still oozes a laid-back Parisian charm and tempts with the sweet

smells of crepes, bruschettas, and croissants. The *croque madame* is as delectable as ever and the beignets can still be ordered by the bagful; the salads, including one with smoked salmon and toasted almonds, don't disappoint either. While its new digs can't quite hope to feel as cozy as its old ones, there's now much more room and plenty of parking to boot.

African

Just next to Hobby Lobby in a strip mall, ★ **Jambo** (2010 Cerrillos Rd., 505/473-1269, 11am-9pm Mon.-Sat., $11) has a menu of spicy, earthy food that's well priced and almost always satisfying. The menu features primarily Indian-inflected dishes from East Africa—lentil stew spiked with chile and softened with coconut, for instance—as well as Caribbean and Moroccan stews.

Asian

Attached to a Quality Inn, **Lu Lu's** (3011 Cerrillos Rd., 505/473-9898, 11am-9pm Mon.-Thurs. and Sun., 11am-9:30pm Fri.-Sat., $7.95-16.95) serves some of the most satisfying Chinese food around. Count on familiar pleasures such as sweet and sour chicken and kung pao, but don't overlook several standout house specialties, including a generous Royal Seafood Pot—scallops, crabmeat, shrimp, fish, and vegetables in a white-wine sauce

Cafés

One of the most dangerous addresses in Santa Fe is an inconspicuous duplex with **Whoo's Donuts** (851-B Cerrillos Rd., 505/629-1678, 7am-3pm daily, $2) and **ChocolateSmith** (851-A Cerrillos Rd., 505/473-2111, 10am-5:30pm Mon.-Sat., noon-5pm Sun.). Bear right for organic maple bacon and blue-corn-and-raspberry cake donuts; bear left for intense hand-dipped truffles.

Counter Culture (930 Baca St., 505/995-1105, 8am-3pm Sun.-Mon., 8am-9pm Tues.-Sat., $12) is generally a locals-only scene, well liked for its catchall menu (including enchiladas, Vietnamese banh mi sandwiches, and tire-size cinnamon buns), its casual-industrial vibe, and its outdoor patio where kids can run around.

Tucked away in the heart of Lena Street's industrial lofts, airy ★ **Iconik** (1600 Lena St., 505/428-0996, 7:30am-6pm Mon.-Sat., 8am-5pm Sun.) is worth seeking out for its heady mix of top-notch pour-overs and drips, bagel sandwiches, and smart decor. It's a large communal space with comfy couches set against a backdrop of coffee-roasting equipment, and features occasional live music. The company also operates the café inside the bookstore **Collected Works** (202 Galisteo St., 505/988-4226, 8am-6pm daily).

SANTA FE METRO AREA
Classic American

On the frontage road for I-25, **Harry's Roadhouse** (96 Old Las Vegas Hwy., 505/989-4629, 7am-9:30pm daily, $13) is an easy detour off the freeway (exit at Old Santa Fe Trail). The pretty patio is usually buzzing, there's a full bar, and the diner-style menu includes everything from fried catfish with grits to turkey meat loaf to pizza, plus coconut cream pie. Expect a line and a packed parking lot; reserve ahead, if possible.

Fresh and Local

For a calmer, more wholesome vibe, keep driving down the road to **Café Fina** (624 Old Las Vegas Hwy., 505/466-3886, 7am-3pm Mon.-Wed., 7am-3pm and 5:30pm-8:30pm Thurs.-Fri., 8am-3pm and 5:30pm-8:30pm Sat., 8am-3pm Sun., $10), also easily accessible at exit 290 off I-25. This is a casual order-at-the-counter place, with a short but flavor-packed menu (including ricotta pancakes, Reubens, and grilled salmon tacos) from mostly locally grown ingredients.

Italian

Chef Enrique Guerrero's handsome and welcoming ★ **El Nido** (1577 Bishop's Lodge Rd., 505/954-1272, 4:30pm-10pm Mon.-Fri., 10:30am-2:30pm and 4:30pm-10pm Sat.-Sun., $14-57) serves up refined and hearty Italian fare in a historical Tesuque adobe. The menu features choice cuts of meat such as a hand-cut strip steak with a potato puree; there are several wood-fired pizzas to choose from as well. Though portions are substantial, think twice about skipping dessert.

Asian

The restaurant at Ten Thousand Waves, **Izanami** (3451 Hyde Park Rd., 505/428-6390,

Izanami

11:30am-10pm Wed.-Mon., 5pm-10pm Tues., $4-22), melds old Japan and new without feeling like a theme restaurant. On the menu, there's pickled burdock root and grilled avocado, as well as wagyu-beef burgers and sake-braised mushrooms in a butter sauce, served in small plates to share. The dining room has a rustic mountain-lodge feel, with an optional shoes-off tatami-mat seating area. Throw in arguably the most extensive sake menu in the Southwest and surprisingly reasonable prices, and it's one of Santa Fe's cooler places to eat, whether you make the drive up for dinner or just wander over after your bath.

Accommodations

Santa Fe offers some great places to stay, but few are particularly cheap. Prices quoted for the bigger hotels are standard rack rates; chances are, you'll find substantially lower ones by calling or booking online, at least at the higher-end properties. Prices spike in July and August, often up to holiday rates. If you're coming for Indian Market or Christmas, try to book several months in advance. On the other hand, despite ski season, rates are often quite low in early December, January, and February.

UNDER $100

As hostels go, **Santa Fe International Hostel** (1412 Cerrillos Rd., 505/988-1153, www.hostelsantafe.com) is best appreciated with rose-colored glasses firmly in place, viewed as an old-school hippie project (it *is* run as a nonprofit). The dorms ($20 per person) and private rooms ($25 single, $35 double) are dim, and cleanliness can be spotty, as you're relying on the previous guests' efforts as part of the required daily chores. The kitchen has free food, but you have to pay for Internet access ($2/day), and everything is cash only.

For camping, the closest tent sites to the center are at **Hyde Memorial State Park** (Hwy. 475, 505/983-7175, www.emnrd.state.nm.us), about eight miles northeast of the city, with both primitive ($10) and developed sites with electricity ($14).

Possibly the best lodging deal in Santa Fe, the **Quaker Meeting House** (630 Canyon Rd., 505/983-7241, www.santa-fe.quaker.org, $45 s, $55 d) rents a guest apartment with a kitchenette. It's a small space, and it has a three-night minimum, but the location on Canyon Road can't be beat. Payment is cash or check only.

Wedged in among the chain hotels on Cerrillos, the self-described kitschy ★ **Silver Saddle Motel** (2810 Cerrillos Rd., 505/471-7663, www.santafesilversaddlemotel.com, $59 d) plays up the retro charm. Cozy rooms may be pretty basic and have cinder-block walls, but they're decked out with Western accoutrements and kept clean—and the price, which includes breakfast, can't be beat. A handful of later-built rooms have a little more space to spread out.

$100-150

The bones of ★ **Santa Fe Sage Inn** (725 Cerrillos Rd., 505/982-5952, www.santafesageinn.com, $114 d) are a standard highway motel, but the super-clean rooms are done in sharp, modern red and black, with Southwestern rugs hung on the walls. Little touches such as free Wi-Fi, plush beds, and an above-average breakfast (fresh bagels, fruit, yogurt, and more) make this an excellent deal. The place even has a swimming pool. It's still walking distance to the center, and it's right across the street from the Railyard Park and the farmers market. The onsite restaurant, Derailed, can be hit or miss, though.

Built around a 1936 motor court, ★ **El Rey Inn** (1862 Cerrillos Rd., 505/982-1931, www.elreyinnsantafe.com, $115 s, $135 d) counts as one of the more charming motels in Santa Fe. Though it has been expanded over the years, its character remains intact, and it has been meticulously kept up and adjusted for modern standards of comfort, with beautiful gardens, a big swimming pool, a hot tub, and a sauna. The 86 rooms, spread over 4.5 acres, vary considerably in style (and in price), from the oldest section with snug adobe walls and heavy viga ceilings to airier rooms with balconies. Guests get a voucher for breakfast at the Pantry, a nice old-timey restaurant next door. The only drawback is that the plaza is too far to walk, but a city bus stops right outside.

$150-200

Santa Fe Motel & Inn (510 Cerrillos Rd., 505/982-1039, www.santafemotel.com, $159 d) is a good budget option close to the center, with rooms done up in simple, bright decor that avoids motel sameness despite the generic layout. A few kitchenettes are available, along with more-private casitas with fireplaces. Lots of nice touches—such as bread from the Sage Bakehouse across the street along with the full breakfast—give the place a homey feel without the tight quarters of a typical bed-and-breakfast.

East of the plaza, two exquisite bed-and-breakfasts under the same ownership offer two kinds of style: The rooms at **Hacienda Nicholas** (320 E. Marcy St., 505/986-1431, www.haciendanicholas.com, $155 d) have a tasteful Southwestern flavor, decorated with a few cowboy trappings and Gustave Baumann prints. Most rooms have fireplaces and there's also a spacious suite. Across the street, **The Madeleine** (106 E. Faithway St., 505/982-3465, www.madeleineinn.com, $155 d) occupies a wood Victorian, with antique furniture offset by rich Balinese fabrics. At both spots, breakfasts show the same attention to sumptuous detail, with items such as blue-corn waffles and a Southwestern frittata.

$200-250

The 100-room **Inn of the Governors** (101 W. Alameda St., 505/982-4333, www.innofthegovernors.com, $199 d) isn't flashy on the outside, but inside it has a personable only-in-Santa-Fe feel, starting with the afternoon "tea and sherry hour," when guests are plied with free drinks and *bizcochitos*. The inn's unique profit-sharing system may account for the exceptionally nice staff. Breakfast is generous, parking is free (unheard-of elsewhere downtown), and there's even a tiny pool. Rooms in the Governors Wing are quietest. The attached Del Charro Saloon serves the best-value meals and margaritas around the plaza.

Inn on the Alameda (303 E. Alameda St., 505/984-2121, www.innonthealameda.com, $229 d) is an ideal choice for those who want adobe style *and* space, and its location near Canyon Road is handy for gallery-hoppers. The big rooms have triple-sheeted beds, wireless Internet access, and overstuffed armchairs that are only lightly dusted with Southwestern flair; most also have a patio or balcony. Gas fireplaces are usually an additional $20. The continental breakfast spread is generous, and there's a wine-and-cheese hour every afternoon.

Downtown's newest and largest property, **Drury Plaza Santa Fe** (828 Paseo de Peralta, 505/424-2175, www.druryplazasantafe.com, $230 d) has a somewhat corporate feel, but it occupies a big historic hospital complex behind the St. Francis Cathedral—a convenient location at a pretty good price for amenities that include a rooftop pool, full breakfast, and free afternoon drinks. Rooms are a little small but comfortably furnished.

A short walk from the plaza, the handsome **La Posada** (330 E Palace Ave, 505/986-0000, $233 d) offers a full range of high-end amenities, including an outdoor pool, a fitness center, and a popular spa. The decor is decidedly Southwestern throughout though not over the top, with earth tones and vigas beams in common areas and guest rooms, the latter of which can vary in size. Some rooms have kiva fireplaces and face out on to the pool; all exude an understated elegance.

A rental condo is a great option if you have a family or group, and those at **Campanilla Compound** (334 Otero St., 800/828-9700, www.campanillacompound.com, $247) are especially nice, with whitewashed walls, fireplaces, and Mexican-tiled kitchens. Each unit has plenty of space inside and out, with a private patio or porch, and, thanks to the location on a hill, some have excellent views of the city and the sunset. There's a three-night minimum in summer, and two nights the rest of the year.

A wonderfully restful spot is ★ **Houses of the Moon** (3451 Hyde Park Rd., 505/992-5003, www.tenthousandwaves.com, $215 d), the guest cottages at Ten Thousand Waves spa. Some have more of a local feel, with viga ceilings and kiva fireplaces, while others are straight from Japan, both samurai era and contemporary anime. Some larger suites have kitchens. Rates include a suitably organic granola breakfast and Japanese teas, as well as free access to the communal and women's tubs.

OVER $250

Hotel Chimayó (125 Washington Ave., 505/988-4900, www.hotelchimayo.com, $259 d) isn't the great value it once was, but it remains one of the best options close to the plaza, though not everyone will like its folksy style, done up with wooden crosses and striped rugs from its namesake village. Upstairs rooms have private balconies, and some suites have fireplaces. Free downtown walking tours are included in the rate.

The iconic, family-owned **La Fonda** (100 E. San Francisco St., 505/982-5511, www.lafondasantafe.com, $259 d) has been offering respite to travelers in some form or another since 1607. A recent renovation has lightened up its guest rooms considerably but also spoiled the impeccable historic feeling in the public areas. The whole place feels more generic and modern as a result, though many rooms do have original folk art, and a few have *latilla* ceilings and kiva fireplaces—along with all the necessary luxuries, such as pillow-top beds. You can soak up most of the place's atmosphere in the public areas, of course, but the location couldn't be better. It helps to have flexible dates—in periods of high demand, the rates can spike to exorbitant levels. Even if you don't stay here, do at least take a spin through the lobby and the mezzanine—there are still traces of the 1920 designs by Mary Colter (best known for the hotels at the Grand Canyon), and some great paintings.

The singular Relais & Chateaux property **The Inn of the Five Graces** (150 E. De Vargas St., 505/992-0957, www.fivegraces.com, $445 suite) can transport you to exotic lands—for at least slightly less than a plane ticket. Outside, it looks like a typical historic Southwestern lodge, a collection of interconnected adobe casitas on Santa Fe's oldest street. But inside, the 24 sumptuous suites are done in the style of an opium dream: antique Turkish kilims, heavy wooden doors, mosaics, and handcrafted furnishings—all courtesy of the boho-style dealers Seret & Sons. Amenities include a Tibetan-themed spa and the most stylish fitness center around. Rates include full breakfast, delivered to your room if you like.

Outside Santa Fe

Less than an hour's drive from Santa Fe are six-century-old ruins of Ancestral Puebloan culture at **Bandelier National Monument**, and the 20th-century atomic developments in **Los Alamos,** home of the Manhattan Project. **Abiquiu,** best known as O'Keeffe Country, is a landscape of rich red rocks bisected by the tree-lined Rio Chama, while green is the predominate color of the endless valleys of the **Valles Caldera National Preserve,** an hour to the northwest of Santa Fe.

The most popular outing from the city is to **Taos**—and even the route there is filled with compelling diversions. The main options are the **low road** along the Rio Grande or the **high road** that passes through tiny mountain villages. You can also take a more roundabout route through **Ojo Caliente,** a village built around hot springs.

PECOS

Santa Fe backs up against the 223,000 acres of the **Pecos Wilderness,** the second-largest nature reserve in New Mexico (after the Gila, in southwestern part of the state). The mountain streams seethe with trout, and elk ramble through emerald-green meadows. The heart of the wilderness is still recovering from the 2011 Pacheco Fire, but day visitors will find plenty to enjoy. The wilderness's gateway is the former logging town of Pecos, where mountain men rub shoulders with alternative healers and monks; south of town are the ruins of **Pecos Pueblo,** the regional power before the Spanish arrived.

On the drive out on I-25, near exit 295, you pass the site of the westernmost Civil War battle in the United States, the **Battle of Glorieta Pass.** It raged March 26-28, 1862; part of a Confederate plan to invade the West with a force of Texans—a plan that was foiled in this decisive rout. The fight is reenacted here annually, and the property owner maintains a makeshift memorial and exhibit on the side of the highway.

Pecos National Historical Park

When the Spanish made first contact with local people in 1540, Pecos was the largest pueblo in the region, population 2,000, in four- and five-story stone buildings sealed with mud. In **Pecos National Historical Park** (Hwy. 63, 505/757-7241, www.nps.gov/peco, 8am-6pm daily June-Aug., 8am-4:30pm Sept.-May, free), the ruins of this complex community are accessible to visitors via a 1.5-mile paved interpretive trail that winds through the remnants of the Pecos Pueblo walls, a couple of restored kivas, and, most striking, the shell of a Franciscan mission. A free **guided walking tour** around the site runs Friday-Sunday in spring and daily at 10am in summer. Additional free **van tours** cover different aspects of local history; check the website for schedules. In winter, the visitors center closes at 4:30pm.

On a ridge looking out onto the plains to the northeast and the mountains behind, the park provides a beautiful view today; around AD 1100, when the area was being settled into the first villages, it also provided a livelihood. The ridge was part of a natural trade path between the Rio Grande farmers and the buffalo hunters of the Great Plains. Both groups met in Pecos, itself an agricultural community, to barter. What began as a series of small villages consolidated in the 14th century into a city, with a layout so orderly it appears to have been centrally planned, and by 1450, the fortress of Pecos was the major economic power in the area.

Perhaps it was the city's trading culture and relative worldliness that made the Pecos Indians welcome Spaniard Francisco Vásquez de Coronado and his men in 1540 with music and dancing rather than bows and arrows.

Outside Santa Fe

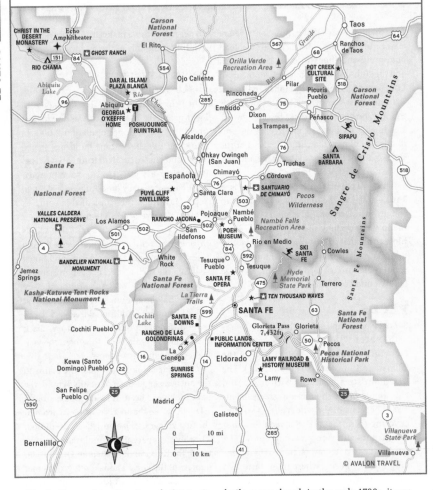

Nearly 60 years later, Don Juan de Oñate visited the area and ordered a mission church built—a giant structure with six bell towers and buttresses 22 feet thick in some spots. The building was destroyed during the Pueblo Revolt, however, and the Pecos people dug a kiva smack in the middle of the ruined convent area—symbolic architecture, to say the least.

But the Spanish returned, and they were even welcomed and aided at Pecos. When they built a new church in the early 1700s, it was noticeably smaller, maybe as a form of compromise. But even as a hybrid Pueblo-Spanish culture developed, the Indian population was falling victim to disease and drought. When the Santa Fe Trail opened up in 1821, Pecos was all but empty, and in 1838, the last city dwellers marched to live with fellow Towa speakers at Jemez Pueblo, 80 miles west; their descendants still reside there today.

Farther Afield: Highway 3 to Villanueva

From exit 323 off I-25, 14 miles southeast of Pecos, **Highway 3** is a beautiful drive south. The two-lane road meanders through a narrow valley with rich red earth cut into small farm plots, dotted by villages such as Ribera and El Pueblo dating to the late 18th century. Stop at the tiny, family-run **Madison Winery** (Hwy. 3, 575/421-8028, 10am-5pm Sat., noon-5pm Sun. in summer, other times by appointment), between El Pueblo and Sena, or visit the small but beautiful **Villanueva State Park** (575/421-2957, www.nmparks.com, $5/car), which occupies a bend in the Pecos River against 400-foot-tall sandstone cliffs. It's rarely crowded—you'll probably have the 2.5-mile Canyon Trail to yourself and the choice of **campsites** (from $8). Spring comes early, filling trails with wildflowers by late April; fall is a burst of red scrub oak and yellow cottonwood leaves, in sharp contrast to the evergreens.

Pecos Wilderness

Stop in at the **Pecos ranger station** (Hwy. 63, 505/757-6121, 8am-4:30pm Mon.-Fri.) on the south end of Pecos town to get maps and information on trail conditions as well as the eight developed campgrounds. At this high elevation, summer temperatures are rarely above 75°F and can dip below freezing at night, so pack accordingly.

Highway 63 is the main access route into the wilderness, running north out of town along the Pecos River. If you've forgotten anything, you can probably get it at the long-running **Terrero General Store** (1911 Hwy. 63, 505/757-6193, 8am-5pm daily in summer), about 13 miles along the two-lane road. The road then narrows and steadily rises, passing fishing access points and campgrounds.

HIKING

About a mile after Mora campground on Highway 63 is the right turn for Forest Road 223, a rough road (ideally, for high-clearance cars only, or proceed slowly) that leads 4.5 miles up to Iron Gate Campground and **Hamilton Mesa Trail** (no. 249), a fairly gentle 3.8-mile hike to a wide-open meadow on an elevated plateau—look for strawberries among the wildflowers.

At Cowles Ponds, a developed fishing area where a mining camp once stood, you can turn left off Highway 63 on Windsor Road to follow a paved one-lane road 1.5 miles to Panchuela campground, the start of **Cave Creek Trail** (no. 288). It's an easy 3.6-mile out-and-back that follows a small waterway up to some caves that have been carved out of the white limestone by the stream's flow. If you go past the caves, up a steep hillside, you reach an area burned in the 2013 Jaroso Fire; hiking here is not recommended, due to the danger of falling trees.

Continuing straight past Cowles on Highway 63 brings you in about three more miles to the scenic Jack's Creek campground and the **Jack's Creek Trail** (no. 257), a 12.5-mile out-and-back that ascends sharply at times to the Pecos Baldy Lake. All trails in this area require a $2 trailhead parking fee; additional fees apply for camping or picnicking, depending on the spot.

Food and Accommodations

For staying the night, the **Pecos Benedictine Monastery** (Hwy. 63, 505/757-6600, www.pecosmonastery.org, $79 d) maintains simple rooms with beautiful views; the rate is a suggested donation and includes meals. Several mountain lodges deeper in the forest, such as **Los Pinos Ranch** (505/757-6213, www.lospinosranch.com, $145 pp), are typically open summers only and offer multiday packages with all meals included and a variety of outdoor activities, including horseback riding.

At the main crossroads in Pecos, where Highway 50 meets Highway 63, **Frankie's at the Casanova** (12 Main St., 505/757-3322, 8am-2pm daily, 5:30pm-8:30pm Fri.-Sat., $9) is the town social center, set in an old adobe dance hall. The food, mainly New Mexican fare and diner staples, isn't always a hit, but it's worth a stop just to see the murals over the bar.

THE PUEBLOS

Between Santa Fe and Taos lie seven **pueblos,** each occupying their own patches of land with their own tribal governments. Unlike scenic Taos Pueblo, these are not notable for their ancient architecture and, with a few small exceptions, do not have any tourist attractions. Some pueblos are closed to visitors all or part of the year, but do make the trip on feast days or for other ceremonial dances if you can.

Tesuque and Pojoaque

Just north of Santa Fe, the highway overpasses are decorated with the original Tewa names of the pueblos. **Tesuque** (Te Tesugeh Owingeh, "village of the cottonwood trees") is marked by **Camel Rock,** a piece of sandstone on the west side of the highway that has eroded to resemble a creature that looks right at home in this rocky desert. The "mouth" of the camel broke off in early 2017, but that hasn't stopped the curious from making the quick stop along Highway 285.

A few miles farther north, the Pojoaque-managed **Poeh Museum** (78 Cities of Gold Rd., 505/455-5041, www.poehcenter.org, 10am-4pm Mon.-Sat., free) occupies a striking old-style adobe building just off the highway. It shows (and sells) local artwork, as well as a permanent installation relating the **Pojoaque** people's path (*poeh*) through history.

Just north of the Cities of Gold Casino is a tasting room for New Mexico's largest craft distillery, **Don Quixote Distillery** (18057-A U.S. 84/285, www.dqdistillery.com, noon-6pm daily). You can sample the husband-and-wife team's blue-corn-based vodka and gin flavored with locally foraged juniper berries and other botanicals. They also make intense vanilla extract, bitters, and port wine based on New Mexican monks' 16th-century recipe.

the high-altitude Hamilton Mesa trail in the Pecos Wilderness

San Ildefonso

Best known for its black-on-black pottery (first by María Martinez and her husband, Julian, and now from a number of skilled potters), the pueblo of **San Ildefonso** is off Highway 502, on the way to Los Alamos. Of all the pueblos just north of Santa Fe, it's the most scenic, with even its newer houses done in faux-adobe style, and the main plaza shaded by giant old cottonwoods. You must first register at the **visitors center** (off Hwy. 502, 505/455-3549, 8am-5pm Mon.-Fri., $10/car), then proceed on foot. There is a small **museum** (8am-4:30pm daily), which is really just an excuse to walk across the village. The only other attractions are pottery shops—which are interesting even if you're not in the market, as it's a chance to peek inside people's homes and chat a bit.

Santa Clara

On the land of **Santa Clara** (Kha P'o, or Shining Water), on Highway 30 south of Española, are the beautiful **Puyé Cliff**

Ceremonial Dances

This is an approximate schedule for dances at pueblos in the Santa Fe area. Pueblo feast days are always on the same date and generally open to all, but seasonal dances (especially Easter and other spring rituals) can vary, and are sometimes closed to visitors. Confirm details and start times—usually afternoon, but sometimes following an evening or midnight Mass—with the **Indian Pueblo Cultural Center** (505/843-7270, www.indianpueblo.org) before setting out.

- **January 1:** Ohkay Owingeh (San Juan), cloud or basket dance; Picurís, various dances

- **January 6:** Picurís: various dances; Nambé, buffalo, deer, and antelope dances

- **January 22:** San Ildefonso, vespers and firelight procession at 6pm

- **January 23:** San Ildefonso: Feast of San Ildefonso, with buffalo and deer dances

- **January 25:** Picurís and Ohkay Owingeh (San Juan), Feast of San Pablo

- **February 2:** Picurís, various dances for Candlemas (Día de la Candelaria)

- **February, first or second weekend:** Ohkay Owingeh (San Juan), deer dance

- **Easter:** various dances at most pueblos

- **June 13:** Ohkay Owingeh (San Juan), Santa Clara, and Picurís, Feast of San Antonio

- **June 24:** Ohkay Owingeh (San Juan), Feast of San Juan Bautista

- **July 4:** Nambé, celebration at the waterfall

- **July 25:** San Ildefonso, Feast of Santiago

- **August 9-10:** Picurís, Feast of San Lorenzo

- **August 12:** Santa Clara, Feast of Santa Clara

- **September 8:** San Ildefonso, corn dance

- **October 4:** Nambé, Feast of San Francisco de Asís

- **November 12:** Tesuque, Feast of San Diego

- **December 12:** Pojoaque, Feast of Nuestra Señora de Guadalupe

- **December 24:** Picurís and Ohkay Owingeh (San Juan), torchlight procession at sundown, followed by Los Matachines; Tesuque and Nambé: various dances, beginning after midnight Mass; San Ildefonso: various dances

- **December 25:** San Ildefonso, Ohkay Owingeh (San Juan), Picurís, and Tesuque: various dances

- **December 26:** Ohkay Owingeh (San Juan), turtle dance

- **December 28:** Picurís: children's dances to celebrate Holy Innocents Day

Tribal Economies in the Gaming Age

North of Santa Fe on U.S. 84/285, Cities of Gold Casino looms beside the road, a sight that would have dazzled any conquistador in search of El Dorado. It was the first of the pueblo casinos, and a much-debated project within the community of **Pojoaque** before it opened in the 1990s. Casinos were effectively permitted by the federal Indian Gaming Regulatory Act in 1988 and then legalized in New Mexico in 1994.

The main argument in Pojoaque for getting into the industry was a need for cash and jobs in communities that had virtually no industry. At the time, up to 72 percent of pueblo residents were jobless, and the average income in many communities was less than $10,000 per year—almost inconceivably below national standards. Now, Pojoaque boasts close to zero unemployment as well as attractive apartment housing and a beautifully appointed museum funded by casino profits (including the Buffalo Thunder Resort, opened in 2008), and many other nearby Rio Grande-area pueblos have followed with their own projects.

More remote pueblos have taken different strategies. Small and somewhat conservative Picurís voted against its own gambling palace; the elders did eventually agree to co-owning the **Hotel Santa Fe**, a venture initiated by a few Anglo entrepreneurs who aimed to capitalize on a unique relationship with a pueblo. Jemez Pueblo attempted to open a casino in southern New Mexico, far from its own land, but its application was denied at the federal level in 2011.

Puebloans and Anglos alike complain about the aesthetics of the gaudy, brightly lit casinos, and others worry about the apparent loss of tradition that goes along with courting lowest-common-denominator tourism. But for many pueblo people who, previously, had been considered to be not much more than a scenic backdrop in New Mexico—a mute patch of "local color"—there's no incongruity at all. As George Rivera, the governor of Pojoaque, has put it, "You don't have to be poor to have your culture."

Dwellings (888/320-5008, www.puyecliffs.com), which were occupied until the early 1600s. They're accessible only by guided tour, and a slightly expensive one at that: $20 for a one-hour walk either along the cliffside or the mesa top, or $35 for both. But tour leaders come from the pueblo and connect the ancient ruins with current culture in an intimate and fascinating way.

At the base of the cliffs is a stone building from the Fred Harvey Indian Detour days of the early 1900s, when carloads of intrepid visitors would trundle off the train and out to these exotic sights; it now houses a small museum. The Puyé Cliffs Welcome Center—better recognized as a gas station on Highway 30—marks the turn to the cliffs; you can buy your tickets here (preferred, so they know you're coming) or up the road at the site. **Tours** run on the hour 9am-5pm daily April-September; the rest of the year, tours run 9am-2pm.

Getting There

From downtown Santa Fe, northbound Guadalupe Street turns into U.S. 84/285, which runs north through Tesuque in 5 miles and Pojoaque in 15 miles. Though this stretch of casinos and tax-free cigarette shops isn't particularly scenic, don't be tempted to race through it—the area is a major speed trap.

To reach San Ildefonso, turn off U.S. 84/285 in Pojoaque at the exit for Highway 502 to Los Alamos; the turn for the pueblo is about 6 miles ahead on the right. From San Ildefonso, you can continue to Santa Clara by turning north on Highway 30; the cliff dwellings are 7 miles ahead on the left. The slightly more direct route to Santa Clara is via Española, following signs for Highway 30; the total drive from the edge of Santa Fe is about 23 miles.

LOS ALAMOS

Unlike so many other sights in New Mexico, which are rooted in centuries of history, **Los Alamos,** home of the atomic bomb, is a product of the modern age. You may spend only a few hours here, visiting the museum and admiring the view from this high plateau, but you'll still sense an atmosphere quite unlike anywhere else in New Mexico. If you can, visit on a weekday, as more businesses are open; weekends are especially sleepy in this town that draws specialized commuters from around the state—and even beyond.

During World War II, the army requisitioned an elite, rugged boys' school on a remote New Mexico mesa in order to build a top-secret laboratory for development of the nuclear bomb. It was home for a time to J. Robert Oppenheimer, Richard Feynman, Niels Bohr, and other science luminaries. The Manhattan Project and its aftermath, the Cold War arms race, led to the establishment of **Los Alamos National Laboratory** (LANL). Only in 1957 did the onetime military base become an actual public town; it's now home to about 18,000 people (if you count the "suburb" of White Rock, just down the hill on Highway 4). The highway up the mountainside is wider than it used to be, but the winding ascent to the mesa of "Lost Almost"—as the first scientists dubbed their officially nonexistent camp—still carries an air of the clandestine. The town can be visually jarring—there is no adobe to be found and the streets have names such as Trinity Drive (named after the first test of a nuclear weapon)—a feeling only enhanced by the dramatic landscape surrounding it.

The town is spread over four long mesas that extend like fingers from the mountain behind. Highway 502 arrives on a middle mesa, depositing you on Central Avenue and the main downtown area. The northernmost mesa is mostly residential, while the southernmost mesa is occupied by LANL and two routes running back down the mountain and connecting with Highway 4.

Los Alamos Historical Museum

Though the manufactured feel of Los Alamos would lead you to believe otherwise, the area's history began long before the construction of LANL. See what the area was like pre-Manhattan Project at the fascinating, recently renovated **Los Alamos Historical Museum** (1050 Bathtub Row, 505/662-4493, www.losalamoshistory.org, 9am-5pm Mon.-Fri., 10am-4pm Sat.-Sun., $5), set in an old building of the Los Alamos Ranch School, the boys' camp that got the boot when the army moved in. The exhibits cover everything from relics of the early Tewa-speaking people up to juicy details on the social intrigue during the development of "the gadget," as the A-bomb was known. Volunteer docents lead two-hour **walking tours** (11am Mon., Fri., and Sat., $10) from the museum late May-early October; if you miss this, pick up a brochure for a self-guided walk.

In front of the museum is **Fuller Lodge Art Center** (2132 Central Ave., 505/662-1635, 10am-4pm Mon.-Sat., free), originally the ranch school's dining room and kitchen. It usually has a community art exhibit downstairs, plus a room upstairs restored to the era when schoolteachers bunked here. The architect John Gaw Meem built the structure in 1928, handpicking more than 700 pine poles to form the walls, and designing the cowboy-silhouette light fixtures in the main hall.

The museum is just west of the main street, Central Avenue—you'll see Fuller Lodge on Central, with the museum set back behind it.

Bradbury Science Museum

Set up by Los Alamos National Laboratory, the **Bradbury Science Museum** (1350 Central Ave., 505/667-4444, www.lanl.gov/museum, 10am-5pm Tues.-Sat., 1pm-5pm Sun.-Mon., free) on the miracles of atomic energy has the feel of a upper-grade science fair, with plenty of buttons to push and gadgets to play with. There's also an air of a convention sales booth—the museum's mission is definitely to sell the public on LANL's work and

Los Alamos

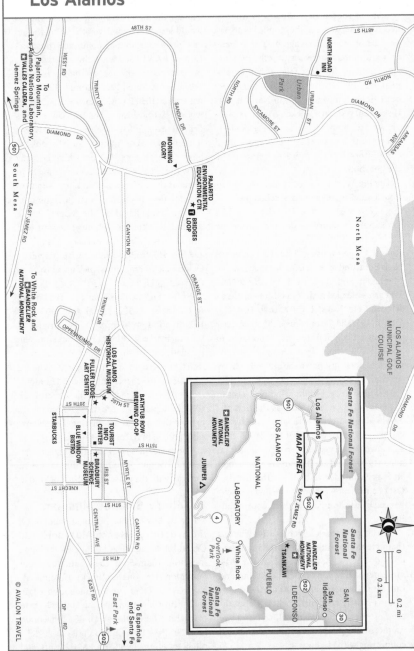

© AVALON TRAVEL

nuclear technology in general, though a public forum corner gives space to opposing views. More interesting are the relics of the early nuclear age: Fat Man and Little Boy casings, gadgetry from the Nevada Test Site, and the like. **Atomic City Van Tours** (505/662-3965, www.atomiccitytours.com, 1:30pm daily Mar.-Oct., $25) leave from the parking lot in front of the museum. The 1.5-hour tour is a good way to see more of the town, which is otherwise a bit difficult to navigate, and learn some of the history. Call ahead to reserve. If you can't make the set tour time, you can download a short self-guided tour from the website; this route takes the free city bus to the main part of LANL, pointing out town landmarks along the way.

Recreation

The mountain behind Los Alamos is recovering from the 2011 Las Conchas Fire, but the canyons below Los Alamos were untouched, and are laced by numerous top-notch hiking and mountain biking trails, easily accessible from the town's main roads. Pick up a map and get recommendations from the visitors center or the smartly designed **Los Alamos Nature Center** (2600 Canyon Rd., 505/662-0460, www.peecnature.org, 10am-8pm Tues.,

10am-4pm Wed. and Fri.-Mon., free), which also is a good place to get to know the plants and animals in the area.

The dramatic **Canyon Rim Trail** skirts the edge of Los Alamos Canyon for 1.5 miles; it provides the best vantage point for appreciating the town's setting atop the finger-like mesas. The trailhead is located along Hwy 502, just shy of two miles east of the town center; count on about 45 minutes to hike to the paved trail's end and back. There are further spectacular views in White Rock, 15 minutes to the southeast, where the **White Rock Rim Trail** runs three miles along the cliff edge—you'll have suburban tract homes to your back and a dizzying canyon out in front of you. Even if you don't much feel like a hike, stop by where the walk starts in Overlook Park, just for the view; follow signs from Highway 4 at the first stoplight in town. You can also take a strenuous hike into the gorge along the **Red Dot Trail,** which passes a few petroglyphs on its way down to the Rio Grande; follow signs from Highway 4 for Overlook Park, at the back end of a subdivision.

A bit of a locals' secret, **Pajarito Mountain** (505/662-5725, www.skipajarito. com, 9am-4pm Fri.-Sun. and holidays) offers good skiing and snowboarding for relatively

Los Alamos Historical Museum

cheap ($49/full day), with five lifts giving access to bunny slopes as well as double-black-diamond trails. The area is just a few miles west of Los Alamos, off Highway 501.

Food

Los Alamos is not exactly bursting with restaurants, and many are open weekdays only. For breakfast and lunch, the family-run **Morning Glory** (1377 Diamond Dr., 505/662-4000, 6am-4pm Mon.-Fri., 7am-1pm Sat., $5) has tasty breakfast burritos, filling lunch specials, such as chicken-fried steak, and a tempting selection of homemade donuts and baked goods.

Blue Window Bistro (1789 Central Ave., 505/662-6305, 11am-2:30pm and 5pm-8:30pm Mon.-Fri., 5pm-9pm Sat., $18) is the fanciest restaurant in town, which in Los Alamos still doesn't mean too fancy. It's a colorful, bustling place; it often feels as if the entire town is crammed inside. Food is typical fresh American: huge salads and hot sandwiches for lunch, creative pasta and steaks in the evening. If you're headed back down the hill for the night, it's not worth staying for dinner, but if you're here overnight, it's your best option.

Tucked away at the end of a small strip mall, **Bathtub Row Brewing Co-Op** (163 Central Park Square, 505/500-8381, 2pm-10pm Mon.-Wed., 2pm-11pm Thurs., noon-11pm Fri.-Sat., noon-10pm Sun.) pours pints of its own brews, such as excellent brown and blonde ales, and select offerings from other New Mexico breweries. It's especially lively when things wind down at the laboratory's day's end.

Starbucks on Central Avenue (1801 Central Ave., 505/661-0100, 5am-8pm Mon.-Thurs., 5am-9pm Fri.-Sat., 6am-7pm Sun.) is the only café in town and is notable just for the deeply scientific conversations on which you can eavesdrop.

Accommodations

The few hotels in Los Alamos cater primarily to visiting engineers, though it's a handy place to bunk if you want to get an early start at Bandelier and the Valles Caldera. The chain hotels are functional; the best of the few remaining options is the **North Road Inn** (2127 North Rd., 505/662-3678, www.northroadinn.com, $89 d), a converted apartment complex in a quiet residential area that has large rooms (some are suites with kitchenettes). Those on the upper level are a bit more private.

Information

Stop at the **tourist info center** (109 Central Park Sq., 505/662-8105, www.visitlosalamos.org, 9am-5pm Mon.-Fri., 9am-4pm Sat., 10am-3pm Sun.) for maps and advice on hikes. There's a bigger office in **White Rock** (115 Hwy 4, 505/672-3183, 8am-6pm daily, 10am-2pm daily in winter), en route to Bandelier. The comprehensive events calendar at www.fyilosalamos.com is the best source of the latest happenings.

Getting There

Los Alamos is 36 miles (45 minutes by car) from downtown Santa Fe via U.S. 84/285 north to Highway 502 west. From Española, it's 20 miles (30 minutes) west on Highway 30 to Highway 502. There is an airport (LAM, www.lam.aero), but the city no longer has commercial service.

★ BANDELIER NATIONAL MONUMENT

One of New Mexico's most entrancing ancient sites, **Bandelier National Monument** (www.nps.gov/band, $20/car) comprises 23,000 acres of wilderness, including the remarkable Frijoles Canyon, lined on either side with cave "apartments," while the remnants of a massive settlement from the 16th century occupy the valley floor.

The place gets so busy in summer that mid-May-mid-October the park is accessible only by shuttle bus from the visitors center in White Rock. The best way to avoid crowds is to arrive early on a weekday, if possible. Another approach is to join a torch-lit, silent **night walk** ($6) into Frijoles Canyon; they're

Bandelier National Monument

the 250 rooms at one time stood several stories tall.

The trail then goes up next to the cliffs, dotted with small caves dug out of the soft stone, and to **Long House,** the remnants of a strip of condo-style buildings tucked into the rock wall. Paintings and carvings decorate the cliff face above. If you're here near sunset, keep an eye on the **bat cave** near the end of the strip, home to thousands of the flying mammals.

Continue another 0.5 mile to the **Alcove House,** accessible by 140 feet of ladders. It's well worth the climb up, if you can handle heights.

Frey Trail

The 1.5-mile **Frey Trail** used to be the main route to Frijoles Canyon, before the access road was built by the Civilian Conservation Corps in the 1930s. Descending from **Juniper Campground** (just off Highway 4 northwest of the park access road), it's a nice approach to the area, offering great views over Tyuonyi and a general sense of what it must have been like to "discover" the canyon. The trail has no shade, however, so it's best hiked early in the day. The shuttle bus can drop you at the trailhead, so you can hike down, then ride back to the depot.

Tsankawi

Well before you reach the main entrance to Bandelier, you pass **Tsankawi** on the east side of Highway 4. (This area is accessible by car year-round.) Unique pottery excavated in this separate section, disconnected from the main park, suggests that it was inhabited by a different people from those who settled in Frijoles Canyon, and some sort of natural border seems to have formed here, despite a shared cliff-dwelling culture: Today the pueblos immediately north of the Bandelier area speak Tewa, while those to the south speak Keresan. A 1.5-mile loop, with ladders to climb along the way, leads past unexcavated ruins, cave houses, and even a few petroglyphs.

typically on Friday nights, but call the visitors center or check online for the schedule.

In the park, another **visitors center** (505/672-3861, 9am-6pm daily mid-May-mid-Oct., 9am-4:30pm mid-Oct.-mid-May) has a museum and the usual array of maps and guides. If you're interested in wildflowers, pick up a Falls Trail guide, as it has good illustrations of what grows in the area. Rangers run free **guided walks** around the main loop a few times a day, or you can pick up the trail guide for $1.

Main Loop Trail and Alcove House Trail

A paved walkway leads out the back of the visitors center into Frijoles Canyon, passing the ruins of the major settlements—or at least the ones that have been thoroughly excavated. You first reach **Tyuonyi** (chew-ON-yee), a circle of buildings that was settled for about 200 years, beginning in the 1300s. Built of bricks cut from tuff (the volcanic rock that makes up most of the area) and adobe plaster, some of

Camping

Juniper Campground ($12), just inside the park's northern border, is usually open year-round, with 94 sites. There are no hookups or showers. No reservations are taken, but it's usually not full. The scenery up on the plateau is a bit bleak, due to the 2011 fire, but you will get an early start on the day if you overnight here.

Getting There

Bandelier is 45 miles (one hour) from downtown Santa Fe via U.S. 84/285 north to Highway 502 and Highway 4 west. From Jemez Springs, it's 41 miles (one hour) via Highway 4 east.

Mid-May-mid-October, access to the park is via free **shuttle bus** only. The service departs from the **White Rock visitors center** (Hwy. 4) every 20 or 30 minutes between 9am and 3pm; before or after that time, you can enter the park by car.

White Rock is a 40-minute drive from Santa Fe via U.S. 84/285 north to Highway 502 and Highway 4 west. From Jemez Springs, it's about an hour's drive via Highway 4 north and east (but you'll have to drive past the Bandelier entrance, and double back in the shuttle bus). The bus also stops at the Frey Trail trailhead en route to the main park.

★ VALLES CALDERA NATIONAL PRESERVE

Spreading out for 89,000 acres to the north of Highway 4, **Valles Caldera National Preserve** (575/829-4100, www.nps.gov/vall, $20/car) is a series of vast green valleys, rimmed by the edges of a volcano that collapsed into a massive bowl millennia ago. At the center is rounded Redondo Peak (11,254 feet). The surrounding meadows are home to herds of elk; the view down into the caldera from Highway 4 when the elk spread out in front of Redondo Peak can be breathtaking. The land has been carefully managed since it was converted from a ranch in 2000, and it is not heavily visited—it's easy to get out into the wilderness and feel utterly alone under the dome of the sky.

To get oriented, drive in two miles to the **Valle Grande Contact Station** (8am-8pm daily mid-May-Sept., 9am-5pm daily Oct.-mid-May), where you can get a hiking map and the latest trail conditions. A full roster of guided activities is available too in winter and summer, including group day hikes, elk sightseeing, and full-moon snowshoeing

Valles Caldera National Preserve

in winter. There is no **camping** available in the preserve.

Hiking and Mountain Biking

Hiking in the preserve no longer requires reservations or is confined to specific days, and there are several trails to choose from. From the contact station, an hour-long trail offers a quick introduction to the preserve. Follow the loop west around the bases of Redondo Peak and neighboring Redonito (10,898 feet) for a relatively flat hike that bisects a few of the preserve's many creeks; short spurs can be tacked on. Further in the preserve, the trails along the slopes of Cerros del Abrigo (10,332 feet) and Cerros Santa Rosa (9,701 feet) are more challenging and heavily forested.

Many of the preserve's hiking trails are also open to **mountain bikers,** but perhaps the most enjoyable ride can be had by simply following the main dirt road that winds through the preserve to the northwest for approximately 10 miles, crossing through rolling grasslands along the way. As cattle still graze on the land in summer, be prepared to negotiate slow-moving herds.

Winter Activities

Over 25 miles of trails are available for **snowshoeing** and **cross-country skiing;** you can also blaze your own trail into the snowy backcountry. The Contact Station hands out maps for winter activities and is also the staging point for guided outings, including skiing and snowshoeing under the moonlight.

Getting There

Valles Caldera is a scenic, and at times hairraising, 30-minute drive west from Los Alamos along Highway 501 and Highway 4. From Valles Caldera, continuing west on Highway 4 will bring you to Jemez Springs in 30 minutes; driving east on Highway 4 will take you to Bandelier National Monument in about 20 miles.

If you're carrying on to Santa Fe, it's another hour's drive (about 40 miles). Continue on Highway 4 through the town of White Rock and join Highway 502. This leads to U.S. 285, which then goes south to the capital.

ESPAÑOLA

Midway between Santa Fe and Taos, **Española** lacks the glamour or scenery of its neighbors. The town of 10,000 is unquestionably rough around the edges, but don't let that deter you from some of the best New Mexican food in the state. And although it doesn't have much in the way of its own sights (except for the ubiquitous lowriders), it is at a convenient crossroads.

Plaza de Española

Clustered around this public space are the town's museums. The tiny **Bond House Museum** (706 Bond St., 505/747-8535, 1pm-3:30pm Mon.-Wed., noon-4pm Thurs.-Fri., free), built at the turn of the 20th century by a Canadian family that established the Española Mercantile, devotes half its space to artwork and the other small room to various historic artifacts. Down the hill, past the replica Alhambra fountain, is the **Misión Museum,** a replica of the town's original mission church, furnished with traditional craft work from around the valley. It is open sporadically—ask at the Bond House if no one is around.

Chimayó Trading Post

No, you haven't made a wrong turn—you're still in Española. The **Chimayó Trading Post** (110 Sandia Dr., 505/753-9414, 10am-4pm Wed.-Sat.), on the west side of the main highway, relocated here in the 1930s, after several decades at its original location in Chimayó. Now it's a listed landmark, as one of the last remaining historic trading posts, and it has everything you'd expect: creaky wood floors, dim lighting, and a jumbled stock of treasures and bric-a-brac that includes Chimayó rugs, as well as Nepalese silver jewelry; cut-tin candleholders, made locally; skeins of handmade wool yarn; postcards; and even free coffee. The remaining elderly owner (one of a pair of airline employees, back in the real jet-set age)

Española

is no longer seriously replenishing his stock, but there are still some nifty finds. Hours can be a bit erratic.

Santa Cruz de la Cañada Church

Midway through Española, take a right turn at Highway 76 to reach the village of Santa Cruz, established in 1695. The sizable **Santa Cruz de la Cañada Church** (varied hours, free) that's here now (turn left at the traffic light after one mile) dates from 1733, and its altar screen is another colorful work attributed to the Laguna Santero, who also painted the reredos at San Miguel Mission in Santa Fe and the church at Laguna Pueblo. It is dated 1795 but was completely painted over—with the same images—in the mid-19th century, presenting a particular challenge to preservationists, who cleaned and restored the piece in 1995. Each panel presents a different combination of the original artist's work and the fresh paint applied half a century later.

Food

Tucked away underneath a stand of cottonwood trees, takeout stand **El Parasol** (603 Santa Cruz Rd., 505/753-8852, 7am-9:30pm Mon.-Sat., 8am-8pm Sun., $5) has a no-nonsense Spanglish menu ("pollo with guacamole taco") of cheap and delicious New Mexican classics. It's an ideal pit stop for those taking the high road to Taos; there are a few picnic tables if you want to linger in the shade.

Next door and one of the forerunners of New Mexican cuisine, **El Paragua** (603 Santa Cruz Rd., 505/753-3211, 11am-9pm Mon.-Thurs., 11am-9:30pm Fri., 10am-9:30pm Sat., 10am-8pm Sun., $12) has been offering similar staples and much more besides for over 50 years, including a baked salmon filet, lamb chops, and beef flautas quesadillas.

Diner-style **JoAnn's Ranch O Casados** (938 N. Riverside Dr., 505/753-1334, 8am-9pm daily, $10) does all-day breakfast, plus good and inexpensive enchiladas, fajitas, and more. The red chile is rich and mellow, and you can get half orders of many dishes.

Easily missed, **Blue Heron Brewing Company** (100 Hwy. 503, 505/747-4506, 1pm-9pm Wed.-Thurs., 1pm-10pm Fri.-Sat., 1pm-8pm Sun., $11) serves some of the best pizza and ales around; snack on appetizers such as beer-battered fries and salt-crusted pretzels with beer mustard, too. Beers on tap rotate but typically include Blue Heron's red ale, IPA, stout, and Scottish ale. The taproom occasionally hosts live music and has frequent game nights.

At **Saints & Sinners** (503 S. Riverside Dr., 505/753-2757, 1pm-10pm Mon.-Thurs., 1pm-midnight Fri.-Sat.), a long-established package liquor store, you can sit down and crack open a beer. It stocks an excellent selection of tequilas, and the neon sign should get landmark status (yes, the store sells souvenir T-shirts). Cash only.

Accommodations

Española is not an obvious choice for staying overnight, but it has some hotels that are so nice, you might rethink your itinerary. They can be especially handy after a night at the Santa Fe Opera, when all the traffic toward Santa Fe is backed up—but the road north is wide open; as well, you'll get more bang for your buck staying here than in Santa Fe. The ★ **Inn at the Delta** (243 Paseo de Oñate, 505/753-9466, www.innatthedelta.biz, $110 s, $140 d) is a beautiful, rambling adobe complex built by a longtime Española family. The positively palatial rooms are decorated with locally made furniture, and each has a fireplace, a porch, and a jetted tub. Rates include breakfast.

A project of the local pueblo, the **Santa Claran Hotel Casino** (460 N. Riverside Dr., 877/505-4949, www.santaclaran.com, $85 d) also has spacious rooms, tastefully done in subdued grays and browns. Perks include fridges and laundry machines, but Internet is wired-only in rooms; there's wireless access in the lobby.

South of town, a couple of minutes off the road to Los Alamos, ★ **Rancho Jacona** (277 County Rd. 84, 505/455-7948, www.ranchojacona.com, $170 d) is a working 35-acre farm dotted with 11 casitas, each with a kitchen and space for 2-11 people. You'll likely get some fresh eggs for breakfast, and kids can frolic in the pool. There's a three-night minimum.

Getting There

Española is about a 35-minute drive from central Santa Fe via U.S. 84/285 north. Leaving Española, take Highway 68 (also called Riverside Drive) north from here to Taos (45 miles), or cross over the Rio Grande and continue on U.S. 84 to Abiquiu (22 miles) or U.S. 285 to Ojo Caliente (25 miles). From an intersection in the middle of Española, Highway 76 leads east to Chimayó (8 miles), then to Truchas and the other high-road towns on the way to Taos. From the old main plaza on the west side of the Rio Grande, Highway 30 is the back road to Los Alamos (20 miles).

OJO CALIENTE

Twenty-six miles north of Española on U.S. 285, **Ojo Caliente Mineral Springs**

(505/583-2233, www.ojocaliente.ojospa.com, 8am-10pm daily) is effectively the center of a tiny settlement that built up around the hot springs here. Established in 1916, it's now a somewhat posh resort. The various paved pools ($20 Mon.-Thurs., $32 Fri.-Sun., $16/$28 after 6pm) have different mineral contents, and there's a mud area with rich local clay, as well as private soaking tubs and a full spa. It's a pretty little place, set up against sandstone bluffs; try to go on a weekday, as it gets busy on weekends.

The handsome onsite **Artesian Restaurant** (7:30am-11am, 11:30am-3pm and 5pm-9:30pm), with its creative use of local ingredients, is worth a visit alone. The hotel rooms at the resort ($149 d, no shower; $189 d, full bath) are no great value (although rates do include access to the springs). But camping ($20) is an option, and the bathroom facilities were upgraded in 2014. **The Inn at Ojo** (505/583-9131, www.ojocaliente.com, $130 d, $110 s), just down the road, is a better value; breakfast is included.

Just behind the springs, the one-mile **Posi Trail** leads into public land; centuries-old pottery shards are visible along the route. The longer **Mica Mine** trail wends its way through a scenic landscape of cacti and arroyos, ultimately reaching its eponymous destination after two miles. The resort office has trail maps on these trails and others in the area.

Getting There

Ojo Caliente is 50 miles from downtown Santa Fe, about an hour's drive north on U.S. 84/285, then U.S. 285 east where it splits, north of Española. From Española, allow a 30-minutes driving time. From Abiquiu, avoid backtracking by going through El Rito; take Highway 554 north to Highway 111 north, coming out on U.S. 285 a few miles north of Ojo Caliente. This route takes about 45 minutes.

From Ojo Caliente, you can continue 41 miles to Taos (about a one-hour drive). Follow U.S. 285 north for 10 miles, then turn right (east) on Highway 567. In nine miles, Highway 567 ends at a T junction; turn left (north) on

Taos County Road and continue about eight miles. You will meet U.S. 64 about one mile west of the Rio Grande Gorge; Taos is to the right (east).

ABIQUIU

Northwest of Española, along U.S. 84, the valley formed by the Rio Chama is one of the most striking landscapes in northern New Mexico. Lush greenery on riverbanks clashes with bright-red mud; roaming sheep and cattle graze by the roadside. The striated hills represent dramatic geological shifts, from purple stone formed in the dinosaur era 200 million years ago to red clay formed by forests, then gypsum from sand dunes, then a layer of lava only eight million years old. Far more recently, **Abiquiu** became inextricably linked with the artist Georgia O'Keeffe, who made the place her home for more than 40 years, entranced by the glowing light and dramatic skyline.

Although Abiquiu often refers to the whole river valley, the unofficial town center is **Bode's** (21196 U.S. 84, 505/685-4422, 6:30am-7pm Mon.-Thurs., 6:30am-8pm Fri., 7am-8pm Sat., 7am-7pm Sun.), pronounced BO-deez. This long-established general store also has gas, breakfast burritos, pastries and green-chile cheeseburgers (11:30am-3pm daily), fishing licenses and tackle, camping gear, and local crafts. In winter, it closes earlier on weekends.

Up the hill opposite Bode's is the actual **village of Abiquiu,** established in 1754 by *genízaros* (Hispanicized Indians) through a land grant from the Spanish Crown. Georgia O'Keeffe's house forms one side of the old plaza; on the other is the Santo Tomás de Abiquiu Church, built in the 1930s after the community opted for the legal status of village rather than pueblo. Past O'Keeffe's house is the village *morada,* dramatically set on a hilltop. You're not really welcome to poke around, however—the village maintains a privacy policy similar to those of the pueblos. So, it's best to visit on a guided tour of the house, or come on the village's feast day, for Santa Rosa de Lima, on the weekend closest to August 25.

Poshuouinge Ruin Trail

About two miles south of Abiquiu proper, on the west side of the road, the 0.5-mile **Poshuouinge Ruin Trail** leads to an ancestral Tewa site, literally the "village above the muddy river," inhabited only AD 1420-1500—why it was abandoned is unclear. The village contained about 137 rooms, as well as surrounding field grids, though there's not much to see today (thorough excavations took place in 1919, and it has been left to melt away since then). Nonetheless, it's a good place to get out and stretch your legs and take in the view from the hilltop.

Georgia O'Keeffe Home

The artist's main residence, where she lived 1949-1984, fronts the small plaza in the village center of Abiquiu. The **Georgia O'Keeffe Home** (505/685-4539, www.okeeffemuseum. org) is open for hour-long guided tours mid-March-November. The price, even for the basic tour, can seem a bit steep, but for fans of modernism of any kind, it's a beautiful place to see. The rambling adobe, parts of which were built in the 18th century, is a great reflection of O'Keeffe's aesthetic, which fused the starkness of modernism with an organic sensuality. If you're on a budget, console yourself with the fact that in many ways the surrounding landscape evokes O'Keeffe's work at least as much as her home does—and stop at Ghost Ranch, for more (and cheaper) info on the painter.

The schedule varies by month, but there are five **tours** ($35) daily on Tuesday, Thursday, and Friday. June-October, tours are also on Wednesday and Saturday, when the price goes up to $45. Longer, special tours with Judy Lopez ($65), who worked with O'Keeffe for more than a decade, run Thursday June-November. A Wednesday- and Friday-night "behind-the-scenes" tour ($65) includes a visit to O'Keeffe's fallout shelter, among other things. Tours depart from the Abiquiu Inn on

Ancient Egypt in New Mexico

"Adobe," the word for the sun-dried mud bricks the Spanish used to build their houses for the first few centuries they lived in New Mexico, is derived from Arabic (al-tub), which in turn comes from Coptic, a language with its roots in Pharaonic Egypt. The etymology came full circle in 1980, when an Egyptian architect named Hassan Fathy came to Abiquiu to build an adobe mosque and madrassa, as the cornerstone of Dar al Islam, a newly established community of American-born Muslims.

Fathy was a lifelong champion of vernacular architecture, especially of adobe. He drew international interest in the 1940s, when he built the village of New Gourna near Luxor in Egypt. Modernists scoffed at his use of mud brick, but it provided cheap, efficient, even elegant housing, which residents could help construct and, later, make their own repairs to.

By the time the Dar al Islam community hired him in 1980, Fathy was in his eighties, but he nonetheless came to New Mexico to help personally with the mosque construction. It was his first and only commission in North America, and he was excited to work so near the pueblos, where, he noted, the proportions of the mud bricks were nearly the same as those that make up the Temple of Hatshepsut. He brought with him two Nubian assistants and hired a team of locals to help.

An awkward culture clash ensued. Fathy had been built up as an expert to New Mexican adoberos, who resented the deference, especially when he was wrong. In particular, they saw that his construction was not adapted to the cold climate, and he used techniques that could not be applied after he left. The minaret proved too expensive, and a plan to build individual homes in Dar al Islam had to be scrapped because modern building codes required framing in adobe structures.

The innovations Fathy did bring are lovely, though: arched doorways and roofs, and—best of all—the signature adobe domes and barrel vaults that the architect had derived from ancient Nubian temples. The gentle curves of the complex's roofline and its rounded, whitewashed interior spaces echo the nearby Plaza Blanca hills, so the building seems beautifully integrated into its natural surroundings—even though it differs from its Spanish-style adobe neighbors.

U.S. 84; you must make reservations at least a month in advance.

Dar al Islam and Plaza Blanca

In another chapter of New Mexico's long utopian history, a few American converts established Dar al Islam (505/685-4515 ext. 21, www.daralislam.org, 10am-4pm Mon.-Fri., free), an intentional religious community, in 1980. It was meant to be a place in which Muslims—some 30 families to start with—could practice their religion in every aspect of life, from education to food. The group set up a ranch and built the Abiquiu Inn and a few other local businesses, but the village concept eventually foundered. More recently, Dar al Islam has been reinvented as a retreat center that's open to visitors.

Anyone interested in architecture will want to see the adobe mosque by Egyptian architect Hassan Fathy, all organic, sinuous lines; the view from the hilltop across the Chama River valley is a beautiful one, too. The head of the center requests that visitors dress modestly (arms, legs, and cleavage covered) and be quiet, so as not to disturb classes or workshops in session. Stop at the office first (back a bit and to the right of the parking area) to introduce yourself.

The community's land, some 8,500 acres, also includes the towering gypsum formations of Plaza Blanca (White Place). The eerie space, bleached as bones, was recorded in a series of Georgia O'Keeffe paintings, and it has also been used for numerous movie shoots. Two main trails lead down from the parking area.

Coming from the south, the community is accessible via Highway 554, which runs east from U.S. 84, just south of Abiquiu (follow signs for El Rito). Immediately after crossing the Chama River, turn left on County

Road 0155. Continue 3.2 miles and turn right through a wooden gate made of telephone poles. Coming from the north on U.S. 84, look for County Road 0155, which is unpaved here, just north of Bode's; the wooden gate will be on the left, 2.3 miles on, shortly after the paving starts. Once through the gate, the road forks after less than a mile: To the left is the entrance to Dar al Islam; to the right, Plaza Blanca.

Abiquiu Lake and the Pedernal

An Army Corps of Engineers dam project in the late 1950s-early 1960s created the 4,000-acre **Abiquiu Lake,** with fingers running into the canyons all around. The view coming in is marred by the power station, but past that the water glimmers at the base of the flat-topped mountain Pedernal ("Flint") Peak, the distinctive silhouette that found its way into so many of O'Keeffe's paintings. ("It's my private mountain," she often said. "God told me if I painted it often enough, I could have it.") The overly paved **Riana campground** (505/685-4561, www.emnrd.state.nm.us) at the lake is open year-round, but water and electric hookups ($14) are available from mid-April to mid-October. There's now a small beach suitable for swimming.

TOP EXPERIENCE

★ Ghost Ranch

Ghost Ranch (U.S. 84, 505/685-1000, www.ghostranch.org), a 21,000-acre retreat owned by the Presbyterian Church, is best known because Georgia O'Keeffe owned a small parcel of the land and maintained a studio here. In the science world, it's also known as the place where, in 1947, paleontologists combing the red hills discovered about a thousand skeletons of the dinosaur *Coelophysis* ("hollow form," for its hollow, birdlike bones), the largest group discovered in the world.

The grounds are open to day visitors ($5 suggested donation) for **hiking.** The best trek, which takes about two hours round-trip, is to **Chimney Rock,** a towering landmark with panoramic views of the entire area. Don't be daunted—the steepest part of the trail is at the start—but do slather on the sunscreen, as there's no shade on this route. **Box Canyon** is an easier, shadier, all-level walk that's about four miles round-trip. **Kitchen Mesa Trail,** which starts at the same point, is much more difficult, requiring some climbing to get up the cliffs at the end (though you could hike the easy first two-thirds, then turn around).

Visitors can also see the **Florence Hawley**

the otherwordly landscape at Plaza Blanca

Ellis Museum of Anthropology and the **Ruth Hall Museum of Paleontology** (both 9am-5pm Mon.-Sat., 1pm-5pm Sun., $5), which display the local finds, including remnants of the prehistoric Gallina culture from the ridge above the valley and an eight-ton chunk of *Coelophysis*-filled siltstone in the process of being excavated. In summer, both museums are also open 1pm-5pm on Sunday.

Guided **tours** (various times, $25-35) of the ranch grounds run mid-March-November, on various topics, from local archaeology to movie settings. One walking tour visits O'Keeffe's painting spot in the red Chinle hills behind the ranch. **Horseback rides** ($85) are another option, visiting various spots key to O'Keeffe's painting life.

Christ in the Desert Monastery

Thirteen miles up a winding dirt road, the Benedictine **Christ in the Desert Monastery** (Forest Rd. 151, 575/613-4233, www.christdesert.org, 8am-6pm Sun.-Fri.) is said to be the remotest monastery in the Western Hemisphere. The drive follows the Chama River through a lush valley, ending at a striking modern church designed in 1972 by the woodworker and architect George Nakashima to blend in with the dramatic cliffs behind. Most of the outbuildings are straw-bale construction, running on solar power, and the monks grow much of their food and brew their own Belgian-style beer, Monks Ale (look for it at Bode's in Abiquiu). A gift shop next to the modern church sells various monastery products. The annual hop harvest, in late August, is a convivial event that draws volunteers from all over. Look for Forest Road 151 off the west side of U.S. 84, north of Ghost Ranch.

For a hike with a view across the valley and the red rocks, **Rim Vista trail** (no. 15) is a good route, climbing up to a mesa in about 2.3 miles one-way. The trailhead is less than one mile in on Forest Road 151, off the north side of the road; turn right, then bear right at the fork and park after 0.25 mile. The trail is best in spring and fall, as there is not much shade here.

Echo Amphitheater

The bandshell-shaped rock formation **Echo Amphitheater** ($2/car) is a natural wonder of acoustics and a great place to let kids run around and yell to their hearts' content. A short, paved trail from the parking area leads up to the Echo Canyon overlook; there

Ghost Ranch

are also several pleasant picnic areas tucked in the brush. It's just over three miles north of Ghost Ranch on U.S. 84, a couple hundred feet from the road.

Food and Accommodations

The **Abiquiu Inn** (21120 U.S. 84, 505/685-4378, www.abiquiuinn.com) functions as the area's visitors center. Lodging ($170 d) consists of some pretty casitas ($240) at the back of the property near the river, and a cluster of motel rooms closer to the front (request one facing away from the road). Two economy rooms ($110) are well kept but best for early risers, as there are skylights over the beds. The inn's restaurant, **Café Abiquiu** (7am-9pm daily, $14) serves a nice mix of traditional New Mexican and more creative food, with especially good breakfasts.

You can also stay at **Ghost Ranch** (U.S. 84, 505/685-4333, www.ghostranch.org) when it's not full for retreats, in various room options. The cheapest are cabins with a shared bath ($74 s, $89 d, with breakfast), which are an especially good deal for solo travelers. Private-bath rooms ($119 s, $139 d) have fine views over the valley. You can also camp (from $25). Rates for rooms (but not campsites) include breakfast, and day visitors can take simple meals (noon-1pm and 5pm-6pm) at the dining hall.

Christ in the Desert Monastery (Forest Rd. 151, 801/545-8567, www.christdesert.org) offers wonderful accommodations (two-night minimum) for a suggested donation ($70 to $150), which includes all meals. At the 11.5-mile mark on the same road abutting the river, the **Rio Chama Campground** (no fee) is preferable to Abiquiu Lake if you really want to get away from it all.

Getting There

Abiquiu is about 50 miles (one hour) from downtown Santa Fe; take U.S. 84/285 north for 26 miles to Española. From Española, continue on U.S. 84 north for 23 miles to Abiquiu. From Taos, it's about 70 miles, or 1.5 hours, via El Rito or Ojo Caliente.

Christ in the Desert Monastery

LOW ROAD TO TAOS

Following the winding Rio Grande up into the mountains is the highlight of this drive north, mostly along Highway 68. The route begins just beyond Española, passing into a narrowing canyon and finally emerging at the point where the high plains meet the mountains. This dramatic arrival makes it the better route for heading north to Taos; you can then loop back south via the high road.

Embudo and Dixon

The village of **Embudo** is really just a bend in the river where the Chili Line railroad from Denver, Colorado, used to stop (the old station is across the river). But it offers an unexpected treat in the form of the roadside **Classical Gas Museum** (1819 Hwy. 68, 505/852-2995, free), a front yard filled with old service station accoutrements. If the gate is open, the owner is probably home, and you can peek inside to see a beautiful collection of neon signs and restored gas pumps. (Note that the museum has been under discussions to move to a much larger space in Santa Rosa in fall 2018.) A short walk away, ★ **Sugar's** (1799 Hwy. 68, 505/852-0604, 11am-6pm Thurs.-Sun., $6), a small roadside trailer, doles out seriously big, bib-worthy food, such as barbecued brisket burritos. It's takeout only, but there are a few plastic picnic tables where you can sit down.

If you're into wine, keep an eye out for the various wineries just north of here: **Vivác** (2075 Hwy. 68, 505/579-4441, 10am-6pm Mon.-Sat., 11am-6pm Sun., standard tasting $8) is on the main highway, and **La Chiripada** (505/579-4437, 11am-5pm Mon.-Sat., noon-5pm Sun.) is down Highway 75 a few miles, in the pleasant little town of **Dixon,** known for its dense concentration of artists, organic farmers, and vintners. The convivial **farmers market** runs early June-early November on Wednesdays (3:30pm-6:30pm) in front of the co-op, and, on the first full weekend in November, check out the long-running **Dixon Studio Tour** (www.dixonarts.org), which showcases over 25 area galleries. A good year-round reason to make the turn is ★ **Zuly's** (234 Hwy. 275, 505/579-4001, 8:30am-3pm Tues.-Thurs., 8:30am-7pm Fri., 9am-7pm Sat., $8), serving strong coffee and classic New Mexican food with a bit of a hippie flair; hours cut back slightly in winter.

Pilar

Beginning just south of the village of **Pilar** and stretching several miles north, **Orilla Verde Recreation Area** (Hwy. 570, $3/car) is public land along either side of the Rio Grande, used primarily as a put-in or haul-out for rafting, but you can camp on the riverbanks as well. There are seven campgrounds in Orilla Verde; Petaca and Taos Junction have the best sites ($9/night).

Running about 1.2 miles one-way along the west edge of the river, the **Vista Verde Trail** is an easy walk with great views and a few petroglyphs to spot in a small arroyo about one-third of the way out. The trailhead is located on the other side of the river, 0.5 mile up the hill from the Taos Junction Bridge off the dirt road Highway 567 (turn left off Hwy. 570 in Pilar, then follow signs into Orilla Verde). Stop first on the main highway at the **Rio Grande Gorge Visitors Center** (Hwy. 68, 575/751-4899, 8:30am-4:30pm daily June-Aug., 10am-3pm daily Sept.-May) for maps and other information.

Across the road, **Pilar Yacht Club** (Hwy. 68, 575/758-9072, 8am-6pm daily mid-May-Aug., 9am-2pm daily Apr.-mid-May and Sept.-Oct.) is the hub of local activity, selling tubes for lazy floats, serving New Mexican

Classical Gas Museum, a shrine to roadside America

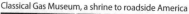

staples and diner food to hungry river rats, and functioning as an office for a couple of outfitters.

Getting There

The low road is more direct than the high road to Taos, and has fewer potential diversions. Driving the 70 miles from downtown Santa Fe to Taos (on U.S. 84/285 and Hwy. 68), with no stops, takes about 1.5 hours. There are no gas stations between Española and Taos.

HIGH ROAD TO TAOS

Chimayó, Córdova, Truchas, Las Trampas, Peñasco—these are the tiny villages strung, like beads on a necklace, along the winding highway through the mountains to Taos. This is probably the area of New Mexico where Spanish heritage has been the least diluted—or at any rate relatively untouched by Anglo influence, for there has been a long history of exchange between the Spanish towns and the adjacent pueblos. The local dialect is distinctive, and residents can claim ancestors who settled the towns in the 18th century. The first families learned to survive in the harsh climate with a 90-day growing season, and much of the technology

that worked then continues to work now; electricity was still scarce even in the 1970s, and adobe construction is common.

To casual visitors, these communities, closed off by geography, can seem a little insular, but pop in at the shops and galleries that have sprung up in a couple of the towns, and you'll get a warm welcome. During the **High Road Art Tour** (www.highroadnewmexico. com), over two weekends in September, modern artists and more traditional craftspeople, famed particularly for their wood-carving skills and blanket weaving, open their home studios.

The route starts on Highway 503, heading east off U.S. 84/285 just north of Pojoaque.

Chimayó

From Nambé Pueblo, Highway 503 continues to a T-junction; make a hard left onto Highway 98 to descend into the valley of Chimayó, site of the largest mass pilgrimage in the United States. During Holy Week, the week before Easter, some 50,000 people arrive on foot, often bearing large crosses. At their journey's end is a small church, seemingly existing in a time long since passed, that holds an undeniable pull.

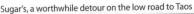
Sugar's, a worthwhile detour on the low road to Taos

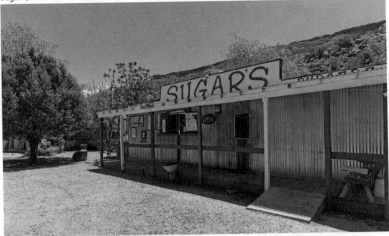

Santuario de Chimayó

★ SANTUARIO DE CHIMAYÓ

The pilgrimage tradition began in 1945, as a commemoration of the Bataan Death March, but the **Santuario de Chimayó** (Hwy. 98, 505/351-9961, www.holychimayo.us, 9am-6pm daily May-Sept., 9am-5pm daily Oct.-Apr.) had a reputation as a miraculous spot from its start, in 1814. It began as a small chapel, built at the place where a local farmer, Bernardo Abeyta, is said to have dug up a glowing crucifix; the carved wood figure was placed on the altar. The building later fell into disrepair, but in 1929, the architect John Gaw Meem bought it, restored it, and added its sturdy metal roof; Meem then granted it back to the archdiocese in Santa Fe.

Unlike many of the older churches farther north, which are now seldom open, Chimayó is an active place of prayer, always busy with tourists as well as visitors seeking solace, with many side chapels and a busy gift shop. (Mass is said weekdays at 11am and on Sunday at 10:30am and noon year-round.) The approach from the parking area passes chain-link fencing into which visitors have woven twigs to form crosses, each set of sticks representing a prayer. Outdoor pews made of split tree trunks accommodate overflow crowds, and a wheelchair ramp gives easy access to the church.

But the original adobe *santuario* seems untouched by modernity. The front wall of the dim main chapel is filled with an elaborately painted altar screen from the first half of the 19th century, the work of Molleno (nicknamed "the Chile Painter" because forms, especially robes, in his paintings often resemble red and green chiles). The vibrant colors seem to shimmer in the gloom, forming a sort of stage set for Abeyta's crucifix, Nuestro Señor de las Esquípulas, as the centerpiece. Painted on the screen above the crucifix is the symbol of the Franciscans: a cross over which the arms of Christ and Saint Francis meet.

Most pilgrims make their way directly to the small, low-ceilinged antechamber that holds *el pocito,* the little hole where the glowing crucifix was allegedly first dug up. From this pit they scoop up a small portion of the exposed red earth, to apply to withered limbs and arthritic joints, or to eat in hopes of curing internal ailments. (The parish refreshes the well each year with new dirt, after it has been blessed by the priests.) The adjacent sacristy displays handwritten testimonials, prayers, and abandoned crutches; the figurine of Santo Niño de Atocha is also said to have been dug out of the holy ground here as well. (Santo Niño de Atocha has a dedicated chapel just down the road—the artwork here is modern, bordering on cutesy, but the back room, filled with baby shoes, is poignant.)

CHIMAYÓ MUSEUM

The only other official sight in the village is the tiny **Chimayó Museum** (Plaza del Cerro, 505/351-0945, www.chimayomuseum.com, 10am-4pm Wed.-Sat. May-Aug., free), set on the old fortified plaza. It functions as a local archive and displays a neat collection of vintage photographs. Look for it behind Ortega's weaving shop.

FOOD AND ACCOMMODATIONS

For lunch, head across the parking lot from the Santuario de Chimayó to **Leona's** (505/351-4569, 10am-5pm Thurs.-Mon., $3), where you can pick up bulk chiles and pistachios as well as delicious tamales and crumbly *bizcochitos*. For a more leisurely sit-down meal, the family-owned ★ **Rancho de Chimayó** (County Rd. 98, 505/351-4444, www.ranchodechimayo.com, 11:30am-9pm daily May-Oct., 11:30am-8:30pm Tues.-Sun. Nov.-Apr., $12) has earned a James Beard America's Classics award for its great local food, such as sopaipilla relleno (fried bread stuffed with meat, beans, and rice), shrimp pesto green-chile enchiladas, and green-chile stew. Enjoy your meal on a beautiful terrace—or inside the old adobe home by the fireplace in wintertime. The place is also open for breakfast on weekends (8:30am-10:30am), and it rents seven rooms (from $69 s, $79 d) in an old farmhouse across the road.

Beyond the Rancho de Chimayó's hacienda, the surrounding area holds a few good options for staying overnight. Not far from the church, off County Road 98, **Rancho Manzana** (26 Camino de Mision, 505/351-2227, www.ranchomanzana.com, $95 d) has a rustic-chic feel, with excellent breakfasts.

En route to Española, **Casa Escondida** (64 County Rd. 100, 505/351-4805, www.casaescondida.com, $122 s, $155 d) is a polished country hideaway with nine modern-Southwest-style rooms and a big backyard with lots of birdlife.

Córdova

From Chimayó, turn right (east) on Highway 76 to begin the climb up the Sangre de Cristo Mountains. Near the crest of the hill, about three miles along, a small sign points to **Córdova,** a village best known for its austere unpainted santos and bultos done by masters such as George López and José Dolores López. Another family member, **Sabinita López Ortiz** (9 County Rd. 1317, 505/351-4572, variable hours), sells her work and that of five other generations of wood-carvers. **Castillo Gallery** (County Rd. 1317, 505/351-4067, variable hours) mixes traditional woodwork with more contemporary sculpture.

Truchas

Highway 76 winds along to the little village of Truchas (Trout), founded in 1754 and still not much more than a long row of buildings set against the ridgeline. On the corner where the highway makes a hard left north is the

Rancho de Chimayó

Walk On, Santo Niño

In northern New Mexico, the figure of **Santo Niño de Atocha** is a popular one. This image of Jesus comes from a Spanish legend, when the Christians were battling the Moors in the medieval period. Around 1300, the Muslims took a number of prisoners after a brutal battle in Atocha, near Madrid, and would not allow the captives' families to visit them. After many desperate prayers on the part of Atocha's Christian women, a mysterious child appeared, carrying food and water, to care for the prisoners. The populace guessed that it must be the child Jesus—thus Santo Niño de Atocha became the patron saint of prisoners, and he is depicted carrying a pail for bread and a gourd for water and wearing a large hat emblazoned with a scallop shell, the symbol of pilgrims.

In **Chimayó** alone, Santo Niño de Atocha is installed in the main church and in a separate 1857 chapel just a block away. He is seen now as a broader intercessor not just for those imprisoned, but also for the chronically ill. New Mexicans have developed a unique folk practice, placing baby shoes at the Santo Niño's feet, on the assumption that his own have worn out while he was walking in the night.

village morada, the meeting place of the local Penitente brotherhood.

Head straight down the smaller road to reach **Nuestra Señora del Rosario de las Truchas Church,** tucked into a small plaza off to the right of the main street. It's open to visitors only June-August—if you do have a chance to look inside the dim, thick-walled mission that dates back to the early nineteenth century, you'll see precious examples of local wood carving. Though many of the more delicate ones have been moved to a museum

for preservation, those remaining display an essential New Mexican style—the sort of "primitive" thing that Bishop Lamy of Santa Fe hated. They're preserved today because Truchas residents hid them at home during the late 19th century. Santa Lucia, with her eyeballs in her hand, graces the altar, and a finely wrought crucifix hangs to the right, clad in a skirt because the legs have broken off.

Just up the road is **The Cordovas Handweaving Workshop** (32 County Rd. 75, 505/689-1124, variable hours Mon.-Sat.),

view of Truchas

an unassuming wooden house that echoes with the soft click-clack of a broadloom, as this Hispano family turns out subtly striped rugs in flawless traditional style, as it has done for generations. Prices are quite reasonable.

Las Trampas

Farther north on Highway 76, the village of **Las Trampas** was settled in 1751, and its showpiece, **San José de Gracia Church** (generally 10am-4pm Sat.-Sun. June-Aug.), was built nine years later. It remains one of the finest examples of New Mexican village church architecture. Its thick adobe walls are balanced by vertical bell towers; inside, the clerestory at the front of the church—a typical design—lets light in to shine down on the altar, which was carved and painted in the late 1700s. Other paradigmatic elements include the *atrio*, or small plaza, between the low adobe boundary wall and the church itself, utilized as a cemetery, and the dark narthex where you enter, confined by the choir loft above, but serving only to emphasize the sense of light and space created in the rest of the church by the clerestory and the small windows near the viga ceiling.

As you leave the town heading north, look to the right—you'll see a centuries-old acequia that has been channeled through a log flume to cross a small arroyo.

Picurís Pueblo

The smallest pueblo in New Mexico, **Picurís** has only about 300 members. It is also one of the few Rio Grande pueblos that has not built a casino. Instead, it capitalizes on its beautiful natural setting, a lush valley where bison roam and aspen leaves rustle. You can picnic here and fish in small but well-stocked Tu-Tah Lake. The **San Lorenzo de Picurís Church** looks old, but it was in fact rebuilt by hand in 1989, following the original 1776 design, a process that took eight years. As at Nambé, local traditions have melded with those of the surrounding villages, and the Hispano-Indian Matachines dances are well attended on Christmas Eve. Start at the **visitors center** (575/587-1099 or 575/587-1071, 9am-5pm Mon.-Sat.) to pick up maps and pay a suggested donation. The pueblo is a short detour from the high road proper: At the junction with Highway 75, turn west, then follow signs off the main road.

Peñasco

Peñasco is best known to tourists as the home of ★ **Sugar Nymphs Bistro** (15046

San José de Gracia Church in Las Trampas

Hwy. 75, 575/587-0311, 11am-4pm and Mon.-Thurs. 11am-8pm Fri.-Sat., 10:30am-3pm Sun., $12), a place with "country atmosphere and city cuisine," where you can get treats like grilled lamb, fresh-pressed cider, piñon couscous, and staggering wedges of chocolate walnut fudge cake. An adjoining **Peñasco Theatre** (www.penascotheatre.org) hosts quirky music and theatrical performances June-September. In winter, restaurant hours are more limited, so call ahead.

This is also the northern gateway to the **Pecos Wilderness Area**—turn on Forest Road 116 to reach Santa Barbara Campground and the Santa Barbara Trail to Truchas Peak, a 23-mile round-trip that requires advance planning. Contact the **Española ranger district office** (1710 N. Riverside Dr., 505/753-7331, 8am-4:30pm Mon.-Fri.) or the one in the town of Pecos for conditions before you hike.

Sipapu

Detouring right (east) along Highway 518, you reach **Sipapu** (Hwy. 518, 800/587-2240, www.sipapunm.com), an unassuming, inexpensive ski resort—really, just a handful of cabins (from $79) and campsites ($12) at the base of a 9,255-foot mountain. Cheap lift tickets ($45 full-day) and utter quiet make this a bargain getaway.

Returning to the junction, continue on to Taos via Highway 518, which soon descends into a valley and passes **Pot Creek Cultural Site** (575/587-2255, 9am-4pm Wed.-Sun. late June-early Sept..), a mildly interesting diversion for its one-mile loop trail through Ancestral Puebloan ruins from around AD 1100.

You arrive in Taos at its southern end—really, in Ranchos de Taos, just north of the San Francisco de Asis Church on Highway 68. Turn left to see the church, or turn right to head up to the town plaza and to Taos Pueblo.

Getting There

From downtown Santa Fe, the high road to Taos is about 90 miles. Follow U.S. 84/285 north for 17 miles to Pojoaque. Turn right (east) on Highway 503, following signs for Nambé Pueblo; turn left where signed, onto County Road 98, to Chimayó, then left again on Highway 76. In about 30 miles, make a hard left onto Highway 518, and in 16 miles, you'll arrive in Ranchos de Taos, just north of the church and about 3 miles south of the main Taos plaza. The drive straight through takes a little more than two hours; leave time to dawdle at churches and galleries, take a hike, or have lunch along the way.

Information and Services

TOURIST INFORMATION

The **Santa Fe Convention and Visitors Bureau** (800/777-2489, www.santafe.org) hands out its visitors guide and other brochures from offices at the **convention center** (201 W. Marcy St., 8am-5pm Mon.-Fri.), at the small **plaza kiosk** next to the First National Bank (66 E. San Francisco St., 10am-6pm daily.) and at the **Rail Runner depot** (401 S. Guadalupe St., 9am-5pm Mon.-Sat.); the depot office is also open for the same hours Sunday May-October. The New Mexico Tourism Department runs a **visitors center** (491 Old Santa Fe Tr., 505/827-7336, www.newmexico.org, 8am-5pm Mon.-Fri.) near San Miguel Mission.

For info on the outdoors, head to the Bureau of Land Management's comprehensive **Public Lands Information Center** (301 Dinosaur Tr., 505/954-2002, www.publiclands.org, 8am-4:30pm Mon.-Fri.), just off Highway 14 (follow Cerrillos Road until it passes under I-25). You can pick up detailed route descriptions for area day hikes, as well as guidebooks, topo maps, and hunting and fishing licenses.

Books and Maps

Santa Fe has several particularly good bookshops in the center of town. **Travel Bug** (839 Paseo de Peralta, 505/992-0418, 7:30am-5:30pm Mon.-Sat., 11am-4pm Sun.) specializes in maps, travel guides, and gear—and has good coffee and baked goods to munch on while you plan your next adventure. For more general books, **Collected Works** (202 Galisteo St., 505/988-4226, 8am-6pm daily) is the place to go for a trove of local-interest titles. **REI** (500 Market St., 505/982-3557, 8am-8pm Mon.-Sat., 8am-6pm Sun.) is well stocked with area outdoor guides and hiking maps.

Local Media

The *Santa Fe New Mexican* is Santa Fe's daily paper. On Friday, it publishes events listings and gallery news in its *Pasatiempo* insert. For left-of-center news and commentary, the *Santa Fe Reporter* is the free weekly rag, available in most coffee shops and cafés.

Radio

KBAC (98.1 FM), better known as Radio Free Santa Fe, is a dynamic community station with eclectic music and talk. Tune in Friday afternoons for news on the gallery scene. Another public station is **KSFR** (101.1 FM), run by Santa Fe Community College.

SERVICES
Banks

First National Santa Fe (62 Lincoln Ave., 505/992-2000, 8am-5pm Mon.-Fri.) is on the west side of the plaza.

Post Office

Santa Fe's **main post office** (120 S. Federal Pl., 505/988-2239, 8am-5:30pm Mon.-Fri., 9am-4pm Sat.) is conveniently just north of the plaza, near the district courthouse.

Laundry

Most self-service laundries are on or near Cerrillos Road. Nearer to the center is **Solana Laundromat** (949 W. Alameda, 505/982-9877, 7am-8pm daily). It also has drop-off service.

Pick up maps, trail information, and gear at REI.

Getting There and Around

AIR

Santa Fe Municipal Airport (SAF, 121 Aviation Dr., 505/955-2900), west of the city, receives direct flights from Dallas and Phoenix (seasonal) with American Airlines, and from Denver with United. Typically, fares are better to the Albuquerque airport (ABQ), an hour's drive away.

Sandia Shuttle Express (888/775-5696, www.sandiashuttle.com) does hourly pickups from the Albuquerque airport 4:45am-6:45pm and every 90 minutes 8pm-12:30am and will deliver to any hotel or B&B ($33 each way).

TRAIN

The **Rail Runner** (866/795-7245, www.riometro.org) goes from Albuquerque to downtown Santa Fe—the final stop is at the rail yard in the Guadalupe district (410 S. Guadalupe St.). The ride takes a little over 90 minutes and costs $10, or $11 for a day pass, and the last train back to Albuquerque leaves at 9pm weekdays, 10:14pm Saturday, and 8:10pm Sunday.

Amtrak (800/872-7245, www.amtrak.com) runs the Southwest Chief once a day through Lamy, 18 miles south of Santa Fe. It's a dramatic place to step off the train—with little visible civilization for miles around, it feels like entering a Wild West movie set. Trains arrive from Chicago and Los Angeles in the afternoon, and Amtrak provides a shuttle van to the city.

BUS AND SHUTTLE

Santa Fe Pick-Up (505/231-2573, www.santafenm.gov, every 10 minutes 6:30am-5:30pm Mon.-Fri., 8:30am-5:30pm Sat., 10am-5:30pm Sun., free) is a service for tourists, with two routes covering all the main sights. It's free and runs more frequently than the regular city bus. The main circuit starts and ends in front of Jean Cocteau Cinema, on Montezuma Avenue just north of the Rail Runner depot, and it stops at the capitol, the St. Francis Cathedral, four points on Canyon Road, Museum Hill, and a few other tourist-friendly spots around town. From the capitol, the second route runs a loop up Canyon Road and out to Museum Hill.

For Cerrillos Road, you can use Route 2 on the city bus system, **Santa Fe Trails** (505/955-2001, www.santafenm.gov), from the handy central depot on Sheridan Street northwest of the plaza. Buses on all routes are not terribly frequent, every 20 minutes at the most. Fare is $1, or you can buy a day pass for $2, payable on board with exact change.

CAR

Having a car in Santa Fe itself is not necessary, though with a car day trips become that much more feasible. Bear in mind that street and garage parking is limited and expensive in the city's center. **Hertz, Budget, Avis,** and **Thrifty** all have branches on Cerrillos Road.

From Albuquerque to Santa Fe, it's a straight shot north on I-25 for 65 miles; you'll reach Santa Fe in about an hour.

Coming from Taos, allow 1.5-2.5 hours, depending on whether you come on the low road (on Hwy. 68 and U.S. 84/285, via Española), via Ojo Caliente (mostly on U.S. 285), or on the high road (mostly on Hwy. 76, via Truchas).

Taos

Sights 113
Entertainment and Events 128
Shopping 131
Sports and Recreation 132
Food 137

Accommodations 142
The Road to Chama 146
The Enchanted Circle 152
Information and Services 159
Getting There and Around 160

A

dobe buildings cluster around a plaza. Snow-capped mountains beckon. Art galleries, organic bakeries, and yoga studios proliferate. But the town of Taos is anything but a miniature Santa Fe.

It's more isolated, reached by two-lane roads along either the winding mountain-ridge route or the fertile Rio Grande Valley, and it has a less polished, more tied-to-the-earth feel. The glory of the landscape, from looming Taos Mountain to the blue mesas dissolving into the flat western horizon, can be breathtaking. The mysticism surrounding Taos Pueblo is intense, as is the often-wild creativity of the artists who have lived here. No wonder people flock here on pilgrimages: to the hip-deep powder at Taos Ski Valley, to the San Francisco de Asis Church that Georgia O'Keeffe painted, to the ranch where D. H. Lawrence lived. Then they wind up staying. The person pouring your coffee at the café just might have a variation on this story.

Taos has long been associated with artists and writers—and, recently, Hollywood types—but this doesn't translate to wealth and exclusivity. Hispano farmers in Valle Valdez are sustained by acequia-fed farm plots as they have been for centuries. The same goes for residents of old Taos Pueblo, the living World Heritage Site that still uses no electricity or running water. Add to that a strong subculture of ski bums, artists, off-the-grid eco-homesteaders, and spiritual seekers, and you have a community that is more loyal and dedicated to preserving its unique way of life than perhaps any other small town in the western United States.

Jump the Taos Gorge on U.S. 64 west out of town for a beautiful drive over the mountains to Tierra Amarilla, where sheepherding continues as it has for centuries. North from here, you're nearly at the Colorado state line in Chama, best known as the depot for a scenic steam train.

North and east from Taos, the so-called Enchanted Circle byway loops around Wheeler Peak, the highest mountain in New Mexico at 13,161 feet. Unlike the rest of northern New Mexico, the area was settled

Look for ★ to find recommended sights, activities, dining, and lodging.

Highlights

★ **Taos Art Museum at Fechin House:** In the early 1930s, Russian artist Nicolai Fechin designed his home in a fusion of Tartar, Spanish, and American Indian styles. His and other artists' paintings hang inside (page 118).

★ **Mabel Dodge Luhan House:** This idiosyncratic home once hummed with artists drawn to Taos by a freethinking woman from New York City, birthing a thriving counterculture (page 119).

★ **San Francisco de Asis Church:** With its massive adobe buttresses and rich earthy glow, this 350-year-old Franciscan mission is one of the most recognizable in the world, thanks to its frequent depiction in paintings and photographs (page 121).

★ **Taos Pueblo:** The stepped adobe buildings at New Mexico's most remarkable pueblo seem to rise organically from the earth. Don't miss the ceremonial dances performed here, about eight times a year (page 122).

★ **Hiking in Taos Ski Valley:** As the road wends ever higher, trailheads beckon, providing access to mountain vistas and some of the most stunning backcountry in the state—not to mention its highest peak (page 133).

★ **Rafting the Rio Grande Gorge:** As jaw-dropping as this 800-foot-deep channel cut through the rock to the west of Taos looks from above, it can't compare to the thrill of rafting its Class III and Class IV rapids (page 134).

★ **Cumbres & Toltec Scenic Railroad:** Ascending the pass through the Rockies into

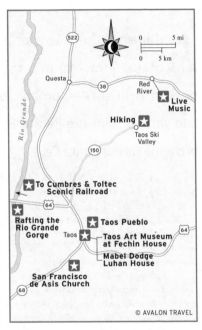

© AVALON TRAVEL

Colorado on this rumbling old steam train, soot and wind in your hair, you'll feel like you've climbed to the top of the world (page 149).

★ **Live Music in Red River:** Though the alpine setting might seem incongruous, the little village of Red River has a surprisingly strong country and bluegrass scene. Catch live acts at packed 1950s-era venues that ooze character (page 156).

Taos Area

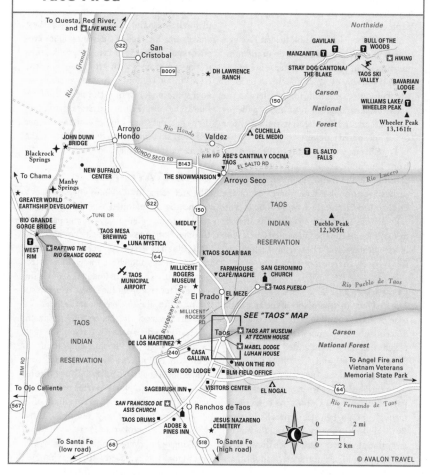

To Questa, Red River, and ✚ LIVE MUSIC

Northside

522

San Cristobal

B009

★ DH LAWRENCE RANCH

GAVILAN

MANZANITA 🚠

BULL OF THE WOODS 🚠

✚ HIKING

STRAY DOG CANTONA/ THE BLAKE

TAOS SKI VALLEY

BAVARIAN LODGE

Rio Grande

Carson

WILLIAMS LAKE/ WHEELER PEAK 🚠

150

National

Wheeler Peak 13,161ft

Forest

Rio Hondo

Arroyo Hondo

Valdez

△ CUCHILLA DEL MEDIO

JOHN DUNN BRIDGE

RIM RD

ABE'S CANTINA Y COCINA TAOS

🚠 EL SALTO FALLS

Rio Lucero

Blackrock Springs

HONDO SECO RD

EL SALTO RD

To Chama

B143

Manby Springs

NEW BUFFALO CENTER

THE SNOWMANSION

Arroyo Seco

GREATER WORLD EARTHSHIP DEVELOPMENT

522

TUNE DR

150

TAOS

RIO GRANDE GORGE BRIDGE

MEDLEY

INDIAN

Pueblo Peak 12,305ft

🚠 WEST RIM

TAOS MESA BREWING

HOTEL LUNA MYSTICA

RESERVATION

✚ RAFTING THE RIO GRANDE GORGE

64

KTAOS SOLAR BAR

Rio Pueblo de Taos

✈ TAOS MUNICIPAL AIRPORT

MILLICENT ROGERS MUSEUM

FARMHOUSE CAFÉ/MAGPIE

SAN GERONIMO CHURCH

El Prado

EL MEZE

TAOS PUEBLO

BLUEBERRY HILL RD

MILLICENT ROGERS RD

SEE "TAOS" MAP

TAOS

Carson

Taos

TAOS ART MUSEUM AT FECHIN HOUSE

LA HACIENDA DE LOS MARTINEZ

MABEL DODGE LUHAN HOUSE

National Forest

INDIAN

240

CASA GALLINA

INN ON THE RIO

To Angel Fire and Vietnam Veterans Memorial State Park

RESERVATION

SUN GOD LODGE

BLM FIELD OFFICE

RIM RD

SAGEBRUSH INN

VISITORS CENTER

EL NOGAL

64

To Ojo Caliente

567

SAN FRANCISCO DE ASIS CHURCH

Ranchos de Taos

Rio Fernando de Taos

TAOS DRUMS

ADOBE & PINES INN

JESUS NAZARENO CEMETERY

0   2 mi

To Santa Fe (low road)

68

518

To Santa Fe (high road)

0   2 km

© AVALON TRAVEL

primarily by miners and ranchers in the late 19th century. Along the way, you can stop at a mining ghost town, a moving Vietnam veterans' memorial, and a couple of less extreme ski resorts, each with their own character—including one with a thriving music scene.

PLANNING YOUR TIME

Taos's busiest tourist season is **summer,** when a day can be spent gallery hopping and museum-going, then settling in to watch the afternoon thunderheads gather and churn,

followed by the sun setting under lurid red streaks across the broad western mesas. **Wintertime** gets busy with skiers November-April, but as they're all up on the mountain during the day, museums scale back their hours, and residents reclaim the town center, curling up with books at the many coffee shops. **Taos Pueblo closes to visitors** for up to 10 weeks in February and March. By May, the peaks are relatively clear of snow, and you can hike to high meadows filled with wildflowers. **Fall** is dominated by the smell of wood smoke and the beat of drums, as the pueblo and the rest of the town turn out for the Feast of San Geronimo at the end of September.

From Santa Fe, it's possible to visit Taos as a **day trip**—as plenty of people do in the summertime—but you'll get a better sense of the place if you stay overnight. A three- or four-night visit gives you time for an afternoon at Taos Pueblo, a couple of mornings at galleries and museums, a hike or skiing, and a day tour of the Enchanted Circle.

For Chama, you can easily make the drive from Taos and back in a day, though if you plan to ride the train, you'll have to get an early start or book a hotel there. As for the **Enchanted Circle,** the 84-mile loop is typically done as a day trip. By no means attempt to visit Taos *and* do the Enchanted Circle loop in a single day—you'd be terribly rushed, and this is hardly the spirit of Taos.

HISTORY

The first human inhabitants of the area at the base of Taos Mountain were Tiwa-speaking descendants of the Ancestral Puebloans (also called Anasazi) who migrated from the Four Corners area around AD 1000. Taos (how Spaniards heard the Tiwa word for "village") was a thriving village when Spanish explorers, part of Francisco de Coronado's crew, passed through in 1540. By 1615, settlers had arrived. By the mid-18th century, Taos was the hub of a large trade in beaver pelts, which drew French fur trappers, Mexican traders, and local settlers to swap meets.

But in 1879, the railroad arrived in Raton, bumping Taos from its position as a trading hub. Fortunes began to turn nearly two decades later, in 1898, when Bert Geer Phillips and Ernest Blumenschein, two painters on a jaunt from Denver, Colorado, "discovered" Taos after their wagon wheel snapped near town. They established the Taos Society of Artists (TSA) in 1915, making names for themselves as painters of the American West and a name for Taos as a destination for creative types. In the 1960s, creativity took a turn to the communal, with groups such as the New Buffalo commune in Arroyo Hondo— an inspiration for Dennis Hopper's film *Easy Rider.* The culture clash at first was fierce, but in the decades since, hippies (and their richer relatives, ski bums) have become part of the town's most basic fabric.

ORIENTATION

The area referred to as Taos encompasses a few nearby communities as well. Arriving via the low road, on Highway 68, you pass first through **Ranchos de Taos;** it's connected to **Taos Plaza** by Paseo del Pueblo Sur, a stretch of chain stores and cheap motels. The intersection with Kit Carson Road (U.S. 64) is the center of town proper (Taos Plaza is just west); for **parking,** there's a pay lot at the light, or a free lot a few blocks farther east on Kit Carson.

Heading north past Kit Carson, the road becomes Paseo del Pueblo Norte. It curves west after 0.5 mile, and a smaller road continues north about two miles to **Taos Pueblo.** Paseo del Pueblo Norte carries on through what is technically the separate village of El Prado, then to a four-way intersection that will forever be known to locals as "the old blinking light," even though the flashing yellow signal was replaced with a newfangled three-color traffic light in the 1990s. Here U.S. 64 shoots **west to the Rio Grande,** and Highway 522 leads northwest to the outlying village of **Arroyo Hondo,** then to Questa and the Enchanted Circle. Highway 150 goes north to **Arroyo Seco,** and eventually to **Taos Ski Valley,** at the base of the slopes.

Sights

TAOS PLAZA

Taos Plaza, enclosed by adobe buildings with deep portals, is easy to miss if you just cruise through on the main road—it's just west of the intersection with Kit Carson Road. Once an informal area at the center of a cluster of settlers' homes, the plaza was established around 1615 but destroyed in the Pueblo Revolt of 1680. New homes were built starting in 1710, as defense against Comanche and Jicarilla raiders. Before long a series of fires gutted the block-style buildings, so the structures that edge the plaza all date from around 1930—and unfortunately virtually all are now filled with rather cheesy souvenir shops.

On the plaza's north side, the **Old Taos County Courthouse** contains a series of Works Progress Administration-sponsored murals painted in 1934 and 1935 by Emil Bisttram and a team of other Taos artists. The door is usually open when the farmers market is on, but not reliably so at other times. Still, it's worth a try: Enter on the ground floor through the North Plaza Art Center and go upstairs, toward the back of the building. On the south side, the **Hotel La Fonda de Taos** harbors a small collection of D. H. Lawrence's "erotic" paintings (10am-6pm daily, guided $6, unguided $3, free to guests). The nine paintings are tame by today's standards, but they flesh out (no pun intended) the story of the writer's time in Taos, some of which is described in his book *Mornings in Mexico*.

In the center is a **monument** to New

Taos: Fact and Fiction

Just as San Francisco de Asis Church has inspired countless painters and photographers, the people of Taos have found their way into novels and short stories.

One of Taos's more revered figures is **Padre Antonio Martinez,** a popular priest in the mid-1800s who clashed with **Bishop Jean-Baptiste Lamy** in Santa Fe. As a result, some Taos residents aren't fond of Willa Cather's *Death Comes for the Archbishop* (New York: Vintage, 1990), even if it is a classic. The 1927 novel is based on the mission of Lamy, with sympathy for his efforts to straighten out "rogue" Mexican priests like Martinez. The padre gets more balanced coverage in *Lamy of Santa Fe* (Middletown, CT: Wesleyan University Press, 2003), a Pulitzer Prize-winning biography by Paul Horgan.

Famous Western novelist Frank Waters, a Taos resident for almost 50 years, fictionalized **Edith Warner,** a woman who ran a small café frequented by Los Alamos scientists while they developed the nuclear bomb. *The Woman at Otowi Crossing* (Athens, OH: Swallow Press, 1987) is his portrait of a woman who seeks isolation in the New Mexico wilderness but is drawn back into the world through the largest event of her time. The novel is fairly true to life, but a biography, *The House at Otowi Bridge: The Story of Edith Warner and Los Alamos* (Albuquerque: University of New Mexico Press, 1973), is stricter with the facts. It's by Peggy Pond Church, who lived at Los Alamos for 20 years before the area was taken over by the government.

Another Taos writer, **John Nichols,** earned acclaim for his 1974 comic novel *The Milagro Beanfield War* (New York: Owl Books, 2000), later made into a film by Robert Redford. The war of the title is an escalating squabble in a tiny village over the acequia, the type of irrigation ditch that's still used in Valle Valdez and other agricultural communities in the area. But if you think it takes comic melodrama and a star such as Redford to make irrigation interesting, look into the beautiful and fascinating *Mayordomo: Chronicle of an Acequia in Northern New Mexico* (Albuquerque: University of New Mexico Press, 1993), **Stanley Crawford**'s memoir about his term as "ditch boss" in the valley where he runs his garlic farm.

Taos

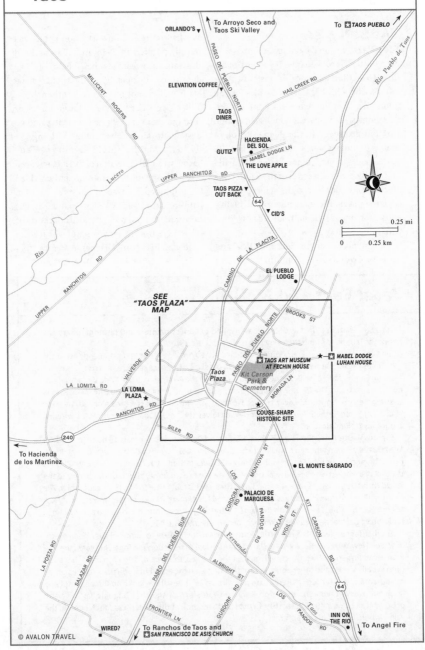

To Arroyo Seco and
Taos Ski Valley

To ⊞ TAOS PUEBLO

ORLANDO'S ▼

ELEVATION COFFEE ▼

HAIL CREEK RD

Rio Pueblo de Taos

MILLICENT ROGERS RD

PASEO DEL PUEBLO NORTE

TAOS
DINER ▼

HACIENDA
DEL SOL ●
MABEL DODGE LN

GUTIZ ▼

THE LOVE APPLE ▼

Lucero

UPPER RANCHITOS RD

TAOS PIZZA ▼
OUT BACK

64

▼ CID'S

Rio

UPPER RANCHITOS RD

0   0.25 mi
0   0.25 km

CAMINO DE LA PLACITA

● EL PUEBLO
LODGE

SEE
"TAOS PLAZA"
MAP

BROOKS ST

PASEO DEL PUEBLO NORTE

VALVERDE ST

Taos
Plaza

⊞ TAOS ART MUSEUM
AT FECHIN HOUSE

★ ⊞ MABEL DODGE
LUHAN HOUSE

Kit Carson
Park &
Cemetery

MORADA LN

LA LOMITA RD

LA LOMA
PLAZA ★

RANCHITOS RD

★ COUSE-SHARP
HISTORIC SITE

SILER RD

240

To Hacienda
de los Martinez

MONTOYA ST

● EL MONTE SAGRADO

LOS

CORDOBA RD

● PALACIO DE
MARQUESA

Rio

PANDOS RD

DOLAN ST

VIGIL ST

KIT CARSON RD

PASEO DEL PUEBLO SUR

Fernando

de

LA POSTA RD

SALAZAR RD

ALBRIGHT ST

Taos

los

64

GUSDORF RD

FRONTIER LN

Pandos

INN ON
THE RIO

To Angel Fire

© AVALON TRAVEL

WIRED? ■

To Ranchos de Taos and
⊞ SAN FRANCISCO DE ASIS CHURCH

Mexicans killed in the Bataan Death March of World War II. The U.S. flag flies day and night, a tradition carried on after an incident during the Civil War when Kit Carson and a crew of his men nailed the flag to a pole and guarded it to keep Confederate sympathizers from taking it down.

In front of the historic La Fonda hotel, a large bronze **statue of Padre Antonio Martinez** gestures like a visionary. This local hero produced the area's first newspaper, *El Crepúsculo de la Libertad* (The Dawn of Freedom), which later became the *Taos News;* he also established a co-ed school, a seminary, and a law school. Bishop Jean-Baptiste Lamy in Santa Fe criticized his liberal views, especially after Martinez defied Lamy's call for mandatory tithing, and Lamy later excommunicated him. Martinez continued to minister to locals at a chapel in his house until his death in 1867. The statue's enormous hands suggest his vast talent and influence in the town.

Harwood Museum of Art

The **Harwood Museum of Art** (238 Ledoux St., 575/758-9826, 10am-5pm Wed.-Fri., noon-5pm Sat.-Sun., $10), set in the sprawling Pueblo Revival-style home of the Harwood

patrons, tells the story of Taos's rise as an art colony, beginning with Ernest Blumenschein's fateful wagon accident, which left him and his colleague Bert Phillips stranded in the tiny town in 1898.

Modern Taos painters are represented in changing exhibit spaces upstairs and down, and it's interesting to see the same material—the mountain, the pueblo, the river, local residents—depicted in different styles over time. Also upstairs is a small but good assortment of Hispano crafts, including some beautiful 19th-century tinwork and a couple of santos by Patrocinio Barela, the Taos wood-carver who modernized the art in the 1930s. A separate back wing is dedicated to seven ethereal abstractions by painter Agnes Martin; a local teacher offers yoga in the gallery every Wednesday. The Arthur Bell Auditorium hosts concerts and artist talks.

E. L. Blumenschein Home

Ernest Blumenschein, one of the founding fathers of the Taos Society of Artists, moved into what is now the **E. L. Blumenschein Home** (222 Ledoux St., 575/758-0505, www.taoshistoricmuseums.org, 10am-5pm Mon.-Sat., noon-5pm Sun. Apr.-Oct., 10am-4pm Mon. and Thurs.-Sat., noon-4pm Sun. Nov.-Mar.,

Taos Plaza

Taos Plaza

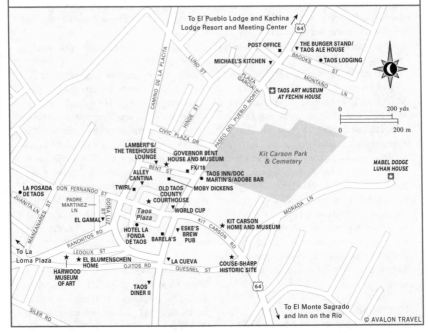

To El Pueblo Lodge and Kachina Lodge Resort and Meeting Center 64

POST OFFICE
THE BURGER STAND/ TAOS ALE HOUSE
MICHAEL'S KITCHEN
BROOKS ST
TAOS LODGING
MONTANO LN
TAOS ART MUSEUM AT FECHIN HOUSE

CAMINO DE LA PLACITA
LUND ST
HINDE ST
PLAZA GARCIA
PASEO DEL PUEBLO NORTE
CIVIC PLAZA DR

0   200 yds
0   200 m

Kit Carson Park & Cemetery

MABEL DODGE LUHAN HOUSE

LAMBERT'S/ THE TREEHOUSE LOUNGE
GOVERNOR BENT HOUSE AND MUSEUM
BENT ST
FX/18
ALLEY CANTINA
TAOS INN/DOC MARTIN'S/ADOBE BAR
LA POSADA DE TAOS
DON FERNANDO ST
TWIRL
OLD TAOS COUNTY COURTHOUSE
MOBY DICKENS
JUANITA LN
PADRE MARTINEZ LN
DOÑA LUZ ST
MANZANARES ST
EL GAMAL
Taos Plaza
WORLD CUP
MORADA LN
KIT CARSON HOME AND MUSEUM
To La Loma Plaza
RANCHITOS RD
LEDOUX ST
HOTEL LA FONDA DE TAOS
BARELA'S
ESKE'S BREW PUB
KIT CARSON RD
EL BLUMENSCHEIN HOME
OJITOS RD
LA CUEVA
COUSE-SHARP HISTORIC SITE
HARWOOD MUSEUM OF ART
QUESNEL ST
TAOS DINER II
64
SILER RD

To El Monte Sagrado and Inn on the Río

© AVALON TRAVEL

$8) in 1919 with his wife, Mary Shepherd Greene Blumenschein, also an accomplished artist. The house's decoration largely reflects her taste, from the sturdy wood furnishings in the dining room to the light-filled studio and the cozy wood-paneled library.

The original rooms of the house feature rotating exhibits, while other rooms, including the "Green Room," are hung with works by their contemporaries, including a beautiful monotype of Taos Mountain by Oscar E. Berninghaus. The main bedroom, entered through a steep arch, is decorated with Mary's lush illustrations for *The Arabian Nights*. Throughout, you can admire the variety of ceiling styles, from rough-hewn split cedar (*rajas*) to tidy golden aspen boughs (*latillas*).

La Loma Plaza

To see what Taos Plaza looked like before the souvenir-shop economy, stroll down Lower Ranchitos Road and turn on Valdez Road to reach **La Loma Plaza.** The center of a fortified settlement created by 63 Spanish families in 1796, the ring of adobe homes around a central open space is dusty and little changed through the centuries. Exit the plaza by continuing uphill and bearing right—this takes you past La Loma's tiny old chapel and onto paved San Antonio Street, which leads downhill and back to Lower Ranchitos.

Governor Bent House and Museum

This dusty little backroom exhibit space is odd, but well worth a visit if it happens to be open (the posted hours aren't always maintained). The **Governor Bent House and Museum** (117 Bent St., 10am-5pm daily, $3) is the former residence of Charles Bent, who, following the onset of the Mexican-American War, was appointed the first governor of the territory of New Mexico in 1846, based on his extensive experience as a

Taos Walking Tour

The major sights around Taos Plaza are listed in the order of a potential walking tour. Stroll quickly to get oriented, or take your time and visit the museums along the way. Either way, you'll pass a few other historical spots as well.

Starting on **Taos Plaza,** walk out the southwest corner to **Ledoux Street** and the museums (such as the **Harwood Museum of Art**). Make a short jog left (southwest) down Lower Ranchitos Road to **La Loma Plaza.** Return to Ranchitos, and then turn left into **Padre Martinez Lane,** where the influential pastor lived until his death in 1867. At the end of the street, turn right and walk to Camino de la Placita, then turn left.

After a couple of blocks, turn right (east) on **Bent Street**, passing **Governor Bent House and Museum,** home of the first American governor, Charles Bent. At Paseo del Pueblo Norte, turn left and walk to **Taos Art Museum at Fechin House,** at least to admire the structure. Backtrack and enter **Kit Carson Park** to find the **cemetery** where many Taos notables are buried. Cut out the back of the park, past the baseball diamonds to Morada Lane—at the end is the **Mabel Dodge Luhan House.**

Take Morada Lane back to **Kit Carson Road,** passing the **Couse-Sharp Historic Site** and the **Kit Carson Home.** Turn right (west) to get back to Paseo del Pueblo, passing Carson's home on the way. Another right turn gets you to a well-deserved drink at the **Taos Inn.**

Western trader (he and his brother had built Bent's Fort, an important trading center in southern Colorado). But Bent died in 1847, at the hands of an angry mob dissatisfied by the new U.S. government.

Amid the slightly creepy clutter, which includes a malevolent-looking ceremonial buffalo head and photos of Penitente rituals from an old *Harper's* magazine, is the very hole in the very wall that Bent's family quickly dug to escape while Bent tried to reason with the murderous crowd. The back room only gets stranger, with weird taxidermy (including an eight-legged lamb), sinister early 1900s doctor's instruments, and lots of old guns. The place may feel like an antiques store where nothing's for sale, but it still gives a surprisingly good overview of the period.

Governor Bent House and Museum

★ Taos Art Museum at Fechin House

This sunny space, the former home of artist and wood-carver Nicolai Fechin, is a showcase not only for a great collection of paintings, but also for Fechin's lovely woodwork. When the Russian native moved to Taos in 1927, hoping to cure his tuberculosis, he purchased seven acres of land, including the small, two-story **Taos Art Museum at Fechin House** (227 Paseo del Pueblo Norte, 575/758-2690, 10am-5pm Tues.-Sun. May-Oct., 10am-4pm Nov.-Apr., $10). He proceeded to hand-carve the lintels, staircases, bedsteads, and more, in a combination of Russian Tartar and local styles. His blending of traditions is flawless and natural—a small altar, also in the dining room, is set with Orthodox icons but could just as easily hold local santos.

The permanent collection rotates through three times a year, so the collection varies at any given time. One thing you can count on is that all will be eclectic: Victor Higgins's 1936 *Indian Nude* recalls Paul Gauguin, while Dorothy Brett's *Rainbow and Indians* from 1942 is more enamored of the powerful landscape. One room is dedicated to Fechin's own portrait work, characterized by broad, dynamic brushstrokes and a canny eye for distinctive facial features. After all the work Fechin did on the house, he stayed in Taos only six years, when his wife divorced him. He moved on to Los Angeles with his daughter, Eya (her sunny study, on the ground floor, contains the child-scale furniture that her father made for her). After her father died in 1955, Eya, by then practicing psychodrama and dance therapy, returned to live in the studio (the back building that also houses the gift shop) and helped establish the main house as a museum.

Kit Carson Park and Cemetery

A shady sprawl of gravestones in a corner of **Kit Carson Park** (211 Paseo del Pueblo Norte, north of the Taos Inn), the **cemetery** was established in 1847 to bury the dead from the Taos Rebellion, a melee incited by wealthy Spanish landowners and Catholic priests anxious about their loss of influence under the Americans. Mobs killed New Mexico's first American governor, the veteran merchant Charles Bent, as well as scores of other Anglo landowners in the area. The cemetery earned its current name when the bodies of Carson and his wife were moved here in 1869, according to his will.

Many of Taos's oldest families, particularly

Taos Art Museum at Fechin House

the merchants of the late 1800s, are buried here. Mabel Dodge Luhan had been a close friend of the trader Ralph Meyers, and they often joked about being buried together. When Mabel died in 1962, a few years after Ralph, writer Frank Waters recalled their wishes and suggested that Meyers's grave be scooted over to make room for Mabel. She was the last person to be buried in the cemetery, in 1962, and her grave is squeezed into the far southwest corner. Other local luminaries at rest here include Padre Antonio Martinez, who stood up to Catholic bishop Lamy, and an Englishman named Arthur Manby, whose grave actually stands outside of the cemetery proper, due to his lifetime of shady business deals, land grabs, and outright swindles perpetrated in town. Manby was found beheaded in his mansion in 1929, and the unsympathetic populace was happy to attribute the death to natural causes.

The park itself is a popular picnic and barbecue spot in summer, when it also holds concerts by local and national acts.

★ Mabel Dodge Luhan House

Now used as a conference center and B&B, the **Mabel Dodge Luhan House** (240 Morada Ln., 575/751-9686, 9am-7pm daily, free) is open to curious visitors as well as overnight guests. Knock at the main building first; the caretaker will give you a history brochure for a self-guided tour around the public areas of the house.

Mabel Dodge, a well-off, freethinking woman who had fostered art salons in New York City and Florence, Italy, decamped to Taos in 1916, following her third husband. Eventually she got married again, to Taos Pueblo member Tony Luhan, and her name became inextricably linked with Taos's 20th-century history, thanks to all the budding artists and writers she encouraged to visit. Novelist D. H. Lawrence dubbed Taos "Mabeltown," and figures as grand and varied as actress Greta Garbo, writer Willa Cather, photographer Ansel Adams, artist Georgia O'Keeffe, poet Robinson Jeffers, and psychiatrist Carl Jung made the long trek to her home.

Bordering the Taos reservation, the house was built to Luhan's specifications starting in 1918. Unsurprisingly, given her artistic taste, she exercised a firm hand in its design. Alongside a small original structure—a low row of adobe rooms that were already a century old at that point—she added a three-story main building, topped with a huge sunroom open on three sides. This, and the

Kit Carson Park and Cemetery

similarly glass-enclosed bathroom on the 2nd floor, scandalized her neighbors, the pueblo residents.

One of them, however, didn't seem to mind: Tony Luhan, the foreman of the construction project, became her next husband. But Mabel's custom love nest brought out some latent prudery even in D. H. Lawrence, who objected to the curtainless bathroom windows; to soothe his sensibilities, if not Mabel's, he painted colorful swirls directly on the glass.

Couse-Sharp Historic Site

Tours of the **Couse-Sharp Historic Site** (146 Kit Carson Rd., 575/751-0369, www.couse-sharp.org, 10am-5pm daily, May-Oct., donation) are by appointment and during open houses (3pm-5pm, first Sat. of the month June-Oct.), but it is well worth arranging to see the interior of painter Eanger Irving Couse's home and studio. Couse, a friend of E. L. Blumenschein's, came to Taos in 1902 with his wife, Virginia, and spent the summers here, working as a figurative painter, until he died in 1936.

Not only has the Couse home and garden been meticulously kept up, as has adjacent property owned by friend and fellow painter

Joseph Henry Sharp, but the tours are led by Couse's granddaughter and her husband, who have a wealth of stories to share. And not only artists will be intrigued; Couse's son, a mechanical engineer who developed mobile repair vehicles, built a vast machine shop here.

Kit Carson Home and Museum

Old photographs, memorabilia, and assorted trinkets from the frontier era conjure the spirit of the legendary scout at the **Kit Carson Home and Museum** (113 Kit Carson Rd., 575/758-4945, www.kitcarsonhomeandmuseum.com, 10am-5pm daily Mar.-Oct., 10am-4pm daily Nov.-Feb., $7), where he lived with his third wife, Josefa Jaramillo, from 1843 until they both died in 1868.

The definitive mountain man, Carson was of the most acclaimed of the many solitary scouts, trackers, and trappers who explored the American West. He was an intrepid adventurer who, after a childhood on the barely settled edge of Missouri, joined a wagon train headed down the Santa Fe Trail; he arrived in Taos in 1826. His talent for tracking, hunting, and translating from Spanish and various Indian languages soon put him in high demand. Whether he was scouting for John

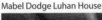

Mabel Dodge Luhan House

C. Frémont as the explorer mapped the trails west to Los Angeles or serving as an officer in the Civil War or, less heroically, forcing the Navajos on the Long Walk to Fort Sumner, he called Taos home.

Taos Inn

Distinguished by its large glowing thunderbird sign, the **Taos Inn** (125 Paseo del Pueblo Norte, 575/758-2233, www.taosinn. com) was as central to previous generations of Taoseños's lives as it is now. Granted, today it's the hotel bar that everyone goes to, but starting in the 1890s, it was the home of T. P. Martin, Taos's first and only county doctor, who had a reputation for accepting chickens or venison from his poorer patients in lieu of cash. His home looked out on a small plaza and a well—which has since been covered over and made into the hotel lobby.

HACIENDA DE LOS MARTINEZ

The word *hacienda* conjures a sprawling complex and fields, but the reality in 19th-century Taos was quite different, as seen at the carefully restored 1804 **Hacienda de los Martinez** (708 Hacienda Rd., off Lower Ranchitos Rd., 575/758-1000, www.taoshistoricmuseums.org, 10am-5pm Mon.-Sat., noon-5pm Sun. Apr.-Oct., 10am-4pm Mon. and Thurs.-Sat., noon-4pm Sun. Nov.-Mar., $8), one of the last remaining homes of its kind in the Southwest. Its builder and owner, Don Antonio Severino Martinez, was a prominent merchant who hosted the Taos trade fairs at the hacienda and eventually became the mayor of Taos in the 1820s. His oldest son was Padre Antonio Martinez, the valley leader who clashed with the French bishop Jean-Baptiste Lamy.

If you plan to visit just Hacienda de los Martinez and the E. L. Blumenschein Home, ask about discounted admission to both places for $12 (as opposed to $8 each).

Despite the family's high social standing, life was fairly rugged, cramped, and dangerous. The 21 simple rooms arranged around two courtyards allowed room for sleeping, cooking, and protection against raids. Some of the spaces have been furnished to reflect their original use; others are dedicated to exhibits, such as an interesting display on slavery in the area, and a wood carving of Doña Sebastiana, Lady Death, with her glittering mica eyes, in the collection of Penitente paraphernalia. During the spring and summer, local craftspeople are on hand to demonstrate weaving, blacksmithing, and the like in the house's workshops; in the fall, the trade fair is reenacted over a weekend.

★ SAN FRANCISCO DE ASIS CHURCH

Just as photographs of the Great Pyramid of Cheops seldom show the sprawl of modern Cairo crowding up to its base, **San Francisco de Asis Church** (east side of U.S. 68 in Ranchos de Taos, 575/758-2754, 10am-4pm daily, Mass 8am, 9:30am, and 11:30am Sun., donation) as depicted in, say, Georgia O'Keeffe's paintings and Ansel Adams's photographs, is a shadow-draped fortress isolated on a hilltop. In fact, the iconic church, completed in the early 19th century as a Franciscan mission, is at the center of a plaza, ringed with buildings.

It's easy to see what has fascinated so many artists: the clean lines, the shadows created by the hulking buttresses, the adobe bathed in the sun's glow. The church is living architecture, as much a part of the earth as something raised above it. As with every traditional adobe structure, it must be refinished every year with a mix of clay, sand, and straw; it is then coated with a fine layer of water and sand, and buffed with sheepskin. This happens over two weeks in June, during which the church is open only at lunchtime and on Sunday.

Inside, the whitewashed walls are covered with the stations of the cross; two Spanish Colonial *reredos* decorate the altars. In the **parish hall** (9am-3:30pm Mon.-Fri., $3) is the 1896 painting *The Shadow of the Cross*, an eight-foot-high canvas in which the figure of Christ can be seen to luminesce—allegedly miraculously.

★ TAOS PUEBLO

Even if you've been in New Mexico for a while and think you're inured to adobe, **Taos Pueblo** (575/758-1028, www.taospueblo. com, 8am-4:30pm Mon.-Sat., 8:30am-4:30pm Sun., 8:30am-4pm daily in winter, closed for 10 weeks Feb.-Mar., $16) is an amazing sight. Two clusters of multistory mud-brick buildings make up the core of this village, which claims, along with Acoma Pueblo, to be the oldest continually inhabited community in the United States. The current buildings, annually repaired and recoated with mud, are from the 1200s, though it's possible that all their constituent parts have been fully replaced several times since then.

About 150 people (out of the 1,900 or so total Taos reservation residents) live here year-round. These people, along with the town's designation as a United Nations Educational, Scientific, and Cultural Organization (UNESCO) World Heritage Site, have kept the place remarkably as it was in the pre-Columbian era, save for the use of adobe bricks (as opposed to clay and stone), which were introduced by the Spanish, as the main structural material. The apartment-like homes, stacked upon each other and reached by wooden ladders, have no electricity or running water, though some use propane gas for heat and light.

You are free to explore, but be mindful not to intrude on private space: Enter only buildings that are clearly marked as shops, and stay clear of the ceremonial kiva areas on the east side of each complex. These round structures form the ritual heart of the pueblo, a secret space within an already private culture.

You're welcome to wander around and enter any of the craft shops and galleries that are open—a good opportunity to see inside the earthen structures and to buy some of the distinctive Taos pottery, which is only lightly decorated but glimmers with mica from the clay of this area. These pots are also renowned for cooking tender beans. On your way out of the pueblo, you may want to stop in at the **Oo-oonah Art Center** (575/779-9566, 1pm-5pm daily Oct.-Apr.), whose gallery displays the work of pueblo children and adults enrolled in its craft classes.

San Francisco de Asis Church

Dennis Hopper in Taos

In 1968, a Taos Pueblo elder told Dennis Hopper, "The mountain is smiling on you!" No wonder the *Easy Rider* actor and real-life renegade claimed the town as what he called his "heart home." His early years here were wild: He's notorious for having ridden his motorcycle across the roof of the Mabel Dodge Luhan House, which he bought in 1969. Over the decades, he mellowed just a bit, and Taos locals came to think of him as one of their own. In 2009, as part of a 40th-anniversary celebration of the Summer of Love, the Harwood Museum mounted an exhibit of his photography and paintings, along with works by some of his compatriots from that era.

Hopper died not long after, in 2010. His funeral was held at the San Francisco de Asis Church, and attended by fellow *Easy Rider* actors Peter Fonda and Jack Nicholson. Following Pueblo tradition, Hopper was buried in a pine box under a dirt mound, in the nearby **Jesus Nazareno Cemetery.** Fans can pay their respects there. To find it, take Highway 518 south; about 0.25 mile along, turn left (east) on Espinoza Road. The cemetery is a short way from here, off the left side of the road. From the main gate, Hopper's grave is near the back, on the right-hand side.

San Geronimo Church

The path from the Taos Pueblo admission gate leads directly to the central plaza, a broad expanse between Red Willow Creek (source of the community's drinking water, flowing from sacred Blue Lake high in the mountains) and **San Geronimo Church.** The church, built in 1850, is perhaps the newest structure in the village, a replacement for the first mission the Spanish built, in 1619, using forced Indian labor. The Virgin Mary presides over the room roofed with heavy wood beams; her clothes change with every season, a nod to her dual role as the Earth Mother. (Taking photos is strictly forbidden inside the church at all times and, as at all pueblos, at dances as well.)

The older church, to the north behind the houses, is now a cemetery—fitting, given its tragic destruction. It was first torn down during the Pueblo Revolt of 1680; the Spanish rebuilt it about 20 years later. In 1847, it was again attacked, this time by U.S. troops sent in to quell the rebellion against the new government, in retaliation for the murder of

Taos Pueblo

Governor Charles Bent. The counterattack brutally outweighed what had sparked it. More than 100 pueblo residents, including women and children, had taken refuge inside the church when the soldiers bombarded and set fire to it, killing everyone inside and gutting the building. Since then, the bell tower has been restored, but the graves have simply intermingled with the ruined walls and piles of dissolved adobe mud. All of the crosses—from old carved wood to newly finished stone—face the sacred Taos Mountain.

EL PRADO AND
WEST ON U.S. 64
Millicent Rogers Museum

A dashing, thrice-married New York City socialite and designer, Millicent Rogers visited Taos in 1947 after breaking things off with actor Clark Gable. After moving to Taos, she brought Southwestern fashion to national attention, as she modeled Navajo-style velvet broomstick skirts, concha belts, and pounds of silver-and-turquoise jewelry for photo spreads in *Vogue* and *Harper's Bazaar*. Though she died just six years after she arrived in Taos, at the age of 51, she managed to accumulate a fantastic amount of local art. The **Millicent Rogers Museum** (1504 Millicent Rogers Rd., 575/758-2462, www.millicentrogers.org, 10am-5pm daily Apr.-Oct., 10am-5pm Tues.-Sun. Nov.-Mar., $10) was established by her son, Paul Peralta-Ramos, and is set in the warren of adobe rooms that make up her former home.

Her belongings form the core collection, with flawless pieces of pottery, rugs, baskets, and jewelry—both local works and her own designs. Peralta-Ramos also contributed his own collection, including beautiful pieces of Navajo rugs and Hispano devotional art. An entire gallery is devoted to the work of San Ildefonso potter Maria Martinez. Aside from the works' individual beauty, they make an excellent broad introduction to the crafts of the area, from ancient times to modern. But it's not all rooted in local culture: Rogers's goofy illustrations of a fairy tale for her children fill the last room. The gift shop here is particularly thorough and includes beautiful vintage jewelry and circa-1900 rugs.

Rio Grande Gorge

Heading west on U.S. 64 from its intersection with Highway 150 and Highway 522, you pass the Taos airstrip on the left; then, after a few more miles, the ground simply drops away. This is the **Rio Grande Gorge** (also called

rafting on the Rio Grande

the Taos Gorge), plunging at its most vertigo-inducing point 800 feet down into malevolent-looking basalt. The river courses below, but it's not just millions of years of rushing water that have carved out the canyon—seismic activity also caused a rift in the earth's surface. The crack extends north to just beyond the Colorado state line and south almost to Española.

The elegant, unnervingly delicate-looking bridge that spans it was built in 1965 to supplement entrepreneur John Dunn's rickety old toll crossing eight miles north. Critics mocked the newer structure as "the bridge to nowhere" because the highway on the western bank had yet to be built, but the American Institute of Steel Construction granted it the Most Beautiful Steel Bridge award in 1966. At 650 feet above the river, the cantilever truss was a stunning engineering feat; it is still the seventh-highest bridge in the United States. On either side of the bridge is the stretch of white water called the Taos Box, two words that inspire wild tales in any seasoned river-runner. This series of Class III and IV rapids is the best place for rafting in New Mexico.

A pedestrian path along the bridge brings the depths below you into extremely sharp relief; viewing the gorge from here at sunset with the mountains looming in the backdrop can make for a stunning end to the day. On the west side of the gorge is a rest area, and the start of the **West Rim Trail,** running south from the parking lot and yielding great views of the bridge to the north.

Greater World Earthship Development

If you brave the slender gorge bridge and continue a mile or so west on U.S. 64, you soon see some whimsically curved and creatively stuccoed houses along the right side of the road. These are Earthships: modular, low-priced homes that function entirely on collected rainwater and wind and solar power. Although they look like fanciful hobbit homes or Mars colony pods, Earthships are made of rather common stuff: The walls, built into hillsides for efficient heating and cooling, are stacks of used tires packed with rammed earth, while bottles stacked with cement and crushed aluminum cans form front walls and colorful peepholes.

Greater World is the largest of three local all-Earthship subdivisions and headquarters of the architecture office that developed the design. The **Earthship visitors center** (2 Earthship Way, 575/613-4409, www.earthship.

fantastical homes at the Greater World Earthship Development

com, 9am-5pm daily in summer, 10am-4pm daily in winter, $8) is the most unconventional model home and sales office you'll ever visit. You can take the self-guided tour of a basic Earthship and watch a video about the building process and the rationale behind the design. If you're hooked, you can, of course, get details on buying a lot in the development or purchasing the plans to build your own place elsewhere. Or try before you buy: You can stay the night in an Earthship here, starting at $130. Look for the green building on the right, 1.5 miles past the bridge.

HIGHWAY 150
Arroyo Seco

When Taos's downtown core becomes too overrun for your liking, it's a good time to make for the village of **Arroyo Seco,** reached by driving past El Prado on U.S. 64 and heading north on Highway 150. This cluster of buildings at a bend in the road to the ski valley feels very much of another era. Sure, there's art up here too, but this diminutive community, though only a half-hour drive from the Taos Plaza, maintains an even more laidback and funky attitude than Taos—if such a thing is possible. It has been a retreat for decades: Frank Waters, celebrated author of *The Man*

Who Killed the Deer and *The Woman at Otowi Crossing,* lived here off and on from 1947 until his death in 1995.

"Downtown" Arroyo Seco, all one block of it, has grown up around the bend in the road and **La Santísima Trinidad Church,** set back from Highway 150 on the left. The church, built in 1834, has adobe walls that are alarmingly eroded in patches, but it sports a cheery red-metal roof; the spare traditional interior is decorated with bultos and retablos, but the doors are often locked. Secular pursuits in this area are more surefire draws: a fine bar and general store, for instance, and El Salto Falls, up the mountain a bit.

The Rim Road

As Highway 150 continues, the road to the ski area eventually makes a hard right, and the so-called rim road heads to the left, along the canyon edge. It gives a great view of **Valle Valdez** below, where tidy farm plots are set along Rio Hondo and the traditional acequia irrigation that has been used here for more than four centuries. In typical modern real-estate distribution, the not-so-well-off native *Taoseños* value their fertile soil, while wealthy *arrivistes* (actress Julia Roberts, most famously) have claimed the swoon-inducing

sleepy Arroyo Seco

New Mexico's Communes

Something about New Mexico's vast empty spaces inspires utopian thinking, as if the landscape were a blank slate, a way to start from scratch and do things right. Spanish settlers felt it in the 16th century. Gold miners banked on it in the 1800s. And in the 1960s, freethinkers, free-lovers, and back-to-the-landers fled crowded cities and boring suburbs to start communities such as the Hog Farm and the New Buffalo commune, both near Taos. For a while, New Mexico was the place to be: Actor Dennis Hopper immortalized New Buffalo in his film *Easy Rider,* singer Janis Joplin chilled out in Truchas, and author Ken Kesey drove his bus, *Further,* through the state. At the end of the decade, some 25 communes had been established.

In most of the rest of the United States, these experimental communities and their ideals were just a brief moment of zaniness—their legacy appears to be Hog Farm leader Wavy Gravy's consecration on a Ben & Jerry's label. But in New Mexico, many of the ideals set down by naked organic gardeners and tripping visionaries took root and sprouted in unexpected ways. Yogi Bhajan, a Sikh who taught mass kundalini yoga sessions in New Mexico in 1969, later became a major contributor to the state economy through all the businesses he established. Buddhist stupas dot the Rio Grande Valley, the product of Anglo spiritual seekers working with Tibetan refugees brought to New Mexico by Project Tibet, cofounded by John Allen, who also ran the commune Synergia Ranch near Santa Fe. Allen was also instrumental in building Biosphere 2, the experimental glass dome in the Arizona desert—probably the most utopian vision yet to have sprouted in New Mexico.

TAOS
SIGHTS

views on the rim road, which was developed only in the later part of the 20th century. On the north side of the valley, the ritzy Turley Mill development is built on the site of a still that produced the powerful bootleg hooch known as "Taos lightning" from the 1700s to 1847. (Also glossed over in the development: The still was burned and its owner and customers killed during the uprising against Governor Bent.) The area is now home to former defense secretary Donald Rumsfeld and other occupants of million-dollar casitas.

Taos Ski Valley

Highway 150 winds relentlessly up through Hondo Canyon, the steep mountain slopes crowded with tall, dense pines that in winter disappear into a wreath of clouds. The paved road ends at the still-growing village of **Taos Ski Valley;** from there it's another two miles along a rough dirt road to the Wheeler Peak and Williams Lake trailhead. When you get out of the car at the village and take in the vertiginous view up to Kachina Peak (elevation 12,481 feet and often white-capped even in July), you'll see why it inspires legions of reverential skiers every winter, when an average of 305 inches of snow falls on the mountain—almost 10 times the amount they get down in town.

For decades, it was *only* skiers here. Snowboarders were banned, allegedly because the slopes were too steep—more than half the trails are rated expert level, and many of them are left ungroomed. But the mountain was opened to all in 2008.

In the summer, the village is increasingly the site of a burgeoning mountain social scene with occasional live music, and Hondo Canyon's many trails make for good hiking or picnicking. The road is dotted on either side with picnic areas and campgrounds—Cuchilla del Medio is a particularly nice area for a picnic. The **visitors center** (575/776-1413, www.taosskivalley.com) in the ski area parking lot stocks trail descriptions and maps.

Entertainment and Events

Taos is a small town: no glitzy dance clubs, no bars where you're expected to dress up. Nighttime fun is concentrated in places where, even after just a couple of visits, you'll get to know the regulars. The various town-wide celebrations—including music and dancing on the plaza on summer Thursdays—draw a good cross section of the population.

NIGHTLIFE
Bars and Clubs

Starting around 5pm, the **Adobe Bar** (125 Paseo del Pueblo Norte, 575/758-2233, 11am-10pm daily), in the lobby of the Taos Inn (look for the neon thunderbird sign), is where you'll run into everyone you've seen over the course of the day, sipping a Cowboy Buddha ($12) or some other specialty margarita—the best in town. Mellow jazz or acoustic guitar sets the mood from 7pm. To give hotel residents a break, the bar closes at 10pm.

Wood-paneled **Eske's Brew Pub** (106 Des Georges Ln., 575/758-1517, 3pm-9pm Mon., noon-9:30pm Tues.-Thurs., 11am-10pm Fri.-Sat., 11am-9:30pm Sun.) is across from the plaza, tucked back from the southeast corner of the intersection of Paseo del Pueblo Sur and Kit Carson Road. It serves its house-made beer and barley wine to a chummy après-ski crowd, and there's often live music. You're in New Mexico—you should at least *try* the green-chile ale.

Everyone's default late-night spot is **The Alley Cantina** (121 Teresina Ln., 575/758-2121, 11:30am-1am Mon.-Sat., 11am-midnight Sun.). This warren of interconnected rooms (one of which is supposedly the oldest in Taos . . . but don't they all say that?) can be potentially baffling after a few drinks. There's shuffleboard for entertainment if you're not into the ensemble onstage, whose name usually ends in "Blues Band"; a cover of $5-10 applies on weekends. The kitchen is open until 11pm.

Wine and Cocktails

Softly lit **The Treehouse Lounge** (123 Bent St., 575/758-1009, 2:30pm-close daily), located on the upper floor of Lambert's, is Taos's most sophisticated late-night option, with a full bar and no shortage of creative cocktails ($10). Happy hour ($6) is 2:30pm-6pm.

On the plaza, the wine shop **Parcht** (103 E. Plaza, 575/758-1194, 2pm-9pm Tues.-Sat.) pops the cork on a dozen bottles a night, offering glasses and tastings along with perfectly paired small plates, such as pear slices with bleu cheese and honey. It's popular with both the après-work and après-ski sets.

Live Music

The **KTAOS Solar Bar** (9 Hwy. 150, 575/758-5826, www.ktao.com, 3pm-9pm Mon.-Thurs., 3pm-11pm Fri.-Sat., 11am-9pm Sun.), the social scene of the KTAO radio station, is a solar-powered smorgasbord of beers, burgers, and spectacular mountain views. You can peek into the radio studios, or dance on the lawn out back, in front of the large stage that hosts major shows. Happy hour (4pm-6pm) sees drinks as low as $3, and kids are usually welcome, with plenty of room to play.

If your style is cramped by old adobes, head out to **Taos Mesa Brewing** (20 ABC Mesa Rd., 575/758-1900, www.taosmesabrewing.com, noon-10pm daily), on U.S. 64 opposite the airport, where there's plenty of room to groove. The metal Mothership looms like a far-flung Burning Man theme camp, and the entertainment roster is suitably eclectic, with everyone from grizzled blues masters to major global artists performing outside (cover from $5 some nights). The crowd is all of Taos's younger hippies, plus hops aficionados of all stripes. The menu features tacos and a couple of filling house-made veggie burgers (from $10) and naturally showcases their own brews, including several IPAs and a potent Scottish ale.

More centrally, the company's "in town" **tap room** (201 Paseo del Pueblo Sur, 575/758-1900, 11am-11pm daily) also hosts bands and fuels the crowd with pizza.

Finally, check the schedule at **Old Martina's Hall** (4140 Hwy. 68, 575/758-3003, www.oldmartinashall.com) for special events in this renovated old adobe theater. It may not get as wild as back in the days when Dennis Hopper owned the joint, but the new wooden dance floor is a treat.

THE ARTS

Given the high concentration of artists of all stripes, it's no surprise that Taos's theater scene is so rich for such a small town. Check at the **Taos Center for the Arts** (133 Paseo del Pueblo Norte, 575/758-2052, www.tcataos.org) to find out what shows may be on; the group also organizes chamber music performances and film screenings at the adjacent Taos Community Auditorium (145 Paseo del Pueblo Norte, 575/758-4677).

SMU in Taos (6580 Hwy. 518, 575/758-8322, www.smu.edu/taos) organizes a summer lecture series at its Fort Burgwin campus about seven miles east of Ranchos de Taos. The Tuesday night gatherings (from 7pm, free), late May-mid-August, bring noted historians, anthropologists, authors, and others with an interest in the Southwest.

The Storyteller (110 Old Talpa Canyon Rd., 575/751-4245, www.storyteller7.com) shows first-run films on seven screens, with an occasional arty option.

FESTIVALS AND EVENTS

Late spring marks the unofficial start of Taos's festival season. The nascent **Music on the Mesa** (www.taosmusiconthemesa.com), held the first weekend in June on three stages at Taos Mesa Brewing, sees some of the best regional acts—and a few national ones too—descending on Taos; of course, there's plenty of locally crafted beer to be had as well.

Things get into full swing in July, beginning with the loopy creativity of the **Arroyo Seco Fourth of July parade,** and then, in the second week, the **Taos Pueblo Powwow** (www.taospueblo.com), a major get-together of Pueblo Indians and tribal members from around the country. Try to be there for the Grand Entry, the massive opening procession. The event takes place at the powwow grounds in El Prado near the Overland Sheepskin store. The next weekend, the town turns out for the **Fiestas de Taos** (www.fiestasdetaos.

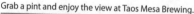

Grab a pint and enjoy the view at Taos Mesa Brewing.

What to Expect at Pueblo Dances

Visiting a pueblo for a ceremonial dance or feast-day celebration is one of the most memorable parts of a trip to New Mexico. But it's important to remember that a pueblo dance is not at all for the benefit of tourists. It is a ceremony and a religious ritual, not a performance—you are a guest, not an audience.

Keep this in mind as a guide to your own behavior. Applause is not appropriate, nor is conversation during the dance. Queries about the meaning of the dances are generally not appreciated. Never walk in the dance area, and try not to block the view of pueblo residents. The kivas, as holy spaces, are always off-limits to outsiders. During feast days, some pueblo residents may open their doors to visitors, perhaps for a snack or drink—but be considerate of others who may also want to visit, and don't stay too long. Photography is strictly forbidden at dances (sometimes with the exception of Los Matachines, which is not a religious ritual). Don't even think about trying to sneak a shot with your smartphone, as tribal police will be more than happy to confiscate it.

On a practical level, be prepared for a lot of waiting around. Start times are always approximate, and everything depends on when the dancers are done with their kiva rituals. There will usually be a main, seasonal dance—such as the corn dance at the summer solstice—followed by several others. If you go in the winter, dress warmly, but in layers. Ceremonies often start inside the close-packed, overheated church, and then dances often proceed outside in the cold.

com), a three-day celebration of Santiago de Compostela and Santa Ana, with a parade, food and crafts booths on the plaza, and the crowning of the Fiestas Queen.

Taos galleries put out their finest at the **Taos Fall Arts Festival** (TFAF, www.taosfallarts.com), a 10-day-long exhibition in late September and early October that shows the works of more than 150 Taos County artists. Taking place at roughly the same time is the three-day-long **Taos Environmental Film Festival,** which is supported by the TFAF and showcases select documentaries on the environment at the Taos Community Auditorium.

Taos's biggest annual festivity (for which many local businesses close) is the **Feast of San Geronimo,** the patron saint assigned to Taos Pueblo by the Spanish when they built their first mission there in 1619. The holiday starts the evening of September 29 with vespers in the pueblo church and continues the next day with footraces and a pole-climbing ritual. Hacienda de los Martinez usually reenacts a 19th-century Taos trade fair, with mountain men, music, and artisans' demonstrations.

On the first weekend in October, the **Taos Wool Festival** (www.taoswoolfestival.org) has drawn textile artists as well as breeders since 1983. Admire the traditional Churro sheep or an Angora goat and then pick up a scarf made from its wool.

In winter, the glow of luminarias and torchlight on snow produces a magical effect. On the first weekend in December, the **tree-lighting ceremony** on the plaza draws the whole town, and the rest of the season sees numerous celebrations, such as the reenactments of the Virgin's search for shelter, called Las Posadas, which take place at Our Lady of Guadalupe Church west of the plaza on the third weekend in December. At the pueblo, vespers is sung at San Geronimo Church on Christmas Eve, typically followed by a children's dance. On Christmas Day, the pueblo hosts either a deer dance or the Spanish Matachines dance.

The end of winter sees the town hosting the Sundance of short film gatherings, the **Taos Shortz Film Fest** (www.taosshortz.com), which screens 150 films from around the globe over one weekend in March.

Ceremonial Dances at Taos Pueblo

In addition to the Feast of San Geronimo, ceremonial dances are open to visitors. This is only an approximate schedule—dates can vary from year to year, as can the particular dances. Contact the **pueblo** (505/758-1028, www.taospueblo.com) for times, or check the listings in the Tempo section of *The Taos News* for that week.

Every night May-October, there are demonstration dances at the **Kachina Lodge** (413 Paseo del Pueblo Norte)—a little touristy, but nice if your trip doesn't coincide with a dance at the pueblo itself.

- **January 1:** Turtle dance
- **January 6:** Deer or buffalo dance
- **Easter:** Various dances
- **May 3:** Feast of Santa Cruz, corn dance
- **June 13:** Feast of San Antonio, various dances
- **June 24:** Feast of San Juan, corn dance
- **July 25-26:** Feast of Santiago and Santa Ana, corn dances and footraces
- **September 29-30:** Feast of San Geronimo
- **December 24:** Sundown procession and bonfire
- **December 25:** various dances

Shopping

ARTS AND CRAFTS

In the Overland Ranch complex about three miles north of the plaza, **Magpie** (1405 Paseo del Pueblo Norte, 781/248-0166, 11am-5:30pm Tues.-Sat.) promises "wonderful things for your nest." The owner, a Taos native returned from living on the East Coast, has selected a colorful array of handcrafted furniture, pottery, handmade jewelry, and more, nearly all produced by Taos residents.

Taos Drums (3956 Hwy. 68, 800/424-3786, 9am-5pm Mon.-Fri., 10am-5pm, Sat., 11am-5pm Sun.) is a giant shop and factory dedicated to making Taos Pueblo-style percussion instruments, from thin hand drums to great booming ones, out of hollow logs. Trying out the wares is encouraged. The shop is located on the west side of the highway five miles south of the plaza.

Taos Clay Studio (1208 Paseo del Pueblo Norte, 307/272-8388, 10am-5pm daily), in El Prado, is a homegrown affair. Local artists turn the ceramics at the on-site studio; classes are available too (individual lessons from $125).

GIFT AND HOME

Fx18 (103-C Bent St., 575/758-8590, 11am-6pm Mon.-Sat., noon-5pm Sun.) has a great selection of assorted goodies, including groovy housewares, lively kids' stuff, and nifty stationery. The selection of contemporary Southwest-style jewelry is particularly good.

Tap into Taos's environmental ethic at **Seconds Eco Store** (120 Bent St.,

575/751-4500, 10am-6pm Mon.-Sat., 11am-6pm Sun.), with nifty upcycled and green goods, such as earrings made of skis and circuit boards turned key chains.

Up Highway 150, **Arroyo Seco Mercantile** (488 Hwy. 150, 575/776-8806, 10am-5:30pm Mon.-Sat., 11am-5pm Sun.) is the town's former general store, now a highly evolved junk shop that has maintained the beautiful old wood-and-glass display cases. Its stock ranges from the practical (books on passive-solar engineering and raising llamas) to the frivolous, with lots of the beautiful, like antique wool blankets.

TOYS

Taos is also home to an exceptionally magical toy store, the nonprofit **Twirl** (225 Camino de la Placita, 575/751-1402, www.twirltaos. org, 10am-6pm daily). Tucked in a series of low-ceilinged adobe rooms, it's crammed with everything from science experiments to wooden trains to fairy costumes. Even the kiva fireplace gets a fantastical 1,001 Nights treatment, and it has the best playground in town out back—it even includes a handcrafted hobbit house.

Sports and Recreation

The wild setting presses in all around Taos, and the mountains frame every town view. Downhill skiing is the main draw in the winter, but snowshoeing and Nordic skiing are also wildly popular. In summer, peak-baggers will want to strike out for Wheeler, the state's highest, and mountain bikers should seek out—but not underestimate—the adrenaline rush that is descending the nearby dedicated trails in the ski valley. Not quite as intense, but no less dramatic, is the ride along the Rio Grande Gorge. In the waters below, kayakers and rafters challenge the churning rapids of the legendary Taos Box (late May and early June, with winter runoff, are the most intense season for this).

Information

Stop in at the **Carson National Forest Supervisor's Office** (208 Cruz Alta Rd., 575/758-6200, 8am-4:30pm Mon.-Fri.) for booklets on recommended trails and maps. Just down the street, the **Bureau of Land Management Taos Field Office** (226 Cruz Alta Rd., 575/758-8851, 8am-4:30pm Mon.-Fri.) can help with rafting or camping trip prep, with plenty of maps and brochures.

The **Taos Youth and Family Center** (407 Paseo del Cañon, 575/758-4160, 8:30am-6pm daily) has a big indoor pool, as well as an ice-skating rink and skate park. Hours are limited in fall and winter.

Sudden thunderstorms are common in summer, as are flash floods and even freak blizzards. Well into May, snow can blanket higher passes, so wherever you go, always carry more warm clothing than you think you'll need. Carry plenty of water with you—your adventures are taking place at over 7,000 feet, after all—and don't skimp on the sunscreen, even when it's below freezing.

HIKING

With Taos Mountain and Wheeler Peak in the backyard, you can ramble along winding rivers or haul up 2,000 feet in less than four miles. Be prepared for a cold snap or storm at any time, and don't plan on anything before May—it takes that long for the snow to thaw. You can still hit white stuff in the alpine meadows well into summer. If you'd like to lighten your load and enjoy unique animal companionship to boot, contact **Wild Earth Llama Adventures** (800/758-5262, www. llamaadventures.com), which runs day hikes with lunch ($125), as well as multiday treks (from $425). What follows are just a few of the many trails worth seeking out.

so many hikes to choose from in the Taos Ski Valley

★ Taos Ski Valley

Highway 150 winds through Hondo Canyon, the paved road ending at the village of **Taos Ski Valley**. The **visitors center** (575/776-1413, www.taosskivalley.com) in the ski area parking lot off Thunderbird Road stocks trail descriptions and maps.

Just before the parking lot for the ski area, **Gavilan Trail** (no. 60) begins at the north side of the road. It's plenty steep but leads to a high mountain meadow. The route is five miles round-trip, or you can connect with other trails once you're up on the rim.

It's another two miles along a rough dirt road to the Wheeler Peak and Williams Lake trailhead. **Wheeler Peak Summit Trail** (no. 67), which scales New Mexico's highest mountain in about four miles (one-way), requires no technical skill, but it's a fairly relentless ascent and should not be undertaken lightly. The first two miles of the route are on the relatively easy and popular **Williams Lake Trail** (no. 62), which starts near the end of Twining Road, a narrow dirt road that leads out of the top of the Taos Ski Valley parking lot. After looking down on the aquamarine waters of Williams Lake (11,040 feet) and negotiating a rocky stretch, the trail is straightforward. Aim to begin your hike early in the morning to avoid afternoon thunderstorms (and to time your return with a well-earned pint at the Bavarian Lodge). In summer, on the night of the full moon, there's a free guided **moonlight hike** to Williams Lake, starting at 7:30pm; check the schedule at www.taosskivalley.com.

If all that sounds too strenuous, in summer you can take the **chairlift** (10am-4pm Thurs.-Mon. June-Aug., $18) up to the top of the mountain, then wander down any of several wide, well-marked trails, all with stunning views.

El Salto Falls

Some theorize that the mysterious "Taos Hum"—the faint, low drone that many in the area claim to hear—emanates from the caves at **El Salto Falls** (575/776-2371, $5), a scenic spot on a patch of private land in Arroyo Seco. That mystery aside, the series of waterfalls is an iconic Taos natural landmark, and an easy hike or a challenging one, depending on just how much you'd like to see. Save this hike for dry weather, unless you have a four-wheel drive—the road is rough when muddy or snowy.

In Arroyo Seco, take El Salto Road east (go straight where Highway 150 makes a hard right); after about a mile is a sign on the left asking visitors to pay. Leave cash in the honor box on the porch of the green house just off the road, and fill out a waiver and a permit to place on your dashboard. Continue driving another 0.7 mile and bear left; from here, it's 0.9 mile up to a green gate and small parking area. Walk in, following the road as it curves left, then bearing right. This leads in just a few minutes to the lowest, largest cave and the first waterfall—though most of the year, it is often just a trickle. Intrepid hikers can climb up to the right of the cave, to ever-smaller falls and notches in the cliff face.

BIKING

Gearing Up (616 Paseo del Pueblo Sur, 575/751-0365, 10am-6pm Mon.-Sat., noon-5pm Sun.) rents mountain and hybrid bicycles for $65 per day. If you're bringing your bicycle with you, consider having it shipped here. The shop will reassemble it and have it waiting when you arrive.

Mountain Biking

Taos has several great trails for mountain biking. A popular ride close to town is **West Rim Trail** along the Rio Grande Gorge, either from the gorge bridge up to John Dunn Bridge, about 15 miles round-trip, or from the gorge bridge south to the Taos Junction Bridge near Pilar, about 18 miles out and back. Either way, you'll have great views and fairly level but rugged terrain. For some serious downhill action, **Taos Ski Valley** offers mountain biking in summer and early fall; the fee-based **Northside** (daily, late June-Oct., $10) contains several exhilarating trails suited for intermediate to advanced riders; the Alpine Wildflower Loop (10.3 miles) offers the best introduction and some of the most dramatic scenery in the area. The 3.6-mile Berminator route, which sets off from the top of the Taos Ski Valley, is a wildly bouncy and heart-pounding descent from 12,500 feet.

Road Biking

For road touring, the pleasant 25-mile loop from Taos through Arroyo Hondo and Arroyo Seco, with no steep grades, is a good way to get adjusted to the altitude. Head north up Paseo del Pueblo Norte, straight through the intersection at Highway 150, then, in Arroyo Hondo, turn right onto County Road B-143. Cross Highway 230, and you arrive in Arroyo Seco, behind The Snowmansion. Turn right on Highway 150 to loop back to Taos.

For a longer road challenge, take on the 84-mile Enchanted Circle—even better if you do so with over 1,000 fellow riders. Held in September, the **Enchanted Circle Century Tour** (800/348-6444, www.redriver.org), the four-decade-old ride kicks off in Red River and is marked by grueling climbs and hairpin descents.

RAFTING AND STAND-UP PADDLEBOARDING

TOP EXPERIENCE

★ Rafting the Rio Grande Gorge

The **Taos Box**, the 16-mile stretch of the Rio Grande between the John Dunn Bridge and Pilar, provides the most exhilarating rafting in New Mexico, with Class III and Class IV rapids with ominous names like Boat Reamer and Screaming Left-Hand Turn. The river mellows out south of the Taos Box, then leads into a shorter Class III section called the **Racecourse**—the most popular run, usually done as a half-day trip. Beyond this, in the Orilla Verde Recreation Area around Pilar, the water is wide and flat, a place for a relaxing float with kids; you can flop in an inner tube if you really want to chill. North of the John Dunn Bridge and accessed only by hiking 1.25 miles down the La Junta trail in the Wild Rivers Recreation Area, is another highly rated run called **La Junta.** It's usually done as a half-day outing and offers some of the best opportunities to see bighorn sheep.

Los Rios River Runners (800/544-1181, www.losriosriverrunners.com) leads trips to all these spots as half-day outings ($54), day trips (from $105), and overnight trips. Another outfitter, **Far Flung Adventures** (800/359-2627, www.farflung.com), can add on rock climbing and horseback riding. With both organizations, you can choose whether you want a paddle boat—where you're actively (and sometimes strenuously) paddling—or an oar boat, where guides row, and you can sit back. Far Flung Adventures and **New Mexico River Adventures** (800/983-7756, www.newmexicoriveradventures.com) also offer stand-up paddleboarding half-day and full-day trips (from $65) on the tamer sections of the Rio Grande. As these outings can be tailored based on skill level, they are suited for those new to the sport as well as those with more experience. All gear is included.

The best month to be on the river is late May-late June, when the water is high from mountain runoff; if the snowmelt is particularly extensive, that period can be extended by a few weeks.

ROCK CLIMBING

From popular rock-climbing spots such as the basalt Dead Cholla Wall in the Rio Grande Gorge to the more traditional routes at Tres Piedras, Taos is a climber's dream. One of the most impressive pitches is at Questa Dome, north of Taos on Highway 378, where the flawless granite on the Questa Direct route is graded 5.10 and 5.11. And climbers are not limited to the summer, as winter sees some terrific ice climbs at higher elevations. **Taos Mountain Outfitters** (113 N. Plaza, 575/758-9292, www.taosmountainoutfitters.com, 9am-6pm Mon.-Wed., 9am-8pm Thurs.-Fri., 9am-8pm Sat., 10am-6pm Sun.) can provide maps, ropes, and more details. For climbing lessons and guided climbs (from $190 for a half day), contact **Mountain Skills** (575/776-2222, www.climbtaos.com) in Arroyo Seco.

SKIING AND SNOWBOARDING

Taos Ski Valley (866/968-7386, www.ski-taos.org, $98 full-day lift ticket) is a mecca for downhill skiing and snowboarding, with an enticing mix of demanding and accessible runs coupled with spectacular mountain scenery and first-class facilities. The resort is open late November-first weekend in April, with over 110 trails served by 15 lifts, and snow-making capacity on all beginner and intermediate areas in dry spells. Having opened a lift to just shy of the 12,481-foot Kachina Peak—making it some of the highest lift-served terrain in North America—much of the focus is currently on improving and expanding the beginner area. Devotees of hike-to terrain still have areas dedicated to them, including a 35-acre tree-skiing area. The highly regarded **Ernie Blake Snowsports School** (866/968-7386) is one of the best places to learn the basics or polish your skills. Group (from $70) and private lessons (from $300) are available; rates are cheaper in the afternoon for the latter.

For cross-country skiing and snowshoeing, **Enchanted Forest** (575/754-6112, www.enchantedforestxc.com, $18 full-day pass), between Elizabethtown and Red River

a rafting adventure with Los Rios River Runners

on the Enchanted Circle loop, offers miles of groomed trails. There are also easy ski access points in the **Carson National Forest**—at Capulin Campground on U.S. 64, for instance, five miles east of Taos, and along Manzanita Trail in Hondo Canyon on Highway 150, four miles before the ski valley.

The family-run **Cottam's Ski Shop** (207-A Paseo del Pueblo Sur, 575/758-2822, 7:30am-7pm Mon.-Fri., 7:30am-8pm Sat.-Sun.) has the area's biggest stock of rental skis, snowboards, and snowshoes. The shop also sells everything else you'll need to get out and enjoy the snow; there's another location at the ski valley (575/776-8719) and one at the Angel Fire ski resort (575/377-3700).

HOT SPRINGS

Two spots along the Rio Grande have natural pools of warm water, by-products of the seismic upsets that formed the gorge. They're popular with locals, and clothing is optional. Don't crowd in if several people are already in the spring, and never leave trash behind.

The easier location to reach is **Blackrock Springs**, accessible by a 0.25-mile hike. From the intersection with U.S. 64, head north on Highway 522 about six miles to where the road dips; immediately after the bridge, turn left on County Road B-005, which runs along the north side of the small Rio Hondo and past the New Buffalo commune. The road crosses the water, then climbs a hill and descends again, toward the Rio Grande. Cross the old John Dunn Bridge to reach the west side, then turn left and park at the first switchback. Hike down the rocks and downstream to the two pools.

Also called Stagecoach Springs, **Manby Springs** are at the edge of the river where the stage road used to meet a bridge and cross to the west side of the gorge. The hike down is on the old road, now quite rocky, and takes about 20 minutes. (In the late afternoon, keep an eye out for bighorn sheep near the trail.) To find the parking area, take U.S. 64 four miles west, just past the airport, and turn right on Tune Drive; follow this to the end, approximately another four miles. The old road is off the southwest side of the parking area.

FISHING AND HUNTING

Taos's mountain streams and lakes teem with fish. The feisty cutthroat trout is indigenous to Valle Vidal, north of Questa, or you can hook plenty of browns in the wild waters of the Rio Grande. Eagle Nest Lake and Cabresto Lake (northeast of Questa) are both stocked every year. If you'd like a guide to show you where to cast, **Cutthroat Fly Fishing** (575/776-5703, www.cutthroatflyfishing.com) and **The Solitary Angler** (866/502-1700, www.thesolitaryangler.com) are two good operators (half-day trips from $175). Stop at the tidy Taos Fly Shop (338 Paseo del Pueblo Sur, 575/751-1312, taosflyshop.com) for tackle and info on flows and other conditions.

Elk are the primary target in hunters' rifle scopes, but you can also bag mule deer, bear, and antelope; **High Mountain Outfitters** (575/751-7000, www.huntingnm.com) is one of the most experienced expedition leaders.

Visit the website of the **New Mexico Department of Game and Fish** (www.wildlife.state.nm.us) for details on seasons, permits, and licenses.

Food

For a town of its size, Taos has no shortage of restaurants that can deliver memorable meals. At one of the New Mexican places, try some posole—it's more common here than in Albuquerque or Santa Fe, often substituted for rice as a side dish alongside pinto beans. Also—especially given the hiking and skiing opportunities nearby—don't overlook the breakfast burrito. This unfussy combo of scrambled eggs, green chile, hash browns, and bacon or sausage in a flour tortilla commonly wrapped in foil makes for the perfect meal on the go. Most restaurants close relatively early, and many smaller places don't take plastic—so load up on cash and get seated by 8pm. You'll need reservations for fine-dining restaurants on the weekends, but the whole scene is relatively casual.

CENTRAL TAOS
New Mexican

A small, festively painted place on the north side of town, the family-run ★ **Orlando's** (1114 Don Juan Valdez Ln., 575/751-1450, 10:30am-2:30pm and 5pm-8:30pm Mon.-Thurs. and Sun., 10:30am-2:30pm and 5pm-9pm Fri.-Sat., $7-14) is invariably the first restaurant named when the question of the best chile comes up. It enlivens all of the New Mexican classics, such as tamales, tostados, and chiles rellenos, most of which are satisfying and freshly made. A standout is the green-chile chicken enchiladas, and the pozole is quite good too—perfectly firm, earthy, and flecked with oregano. The restaurant is always busy, but a fire pit outdoors makes the wait more pleasant on cold nights.

Mexican

Tiny ★ **La Cueva** (135 Paseo del Pueblo Sur, 575/758-7001, 10am-3pm daily, $7-14) looks like a New Mexican restaurant at first glance, as it has all the usual green-chile-smothered dishes. But its owners are from south of the border and round out the menu with fantastically fresh and homemade-tasting dishes such as chicken mole enchiladas and a heaping steak and relleno, as well as exceptionally savory beans. Breakfasts are especially inexpensive. No alcohol, though.

Fine Dining

★ **El Meze** (1017 Paseo del Pueblo Norte, 575/751-3337, 5:30pm-9:30pm Mon.-Sat., $17-32) just might be Taos's best restaurant, thanks to both its exceptional food and thoughtful touches such as complimentary mineral water and plush blankets for cool evenings outside. Chef Frederick Muller draws inspiration from the enduring influences of Spain, North Africa, and the Middle East in dishes that are both brainy and deep-down satisfying. Mouthwatering mountain trout covered in Moroccan butter is seasoned with mint and garlic and served with an invigorating watercress and fennel salad, while fried green olives stuffed with blue cheese remain the bar snack to beat in all of New Mexico. The setting is cozy in winter, inside a thick-walled hacienda, and expansive in summer, with a large patio with a view of Taos Mountain. No matter the time of the year, treat yourself to the immensely satisfying purple adobe lavender crème bruleé.

Set inside a cozy adobe house, **Lambert's** (123 Bent St., 575/758-1009, 11:30am-2:30pm and 5:30pm-9pm Mon.-Sat., 5:30pm-9pm Sun., $23-38) is a Taos favorite, long a popular choice for celebrations and special occasions. Its New American menu is a bit staid, but everything is executed perfectly. The filet mignon in a peppercorn veal reduction is fantastic; less obvious, but equally gratifying, is the zucchini pasta with arugula pesto and seasonal mushrooms. The summer Sunday brunch (11:30am-2:30pm) is well worth it for the shrimp and grits alone. A full liquor license means good classic cocktails, which you can also enjoy upstairs at **The Treehouse Lounge** (11:30am-close daily).

Fresh and Local

★ **The Love Apple** (803 Paseo del Pueblo Norte, 575/751-0050, 5pm-9pm Tues.-Sun., $17-25) wears its local, organic credentials on its sleeve, and the food delivers in simple but powerful flavor combinations. The menu is seasonal, with dishes such as a baked tamale with a red-chile mole sauce and chicken confit taco with green-chile coconut creamed corn. There's an extensive wine list, too. Set inside a thick-walled adobe chapel dating back to the early 19th century, the place oozes atmosphere, with candles glimmering softly against whitewashed walls. It's one place in town where reservations are useful, and in an old-school move, it only accepts cash only.

Burgers

★ **The Burger Stand** (401 Paseo del Pueblo Norte, 575/758-5522, 11am-11pm daily, $9) is an outpost of a Kansas restaurant—but it fits right in in Taos, in large part because it makes not one but two killer veggie burgers. We recommend the one topped with feta cheese, pickled green beans, and toasted almonds. The beef and lamb burgers are great

too, and decked out in similarly creative ways. The same can be said for the fries; try a basket tossed in a white truffle oil. It doesn't hurt that the restaurant's set inside the lively Taos Ale House, where there's a strong beer selection, and it's open relatively late.

Italian

Taos Pizza Out Back (712 Paseo del Pueblo Norte, 575/758-3112, 11am-9pm Mon.-Thurs. & Sun., 11am-10pm Fri.-Sat., $4.25-10) serves up the best pie in town, using mostly local and organic ingredients. Sure, you can design your own pizza, but there's little need to with specialty options such as marinated chicken, peppers, onions, and garlic with a honey chipotle chile sauce and smoked mozzarella or basil pesto, green chile, smoked mozzarella, feta, roasted garlic, and fresh tomatoes.

Breakfast and Lunch

A down-home, wood-paneled family restaurant, **Michael's Kitchen** (304-C Paseo del Pueblo Norte, 575/758-4178, 7am-2:30pm Mon.-Thurs., 7am-8pm Fri.-Sun., $8) is filled with chatter, the clatter of dishes, and the sense that your fellow patrons have been here many times before. It's famous for New Mexican breakfast items like huevos

The Love Apple

rancheros and blue-corn pancakes with pine nuts, served all day, but there's quite a bit more on the extensive menu. "Health Food," for instance, is a double order of chile-cheese fries and there are blintzes, deli sandwiches, and a handful of steak dishes, too. The front room is devoted to gooey doughnuts, Frisbee-sized cinnamon rolls, and pie.

Taos Diner (908 Paseo del Pueblo Norte, 575/758-2374, 7am-2:30pm daily, $10) is as straightforward as its name. Still, there is a pleasant surprise: Much of the enchiladas, egg plates, pancakes, and the like is prepared with organic ingredients. Plus, the largely local scene provides good background theater to your meal—the servers seem to know everyone. There's a second outpost, **Taos Diner II** (216-B Paseo del Pueblo Sur, 575/751-1989, 7am-3pm daily), just south of the plaza.

Euro-Latino might be the best catch-all term for the menu at ★ **Gutiz** (812-B Paseo del Pueblo Norte, 575/758-1226, 8am-3pm Tues.-Sun., $8-16), which borrows from France and Spain and adds a dash of green chile. Start your day with a chocolate croissant or an impressive tower of scrambled eggs and spinach. Lunch sees traditional croques monsieurs, cumin-spiced chicken sandwiches,

and a paella that doesn't skimp on the scallops, shrimp, and mussels.

Set in bucolic gardens with a view of Taos Mountain, **Farmhouse Café** (1405 Paseo del Pueblo Norte, 575/758-5683, 8am-5pm daily, $8-16) is a beautiful spot to revive over a hearty salad, veggie lasagna, or a bison burger. There are several gluten-free options too, including a shepherd's pie and a chocolate-peanut-butter crispy-rice bar. Service can be a little spotty, but the meals are worth the wait.

Just west of the plaza, **El Gamal** (112 Doña Luz St., 575/613-0311, 9am-5pm Mon.-Wed., 9am-9pm Thurs.-Sat., 11am-3pm Sun., $5-12) brings the best of Israeli street food to Taos, with *shakshuka* (spicy scrambled eggs) and boiled bagels for breakfast and falafel and *sabich* (hummus, eggplant, and egg) sandwiches at lunch, washed down with a fizzy yogurt soda.

In the Taos Inn, elegant **Doc Martin's** (125 Paseo del Pueblo Norte, 575/758-1977, 11am-3pm and 5pm-9pm Mon.-Fri., 7:30am-2:30pm and 5pm-9:30pm Sat.-Sun., $8-15) is fine at dinner, but weekend brunch is when the kitchen really shines—especially on dishes such as the Kit Carson (poached eggs on yam biscuits topped with red chile), bagel with house-cured salmon, and blue-corn pancakes

Doc Martin's

with blueberries. The lunch menu is also tasty and doesn't reach the comparatively high dinner prices.

Cafés

★ **Elevation Coffee** (1110 Paseo del Pueblo Norte, 575/758-3068, 6:30am-4pm daily, $3) boasts the best coffee in town without a whiff of snobbery—in fact, its knowledgeable baristas are some of the friendliest around. The fancifully designed mochas are as tasty as they look, while the pour-overs are consistently on the mark. Grab a seat with your drink and admire the art; there's a small patio, too. Cash only.

The location of **World Cup** (102 Paseo del Pueblo Norte, 575/737-5299, 7am-7pm daily, $3) on the corner of the plaza makes it a popular pit stop for both tourists and locals—the latter typically of the drumming, dreadlocked variety, lounging on the stoop.

Markets

If you're planning a picnic or a meal in, stop at **Cid's Grocery** (623 Paseo del Pueblo Norte, 575/758-1148, 8am-8pm Mon.-Sat.) for great takeout food, as well as freshly baked bread and a whole range of organic and local goodies, from New Mexican wines to fresh elk steaks.

The excellent **Taos Farmers Market** (www.taosfarmersmarket.org, 8am-12:30pm Sat.) takes place on the plaza mid-May-late October. As well as fresh produce and meats, vendors sell prepared food and locally made gifts such as honey, jams, and spices.

RANCHOS DE TAOS

Just off the plaza near the church, **Ranchos Plaza Grill** (6 St. Francis Plaza, 575/758-5788, 11am-3pm and 5pm-8:30pm Tues.-Sat., 8am-3pm Sun., $11) is a casual spot, known for its red-chile *caribe,* made from crushed, rather than ground, chiles, for a really rustic effect.

Across the road from the turn to St Francis de Asis, **Old Martina's Hall** (4140 Hwy. 68, 575/758-3003, www.oldmartinashall.com, 7am-9:30pm Mon. and Wed.-Sat., 9am-2pm

Plan your day's adventures at Elevation Coffee.

Sun., $19-48), a once-derelict adobe theater with a soaring ceiling that has been lovingly redone, is a wonderfully welcoming place with a menu of sophisticated regional standbys as well as more than a few surprises. There is green chile, but it's dialed down and accentuates rather than overtakes. The *pollo Yucatan* is excellent, as are the blackened sea scallops with a light mango sauce. It's more casual for breakfast and lunch ($10 for sandwiches). Check out all the rooms and levels.

TAOS PUEBLO

On the road to the center of Taos Pueblo, **Tiwa Kitchen** (328 Veterans Hwy., 575/751-1020, 11am-4pm Wed.-Mon., $9-15) is a friendly, family-run place that specializes in Pueblo food, much of which is laced with chile. The hearty lunch options include stuffed fry bread and a red chile beef and vegetable stew; for dessert there are homemade baked goods to choose from, including a decadent chocolate squash cake.

ARROYO SECO

A creaky, old, all-purpose general store/diner/saloon, ★ **Abe's Cantina y Cocina** (489 Hwy. 150, 575/776-8643 7am-5pm Mon.-Fri., 7am-1:30pm Sat., $4) has earned fans from all over for serving a breakfast burrito that is both cheap and satisfying. There's a full menu of tacos and green-chile cheeseburgers, an impressive beer list featuring several top-notch regional ales, and a nice shaded back patio. Don't miss the sweet, flaky empanadas next to the cash register in the store.

For coffee, though, you'll want to go next door to **Taos Cow** (485 Hwy. 150, 575/776-5640, 7am-6pm daily, $3-9.50), a chilled-out coffee bar par excellence, with writers scribbling in one corner and flute players jamming in another. But it's the ice cream that has made the Taos Cow name (you'll see it distributed all around town, and elsewhere in New Mexico and Colorado). The most popular flavors are tailored to local tastes: Café Olé blends cinnamon and Mexican chocolate chunks in its coffee ice cream, while Cherry Ristra is cherry with piñon nuts and dark chocolate. There are plenty of breakfast options too, including a bagel sandwich with lox, cream cheese, and capers.

The husband-and-wife chef team at the restaurant, bar, and wine shop **Medley** (100 N.M. 150, 575/776-8787, 3pm-9pm Mon.-Fri., 10am-2pm and 3pm-9:30pm Sat.-Sun., $17-38) have cooked all over the world. Their menu mixes eclectic global flavors (chimichurri, aioli, saffron) with New American staples such as roasted red peppers. The food is great, if not flawless—even the bread plate is worthy of a lengthy post-dinner recap—and the atmosphere is casual.

TAOS SKI VALLEY

For nourishment in the ski village, fortify yourself with a green-chile cheeseburger or a bowl of smoky-hot green-chile stew at the **Stray Dog Cantina** (105 Sutton Pl., 575/776-2894, 8am-9pm daily in winter, $12), which gets busy after 3pm, when tired skiers come down from a day on the slopes. In the summer, it doesn't open till 11am on weekdays, but it's a nice destination for a drive, as you can sit on the deck and listen to the river flow by.

More adventurous drivers should head for ★ **Bavarian Lodge** (100 Kachina Rd., 575/776-8020, 11:30am-9pm daily in ski season, $15), way up Twining Road near the southeast edge of the ski area and Kachina Lift 4. You'll need four-wheel drive in winter; in summer, the huge front deck is a lovely place

Hearty German fare awaits at the Bavarian Lodge.

to have a stein of ale (served by actual German speakers) in the pines, though note that it's open only around the weekend (11:30am-close Thurs.-Sun.). The menu is hearty Wiener schnitzel and spaetzle; the bread pudding with pretzel pieces is as dense as it sounds—and delicious, too.

Accommodations

Taos hotels can be overpriced, especially at the lower end, where there are few reliable bargains. But because Taos is awash in centuries-old houses, bed-and-breakfasts have thrived. For those skeptical of B&Bs, don't despair: The majority have private bathrooms, separate entrances, and not too much country-cute decor. Certainly, just as in Santa Fe, the Southwestern gewgaws can be applied with a heavy hand, but wood-burning fireplaces, well-stocked libraries, hot tubs, and big gardens make up for that.

For better deals, consider staying outside of Taos proper. Arroyo Seco is about a half-hour drive from the plaza, and rates here and in Ranchos de Taos can be a little lower. In the summer, the lodges in the ski valley cut prices by almost half—a great deal if you want to spend time hiking and don't mind driving for food and entertainment.

CENTRAL TAOS
Under $100
Of the various motels on the south side, none is excellent—or all that memorable in a good way, for that matter—but **Sun God Lodge** (919 Paseo del Pueblo Sur, 575/758-3162, www.sungodlodge.com, $65 d) is better than most. Maintenance can be spotty, but rooms are set around a big, grassy, tree-shaded courtyard and, in back, a small hot tub. that the latter can foster a somewhat rowdy atmosphere, especially in ski season or after big summer events.

Not a hotel at all, but simply a clutch of well-maintained one- and two-bedroom private casitas, **Taos Lodging** (109 Brooks St., 575/751-1771, www.taoslodging.com, $75 studio) is in a quiet, convenient block about a 10-minute walk north from the plaza. Here, eight cottages, arranged around a central courtyard, have assorted floor plans, but all have porches, full kitchens, living rooms, and fireplaces as well as access to a shared outdoor hot tub. The smallest, a 350-square-foot studio, sleeps two comfortably; the largest ($140 for two) sleep up to six. The same group manages two additional properties nearby, for those who want a larger condo.

The **Kachina Lodge Resort and Meeting Center** (413 Paseo del Pueblo Norte, 575/758-2275, kachinalodge.com, $72), a sprawling former Best Western property, has seen better days and is in need of improvements—cosmetic and otherwise—but it is a dependable and well-run option with more character than most in this price bracket. Rooms are comfortable and nicely decorated, though dated, with basic amenities.

$100-150
In addition to being a tourist attraction, the **Mabel Dodge Luhan House** (240 Morada Ln., 575/751-9686, www.mabeldodge-luhan.com, $116 d) also functions as a homey bed-and-breakfast. Even the least expensive rooms, in a 1970s outbuilding, feel authentically historic and cozy, with wood floors and antique furniture. In the main house, Mabel's original bedroom ($220) is the grandest (you can even sleep in her bed). The pick of the 21 rooms, though—if you don't mind waking at the crack of dawn—is the upstairs solarium ($145), which is gloriously sunny, with gorgeous views of the mountain. Either way, you'll feel a little like you're bunking in a museum (which means those who want modern amenities like air-conditioning should look

elsewhere). Breakfast is a cut above standard B&B fare.

Of the two landmark hotels in town, **Hotel La Fonda de Taos** (108 S. Plaza, 575/758-2211, www.lafondataos.com, $149 d) has a few more modern perks, such as gas fireplaces in some rooms and mostly reliable Internet. As can be expected of an older hotel, rooms tend to be on the small side, and you're certainly paying a premium for its history. Its location can't be beat if you're looking for something central—plus, it can feel quite grand opening your balcony doors over the plaza (though you may also be subjected to predawn street-cleaning noise).

Walking distance from the plaza, **El Pueblo Lodge** (412 Paseo del Pueblo Norte, 575/758-8700, www.elpueblolodge.com, $150 d) is a budget operation with nice perks such as a full breakfast and free use of barbecue grills. The cheerful rooms vary from a snug nook in the oldest adobe section to new, slick motel rooms complete with gas fireplaces. Those in the 1960s motel strip are a good combo of atmosphere and amenities. The grounds are pleasant and shaded, with a hot tub and a heated pool in the summertime.

★ **Inn on the Rio** (910 E. Kit Carson Rd., 575/758-7199, www.innontherio.com, $125 d) might be more accurately called Motel on the Creek. But what a motel: Each of the 12 thick-walled rooms has been decorated with rich colors and retro Western details. The vintage wall heaters, still cranking from the old motor-court days, keep the rooms as toasty as a fireplace would. A hot tub and summer-only pool between the two wings, plus luxe sheets and locally made bath gels, are nice upgrades. Pair this with longtime resident owners and a great morning meal, and you have all the benefits of a bed-and-breakfast without the feeling that you have to tiptoe in late at night. Rates are lower on weekdays in summer.

$150-200

Everything at **Hacienda del Sol** (109 Mabel Dodge Ln., 575/758-0287, www.taoshaciendadelsol.com, $160 d) is built in relation to Taos Mountain. With this view, even the smallest of the 11 rooms in the adobe complex feel expansive. The style is cozy without being too oppressively Southwestern. Once owned by Mabel Dodge Luhan, the house was where she often put up guests; perks like plush robes and kiva fireplaces make it feel homey; some rooms have skylights.

The seven rooms at the central **Dream-catcher** (416 La Lomita Rd., 575/758-0613,

Hotel La Fonda de Taos, on the main plaza

TAOS
ACCOMMODATIONS

143

www.dreambb.com, $155 d) look out on to a pretty courtyard with hammocks. Three of the rooms are attached to the main house, while the four others are split between two cute casitas. All are thoughtfully designed and appointed and evoke the region; think warm earth tones, wood furniture and Native American rugs and artwork; some have kivas as well.

The **Historic Taos Inn** (125 Paseo del Pueblo Norte, 575/758-2233, www.taosinn.com, $189 d), established in 1936 in the former home of the town doctor, like La Fonda, has long been intertwined with the town's past and present, though it is cozier and slightly overpriced. Rooms in the main building have more character and are cheaper (about $129 in high season); in the courtyard section or other outbuildings, you may get a kiva fireplace. All 44 rooms offer free Wi-Fi and access to the onsite fitness center and yoga studio.

Decorated with an artist's eye, the five bright and colorful guest cottages at **Casa Gallina** (613 Callejon, 575/758-2306, www.casagallina.net, $195 d) showcase beautiful handicrafts from Taos and around the globe. All are well appointed and cared for and the kitchens can be stocked with occasional goodies from the garden and eggs from resident hens (they're also pressed into service for the fresh and delicious breakfasts).

Over $250

A somewhat storied and star-crossed luxury hotel, **El Monte Sagrado** (317 Kit Carson Rd., 575/758-3502, www.elmontesagrado.com, $299) is now owned by the excellent New Mexico company Heritage Hotels and Resorts, which recently enlivened the overall look and restored some of its eco-friendly infrastructure. The hotel has eclectic style in the Global Suites ($499 and up), but entry-level Taos Mountain rooms, while a little generic with their white linens and dark wood, are reasonably priced and have balconies. The grounds are immaculate, and there's a lovely spa.

Palacio de Marquesa (405 Cordoba Rd., 575/758-4477, www.marquesataos.com, $279

d) is an exquisite eight-room inn, also run by Heritage Hotels and Resorts. The rooms have an air of what might be called pueblo minimalism: dark viga ceilings, with white walls, white leather chairs, and marble baths. What could come off as too austere is warmed up with pops of color, skylights, and kiva fireplaces. Rooms are dedicated to Taos women of influence, such as Mabel Dodge Luhan and Agnes Martin. Spa services and the option of a made-to-order breakfast delivered to your room add to the cocoon-like feel.

ARROYO SECO
Under $100

The best bargain option in the area is **The Snowmansion** (Hwy. 150, Arroyo Seco, 575/776-8298, www.snowmansion.com). Conveniently set midway to the Taos Ski Valley in bustling "downtown" Arroyo Seco, this cheerful place offers bunks in dorm rooms ($35) and private rooms (from $74). In the summer, you can also camp (from $30) or sleep in a tepee ($74), and nosh on veggies from the hostel garden. But as the name suggests, winter sports fanatics are the main clientele, and if you don't want to be woken by skiers racing for the Chile Line bus outside, opt for an individual cabin with shared bath ($65).

TAOS SKI VALLEY
Over $250

When ★ **The Blake** (116 Sutton Pl., 575/776-8298, www.skitaos.com, $275) opened in February 2017, it was the clearest signal yet of the Taos Ski Valley's intent to position itself squarely among the top ski resorts in the West. A model of sustainability and replete with thoughtful touches and features, the property at once pays homage to the ski valley's European roots and proudly displays the area's Native American and Southwestern influences. Rooms vary in size from two queen beds or a king to lavish 1400-square-foot suites. All are handsomely designed and include access to a hot tub, pool, spa services, and breakfast at the onsite 192 at The Blake restaurant. Hitting the slopes from here couldn't be any easier—there's a ski lift outside the doors and a full equipment shop onsite.

RANCHOS DE TAOS
$150-200
At the south edge of Ranchos de Taos, ★ **Adobe & Pines Inn** (4107 Hwy. 68, 575/751-0947, www.adobepines.com) is built around an 1830s hacienda, shaded by old trees and overlooking a lush garden. Of the eight rooms, six are quite large (from $179), with especially lavish bathrooms. But even the two smallest rooms ($115 and $125) have fireplaces—and everyone gets the exceptionally good breakfasts, with fresh eggs from the on-site chickens and veggies from the garden.

NORTH AND EAST OF TAOS
Under $100
Hotel Luna Mystica (25 ABC Mesa Rd., 575/977-2424, www.hotellunamystica.com, $95), conveniently located across the road from the Taos Mesa Brewing, offers cheerful accommodation in an assortment of vintage trailers from the 1950s and '60s. All are smartly appointed and comfortable, and the morning coffees from their decks can't be beat. There are also several dozen primitive campsites ($10) equipped with hammocks for some of the best stargazing around.

$100-150
Nestle into a snug sheepherder's cabin at **Taos Goji Eco Lodge** (Old State Rd. 3, 575/776-3971, www.taosgoji.com, $120 d), in the village of San Cristobal, 11 miles north of Taos. Blessedly devoid of Internet access and TVs, the 10 cozy and comfortable cabins, each over a century old, have wood stoves and kitchens, and the surrounding 40-acre farm is lively with sheep, goats, and chickens.

$150-200
For an only-in-Taos experience, stay the night in an **Earthship** (U.S. 64, 575/751-0462, www.earthship.com, from $185 d). Five of the curvy, off-the-grid homes are available, with room for up to six people in the largest one. Evoking a stay in a hobbit house with banana trees (in the south-facing greenhouse areas), you're out in the larger, all-Earthship subdivision, with great views of the mountain. And, yes, you'll have running water, a refrigerator, and all the other comforts. It's a bit of a drive from town (west of the Rio Grande), but it's well worth it. It's now also possible to stay in the Earthship that started it all ($140 d), a short drive east of the Taos Plaza.

The Blake

The Road to Chama

U.S. 64 leads west out of Taos into an undulating landscape of thick patches of forest and open grassy plains interrupted sparingly by resolute ranching communities, most of which have long since passed their heyday. After winding through mountains, a dramatic descent brings you into the lush Chama Valley and the likeable town of Chama, a few miles from the border with Colorado.

TRES PIEDRAS

This settlement about 30 miles west of Taos is not much more than a handful of houses scattered around the crossroads of U.S. 64 and U.S. 285and the welcoming **Chili Line Depot Café** (38429 U.S. 285, 575/758-1701, 8am-7pm daily, $7), just north of the intersection. With friendly staff, hearty burritos, and green-chile cheeseburgers, it's well worth the detour. Call ahead to check hours; the restaurant may close early if business is slow. It also has a couple of cozy guest rooms with breakfast and dinner included ($95).

TIERRA AMARILLA AND LOS OJOS

U.S. 64 climbs up and over the Brazos Mountains, the view from the pass taking in the sheer limestone of 3,000-foot-high cliffs to the north. Descending into the golden valley along the Rio Chama, you soon reach the junction with U.S. 84 and the village of Tierra Amarilla, off the east side of the highway. Most of the buildings have long been vacant, but next door to the courthouse is the excellent **Three Ravens Coffeehouse** (15 Hwy. 531, 575/588-9086, 7am-4pm Mon.-Fri., also Sat. May-Sept., $6), a labor of love, and the active community center; ask the owner about how he renovated the ancient adobe building. Aside from the coffee, the menu features paninis, croissants, and smoothies.

Just a few miles north of Tierra Amarilla and west of the highway, Los Ojos is a two-block-long main street of adobe and Victorian wood-frame buildings, most connected in some way with **Ganados del Valle,** a cooperative established in 1983 to preserve the economy in the region, which for hundreds of years had been based on raising sheep and selling their products. But young people could no longer earn a living from this, and many of the most traditional weaving and spinning techniques had already been lost. The cooperative was gradually able to provide employment for dozens of artists, administrators, and sheepherders, and in 1990, one of its founders, Maria Varela, who got her start as a Chicana activist in the Student Nonviolent Coordinating Committee in the 1960s, earned a MacArthur "genius grant" for her efforts.

Once a Ganados project, though now a consignment shop, **Tierra Wools** (91 Main St., 575/588-7231, www.handweavers.com, 9am-6pm Mon.-Sat., 11am-4pm Sun. Apr.-Oct., 10am-5pm Mon.-Sat. Nov.-May) has become a pilgrimage site for anyone engaged in fiber arts. The shop showcases the work of local weavers—rugs, pillows, ruanas—as well as brilliantly dyed skeins of handwoven wool yarn from the hardy, four-horned Churro sheep, a breed the conquistadors introduced to New Mexico. If you're interested in the process, you can join a weeklong class ($525) or try your hand at it for a day ($130) at their Rio Grande Weaving School. The last weekend in April, the **Spring Harvest Festival** involves demonstrations of sheep-shearing, hand-spinning, and more, along with music and other entertainment. The shop also offers two lodgings in a sweet rental **casita** (from $95), for those who'd like a taste of village life.

EL VADO LAKE AND HERON LAKE STATE PARKS

The two reservoirs west of Tierra Amarilla are nearly linked; **El Vado Lake State Park**

Greater Taos

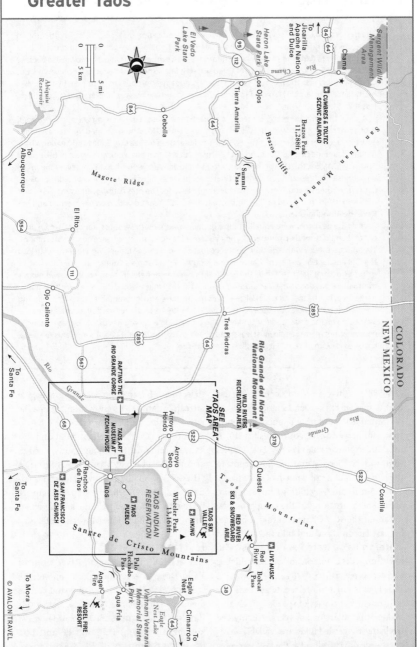

To Jicarilla Apache Nation and Dulce

84
84
95
112

Chama
Rio Chama

Sargent Wildlife Management Area

Heron Lake State Park

El Vado Lake State Park

Los Ojos

Tierra Amarilla

★ CUMBRES & TOLTEC SCENIC RAILROAD

▲ Brazos Peak 11,288ft

Brazos Cliffs

64

Abiquiu Reservoir

84

Cebolla

To Albuquerque

Magote Ridge

Summit Pass

San Juan Mountains

554

El Rito

111

Ojo Caliente

285

COLORADO
NEW MEXICO

Tres Piedras

285

64

567

Rio Grande

RAFTING THE RIO GRANDE GORGE ★

To Santa Fe

68

★ TAOS ART MUSEUM AT FECHIN HOUSE

Arroyo Hondo

Arroyo Seco

522

150

SEE "TAOS AREA" MAP

Rio Grande del Norte National Monument

WILD RIVERS RECREATION AREA ■

378

Rio Grande

285

Questa

522

Costilla

▲ Ranchos de Taos

★ SAN FRANCISCO DE ASIS CHURCH

Taos

★ TAOS PUEBLO

TAOS INDIAN RESERVATION

Wheeler Peak 13,161ft

TAOS SKI & SNOWBOARD AREA
TAOS SKI VALLEY
★ HIKING

Taos Mountains

RED RIVER SKI & SNOWBOARD AREA

Red River

★ LIVE MUSIC

Bobcat Pass

To Santa Fe

Sangre de Cristo Mountains

Palo Flechado Pass

Angel Fire
Agua Fria

Vietnam Veterans Memorial State Park

ANGEL FIRE RESORT

To Mora

Eagle Nest

Eagle Nest Lake

38

Cimarron

64
To

© AVALON TRAVEL

0   5 mi
0   5 km

King Tiger and the *Mercedes*

The pastoral village of **Tierra Amarilla** gives little indication that it was once a battleground in the Chicano rights movement and the local Hispano fight for land-grant restitution. The Tierra Amarilla *merced* (land grant) was established in the 19th century, and when Nuevo México became a U.S. territory in 1848, the Treaty of Guadalupe Hidalgo specified it would be preserved. But cattle ranchers and the national forest system gradually appropriated it, so that, by the 1960s, many families in largely Hispano Rio Arriba County found themselves landless and subsisting on less than $1,500 per year.

Around this time, Reies López Tijerina, a charismatic activist in the growing Chicano movement, took up the land-grant cause. In 1967, he and more than 150 local men stormed the Tierra Amarilla courthouse, calling themselves the Political Confederation of Free City States and bearing a banner proclaiming "Give Us Our Land Back." Their plan was to make a citizen's arrest of the district attorney (DA). But the DA was nowhere around, the activists wound up taking everyone in the courthouse hostage, and 300 National Guard troops were called in. The incident made headlines across the country, and Tijerina was an overnight legend. The press dubbed him King Tiger, and he was praised in the ballad "El Corrido de Rio Arriba," penned within weeks by the band Los Reyes de Albuquerque.

Trials the next year were equally gripping: Tijerina wept on the witness stand, a lawman present at the raid turned up murdered, and even New Mexico's governor gave heartfelt testimony. Tijerina came away with a minimal sentence for second-degree kidnapping. He went on to lead the Chicano faction as part of Martin Luther King Jr.'s Poor People's Campaign.

In Tierra Amarilla, meanwhile, the battle lines became hopelessly tangled. With seed money from a generous donor, the Sierra Club announced in 1970 that it would donate a new "land grant" to the area, but it failed to materialize—perhaps because environmentalists soon were battling the local sheepherders over the effects of grazing. In 1995, a local shepherd successfully sued the Sierra Club for the never-applied donation, and the economic situation in the valley has somewhat improved. But many people must lease land on which to graze their sheep, resentments run deep, and the activism of King Tiger is still recalled with feeling.

(575/588-7247, www.nmparks.com, $5/car day use) is smaller but busier, as motorboats are permitted here, and it's a popular recreation spot, with large **campgrounds** (sites $10) at its south end (accessible via Hwy. 112, 17 miles southwest of Tierra Amarilla; the turnoff to the park is about 2 miles north of the village).

A 5.5-mile one-way hiking trail leads from Shale Point, north of all the campgrounds, up along the Rio Chama, across a bridge, up past Heron Dam, and into the south end of **Heron Lake State Park** (575/588-7470, www.nmparks.com, $5/car day use), which is also accessible via U.S. 64/84 and Highway 95. This lake is much more sedate as boats can only operate at no-wake speeds, which also makes it popular for kayakers. During the week, free ranger-led hikes are available on request—ideally, call ahead to the visitors center

to let the staff know you're coming. Scores of attractive **campsites** (sites from $8) line the park's southern and eastern shores.

Both lakes offer excellent trout and kokanee salmon fishing, though you'll need to arrange for a boat at **Stone House Lodge** (Hwy. 95, 575/588-7274, www.stonehouselodge.com, from $175/four hours), as there are no rentals at the lake itself; the lodge is about 14 miles west of the U.S. 64/84 turnoff.

Rafting

The stretch of the Chama River from El Vado Dam to Abiquiu Lake is one of the state's more scenic rafting runs and can be done as a leisurely multiday trip. **Kokopelli Rafting Adventures** (505/983-3734, www.kokopelliraft.com) in Santa Fe and **Los Rios River Runners** (575/776-8854, www.

losriosriverrunners.com) in Taos both run trips through these remote canyons; expect to pay about $115 for a one-day outing and $359 for a two-day trip.

CHAMA

A picturesque high-mountain town, **Chama** is the last population center of any size until you're well inside Colorado. With just 1,000 residents, the place has always been centered on the railroad that begins here and threads its way northeast between the mountains and over the state line to Antonito. Even if the steam train isn't your thing, you can drive north on Highway 17 for the views, though note that when the train isn't running, neither is much of the town; check for winter closures.

Chama is bordered on both sides by land belonging to the Jicarilla Apache. The tribe operates an elite hunting ranch south of town, The Lodge at Chama, that's a favorite politico getaway. But the natural attractions here are accessible to all—with the Rio Chama running right through town, you could theoretically walk out the front door of your (affordable) rental cabin, snag a trout, and cook it for dinner. On a day visit, the star of the show is the great steam train. If you stay a little longer, you'll have a chance to appreciate

the remarkable vistas—particularly in the fall, when the mountains are blanketed with a thick patchwork of color.

★ Cumbres & Toltec Scenic Railroad

The biggest attraction in Chama is the historic steam-driven **Cumbres & Toltec Scenic Railroad** (575/756-2151, www.cumbrestoltec. com), which has been running 64 miles from Chama up to Antonito, Colorado, since 1880. It is now jointly owned by the two neighboring states and maintained as a sort of museum.

You can travel the route in several ways, depending on how long of an outing you want. The shortest ride is the four-hour Sunday Express, running only that day in summer. The year-round standard outing is from Chama to the midpoint, the ghost town of Osier, just over the state border—you hop off there, have lunch, stroll around, and get back on the train for the ride back down the pass (from $95 adults, $50 kids). The whole trip takes a little more than six hours. Hard-core rail fans can go the whole way to Antonito—stopping in Osier for lunch—and return to Chama by bus, which takes eight hours ($95 adults, $50 kids); this way, you'll get to see the dramatic Toltec Gorge, just north of Osier.

the Cumbres & Toltec Scenic Railroad

Trains run most frequently in June, July, and early August, then again late September-mid-October, for autumn leaf season. Reservations are advised, and you can choose from three classes of service (windows open in tourist class, which is fun, but soot from the steam engine can make things a little gritty). The hot lunch included in the ticket price is pretty generous, with turkey and all the standard vegetables, plus pie to finish.

You can also prowl around the depot and rail yards. Pick up a flyer at the station that identifies all the structures, as well as distinguishes between drop-bottom gondolas, flangers, and other specialized train cars.

Recreation

Elk are prevalent throughout the mountains around Chama, and in the fall, the elk's distinctive mating call, or bugle, can be heard. North of town, accessed at the end of Pine Street, the **Edward Sargent Wildlife Management Area** (575/476-8000, www.wildlife.state.nm.us) has a viewing spot just inside the borders of the reserve, overlooking a big basin where the animals often graze. You can also hike into the center of the 20,000 acres, along the Rio Chama (for excellent fishing)—ask at the Chama visitors center for more information and other area hiking spots. If you want to hike or explore further, you'll need a Gaining Access into Nature (GAIN) permit, which you can pick up at the Chama Valley Supermarket.

Food

For an honest steak and potato, plus grilled local trout and cold beer, head to the **High Country Restaurant & Saloon** (2289 S. Hwy. 17, 575/756-2384, 11am-10pm Mon.-Sat., 8am-10pm Sun., $10-20), a big wood-paneled operation that's popular with through-bikers as well as locals; the wait for your meal can be lengthy. It serves a massive breakfast buffet on Sunday 8am-noon.

Across the street from the train yard, **Box Car Cafe** (425 Terrace Ave., 575/756-2706, 7am-3pm Mon.-Tues., Wed.-Sat. 7am-8:30pm,

the Rio Chama

7am-3pm Sun. Apr.-Nov., $8) serves hearty breakfast burritos (smothered in piquant chile) and juicy burgers for lunch. The menu is fairly limited, but the food is good and priced well.

Occupying a pine building straight out of a Wild West film set, the central **Brew House** (587 Terrace Ave., 575/756-1259, 1pm-10pm Wed.-Sun.) serves local beer, wine, hard cider, and mead made with wild honey. Stop in for a drink and occasional live music.

Accommodations

Chama has a reasonable selection of places to stay. The south side of town is largely devoted to rustic riverside cottage operations. **Chama River Bend Lodge** (2625 Hwy. 64, 575/756-2264, www.chamariverbendlodge.com) offers clean, basic rooms in a motel-like strip (from $89 d), as well as cabins closer to the water (from $119). Neighboring **Vista del Rio Lodge** (2595 Hwy. 64, 575/756-2138, www.

vistadelriolodge.com, $90 d) is one of the nicest in town. Spacious, rooms are furnished in a contemporary Southwest style and have modern bathrooms.

Up near the depot, the lodging is a bit less rustic. The pretty ★ **Chama Station Inn** (423 Terrace Ave., 575/756-2315, www. chamastationinn.com, May-mid-Oct., $95 d) is just across from the train depot. Most of the nine rooms have wood floors, and all are decorated sparingly with country touches; the extra $10 for a deluxe room is well worth it, as it gets you a kiva fireplace, a graceful high ceiling, and a little more space.

One of the least expensive beds can be found at **The Hotel** (501 S. Terrace Ave., 575/756-2416, www.thehotel.org, $67 d), a 1930s building with small rooms that are nonetheless clean, and a pleasant throwback. The property has been for sale for a few years—check that a change in owners hasn't changed the quality.

Campers will do well at the **Rio Chama RV Park** (U.S. 64, 575/756-2303, www.riochamarv.com, May-mid-Oct.), on the north edge of town, where tent sites ($16) are nestled amid tall trees, and the river flows right by.

Information and Services

Chama's **visitors center** (575/756-2235, 8am-6pm daily) is located at the junction of U.S. 64/84 and Highway 17, on the southern edge of town. In addition to maps and other info (for the whole state), it also provides free Internet access and coffee. In the winter, the office closes at 5pm.

JICARILLA APACHE NATION

The village of **Dulce** is the main town of the 750,000-acre **Jicarilla Apache Nation** (575/759-3255), which stretches north to the state line and south almost to the town of Cuba. The area is not the ancestral homeland of this band of Apache—originally, they had lived around the Platte and Arkansas Rivers in what is now central Colorado. But they were pushed south by white settlers in

the 19th century, eventually scattering to live with other tribes as far south and east as Tucumcari. The current reservation wasn't designated until 1887, when the band's numbers had dwindled to just 330 and the group had split into two factions. Although the land was hard-won, it proved fortunate when oil and gas were discovered on it in the 1930s. Profit from these resources, as well as a casino in Dulce and the luxurious Lodge at Chama, has made this a relatively prosperous reservation.

The tribe now numbers about 3,000 members, with 2,500 or so based in Dulce, 25 miles west of Chama on U.S. 64. The village is set in a high, grassy valley that feels hidden away from the rest of the world, with bison, cattle, and sheep grazing beneath the snowcapped Rockies. The **Jicarilla Cultural Center** (U.S. 64, 575/759-1343, 8am-5pm Mon.-Fri., free) has a small museum that describes the role of buffalo, medicinal herbs, and other heritage. In a trailer south of the tribal headquarters, the **Arts and Crafts Museum** (U.S. 64, 575/759-3242, 8am-5pm Mon.-Fri., free) is more of a shop, where you can also see people making the intricate baskets for which the tribe is known.

Festivals and Events

On the third week in July, the **Little Beaver Roundup** is a well-attended powwow and rodeo in Dulce that's open to visitors, and photography is permitted. Similar events, plus traditional footraces, mark **Go-Jii-Ya,** the tribe's feast day on September 15; it takes place at Stone Lake.

Recreation

Most visitors come here to hunt mule deer and elk on the reservation lands, or to fish in one of the many lakes; contact **Jicarilla Game and Fish** (575/759-3255, www.jicarillahunt. com) for rules and permits. **Stone Lake** ($5, or free with fishing and hunting licenses), 18 miles south of Dulce, has pretty campsites around its three miles of shoreline.

The Enchanted Circle

The **Enchanted Circle,** the loop formed by U.S. 64, Highway 38, and Highway 522, is named for its breathtaking views of the Sangre de Cristo Mountains, including Wheeler Peak. The area is a cultural shift from Taos, much of it settled by Anglo ranchers and prospectors in the late 1800s and currently populated by transplanted flatlander Texans enamored of the massive peaks. The main towns on the route—Angel Fire and Red River—are ski resorts. As the scenery is really the thing, you can drive the 84-mile route in a short day, with time out for a quick hike around Red River or a detour along the Wild Rivers scenic byway. If you like country music, you might want to plan to be in Red River for the evening.

Driving counterclockwise around the loop, as described below, gives you the arresting descent into the Taos Valley from Questa—not to be missed, if you can manage it. Avoid driving the circle on a Sunday and early in the week, as significantly more attractions and businesses are closed.

To start, head east out of Taos on Kit Carson Road, which turns into U.S. 64, winding along next to the Taos River and past numerous campgrounds and hiking trails. At Palo Flechado Pass, the road descends into the high Moreno Valley, a gorgeous expanse of green in early spring and a vast tundra in winter.

ANGEL FIRE

After about 20 miles, a right turn up Highway 434 leads to this tiny ski village, a cluster of timber condos at the base of a 10,600-foot mountain. In comparison with Taos Ski Valley, **Angel Fire Resort** (800/633-7463, www.angelfireresort.com, $73 full-day lift ticket) looks like a molehill, with a vertical drop of 2,077 feet. But it's friendly to families, has two freestyle terrain parks, and is the only place in the state for night skiing. For those with no snow skills at all, the 1,000-foot-long tubing hill provides an adrenaline rush.

In summer, the resort transforms itself with a full slate of activities on offer, though mountain biking is the clear highlight. Rightly acclaimed by regional riders, the **Angel Fire Bike Park** ($49/day) is larger than the nascent one at Taos Ski Valley and has more varied runs, including a handful that are suitable for beginners. Near the resort, the storied **South Boundary Trail** (no. 164) runs from a trailhead off Forest Road 76 south of Angel Fire. The route to Taos is about 5 vertical-seeming miles over the pass, then another 22 or so back to El Nogal trailhead on U.S. 64, a couple of miles east of Taos. **Gearing Up** (129 Paseo del Pueblo Sur, 575/751-0365) offers shuttle service ($55), so you can bike one-way.

The cool alpine waters of the resort's **Monte Verde Lake** are particularly appealing at the height of summer. Try your hand at stand-up paddleboarding ($20/hour) and fishing ($25/person), or enjoy the elaborate zipline course ($119). Off the slopes, **Roadrunner Tours** (Hwy. 434 in town, 575/377-6416, www.rtours.com) offers trail rides on horseback into the mountains.

Food

Before hitting the slopes, stop in at **The Bakery & Cafe** (3420 Mountain View Blvd., 575/377-3992, 7am-2:30pm daily, $7-11) for generous portions of tasty migas, biscuits and gravy, and chicken-fried steak and eggs.

Hail's Holy Smoked BBQ (3400 Hwy. 434, 575/377-9938, 6am-3pm Tues.-Sat., $5-16) proudly serves a no-nonsense Texas lunch, with smoked brisket, cowboy beans, and

The Enchanted Circle

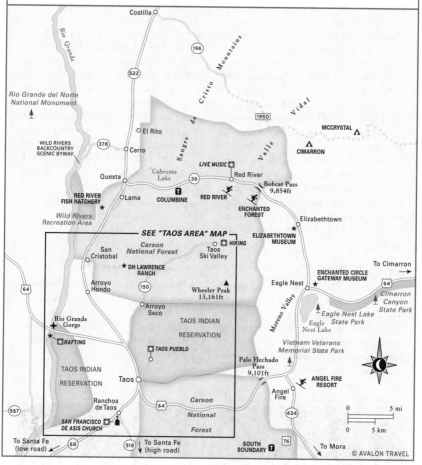

house-made desserts. Hail's does meat by the pound too, and its breakfast options are pretty inexpensive.

If you're around for dinner, **Angel Fired Pizza** (3375 Mountain View Blvd., 575/377-22774, 11am-9pm Tues.-Sun.) is the place to go. As well as several thin-crust whole wheat pizza specialties, it serves a green-chile carbonara and an unwieldy, but supremely tasty, meatball sub.

Information

The Angel Fire CVB maintains a **visitors center** (3365 Hwy. 434, 575/377-6555, www.angelfirefun.com, 9am-5pm daily) just south of the T intersection with Angel Fire Road. The **Angel Fire Chamber of Commerce** (3407 Hwy. 434, 575/377-6353, www.angelfirechamber.org, 9am-5pm Mon.-Fri.) has its own office where the lobby is open 24 hours, so you can pick up brochures and maps anytime.

VIETNAM VETERANS MEMORIAL STATE PARK

Back on U.S. 64, a little more than a mile past the turn for Angel Fire, a swooping white structure rises on the hill to your left. This is the **Vietnam Veterans Memorial State Park** (575/377-2293, www.emnrd.state.nm.us, 9am-5pm Thurs.-Mon.; chapel open 24 hours), built by Victor "Doc" Westphall as a remembrance of his son David, who was killed in the war. When Westphall commissioned Santa Fe architect Ted Luna to design the graceful white chapel in 1968, it was the first such memorial dedicated to the casualties of Vietnam. An adjacent visitors center was built later and now holds a small but moving museum about the conflict and its aftermath. In the garden are a Huey helicopter and the graves of Victor Westphall and his wife, Jeanne.

EAGLE NEST

At the junction of U.S. 64 and Highway 38, **Eagle Nest** is a small strip of wooden buildings, all that's left of what was a jumping gambling town in the 1920s and 1930s, when bars hosted roulette and blackjack, and enterprising businesspeople would roll slot machines out onto the boardwalks to entice travelers en route to Raton and the train. The pretty lake here now is the main focus of fun, but there's also good hiking just east in Cimarron Canyon State Park.

Eagle Nest Lake State Park

East of U.S. 64, south of town, **Eagle Nest Lake** was created in 1918 with the construction of a privately financed dam on the Cimarron River. Today it's a state park, stocked with trout, and a popular recreation spot—the Fourth of July fireworks display and winter ice fishing are legendary. For the marina and **visitors center** (575/377-1594, www.emnrd.state.nm.us, 8am-4:30pm daily, $5/car day use), look for the turn off U.S. 64 marked by a large RV park sign. Stop here for an exhibit on the dam, as well as camping ($10).

Enchanted Circle Gateway Museum

The **Enchanted Circle Gateway Museum** (U.S. 64, 575/377-5978, 9:30am-4pm Mon.-Sat., 11am-4pm Sun., donation), at the eastern edge of Eagle Nest, gives an overview of the good old days and often hosts events, such as a mountain-man rendezvous.

the chapel at the Vietnam Veterans Memorial State Park

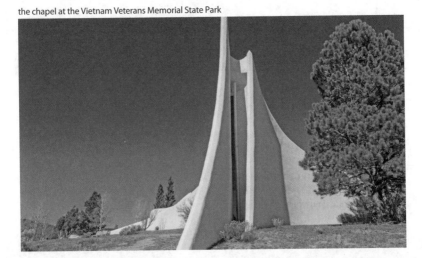

Farther Afield: Cimarron

From Eagle Nest, continuing east on U.S. 64 takes you through **Cimarron Canyon State Park** (575/377-6271, www.emnrd.state.nm.us, $5/car), known for excellent trout fishing in the Cimarron River, the dramatic granite palisades that form the canyon walls, and a few scenic hikes. Of the three campgrounds (sites from $10) along the river banks, Maverick and Ponderosa are closest to the trails. Twelve miles east of the canyon, you reach the town of Cimarron, where the **St. James Hotel** (Hwy. 21, 575/376-2664, www.exstjames.com, $85 d shared bathroom, $120 private bathroom) is one of the state's most historic hotels, notorious for gunfights in the years of the Colfax County War and still rich with atmosphere. Fill up on sandwiches, breakfast burritos, and sizable baked goods at **The Porch** (636 E. 9th St., 575/376-2228, 5-8pm Thurs., 10am-2pm & 5-8pm Fri., 5-8pm Sat., 10am-2pm Sun., $6).

Food and Accommodations

The atmosphere inside **Calamity Jane's** (51 Therma Dr., 575/377-9530, 11am-8pm Thurs.-Mon., $10), the town's main restaurant, can't be beat. Built out of old railroad ties and located within the Eagle Nest's oldest hotel—Laguna Vista Lodge—it endearingly evokes a bygone era, though the steakhouse food is often hit or miss.

Retro **Kaw-Lija's** (Therma Dr., 575/377-3424, 8am-8pm daily May-Sept., $6) is the most reliable place to eat here, with burgers, chicken-fried steak, and the like; there's homemade ice cream, too. Opening hours can be erratic, and it closes in the winter.

Laguna Vista Lodge (51 Therma Dr., 575/377-6522, www.lagunavistalodge.com, $85-125 d) has standard motel rooms connected by a screened porch, as well as cabins and apartments with a view of the lake.

Information

The **Eagle Nest Chamber of Commerce** runs a **visitors center** (50 Therma Dr., 575/377-2420, www.eaglenestchamber.org, 8am-4pm Mon.-Fri. mid-May-mid-Oct.) with an enthusiastic staff and plenty of local and regional information.

ELIZABETHTOWN

Blink and you'll miss it: A small sign on the right side of the road 4.8 miles past Eagle Nest points to a left turn to the former gold rush site of **Elizabethtown**, the first incorporated village in New Mexico. When gold was discovered in 1866, it grew to more than 7,000 people, then faded to nothing after a dredge-mining project failed in 1903. It's now a barely discernible ghost town, with the meager stone ruins of the Mutz Hotel, the former center of social activity. The only signs of life are, ironically, in the **cemetery**, which is still used by residents of Colfax County and contains graves dating as far back as 1880, and in the **museum** (505/312-3800, call for hours, donation suggested), which provides a surprisingly good sense of what life was like in the village's heyday.

RED RIVER

The ski village of **Red River** is a cluster of tidy rows of wooden buildings, all done up in Old West facades, complete with boardwalks and swinging saloon doors. Like Elizabethtown, this was once a community of wild prospectors, but when mining went bust, the town salvaged itself by renting out abandoned houses to vacationers escaping the summer heat. Just when air-conditioning started to become widespread in the 1950s, the ski area opened, saving the town from a major slump. Red River still thrives, with a year-round population of only about 500.

The town hosts several outsized events throughout the year, including a rowdy **Memorial Day Motorcycle Rally,** a large Fourth of July parade, the **Enchanted Circle Century Tour** and the **Red River**

Folk Festival (http://redriverfolk.com) in September, and a Mardi Gras street party; contact the **Red River Chamber of Commerce** (575/754-2366, www.redriver-chamber.org) for more details.

Skiing

Compared with Taos Ski Valley, **Red River Ski & Summer Area** (575/754-2223, www.redriverskiarea.com, $73 full-day lift ticket) may be a bunny hill, but it's nothing if not convenient: The trails run into town, so the two chairlifts are walking distance from anywhere in town.

Cross-country skiers should follow Highway 38 east of town, to the **Enchanted Forest** cross-country ski area (575/754-6112, www.enchantedforestxc.com, $18 full-day pass), which has more than 20 miles of groomed trails through the trees and up the mountainside. Nonskiers can rent snowshoes. And, for a special overnight experience, you can trek in to a **yurt** ($40-150, depending on season), nicely appointed with a woodstove. It's available year-round, and snowmobile delivery of your gear is an option in winter.

Hiking

The town abuts the back side of Wheeler Peak, so the ascents here are much more gradual, while still yielding dramatic views. Stop in at the **visitors center** (101 W. River St., 575/754-3030, www.redriver.org, 8am-5pm daily), in the town hall, for area maps and trail guides. The easy **Red River Nature Trail** can be accessed behind the conference center just past the covered bridge and runs one mile round-trip, with signs identifying plants and geological formations. The more demanding and scenic **Pioneer Creek Trail** (FR 485) starts next to the Arrowhead Lodge off Pioneer Street and follows an old mining road through the forest for 3.4 miles before ending at just over 10,000 feet; there are a few signs of long-closed silver and copper mines along the way.

West of town, Highway 38 leads past a number of trailheads that make for a good amble. **Columbine Trail** (no. 71), on the left (south), eight miles out (or about four miles east of Questa), at the back of the Columbine Campground, is the one to choose if your time is limited. The trail starts out easy, crossing Deer Creek, but soon climbs switchbacks that lead through a large aspen grove, then above the tree line to the ridge, a total of about five miles. As an incentive, wild berry bushes flourish alongside the trail in late summer. The right side of the road, however, is a little less scenic because a molybdenum mine has stripped a good chunk of the mountain.

In summer, you can ride the **Platinum Chairlift** ($19) to the ski area, where you can hike around the summit and negotiate the steep trail back into town; it's also popular with experienced mountain bikers. The 360-degree views from the top are worth the trip up alone.

★ Live Music

Red River has a lively country music scene, heavily influenced by the Texans and Oklahomans who have long come here for vacation. "Outlaw country" singer and songwriter Michael Martin Murphey, whose song "The Land of Enchantment" is the official state ballad, has long been active in the music scene here, and he performs regularly July-first week of September at **Rockin' 3M Chuckwagon Amphitheater** (178 Bitter Creek Rd., 575/754-6280, 3pm-2am daily).

The barn-like Texas Reds holds two live music venues: the adjacent **Motherlode Saloon** (406 E. Main St., 575/754-6280, 6pm-2am daily) and the aptly named **Lost Love Saloon** (400 E. Main St., 575/754-2922). Local rock and country acts take the stage at the former and make it the most rollicking place in town on weekends; the latter features more sedate country and western crooners throughout the week.

Bobcat Pass (1670 Hwy. 38, 575/754-2769, www.bobcatpass.com, 5:30pm Tues., Thurs., and Sat. mid-June-late Aug.), offers horseback rides by day (from $45) and hosts "cowboy evenings," which include a home-style steak dinner along with a night of singing and picking and a bit of poetry.

Food

The largest selection of lunch options on the Enchanted Circle is in Red River, but none of them is particularly remarkable. Business turnover can be high here, but at least **Texas Reds** (400 E. Main St., 575/754-2922, 4:30pm-9pm Mon.-Thurs., 11:30am-3pm and 4:30pm-9pm Fri.-Sun., $15) is consistent; it packs 'em in with Texas-sized steaks and elk burgers in a wood-paneled Western-look room, the floors scattered with peanut shells.

For Tex-Mex, including gut-busting stuffed sopaipillas, **Sundance** (401 High St., 575/754-2971, 5pm-9pm Thurs.-Tues., $13) is equally reliable—it's on the street uphill and parallel to the main drag.

For a quick in-and-out meal, **Dairy Bar** (417 E. Main St., 575/754-9969, 11am-9pm daily in summer, 11am-7pm Thurs.-Mon. in winter, $5) does burgers, chile, quesadillas, and, of course, soft-serve ice cream.

The best place in town to stock up for a picnic and hike is the central **Der Market** (307 W. Main St., 575/754-2974, 5am-8pm daily).

Accommodations

Red River is an ideal base for exploring the Enchanted Circle's hiking and skiing options; there are plenty of choices, and most are pleasant and reasonably priced, if somewhat dated. **Golden Eagle Lodge** (1100 Main St., 575/754-2227, $90), on the village's eastern edge, is one of the better representatives of what's on offer. It's a quaint, family-run place with various-sized apartments that are comfortable and well cared for.

Spread along the river, the Bavarian-themed **Alpine Lodge** (417 W. Main St., 575/754-2952, $115 d) is the best deal in the village. Accommodations range from nicely appointed rooms with balconies in the hotel to spacious log cabins that can fit up to twelve. The property has its own private park and you can even cast a line in the river out back.

Information

The chamber of commerce staffs a **visitors center** (101 W. River St., 575/754-3030, 8am-5pm daily) inside the town hall, off the north side of the main drag.

QUESTA

Arriving in **Questa,** at the junction of Highway 38 and Highway 522, it's hard not

Motherlode Saloon in Red River

to get a sense you're back in Spanish New Mexico. The town, which now has a population of about 1,700, was established in 1842 and is still primarily a Hispano farming village, though a few Anglo newcomers have set up art spaces here. **Ocho** (8 Hwy. 38, www.ochozone.org, gallery 11am-5pm Fri.-Sun.) is one; it hosts community music jams and other events.

Across the road is the **visitors center** (Hwy. 38, 575/613-2852, www.questa-nm.com/visitor-center, 9:30am-5pm daily June-Aug.), though it has little to share. The heart of town, a few blocks back, is the 1841 **San Antonio Church,** which was restored in 2016 by volunteers over about eight years of night-and-weekend work.

Of the few places to grab a bite to eat, **The Wildcat's Den** (2457 Hwy. 522, 575/586-1119, 11am-6pm Tues.-Fri., 11am-4pm Sat., $7) is the best bet; its burgers are rightly revered by locals. For a meal more in line with Questa's roots, head north a bit to **My Tia's Café** (107 Hwy. 378, 575/586-2203, 11am-6pm Mon. and Thurs.-Fri., 8am-7pm Sat.-Sun., $7), which does New Mexican home cooking, including chiles rellenos and taco salads.

Wild Rivers Recreation Area

In 2014, the **Río Grande del Norte National Monument** (575/758-8851, www.blm.gov) was established, protecting the river from the Colorado state line to Pilar, south of Taos. Perhaps the wildest section of the land is found north of Questa, in the **Wild Rivers Recreation Area,** where the Red River meets the Rio Grande. Red-tailed hawks circle over gnarled, centuries-old piñon and juniper trees, and river otters thrive here, after their reintroduction in 2008. White-water **rafting** is popular in the Class III rapids of the Red River Confluence run; contact an outfitter in Taos.

The access road to the recreation area is three miles north on Highway 522 from the main Questa intersection, then west on Highway 378, which leads through the town of Cerro and to the area's **visitors center**

(575/586-1150, 9am-6pm daily June-Aug., $3/car day use).

Steep **hiking** trails lead down into the gorge and along the river, so you can make a full loop, starting down from **La Junta Point,** then taking **Little Arsenic Trail** back up (about 4.5 miles total), or **Big Arsenic Trail** for a longer hike (6 miles). If you'd prefer not to descend (and, necessarily, ascend) the canyon, follow the more level 1.7-mile **Pescado Trail** along the Red River rim and gently down to the Red River Fish Hatchery.

Five developed **campgrounds** (but no RV hookups; $7/car) on the rim can be reached by car, or you can hike in to campsites by the river ($5).

D. H. LAWRENCE RANCH

After Questa, the view opens up as you descend into Taos Valley, with mesas stretching far to the west. Five miles east on the rutted San Cristobal Road is the 160-acre **D. H. Lawrence Ranch** (575/776-2245, 10am-2pm Thurs.-Fri., 10am-4pm Sat June-Oct.), also known as the Kiowa Ranch, where English writer and provocateur D. H. Lawrence lived 1924-1925 with his wife, Frieda, and the painter Dorothy Brett. The ranch was closed to visitors for several years, but reopened in 2014, with a docent on-site to answer questions. Though there's not much to see, it is as good a reason as any to drive up a back road and into the fragrant pine forests. (Don't bother driving up on a closed day—the property is fully fenced and locked up.)

The 160-acre spread was a gift from Mabel Dodge Luhan—generous, but nonetheless a bare-bones existence, as you can see in the cabins the artists occupied. Lawrence soon returned to Europe, but Frieda stayed on. Years after the writer died of tuberculosis in France in 1930, Frieda exhumed and cremated his body and brought the ashes to New Mexico. This plan sparked anger among Lawrence's friends, including Mabel, who characterized Frieda's planned site for the ashes as "that outhouse of a shrine." Tales abound about how the ashes never made the trip. Some of the earliest visitors to pay their respects at the ranch include playwright Tennessee Williams and artist Georgia O'Keeffe, whose painting *The Lawrence Tree* was inspired by the view from the base of a gnarled pine in front of the Lawrences' cabin.

Coming from the north, turn left at the *second* sign for County Road B-009 (the first is in the town of San Cristobal). Coming up from Taos, look for the historical marker on the right side of the road, immediately before the turn.

Information and Services

TOURIST INFORMATION

A few miles south of the plaza, the **Taos Visitor Center** (1139 Paseo del Pueblo Sur, 575/758-3873, www.taos.org, 9am-5pm daily) is helpful, as long as you don't show up right before closing time. Stop here for flyers and maps galore, free coffee, and the thorough weekly news and events bulletin (also posted online), which includes gallery listings, concerts, festivals, and more.

Books and Maps

Op.cit. (124-A Bent St., No. 6 Dunn House, 575/751-1999, 10am-6pm daily) stocks new and used books, local titles, and maps, and hosts author readings.

Local Media

The *Taos News* comes out every Thursday; its Tempo entertainment section covers music, theater, and film listings. Many hotels offer free copies of Tempo to their guests. The *Albuquerque Journal North*, which covers northern New Mexico, publishes daily.

Radio

While you're in town, don't miss tuning in to **KTAO** (101.9 FM), a solar-powered local radio station. The musical programming is broad, and you're sure to learn interesting tidbits about the community as well.

SERVICES

Banks

US Bank (120 W. Plaza, 575/737-3540,

Op.cit. bookstore in Taos

9am-5pm Mon.-Fri.), just off the southwest corner of the plaza, is the most convenient bank and ATM while on foot. The drive-through service at **Centinel Bank of Taos** (512 Paseo del Pueblo Sur, 575/758-6700, 9am-5pm Mon.-Fri.) is easily accessible from the main drag.

Post Offices

The Taos **post office** (710 Paseo del Pueblo Sur, 575/751-1801, 9am-1pm and 2pm-4:30pm Mon.-Fri.) is on the south side; there's another on the north side (318 Paseo del Pueblo Norte, 575/758-2081, 8:30am-5pm Mon.-Fri.).

Internet

The one-stop **Wired?** (705 Felicidad Ln., 575/751-9473, www.wiredcoffeeshop.com, 8am-5pm daily), behind Albertsons off La Posta Road, is a laid-back Internet café, print shop, book store, and gallery, with a big garden, good veggie and raw-food meals, and free wireless access for laptops; computer use is $2 for 15 minutes.

Getting There and Around

CAR

From Santa Fe, the drive to Taos takes about 1.5 hours (70 miles) along the direct "low road" through the river valley (via Española, U.S. 84/285 to Hwy. 68). If taking the "high road" (via Chimayó and Truchas, mostly on Hwy. 76), plan on at least 2 hours for the 80-mile drive.

From Albuquerque, add at least an hour's travel time for the 60-mile drive up I-25 (the most direct route) to Santa Fe.

Once in Taos, you will need a car to get to outlying sights but will also have to bear the daily traffic jams on Paseo del Pueblo. There are paid parking lots close to the plaza, and a free one less than 0.25 mile down Kit Carson Road. Of the rental car options, **Enterprise** (1350 Paseo del Pueblo Sur, 575/758-5333, www.enterprise.com, 8am-5pm Mon.-Fri., 9am-noon Sat.) is the most convenient, a block south of the visitors center.

BUS AND SHUTTLE

For pickup at the Albuquerque airport, **Twin Hearts Express** (575/751-1201, www.twin-heartsexpress.com, $60 one-way, cash only) runs a shuttle four times a day (11:30am, 1:30pm, 3:30pm, and 5:30pm), with drop-offs at most hotels. Allow at least 2.5 hours for travel time; reservations are required.

From Santa Fe, there's great weekend service from city-sponsored **Taos Express** (575/751-4459, www.taosexpress.com, $10 round-trip), which runs from Taos and back once on Saturday and Sunday, completing a loop in the morning and another in the afternoon. The one-way trip takes 1 hour and 50 minutes.

In Santa Fe, the bus picks up passengers near the Rail Runner main depot (Montezuma at Guadalupe) and at the South Capitol station (Sunday). In Taos, it drops off at Our Lady of Guadalupe parking lot, one block west of the plaza; going back south, it also picks up passengers at the Sagebrush Inn (1508 Paseo del Pueblo Sur). The schedule syncs with the Rail Runner's arrival in Santa Fe (and it can carry bicycles), making it a potentially seamless three-hour trip all the way from Albuquerque.

Within Taos, the **Chile Line bus** runs north-south from the Ranchos de Taos post office to the Taos Pueblo, approximately every 40 minutes 7:30am-5:30pm Monday-Friday. In town, it's free. Mid-December-April, a **ski shuttle** ($1 one-way) runs to Taos Ski Valley, with five buses daily making stops at key motels en route to the mountain; not all buses stop at all hotels. Contact **Taos's transportation division** (575/751-4459, www.taosgov.com) for maps and schedules.

Albuquerque

Sights 166

Entertainment and Events 181

Shopping...................... 186

Sports and Recreation 188

Food 191

Accommodations.............. 197

Outside Albuquerque.......... 200

Information and Services 214

Getting There and Around..... 215

Look for ★ to find recommended sights, activities, dining, and lodging.

Highlights

★ **ABQ Trolley Co.:** The best tour in the state, aboard an open-sided, faux-adobe tram-on-wheels, with the lively, knowledgeable owners sharing Albuquerque lore (page 166).

★ **KiMo Theatre:** A fantasia of Southwestern decorative styles, this former cinema is one of the few examples of Pueblo Deco style. Restored and run with city money, it's the showpiece of downtown (page 173).

★ **Sandia Peak Tramway:** Zip up the world's longest single-cable tram to the crest of the mountain that looms over the east side of Albuquerque. At the top, you'll get a vertigo-inducing view across the whole metro area and out to the hazy western horizon (page 177).

★ **Petroglyph National Monument:** Basalt boulders throughout the city's West Mesa are covered with several thousand fine rock carvings etched centuries ago by the ancestors of the local Pueblo people (page 178).

★ **Ballooning:** In the American hot-air balloon capital, enjoy a dawn flight—or at least witness hundreds of brightly colored balloons take part in the wildly popular Balloon Fiesta (page 188).

★ **Acoma Pueblo:** This windswept village on a mesa west of Albuquerque is one of the oldest communities in the United States. Visit for a glimpse into this remarkable community's perseverance as well as for the delicate black-on-white pottery made only here (page 200).

★ **Bosque del Apache:** Nothing quite prepares you for the sight of thousands of snow geese suddenly taking flight against the backdrop of a burnt orange sky at one of North

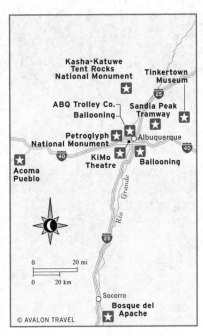

America's premier birding destinations (page 205).

★ **Tinkertown Museum:** An enthralling collection of one man's lifetime of whittling projects, this folk-art exhibit delights kids and adults alike (page 206).

★ **Kasha-Katuwe Tent Rocks National Monument:** Break up the otherwise unremarkable freeway drive to Santa Fe with a hike in this eerie canyon landscape marked by dozens of bleached-white conical formations (page 214).

As a tourist destination, Albuquerque has long labored in the shadow of the arts colonies to the north, but times are changing—and rightly so. The Duke City is fun, down-to-earth, and affordable.

If Santa Fe is the "City Different" (a moniker Albuquerqueans, or *Burqueños*, razz for its pretentiousness), then New Mexico's largest city, with a population of 900,000 in the greater metro area, is proudly the "City Indifferent," unconcerned with fads and fanciful facades.

The city does have its pockets of historic charm—they're just not visible from the arteries of I-40 and I-25, which intersect in the center in a graceful tangle of turquoise-trimmed bridges. Albuquerque was founded three centuries ago, its cumbersome name that of a Spanish nobleman (hence its nickname, the Duke City) but its character the product of later eras: the post-1880 downtown district; the University of New Mexico campus, built in the early 20th century by John Gaw Meem, the architect who defined Pueblo Revival style; and Route 66, the highway that joined Albuquerque to Chicago, Illinois, and Los Angeles, California, in 1926.

Spread out on either side of the Rio Grande, from volcanic mesas on the west to the foothills of the Sandia Mountains along the east, Albuquerque has accessible hiking and biking trails that run through diverse landscapes. In the morning, you can stroll under centuries-old cottonwood trees near the wide, muddy river; in the afternoon, you can hike along the edge of a windswept mountain range with views across the vast empty land beyond the city grid. And at the end of the day, you'll see Albuquerque's most remarkable feature, the dramatic light show on the Sandia Mountains—Spanish for "watermelon," for the bright pink hue they turn at sundown.

The city is also an excellent base for exploring the many interesting pueblos and natural attractions nearby. In the Manzano Mountains southeast of town, for instance, lie a series of ruined pueblos, last inhabited during the early years of the Conquest. The road that links them also winds past a canyon

---

Previous: the KiMo Theatre; Acoma Pueblo. **Above:** Petroglyph National Monument.

Albuquerque

PETROGLYPH NATIONAL MONUMENT

VISITORS CENTER

UNSER BLVD

ATRISCO DR

MONTAÑO RD

COORS BLVD

CENTRAL AVE

COORS BLVD

RIO BRAVO BLVD

SOUTH VALLEY

SANDIA PEAK INN

NATIONAL HISPANIC CULTURAL CENTER

AMC ALBUQUERQUE MODELO

ISLETA BLVD

2ND ST

BROADWAY

BRIDGE BLVD

To Volcanos-Day Use Area, Laguna Pueblo, and ACOMA PUEBLO

To Casa/San Ysidro, Coronado Historic Site, Hyatt Tamaya, and Jemez

CORRALES

Rio Grande

CORRALES RD

BALLOONING

Balloon Fiesta Park

SARABANDE B&B

SOPHIA'S PLACE

FARM & TABLE

PEREA'S

LOS RANCHOS

LOS POBLANOS INN

FLYING STAR/ BOOKWORKS

CINNAMON MORNING

ANNAPURNA

4TH ST

EDITH BLVD

ANNAPURNA

2ND ST

4TH ST

NORTH VALLEY

RIO GRANDE NATURE CENTER STATE PARK

INDIAN PUEBLO CULTURAL CENTER

TINGLEY BEACH

KIMO THEATRE

Paseo del Bosque

SEE "OLD TOWN" MAP

SEE "DOWNTOWN ALBUQUERQUE" MAP

SEE "UNIVERSITY AREA" MAP

MARY & TITO'S CAFE

LA CUMBRE BREWING

MENAUL BLVD

CHAMA RIVER BREWING

SEASONAL PALATE

JEFFERSON ST

GRUET WINERY

NATIVO LODGE

ALAMEDA

ANDERSON ABRUZZO INTERNATIONAL BALLOON MUSEUM

Balloon Fiesta Park

To KASHA-KATUWE TENT ROCKS NATIONAL MONUMENT and Santa Fe

SANDIA CASINO

SANDIA PUEBLO

SANDIA PEAK TRAMWAY

NOB HILL

VORTEX THEATRE

GREEN JEANS FARMERY

FRENCH-ISH

HUMBLE COFFEE

NEON

ABSOLUTELY

TALIN MARKET/ CODA BAKERY

FAIRGROUNDS/ FLEA MARKET

FORK & FIG

NORTHEAST HEIGHTS

CARLISLE BLVD

SAN MATEO BLVD

SAN PEDRO BLVD

LOUISIANA BLVD

WYOMING BLVD

EUBANK BLVD

JUAN TABO BLVD

MONTGOMERY BLVD

CANDELARIA BLVD

CENTRAL AVE

INDIAN SCHOOL RD

LOMAS BLVD

TRAMWAY BLVD

PASEO DEL NORTE

ACADEMY BLVD

JUAN TABO BLVD

TIA B'S LA WAFFLERIA

FLYING STAR

ISOTOPES PARK

THE PIT

UNIVERSITY BLVD

EXIT 221

BERNALILLO CO/SUNPORT RAIL RUNNER STATION

ALBUQUERQUE INTERNATIONAL SUNPORT

GIBSON BLVD

NATIONAL MUSEUM OF NUCLEAR SCIENCE & HISTORY

TRACTOR BREWING

KIRTLAND AIR FORCE BASE

To BOSQUE DEL APACHE NATIONAL WILDLIFE REFUGE

Embudo Canyon Park

Elena Gallegos Picnic Area

Juan Tabo Picnic Ground

Sandia Peak 10,678ft

SANDIA PEAK

SANDIAGO'S

SANDIA PEAK TRAMWAY

LA LUZ

CAPULIN SPRINGS SNOWPLAY AREA

SANDIA CREST RD

TINKERTOWN MUSEUM

To Tijeras, Turquoise Trail, and Salinas Pueblo Missions National Monument

0   25 km
0   25 mi

© AVALON TRAVEL

known for its fall colors and a historic hotel in a distinctly New Mexican style.

Albuquerque is also just an hour's drive to Santa Fe, with easy day trips or scenic drives through the mountains in between. The most direct is I-25, which cuts through dramatic rolling hills; take a short detour to Kasha-Katuwe Tent Rocks National Monument, where pointed white rocks tower above a narrow canyon. Beginning east of Albuquerque, the historic Turquoise Trail winds along the back side of the Sandias, then through the former mining town of Madrid, resettled as an arts colony, with galleries occupying the cabins built against the black, coal-rich hills. The most roundabout route north is along the Jemez Mountain Trail, a scenic byway northwest of Albuquerque through the brick-red rocks surrounding Jemez Pueblo, then past natural hot springs.

PLANNING YOUR TIME

Precisely because it's not so full of must-see historic attractions, Albuquerque fares best as the primary focus of a trip, so you have time to enjoy the natural setting, the food, and the people. It makes financial sense, too: Your money will go further here than it will farther north, especially when it comes to hotels, which offer great value and don't dramatically hike rates for **summer** high season, as is standard in Taos and Santa Fe. Ideally, you would spend a leisurely **four days** here, soaking up a little Route 66 neon, enjoying the downtown entertainment, hiking in the Sandias, taking scenic drives, and bicycling along the Rio Grande.

But if you're also planning to visit other parts of the state, it is difficult to recommend more than a **couple of days** in Albuquerque—preferably on the way out, as the city's modern, get-real attitude is best appreciated after you've been in the adobe dreamland of Santa Fe for a bit. Spend a day cruising the neighborhoods along Central Avenue, and for a last dose of open sky, take the tramway up to Sandia Peak and hike along the Crest Trail. At the end of your trip,

you'll be able to handle the elevation with no problem.

In the city proper, most of the year is enjoyable. **Winters** are mild in the low basin around the river, though the Sandias often get heavy snow. Note that a **summer** day here can be 5-10°F hotter than father north, though, as elsewhere in the state the heat of July and August is usually broken by heavy afternoon rainstorms (though May and June are typically hot and dry). And because Albuquerque is seldom at the top of tourists' lists, there's never a time when it's unpleasantly mobbed.

HISTORY

Albuquerque was established in 1706 as a small farming outpost on the banks of the Rio Grande, where Pueblo Indians had been cultivating crops since 1100, and named after a Spanish duke. Decades later, the Villa de San Felipe de Alburquerque (the first "r" was lost over the years) flourished as a waypoint on the Camino Real trade route.

The city began to transform in 1880, when the railroad arrived, two miles from the main plaza—this sparked the growth of "New Town" (now the downtown business district) and drew tuberculosis patients, who saw the city's crisp air as beneficial. By 1912, these patients made up nearly a quarter of the state's population.

More modernization and growth came from Route 66, which was laid down Central Avenue in the 1930s, and the establishment of Sandia National Labs in 1949, in response to the escalating Cold War. Tourism boomed (and neon signs buzzed on), and new streets were carved into the northeast foothills for lab workers' tract homes. In the 1940s, the population exploded from 35,000 to 100,000; by 1959, 207,000 people lived in Albuquerque.

Growth has been steady ever since, and recent development has been spurred by a growing film industry and other technical innovations. Subdivisions have spread across the West Mesa, and small outlying communities have become suburbs—though portions along the river retain a village feel that's not too far from the city's roots as a farming community three centuries back.

ORIENTATION

Albuquerque's greater metro area covers more than 100 square miles, but visitors will likely see only a handful of neighborhoods, all linked by Central Avenue (historic Route 66), the main east-west thoroughfare across town. Completed in early 2018, the Albuquerque Rapid Transit (ART; www.brtabq.com) project significantly upgraded and enhanced bus options along Central Avenue, though with fewer lanes available, travel times by car can be a bit longer.

Visitors typically start exploring in **Old Town:** The best museums are clustered here, a few blocks from the Rio Grande, which runs north-south through the city. East from Old Town lies **downtown,** with most of the city's bars and clubs, along with the bus and train depots. Central continues under I-25 and past the **University of New Mexico** campus, followed by the **Nob Hill** shopping district, which occupies about 10 blocks of Central. After this, the rest of Albuquerque blurs into the broad area known as the **Northeast Heights;** the main attractions up this way are hiking trails in the foothills and the Sandia Peak Tramway. The other notable parts of town—technically, separate villages—are **Los Ranchos de Albuquerque** and **Corrales.** These are two districts in the North Valley—the stretch of the river north of Central—that contain a few of the city's better lodging options; from Old Town, head north on Rio Grande Boulevard to reach Los Ranchos, then jog west over the river and north again to Corrales.

To keep your bearings, remember that the mountains run along the east side of the city. Street addresses are followed by the city quadrant (NE, NW, SE, SW); the axes are Central and 1st Street. When locals talk about "the Big I," they mean the relatively central point where I-40 and I-25 intersect.

Sights

Most sightseeing destinations are somewhere along Central Avenue (historic Route 66), with a few destinations elsewhere in the greater metro area.

OLD TOWN

Until the railroad arrived in 1880, this wasn't just the old town—it was the *only* town. The labyrinthine old adobes have been repurposed as souvenir emporiums and galleries; the city's major museums are nearby on Mountain Road. Despite the chile-pepper magnets and cheap cowboy hats, the residential areas surrounding the shady plaza retain a strong Hispano flavor, and the historic **Old Town** buildings have a certain endearing scruffiness—they're lived-in, not polished.

★ ABQ Trolley Co.

To cruise the major attractions in town and get oriented, put yourself in the hands of the excellent locally owned and operated **ABQ Trolley Co.** (800 Rio Grande Blvd. NW, 505/240-8000, www.abqtrolley.com)—even if you're not normally the bus-tour type. The difference here is, first of all, in the bus itself: in summer, a goofy faux-adobe open-sided trolley-bus; in winter, a stealthy black van. But much more important are the enthusiastic owners, who give the tours themselves. Their love of the city is clear as they wave at pedestrians and tell stories about onetime Albuquerque resident and Microsoft founder Bill Gates.

All tours depart from the Hotel Albuquerque at Old Town. The 85-minute **standard tour** (10am, noon, and 2pm daily, $30) runs through downtown and some off-the-beaten-track old neighborhoods, passing many TV and movie locations. There's also

Old Town Albuquerque

© AVALON TRAVEL

a periodic *Breaking Bad* **tour** (3.5 hours, $65) that remains a big draw—book well in advance for this. Or join one of the monthly nighttime theme tours—such as The Hopper, a brew-pub crawl—that draw locals as well. Buy tickets online to guarantee a spot; the tickets also get you discounts around town, so it's good to do this early in your visit.

ABQ BioPark

The earnest **ABQ BioPark** (505/768-2000, www.cabq.gov/biopark, 9am-5pm Mon.-Fri., 9am-6pm Sat.-Sun. June-Aug.) is made up of several components, linked by parkland along the river. On the riverbank just west of Old Town (2601 Central Ave. NW) are an **aquarium** and **botanical gardens.** The aquarium is small but well stocked, with a giant shark tank and displays on underwater life from the Gulf of Mexico and up the Rio

Grande. The well-conceived adjoining gardens include a desert hothouse, a butterfly habitat, a Japanese garden, a garden railroad, and a surprisingly compelling "BUGarium" full of insects in close approximations of their natural habitats. The gardens also include the 10-acre **Rio Grande Heritage Farm,** a re-creation of a 1930s operation with heirloom apple orchards and rare types of livestock, such as Percheron horses and Churro sheep, in an idyllic setting near the river. The whole facility is of course very kid friendly, but in the desert rose garden, there's a pleasant **mini café** where you can enjoy a glass of wine too.

A few blocks away is the **zoo** (903 10th St. SW), which you can reach from the aquarium via a miniature train. The zoo is not particularly groundbreaking, but there's plenty of space for kids to run around within earshot of trumpeting elephants and screeching peacocks; the window into the gorilla nursery is probably the most fascinating exhibit. Tickets for each section (zoo or aquarium/gardens) are $14.50, and a combo ticket for entry to all three, which includes the mini-train ride, is $22. Ticket booths close 30 minutes before the attractions' closing times.

The land between the zoo and aquarium, on the east bank of the river, south of Central, is so-called **Tingley Beach** (1800 Tingley Dr. SW, sunrise-sunset, free), 18 acres of paths and ponds for fishing; you can also rent paddleboats and bicycles here.

Albuquerque Museum of Art and History

The **Albuquerque Museum of Art and History** (2000 Mountain Rd. NW, 505/243-7255, www.cabq.gov/museum, 9am-5pm Tues.-Sun., $4) has a permanent collection ranging from a few choice Taos Society of Artists members to contemporary work by the likes of Nick Abdalla, whose sensual imagery makes Georgia O'Keeffe's flower paintings look positively literal. The history wing covers four centuries, with emphasis on Spanish military trappings, Mexican cowboys, and Albuquerque's early railroad years. Free guided tours run daily around the sculpture

garden, or you can join the informative **Old Town walking tour** (11am Tues.-Sun. mid-Mar.-mid-Dec.). The museum has free admission Saturday afternoon (after 2pm) and Sunday morning (9am-1pm), as well as the third Thursday night of the month, when it's open till 8:30pm.

American International Rattlesnake Museum

You'd never guess that a small storefront just off the plaza houses the largest collection of live rattlesnakes in the world. An outsized gift shop tempts at the entrance to the **American International Rattlesnake Museum** (202 San Felipe St. NW, 505/242-6569, www.rattlesnakes.com, 10am-6pm Mon.-Sat., 1pm-5pm Sun. June-Aug., $5); press past the snake swag to view the live critters in the back. You'll also see some fuzzy tarantulas and Gila monsters; the enthusiastic staff are usually showing off some animals outside to help educate the phobic. In the off-season, September-May, weekday hours are 11:30am-5:30pm (10am-6pm Sat., 1pm-5pm Sun.).

Capilla de Nuestra Señora de Guadalupe

One of the nifty secrets of Old Town, the

The ABQ Trolley Co. offers a great introduction to the Duke City.

Breaking Bad

The Candy Lady tempts *Breaking Bad* viewers with bags of blue treats.

Walter White and Jesse Pinkman may be gone from television (at least, neither have yet to appear in the *Breaking Bad* prequel *Better Call Saul*), but their legacy lives on in Albuquerque. The AMC show about a high school chemistry teacher turned meth cook, *Breaking Bad* was originally written for a California setting, but production moved to Albuquerque following tax incentives. It was a happy accident, and unlike other productions shot here anonymously, *Breaking Bad* was explicitly down with the 505.

Dedicated fans can book the twice-monthly "BaD Tour" with the **ABQ Trolley Co.** (800 Rio Grande Blvd. NW, 505/240-8000, www.abqtrolley.com, May-Nov., 3.5 hours, $65)—though its standard route passes a few filming locations as well. The bike rental company **Routes** (404 San Felipe St. NW, 505/933-5667, www.routesrentals.com, $60) offers "Biking Bad" tours every other Saturday.

A few other sights around town include:

- The **Dog House** hot dog stand, with its exceptionally fine neon sign, is at 1216 Central Avenue Southwest, near Old Town.

- **Los Pollos Hermanos** is actually Twisters, at 4257 Isleta Boulevard Southwest, but the PH logo is painted on the wall outside.

- Walt and Skyler's **A1A Car Wash** is at Menaul and Eubank (9516 Snow Heights Circle NE, for your GPS).

- **The Grove** (600 Central Ave. SE), where Lydia loved her Stevia too well, is a popular café downtown.

As souvenirs of your Albuquerque visit, **Great Face & Body** (123 Broadway SE, 505/404-6670) sells "Bathing Bad" blue bath salts. **The Candy Lady** (424 San Felipe St. NW, 505/243-6239), which cooked the prop "meth" for a few episodes, sells its blue hard candy in zip-top plastic bags.

Better Call Saul's ties to the city are just as strong, though Jimmy McGill (aka Saul) and his escapades have not yet been immortalized with an exclusive tour.

tiny adobe **Capilla de Nuestra Señora de Guadalupe** (404 San Felipe St. NW) is tucked off a small side alley. It's dedicated to the first saint of Mexico; her image dominates the wall facing the entrance. The dimly lit room, furnished only with heavy carved seats against the walls, is still in regular use (although, unfortunately, a fire put an end to lit votive candles, and the image of the Virgin was repainted in a more modern style). Despite the building's diminutive size, it follows the scheme of many traditional New Mexican churches, with a clerestory that allows sunlight to shine down on the altar.

¡Explora!

A 50,000-square-foot complex adjacent to the natural history museum, **¡Explora!** (1701 Mountain Rd. NW, 505/224-8300, www.explora.us, 10am-6pm Mon.-Sat., noon-6pm Sun., adults $8, children $4) is dedicated to thrilling—and educating—with science. Its colorful geodesic-dome top reflects the enthusiastic and engaging tone within; inside, more than 250 interactive exhibits demonstrate the scientific principles behind everything from high-wire balancing to optical illusions. Kids can even build robots using Lego systems,

and, since this is the desert, a whole section is dedicated to water.

Museum of Natural History and Science

The **Museum of Natural History and Science** (1801 Mountain Rd. NW, 505/841-2800, www.nmnaturalhistory.org, 9am-5pm daily) is a large exhibit space containing three core attractions: a **planetarium** and observatory, a wide-format **theater** screening the latest vertigo-inducing nature documentaries, and an **exhibit** of Earth's geological history. Admission is $8 to the main exhibit space or $7 each for the planetarium and the theater, though there are discounts if you buy tickets to more than one.

The museum section devotes plenty of space to the crowd-pleasers: dinosaurs. New Mexico has been particularly rich soil for paleontologists, and several of the most interesting finds are on display, such as *Coelophysis* and *Pentaceratops*. In addition, the *Startup* exhibit details the early history of the personal computer in Albuquerque and elsewhere. The show was funded by Paul Allen, who founded Microsoft here with Bill Gates, *then* moved to Seattle, Washington.

inside the diminutive Capilla de Nuestra Señora de Guadalupe

San Felipe de Neri Church

Established in 1706 along with the city itself, **San Felipe de Neri Church** (2005 N. Plaza St. NW) was originally built on what would become the west side of the plaza—but it dissolved in a puddle of mud after a rainy season in 1792. The replacement structure, on the north side, has fared much better, perhaps because its walls, made of adobe-like *terrones* (sun-dried bricks cut out of sod) are more than five feet thick. As they have for two centuries, local parishioners attend Mass here, which is conducted three times a day, once in Spanish.

Like many religious structures in the area, this church received a late-19th-century makeover from Eurocentric bishop Jean-Baptiste Lamy of Santa Fe. Under his direction, the place got its wooden folk Gothic spires, as well as new Jesuit priests from Naples, who added such non-Spanish details as the gabled entrance and the widow's walk. The small yet grand interior has brick floors, a baroque gilt altar, and an elaborate pressed-tin ceiling with Moorish geometric patterns. A tiny **museum** (9:30am-5pm Mon.-Sat., free), accessible through the gift shop, contains some historic church furnishings.

Turquoise Museum

The **Turquoise Museum** (2107 Central Ave. NW, 505/247-8650, tours 11am and 1pm Mon.-Sat., $10) is much more substantial than it looks from its strip-mall facade. Exhibits present the geology and history of turquoise, along with legendary trader J. C. Zachary's beautiful specimens from all over the world. But most folks can't help but think how this relates to all the jewelry they plan to buy. So come here to learn the distinction between "natural" and "real" turquoise and arm yourself for the shopping ahead. Admission is by **guided tour** only (1.5 hours).

DOWNTOWN

Albuquerque's **downtown** district, along Central Avenue between the train tracks and Marquette Avenue, was once known as bustling New Town, crowded with mule-drawn streetcars, bargain hunters, and wheeler-dealers from the East Coast. At Central Avenue and 4th Street, two versions of Route 66 intersect. When the original highway was commissioned in 1926, the road from Chicago to the West Coast ran along 4th Street; after 1937, the route was smoothed so that it ran east-west along Central. The route brought more business, but spread it through the city: In the

San Felipe de Neri Church

Downtown Albuquerque

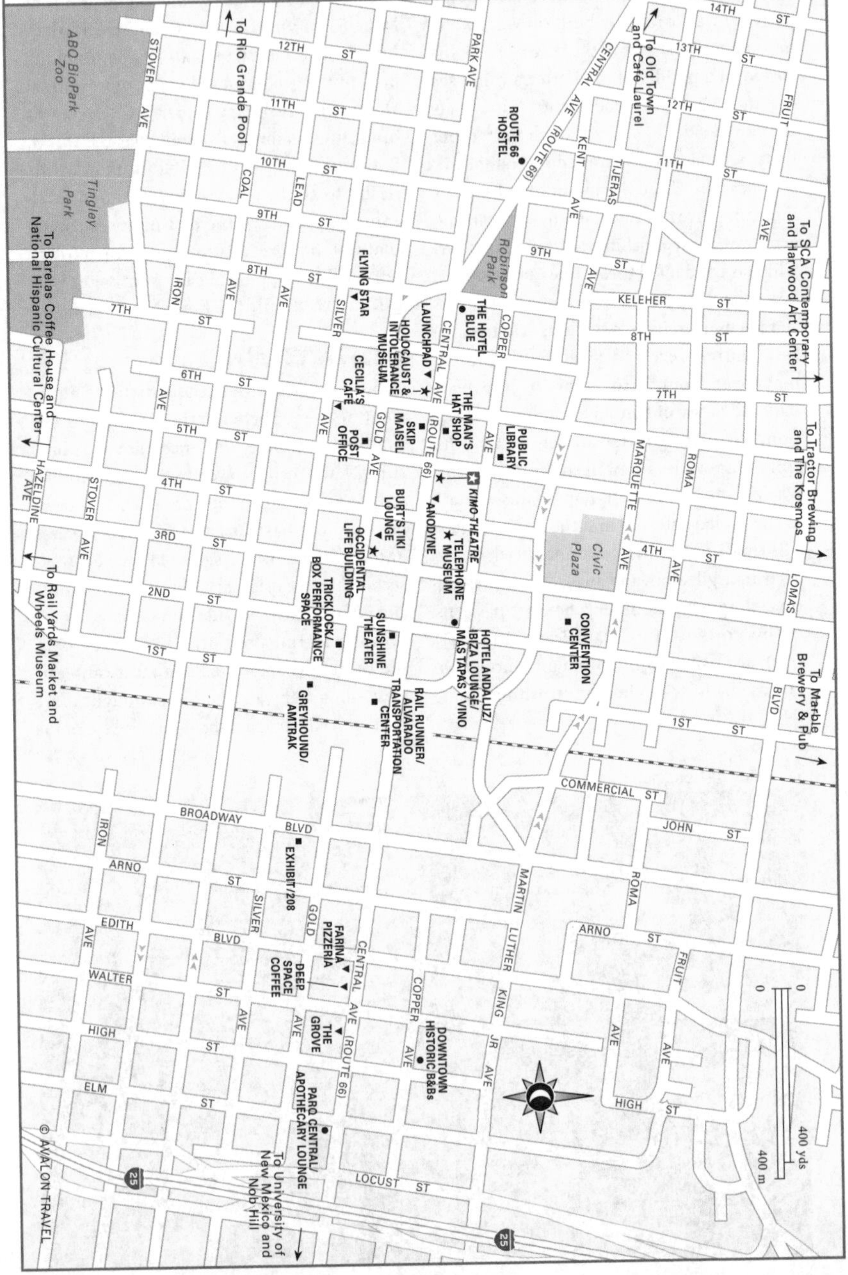

To Rio Grande Pool
To Old Town and Café Laurel
ABQ BioPark Zoo
Tingley Park
To Barelas Coffee House and National Hispanic Cultural Center
To Rail Yards Market and Wheels Museum
To SCA Contemporary and Harwood Art Center
To Tractor Brewing and The Kosmos
To Marble Brewery & Pub
To University of New Mexico and Nob Hill
ROUTE 66 HOSTEL
Robinson Park
THE HOTEL BLUE
FLYING STAR
LAUNCHPAD
HOLOCAUST & INTOLERANCE MUSEUM
CECILIA'S CAFÉ
THE MAN'S HAT SHOP
SKIP MAISEL
POST OFFICE
PUBLIC LIBRARY
KIMO THEATRE
ANODYNE
BURT'S TIKI LOUNGE
OCCIDENTAL LIFE BUILDING
TELEPHONE MUSEUM
Civic Plaza
CONVENTION CENTER
HOTEL ANDALUZ/ IBIZA LOUNGE/ MÁS TAPAS Y VINO
SUNSHINE THEATER
TRICKLOCK/ BOX PERFORMANCE SPACE
RAIL RUNNER/ ALVARADO TRANSPORTATION CENTER
GREYHOUND/ AMTRAK
EXHIBIT/208
FARINA PIZZERIA
DEEP SPACE COFFEE
THE GROVE
DOWNTOWN HISTORIC B&Bs
PARQ CENTRAL/ APOTHECARY LOUNGE
CENTRAL AVE (ROUTE 66)
14TH ST
13TH ST
12TH ST
11TH ST
10TH ST
9TH ST
8TH ST
7TH ST
6TH ST
5TH ST
4TH ST
3RD ST
2ND ST
1ST ST
STOVER AVE
PARK AVE
COAL AVE
LEAD AVE
IRON AVE
SILVER AVE
GOLD AVE
COPPER AVE
KENT AVE
TIJERAS AVE
FRUIT AVE
KELEHER
MARQUETTE AVE
ROMA AVE
LOMAS BLVD
HAZELDINE AVE
COMMERCIAL ST
JOHN ST
BROADWAY BLVD
ARNO ST
EDITH BLVD
WALTER ST
HIGH ST
ELM ST
LOCUST ST
MARTIN LUTHER KING JR AVE
0 400 yds
0 400 m
25
© AVALON TRAVEL

the iconic facade of the KiMo Theatre

505/768-3522 or 505/768-3544, www.cabq.gov/kimo). In 1927, local businessman and Italian immigrant Carlo Bachechi hired Carl Boller, an architect specializing in movie palaces, to design this marvelously ornate building. Boller was inspired by the local adobe and native culture to create a unique style dubbed Pueblo Deco—a flamboyant treatment of Southwestern motifs, in the same vein as Moorish- and Chinese-look cinemas of the same era. The tripartite stucco facade is encrusted with ceramic tiles and Native American iconography (including a traditional Navajo symbol that had not yet been appropriated by WWII Germany's Nazi Party when the KiMo was built).

To get the full effect, take a **self-guided tour** (11am-8pm Wed.-Sat., 11am-3pm Sun.) of the interior to see the cow-skull sconces and murals of pueblo life; enter through the business office, just west of the ticket booth.

Occidental Life Building

On Gold Avenue at 3rd Street, the one-story **Occidental Life Building** is another of Albuquerque's gems, built in 1917 by H. C. Trost, whose work defines downtown El Paso, Texas. With its ornate facade of white ceramic tile, it looks a bit like the Doge's Palace in Venice rendered in marshmallow fluff. After a 1933 fire, the reconstructing architects added even more frills, such as the crenellations along the top. The entire building is surfaced in white terra-cotta; the tiles were made in a factory in Denver, Colorado, that sprayed the ceramic glaze onto concrete blocks, each individually molded and numbered, and the blocks were then assembled in Albuquerque according to an overall plan. (The building is owned by local-boy-made-good Jared Tarbell, a cofounder of Etsy, the online craft site. Tarbell's toy- and art-manufacturing company, Levitated, is located nearby, on Silver Avenue at 7th Street.)

1950s and 1960s, shopping plazas farther east in Nob Hill and the Northeast Heights drew business away from downtown. By the 1970s, the neighborhood was a wasteland of government office buildings. Thanks to an aggressive urban-renewal scheme initiated in 2000, downtown has regained some of its old vigor, and Central is now a thoroughfare best known for its bars.

By day there aren't many attractions to detain you, but you can join a walking tour with **Albuquerque Tourism & Sightseeing Factory** (219 Central Ave. NW, 505/200-2642, www.atsfworks.com), the friendly, informed crew that also runs the city trolley tours. Walks include Albu-Quirky (1.5 hours, $20), a daytime stroll pointing out architectural details and the odd stories behind them, and Albucreepy (1.5 hours, $20), a nighttime ghost tour.

★ KiMo Theatre

Albuquerque's most distinctive building is the **KiMo Theatre** (423 Central Ave. NW,

Museums

Production value is basic at the storefront **Holocaust and Intolerance Museum**

(616 Central Ave. SW, 505/247-0606, 11am-3:30pm Tues.-Sat., free), but the message is compelling. Displays cover not just World War II, but also the Armenian genocide, actions against Native Americans, and a new permanent exhibit on African Americans and slavery. Nearby, the surprisingly detailed three-story **Telephone Museum** (110 4th St. NW, 505/841-2932, 10am-2pm Mon., Wed., and Fri., $2) is worth a visit—if you happen to get there during its laughably narrow open time.

The **Wheels Museum** (1100 2nd St. SW, 505/243-6269, www.wheelsmuseum.org, donation) is dedicated to Western transportation, with a special focus on trains—fitting its location in the city rail yard. It displays some great interviews with former workers in the old Santa Fe workshops. At the time of writing, the place was under development with no set hours; call for regular hours. It is somewhat reliably open during the **Rail Yards Market** (777 1st St. SW, www.railyardsmarket.org, 10am-2pm Sun. May-Oct.), however; model-train fans will be well rewarded.

THE UNIVERSITY AND NOB HILL

When it was established in 1889, what's now the state's largest university was only a tiny outpost on the far side of the railroad tracks. Surrounding the campus, which sprawls for blocks, is the typical student-friendly scrum of cheap-pizza places and dilapidated bungalow rentals. The next neighborhood east along Central is Nob Hill, developed around a shopping plaza in the late 1940s and still showing that decade's distinctive style in marquees and shop facades.

The University of New Mexico

More than 25,000 students are enrolled at the **University of New Mexico** (UNM) campus, the core of which is bounded by Central Avenue and University Boulevard. The school's oldest buildings are a distinct pueblo-inspired style, commissioned in the early 1900s by college president William George Tight. Trustees later fired Tight in part for his non-Ivy League aesthetics, but the style was in motion. Pueblo Revival pioneer John Gaw Meem carried on the vision through the 1940s, and even with contemporary structures now set among the original halls, it's still a remarkably harmonious vision, uniting the pastoral sanctuary feel of the great East Coast campuses with a minimalist interpretation of native New Mexican forms.

Visitors can park in a complex just inside the UNM campus across from Cornell Street. The info center, where you can pick up a detailed map, is in the southwest corner of the structure. Just across the way, the **University Art Museum** (203 Cornell Dr. NE, 505/277-4001, www.unmartmuseum.org, 10am-4pm Tues.-Fri., 10am-8pm Sat., $5 donation) displays treasures from the permanent fine art collection of more than 30,000 pieces from all over the globe.

Elsewhere on the grounds, you'll see such classic Meem buildings as **Mesa Vista Hall** and **Zimmerman Library.** Rest up at the bucolic duck pond, then head for the **Maxwell Museum of Anthropology** (off University Blvd., north of M. L. K. Jr. Blvd., 505/277-4405, 10am-4pm Tues.-Sat., free), a Meem building designed as the student union. The museum has a strong overview of Southwestern Indian culture, numerous Native American artifacts from university-sponsored digs all over the state, and a surprisingly extensive collection of objects depicting cultures from around the world.

Nob Hill

At Girard Street, a neon-trimmed gate marks the start of the **Nob Hill** district, which extends east along Central Avenue about 10 blocks to Washington Boulevard. The area began to grow after 1937, when Route 66 was rejiggered to run along Central. The Nob Hill shopping plaza, at Central and Carlisle, signaled the neighborhood's success when it opened as the glitziest shopping district in town a decade later. It's still a lively district,

University Area

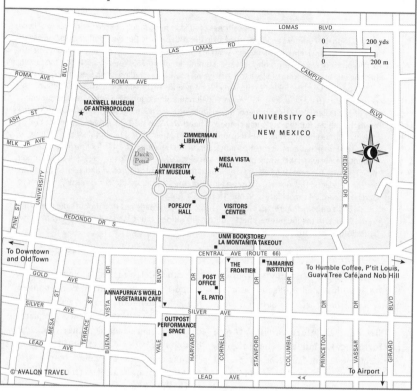

with more refined bars and restaurants than downtown, and good, quirky shops.

The area went through a slump from the 1960s through the mid-1980s, but it's again lined with brightly painted facades and neon signs, making it a lively district where the quirk factor is high—whether you want designer underwear or an antique Mexican mask, you'll find it here. Head off of Central on Monte Vista and keep an eye out for the **Bart Prince House** (3501 Monte Vista Blvd. NE), the home and studio of one of the city's most celebrated contemporary architects, whose favorite forms seem to be spaceships and antennae—it's the residential counterpart to the eccentric businesses that flourish in this area.

NORTH VALLEY

The stretch of the river north of Central is one of Albuquerque's prettier areas, shaded with cottonwoods and spotted with patches of farmland. The scenic route is Rio Grande Boulevard; the commercial strip is 4th Street.

Indian Pueblo Cultural Center

Just north of I-40 from Old Town, the **Indian Pueblo Cultural Center** (2401 12th St. NW, 505/843-7270, www.indianpueblo.org, 9am-5pm daily, $8.40) is a must-visit before heading to any of the nearby Indian communities. The horseshoe-shaped building (modeled after the Pueblo Bonito ruins in Chaco Canyon in northwestern New Mexico) houses a large museum that traces the history of the

The Rebirth of Route 66

Route 66 is one of the biggest repositories of American nostalgia, a little neon ribbon of cool symbolizing the country's economic growth in the 20th century. But the "mother road," on which so many Dust Bowl refugees made their way west and so many beatniks got into their grooves, officially no longer exists; the highway was decommissioned in 1985. You can still follow the brown historic-marker signs from Chicago to Los Angeles, however, including along **Central Avenue.**

The businesses that thrived in the early highway era—especially the numerous 1940s motor courts—fell on hard times long ago. As part of Albuquerque's aggressive urban-renewal program, city planners demolished a number of motels, leaving dead neon signs standing like tombstones amid the rubble. But the city had a change of heart with the 1939 **De Anza,** on the east edge of Nob Hill, and bought it in 2003 to protect, among other things, beautiful interior murals by American Indian painters. In the meantime, *Burqueños* developed fresh affection for their neon-lit heritage. So, when the owner of the **El Vado Motel,** near Old Town, threatened his vintage property with the wrecking ball, the city bought that too. At the time of writing, construction was well under way on El Vado to turn it into a motor-themed boutique hotel complete with a taproom and restaurants. A similar fate is planned for the De Anza.

The city's ongoing interest in preserving its Route 66 heritage just might yield similar rebirths in the future. In the meantime, check out the self-guided tour of the fabled highway at www. visitalbuquerque.org.

first settlers along the Rio Grande. Renovated in 2016, it is illustrated with some beautiful artifacts and showcases the best craftwork from each pueblo.

The central plaza hosts **dance performances** (11am and 2pm Sat.-Sun. Apr.-Oct., noon Sat.-Sun. Nov.-Mar.), one of the only places to see them outside of the pueblos themselves. The extensively stocked gift shop is a very good place to buy pottery and jewelry; you can also have a lunch of stew and fry bread at the Pueblo Harvest Café. Don't miss the south wing, which contains a gallery for contemporary art. At the information desk, check on ceremony schedules and get directions to the various pueblos.

Rio Grande Nature Center State Park

Explore a secluded wetland landscape at the **Rio Grande Nature Center State Park** (2901 Candelaria St. NW, 505/344-7240, www. emnrd.state.nm.us, 8am-5pm daily, $3/car). The sleek, concrete **visitors center** (10am-5pm daily) houses an exhibit on water conservation and river ecology, while just beyond is a comfortable glassed-in "living room," where

you can watch birds on the pond from the comfort of a lounge chair, with the outdoor sounds piped in through speakers.

Outside, several **paved trails** run across irrigation channels and along the river, shaded by towering cottonwoods. In the spring and fall, the area draws all manner of migrating birdlife. Borrow binoculars from the staff if you want to scout on your own, or join one of the frequent **nature walks** (including full-moon tours) that take place year-round.

Los Ranchos and Corrales Scenic Byway

For a pretty drive (or bike ride) through these villages that have been all but consumed by greater Albuquerque, head north from Old Town on Rio Grande Boulevard; you first reach **Los Ranchos,** then cross the river at Alameda to Corrales Road and continue up the west bank. These districts remain pockets of pastoral calm, a practical melding of old agricultural heritage with modern suburban trappings.

The only real sights are in central **Corrales,** two blocks west of the main road. The folk Gothic **Old San Ysidro Church**

(505/897-1513, 1pm-4pm Sat.-Sun. June-Oct.) stands where the center of the village was in 1868, when its bulging adobe piers were first constructed. Every spring, the church gets a fresh coat of mud from the community. Across the road, **Casa San Ysidro** (973 Old Church Rd., 505/898-3915, www.cabq.gov/museum, $4) was the home of obsessive collectors Alan and Shirley Minge. While they lived in the place, 1952-1997, they heated with firewood and squirreled away New Mexican antiques and craftwork. It is a lovingly preserved monument to a distinct way of life. The Albuquerque Museum gives **tours** (10:30am, noon, and 1:30pm Tues.-Sat. June-Aug.) of the interior with its beautiful brickwork and wood carving; tours are less frequent September-November and February-May (9:30am and 1:30pm Tues.-Fri., 10:30am, noon, and 1:30pm Sat.). You can just turn up, but it's a good idea to call to confirm the times.

ALBUQUERQUE METRO AREA

Beyond Central Avenue, Albuquerque is largely a haze of nondescript houses and shopping centers built during the 1960s and later—decades one local journalist dubbed the city's Asphalt Period. A few sights are well worth seeking out, however.

National Hispanic Cultural Center

Just south of downtown (but not quite walking distance), the modern **National Hispanic Cultural Center** (1701 4th St. SW, 505/246-2261, www.nhccnm.org) lauds the cultural contributions of Spanish speakers the world over. It has had a positive influence in the down-at-the-heels district of Barelas (even the McDonald's across the street mimics its architecture), but numerous houses—occupied by Hispanics, no less—were demolished for its construction. One woman refused the buyout, and her two small houses still sit in the parking lot, a kind of exhibit of their own.

The central attraction is the **museum** (10am-5pm Tues.-Sun., $6), which shows work ranging from the traditional *bultos* and *retablos* by New Mexican craftspeople to contemporary painting, photography, and even furniture by artists from Chile, Cuba, Argentina, and more. If you can, visit on Saturday or Sunday, when the *torreón* (tower) is open (noon-5pm) to show Frederico Vigil's amazing fresco *Mundos de Mestizaje,* a decadelong project depicting the many strands—Arab, Celtic, African—that have contributed to Hispanic culture today.

Adjacent to the museum is the largest Hispanic genealogy library in existence, as well as the giant **Roy E. Disney Center for Performing Arts.**

National Museum of Nuclear Science & History

The spiffy **National Museum of Nuclear Science & History** (601 Eubank Blvd. SE, 505/245-2137, www.nuclearmuseum.org, 9am-5pm daily, $12) covers everything you wanted to know about the nuclear era, from the development of the weapon on through current energy issues. Exhibits cover the ghastly elements of the atomic bomb, but also wonky tech details (check out the display of decoders set in suitcases for emergency deployment) and pop-culture artifacts, such as "duck and cover" films from the Cold War. Don't miss the beautiful posters by Swiss American artist Erik Nitsche.

★ Sandia Peak Tramway

The longest tramway of its type in the world, the **Sandia Peak Tramway** (505/856-7325, www.sandiapeak.com, $1 parking, $25 round-trip, $15 one-way) whisks passengers 2.7 miles and 4,000 feet up, along a continuous line of Swiss-made cables. The ride from Albuquerque's northeast foothills to the crest takes about 15 minutes; the view of the cityscape and beyond along the way can be breathtaking. It's a convenient way to get to the ski area in winter too, and in summer and fall, you can hike along the ridgeline a few miles to the visitors center. There's a so-so restaurant at the top and a small exhibit about local flora and fauna. The service runs frequently year-round (9am-9pm daily June-Aug., 9am-8pm Wed.-Mon., 5pm-8pm Tues. Sept.-May)—but check the website for periodic maintenance closures in fall and spring.

At the base of the tram, there's a small, free museum about skiing in New Mexico, and even from this point, the view across the city is very good. The remodeled Mexican restaurant here, **Sandiago's** (38 Tramway Rd. NE, 505/856-6692, 11am-9pm Mon., Wed.-Sun., 4:30pm-9pm Tues., $14-28), has morphed into a sophisticated choice for a sunset margarita—the cucumber spritzer is especially refreshing in the summer months.

★ Petroglyph National Monument

Albuquerque's west side is marked by the black boulders of **Petroglyph National Monument,** some of which are the canvas for 20,000 carved lizards, birds, and assorted other beasts. Most of the images, which were created by chipping away the dark "varnish" of the volcanic rock to reach the paler stone beneath, are 400-700 years old, while others may date back three millennia. A few later examples of rock art include Maltese crosses made by Spanish settlers and initials left by explorers (not to mention a few by idle teenagers in more recent years).

Stop in first at the **visitors center** (Unser Blvd. at Western Tr., 505/899-0205, www.nps.gov/petr, 8am-5pm daily) for park maps, flyers on flora and fauna, and general orientation. From here, you will have to drive to the major trails that crisscross the monument's 7,500 acres: **Boca Negra Canyon,** a short, paved loop and the only fee area ($1/car on weekdays, $2 on weekends); **Piedras Marcadas Canyon,** a 1.5-mile unpaved loop; and **Rinconada Canyon,** an out-and-back hike (2.2 miles round-trip) that can be tedious going in some spots because the ground is sandy. The clearest, most impressive images can be found here, in the canyon at the end of the trail. Everywhere in the park area, keep an eye out for millipedes, which thrive in this environment; dead, their curled-up shells resemble the spirals carved on the rocks—coincidence?

For the best overview (literally) of this area's geology, head for the back (west) side of the parkland, the **Volcanoes Day Use Area** (9am-5pm daily), where three cinder cones mark Albuquerque's western horizon. Access is via Atrisco Vista Boulevard (exit 149) off

Spectacular views await on the Sandia Peak Tramway.

I-40; turn right (east) 4.3 miles north of the highway at a dirt road to the parking area.

From this vantage point, you can look down on the lava "fingers" that stretch east to form the crumbled edges of the escarpment where the petroglyphs are found. The fingers were formed when molten rock flowed between sandstone bluffs, which later crumbled away. The volcanoes were last reported emitting steam in 1881, though a group of practical jokers set smoky fires in them in the 1950s, briefly convincing city dwellers of an impending eruption. But the peaks are not entirely dead: Patches of green plants flourish around the steam vents that stud the hillocks, particularly visible on the middle of the three volcanoes.

Anderson Abruzzo Albuquerque International Balloon Museum

Boosters of Albuquerque's hot-air balloon scene—which has been flourishing since the first rally in 1972—include locals Ben Abruzzo, Larry Newman, and Maxie Anderson, who in 1978 made the first Atlantic crossing by balloon in the *Double Eagle II* helium craft. Abruzzo and Anderson also crossed the Pacific and set a long-distance record (5,678 miles) in the *Double Eagle V.*

These pioneers are honored at the so-called **BaMu** (9201 Balloon Museum Dr. NE, 505/768-6020, www.balloonmuseum.com, 9am-5pm Tues.-Sun., $4), in Balloon Fiesta Park just off Alameda Boulevard. The displays are a great mix of historical background, interactive physics lessons, and inspiring footage of record-setting balloon ventures. As long as you don't dwell too long on the zeppelin exhibit, complete with china and tableware from the *Hindenburg,* you may come away sufficiently inspired by the grace of balloons to seek out a ride in one yourself.

Coronado Historic Site

Though named for Spanish explorer Francisco Vásquez de Coronado, who camped on this lush riverside spot during his 1540 search for gold, the **Coronado Historic Site** (485 Kuaua Rd., Bernalillo, 505/867-5351, 8:30am-5pm Wed.-Mon., $5) is actually a Native American relic, the partially restored pueblo of Kuaua (Tiwa for "evergreen"), inhabited between 1300 and the early 1600s. The centerpiece is one of the partially sunken kivas, or ceremonial chambers, inside which murals of life-size human figures and animals were

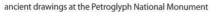

ancient drawings at the Petroglyph National Monument

Albuquerque's Hot-Air History

How did it come to be that one of the most iconic sights in Albuquerque is a 127-foot-tall Mr. Peanut figure floating in front of the Sandias? Albuquerque, it turns out, enjoys the world's most perfect weather for navigating hot-air balloons. A phenomenon called the Albuquerque Box, created by the steep mountains adjacent to the low river bottom, enables pilots to move at different speeds at different altitudes, and even to backtrack, if necessary. Combine that with more than 300 days of sunshine per year, and it's no wonder that now more than 700 balloons—including "special shapes" such as Darth Vader and Yoda—convene each October to show off their colors and compete in precision flying contests.

The city's air currents were discovered to be friendly to balloons for the first time in 1882. That was when an adventurous bartender piloted a hydrogen-filled craft into the sky as part of the New Town's Fourth of July celebrations, much to the delight of the assembled crowd, which had waited almost two days for *The City of Albuquerque*, as the balloon was dubbed, to fill. "Professor" Park Tassell, the showman pilot, went aloft alone and landed successfully; the only mishap was that a ballast sandbag was emptied on a spectator's head.

A balloon ride offers unparalleled views of the city.

Ninety years passed, and in 1972, Albuquerque again drew attention to this venerable pursuit. This was the year the first balloon fiesta was held, with 13 aircraft participating. The gathering, a rudimentary race, was organized as a publicity stunt for a local radio station's 50th-anniversary celebration. The spectacle drew 20,000 people, most of whom had never even seen a hot-air balloon before—but within a few short years, the event was internationally renowned, and the **Balloon Fiesta** has been a hugely popular annual event ever since.

discovered in the 1930s. The images were carefully salvaged, then reproduced in the kiva by Velino Herrera (Ma Pe Wi), a member of a key group of early American Indian figurative painters who also painted murals in the U.S. Department of the Interior in Washington DC.

With Herrera's reproductions in place, this is the only opportunity to witness the usually protected, sacred space of a kiva close to how it originally appeared. And once you've seen the complete images, it's easier to pick out the representations on the original frescoes mounted in the visitors center—some of the oldest examples of indigenous art on display anywhere in the United States.

Join a tour of the kiva, if possible—the guides add a lot to the story. On occasional

weekends, there are traditional craft demonstrations as well. And even if none of that is going on, this is a beautiful spot for a picnic. Facing the river and the mountains, with the city hidden from view behind a dense screen of cottonwoods, you get a sense of the lush, calm life along the Rio Grande in the centuries before the Spanish arrived. To reach the monument, exit I-25 in Bernalillo and head west on Highway 550; Kuaua Road is on your right, before the Santa Ana Star casino.

Gruet Winery

The Spanish planted the first vineyards in North America in New Mexico in the 17th century, and the industry persisted until a series of floods finally wiped out the vines by the 1920s. So New Mexico's current wine scene, while strong, is still somewhat young. One of the state's best wineries, **Gruet** (8400 Pan American Fwy. NE, 505/821-0055, www.gruetwinery.com, 10am-7pm Mon.-Fri., noon-7pm Sat., noon-6pm Sun.) began producing its excellent sparkling wines (the Gruet family hails from Champagne, France) only in 1987; look out especially for its nonvintage sparkling rosé, which is delicious and affordable. The tasting room serves five pours for $7; **tours** of the winery are at 2pm.

Entertainment and Events

NIGHTLIFE

Because Albuquerque doesn't have enough members of any one particular subculture to pack a whole bar, the city's drinking dens can host a remarkable cross section, and even the most chic-appearing places might see an absentminded professor and a veteran Earth Firster propping up the bar next to well-groomed professionals.

That said, the city's main bar and club scene, in a few square blocks of downtown, can feel a bit generic, with free-flowing beer specials for non-choosy students. It ends in a rowdy scene after closing time on weekends, when crowds spill out onto several blocks of Central that are closed to car traffic. So, although this area does have a few good bars, you'll find more interesting entertainment elsewhere.

Downtown

The **Hotel Andaluz lobby** (125 2nd St. NW, 505/923-9080) touts itself as "Albuquerque's living room"—hotelier Conrad Hilton's original vision for the place—and it's a comfy spot to sip cocktails and nibble Spain-inspired snacks, especially if you reserve one of the private booths ("casbahs") on the weekend.

A great spot to watch the Sandia Mountains turn pink at sunset, the **Apothecary Lounge** (806 Central Ave. SE, 505/242-0040, 3pm-10:30pm Mon.-Thurs., 3pm-1am Fri.-Sun.) is the rooftop bar at the Parq Central hotel in East Downtown. Fitting with the historic atmosphere of the hotel, the bar is good at vintage cocktails (if sometimes a bit slow).

The best all-purpose casual bars downtown are at the same address. Upstairs, **Anodyne** (409 Central Ave. NW, 505/244-1820, 4pm-2am Mon.-Sat., 7pm-midnight Sun.) is a long, wood-floored room filled with pool tables and thrift-store sofas. Choose from more than a hundred beers, and get some quarters to plug in to the good collection of pinball machines. Happy hour is 4pm-8pm Monday-Thursday, and till 9pm on Friday. Downstairs, the more cavernous **Sister** (505/242-4900, www.sister-thebar.com, 11am-2am Mon.-Sat., 11am-midnight Sun.) has tacos, live bands, and more pinball.

With free live music and a pool table, **Burt's Tiki Lounge** (515 Central Ave. NW, 505/247-2878, www.burtstikilounge.com, 4:30pm-2am Mon.-Sat., 4:30pm-midnight Sun.) has a funky feel and an eclectic bill, from British psychedelia to reggae.

The University and Nob Hill

In the Nob Hill shopping plaza, **Gecko's** (3500 Central Ave. SE, 505/262-1848, 11:30am-late Mon.-Fri., noon-late Sat.-Sun.) is a good place for finger food (anything from Thai curry shrimp to chipotle hot wings) and a drink in the sidewalk seats. Sporting its own breezy patio, **O'Niell's** (4310 Central Ave. SE, 505/255-6782, 11am-midnight daily) is a great Irish pub that draws a varied crowd, whether for quiz night or weekend folk bands; the kitchen is open until 11pm. There's a second location in the Northeast Heights with the same hours (3301 Juan Tabo Blvd. NE, 505/293-1122).

Albuquerque Beer Culture

Burque's beer scene is so lively that the *Albuquerque Journal* has a dedicated Brews News beat. These are some of the best spots in town; for more, see the **New Mexico Brewers Guild** (www.nmbeer.org). For car-free sampling, check out **The Hopper** trolley tour (www.abqtrolley. com; last Friday evening of the month; $20).

- **Il Vicino** (3403 Central Ave. NE, 505/266-7855, 11am-11pm Sun.-Thurs., 11am-11pm Fri.-Sat.): This Nob Hill pizza parlor has been brewing its own beer since 1994 and now has a large brewing facility, the **Canteen Brewhouse,** at 2381 Aztec Road Northeast (3pm-10pm Mon.-Thurs., 11am-1pm Fri.-Sat., noon-10pm Sun.).

- **Kellys Brew Pub** (3222 Central Ave. SE, 505/262-2739, 11am-10pm Mon.-Thurs., 11am-11pm Fri., 8am-11pm Sat., 8am-10pm Sun.): Another long-established Nob Hill brewery, set in an old car showroom. Great outdoor seating.

- **Matanza** (3225 Central Ave. NE, 505/312-7305, 4pm-9pm Mon., 11:30am-10pm Tues.-Thurs., 11:30am-11pm Fri.-Sat., 11:30am-9pm Sun.): The newest on the Nob Hill scene, with 100 craft beers on tap and tasty "sangwiches" and other bar food with New Mexican flair.

- **Marble Pub** (111 Marble Ave. NW, 505/243-2739, noon-midnight Mon.-Sat., noon-10:30pm Sun.): Pleasantly out of the downtown fray, with a dog-friendly outdoor area featuring eclectic bands.

- **Boese Brothers** (601 Gold Ave. SW, 505/382-7060, 3pm-midnight Sun.-Mon., 3pm-midnight Tues.-Thurs., 3pm-2am Fri., 1pm-2am Sat., 3pm-10pm Sun.): This downtown brewery, opened in 2015, is big and lively, usually with six house brews on tap.

- **Tractor Brewing**: This popular place has three locations: its brewery, in the industrial area north of downtown (1800 4th St. NW, 505/243-6752, 3pm-late Mon.-Thurs., 1pm-late Fri.-Sat., 1pm-midnight Sun.), a bar in Nob Hill (118 Tulane St. SE, 505/433-5654, noon-midnight Sun.-Thurs., noon-2am Fri.-Sat.), and a newer outpost in Four Hills (13170-C Central Ave. SE, 505/554-2462, 11am-midnight Sun.-Thurs., 11am-2am Fri.-Sat.). All three have low-fi live music.

- **La Cumbre Brewing** (3313 Girard Blvd. NE, 505/872-0225, noon-late daily): La Cumbre is in a fairly isolated industrial area, with only the occasional food truck for sustenance, but locals love this beer.

THE ARTS

Albuquerque has the liveliest theater scene in the Southwest, with over 30 troupes in action. The standbys are the black box **Vortex Theatre** (2900 Carlisle Blvd. NE, 505/247-8600, www.vortexabq.org), running since 1976, and the more standard repertory **Albuquerque Little Theatre** (224 San Pasquale St. SW, 505/242-4750, www. albuquerquelittletheatre.org), founded in 1930 and performing in an intimate 500-seat Works Progress Administration-era building. Up in the North Valley, the **Adobe Theater** (9813 4th St. NW, www.adobetheater.org) has been running in some form since 1957. At the time of writing, it was temporarily closed for renovations. It frequently features plays by local playwrights.

The 70-seat **Cell Theatre** (700 1st St. NW, www.liveatthecell.com) is home to the long-running FUSION, a theater company of professional union actors. It often runs recent Broadway dramas.

A more avant-garde group is the two-decade-old **Tricklock** (110 Gold Ave. SW, 505/414-3738, www.tricklock.com), which develops physically oriented shows at its "performance laboratory" downtown. It also hosts an international theater festival (in Jan. and Feb.). The neighboring **Box Performance Space** (114 Gold Ave. SW, 505/404-1578, www.theboxabq.com) hosts various improv groups and satirical comedians, and it conducts workshops.

Also see what **Blackout Theatre** (505/672-8648, www.blackouttheatre.com) is up to—it doesn't have its own space, but it mounts interesting shows in interesting places: improv Dickens, for instance, or an interactive alien invasion commemorating the UFO incident at Roswell. Other groups of note include the **Duke City Repertory Theatre** (505/797-7081, www.dukecityrep.com) and **Mother Road Theatre Company** (505/243-0596, www.motherroad.org).

CINEMA

Century 14 Downtown (100 Central Ave. SW, 505/243-9555, www.cinemark.com) and **AMC Albuquerque** (3810 Las Estancias Way SW, 505/544-2360, www.amctheatres.com) both devote most of their screens to blockbusters, while the latest indie and art films are shown at **The Guild** (3405 Central Ave. NE, 505/255-1848, www.guildcinema.com), a snug single screen in Nob Hill.

LIVE MUSIC

Albuquerque's arts scene graces a number of excellent stages. The most beautiful is the city-owned **KiMo Theatre** (423 Central Ave. NW,

505/768-3544, www.cabq.gov/kimo), often hosting locally written plays and dance, as well as the occasional musical performance and film screening.

Bigger classical and folkloric acts perform at the **Roy E. Disney Center for Performing Arts** at the National Hispanic Cultural Center (1701 4th St. SW, 505/724-4771, www.nhccnm.org), a modernized Mesoamerican pyramid that contains three venues, the largest of which is a 691-seat proscenium theater. This is the place to catch a performance by visiting or local flamenco artists—with the National Institute of Flamenco headquartered in Albuquerque, there's often someone performing.

UNM's **Popejoy Hall** (UNM campus, 505/277-3824, www.popejoyhall.com) hosts the New Mexico Symphony Orchestra (which also plays at the Rio Grande Zoo in the summer).

A more intimate classical event is **Chatter Sunday** (505/234-4611, www.chatterabq.org, 10:30am Sun., $15). Originally known as Church of Beethoven, this chamber-music show aims to offer all the community and quiet of church, with none of the religious overtones. It takes place at the funky coffeehouse **The Kosmos** (1715 5th St. NW), part of a larger warehouse-turned-art-studios

Sunshine Theater is a frequent stop of touring indie bands.

complex. The "service" lasts about an hour, with two musical performances, interspersed with a poem and a few minutes of silent contemplation. It's all fueled by free espresso.

Flamenco enthusiasts should check the schedule at **Casa Flamenca** (401 Rio Grande Blvd. NW, 505/247-0622, www.casaflamenca.org) in Old Town. The dance school in an old adobe house hosts a monthly *tablao*, in which local teachers and visiting experts perform.

For rock concerts, the biggest venue in town is **Isleta Amphitheater** (5601 University Blvd. SE, www.isletaamphitheater.net), with space for some 12,000 people. The next step down is one of the Albuquerque-area casinos, the ritziest of which is **Sandia Casino** (I-25 at Tramway, 800/526-9366, www.sandiacasino.com), which has a 4,000-seat outdoor amphitheater. **Isleta Casino** (11000 Broadway SE, 505/724-3800, www.isleta.com), not to be confused with the amphitheater, has a smaller indoor venue, as does Laguna Pueblo's **Route 66 Casino** (14500 Central Ave. SW, 866/352-7866, www.rt66casino.com).

Also see what's on at **El Rey Theater** (620 Central Ave. SW, 505/510-2582, www.elreytheater.com) and **Sunshine Theater** (120 Central Ave. SW, 505/764-0249, www.sunshinetheaterlive.com)—both converted movie houses, they have excellent sightlines. **Outpost Performance Space** (210 Yale Blvd. SE, 505/268-0044, www.outpostspace.org) books very good world music and dance acts. To catch touring indie rockers or the local crew about to hit it big, head to the very professional **Launchpad** (618 Central Ave. SW, 505/764-8887, www.launchpadrocks.com).

FESTIVALS AND EVENTS

The city's biggest annual event is the **Albuquerque International Balloon Fiesta** (505/821-1000, www.balloonfiesta.com, $10), nine days in October dedicated to New Mexico's official state aircraft, with more than 700 hot-air balloons of all colors, shapes, and sizes gathering at a dedicated park on the north side of town, west of I-25. During the

Christmas luminarias

fiesta, the city is packed with "airheads," who claim this is the best gathering of its kind in the world. If you go, don't miss an early morning mass ascension, when the balloons glow against the dark sky, then lift silently into the air in a great wave. Parking can be a nightmare—take the park-and-ride bus, or ride a bike (valet parking available!).

In April is the equally colorful **Gathering of Nations Powwow** (505/836-2810, www.gatheringofnations.com), the largest tribal get-together in the United States, with more than 3,000 dancers and singers in full regalia from over 500 tribes coming together at the Tingley Coliseum and Expo New Mexico. Miss Indian World earns her crown by showing off traditional talents such as spearfishing or storytelling.

The eclectic and never dull two-day world-music fest **¡Globalquerque!** (www.globalquerque.com) runs in mid-September. It draws top-notch pop and traditional performers from around the world as well as plenty of international arts and crafts and cuisine. Concerts take place at the National Hispanic Cultural Center.

Just after Labor Day, the state's agricultural roots get their due at the **New Mexico State Fair** (www.exponm.com), two weeks of fried

Ceremonial Dances

This is an approximate schedule for dances at Albuquerque-area pueblos. Pueblo feast days are always on the same date and generally open to all, but seasonal dances (especially Easter and other spring rituals) can vary, and are sometimes closed to visitors. Confirm details and start times with the **Indian Pueblo Cultural Center** (505/843-7270, www.indianpueblo.org) before setting out.

- **January 1:** Jemez: Los Matachines; Kewa (Santo Domingo, corn dance
- **January 6:** Most pueblos, various dances to honor new tribal officials
- **Easter:** Most pueblos, various dances
- **May 1:** San Felipe, Feast of San Felipe
- **Memorial Day weekend:** Jemez craft show and powwow
- **June 13:** Sandia, Feast of San Antonio
- **June 29:** Santa Ana and Kewa (Santo Domingo), Feast of San Pedro
- **July 14:** Cochiti, Feast of San Bonaventura
- **July 26:** Santa Ana, Feast of Santa Ana
- **August 2:** Jemez, Feast of Santa Persingula
- **August 4:** Kewa (Santo Domingo), Feast of Santo Domingo
- **August 10:** Jemez, Pueblo Independence Day and Fair
- **August 15:** Zia, Feast of the Assumption of Our Blessed Mother
- **August 28:** Isleta: Feast of San Agustín (ends September 4)
- **Labor Day:** Kewa (Santo Domingo), craft market
- **November 12:** Jemez, Feast of San Diego
- **December 12:** Jemez, Los Matachines
- **December 25:** Santa Ana, Kewa (Santo Domingo), and Zia, various dances
- **December 26-28:** Kewa (Santo Domingo), corn dance; also dances at most other pueblos

foods, prizewinning livestock, midway rides, and really excellent rodeos, which often end with shows by country music legends.

In early November, don't miss the **Marigold Parade** (505/363-1326, www.muertosymarigolds.org), celebrating the Mexican Day of the Dead and general South Valley pride. The parade is a procession of skeletons, cars bedecked in flowers, and a little civil rights activism.

For the **winter holiday season,** the city is trimmed with luminarias (paper-bag lanterns), especially in Old Town and the Country Club neighborhood just to the south. The Albuquerque Botanic Garden (www.abq.gov/biopark) is decked out with holiday lights and model trains for much of December, and ABQ Ride, the city bus service, offers a bus tour around the prettiest neighborhoods on Christmas Eve.

Shopping

Old Town and its environs are where you can pick up traditional American Indian jewelry and pottery for very reasonable prices, while **Nob Hill** is the commercial center of Albuquerque's counterculture, with body-piercing studios adjacent to comic book shops next to herbal apothecaries.

OLD TOWN

The galleries and gift shops around the plaza can blur together after just a little bit of browsing, but the **Blue Portal Gallery** (2107 Church St. NW, 505/243-6005, 10am-4:30pm Mon.-Sat.) is a nice change, with well-priced and often very refined arts and crafts, from quilts to woodwork, by Albuquerque's senior citizens. And the **street vendors** set up on the east side of the plaza are all artisans selling their own work, at fair prices.

For a great selection of interesting New Mexico gifts and books, as well as local herbal treatments, visit **Duran Central Pharmacy** (1815 Central Ave. NW, 505/247-4141, 8:30am-7pm Mon.-Fri., 8:30am-3pm Sat., 9am-3pm Sun.), just outside Old Town.

DOWNTOWN

An emporium of American Indian goods, **Skip Maisel's Indian Jewelry & Crafts** (510 Central Ave. SW, 505/242-6526, 9am-5:30pm Mon.-Sat.) feels like a relic from downtown's heyday. Whether you want a warbonnet, a turquoise-studded watch, or deerskin moccasins, it's all here in a vast, overstocked shop with kindly salespeople. Don't miss the beautiful murals above the display windows and in the foyer; they were painted in the 1930s by local Indian artists such as Awa Tsireh, whose work hangs in the New Mexico Museum of Art in Santa Fe.

Set in the old Santa Fe workshops south of downtown, **Rail Yards Market** (777 1st St. SW, www.railyardsmarket.org, 10am-2pm Sun. May-Oct.) is a festive gathering of arts and crafts, produce, snacks, and live music. It's a good place to shop for offbeat souvenirs—and it's a great chance to see inside the majestic old buildings where locomotives for the Santa Fe line were built from the ground up.

THE UNIVERSITY AND NOB HILL

Among the various quirky boutiques in this area, of note is **Absolutely Neon** (3903 Central Ave. NE, 505/265-6366, 11am-6pm Mon.-Sat.), a gallery of new and vintage signs. And on the east edge of Nob Hill is a slew of **antiques marts**.

NORTH VALLEY

For excellent crafts, head to **Shumakolowa Native Arts** (2401 12th St. NW, 505/843-7270, www.indianpueblo.org, 9am-5:30pm daily), the shop at the Indian Pueblo Cultural Center. Not only are prices reasonable, but the staff is happy to explain the work that goes into various pieces.

Los Poblanos Farm Shop (4803 Rio Grande Blvd. NW, 505/938-2192, 9am-5pm daily) sells soaps, bath salts, and lotions scented with the organic lavender grown in the adjacent field. It also stocks an excellently curated selection of garden gear, books, kitchen supplies, and locally made snacks.

ALBUQUERQUE METRO AREA

Every Saturday and Sunday, Albuquerque's **flea market** (505/315-7661, $5 parking) takes place at the fairgrounds (enter at Gate 1, on Central just west of Louisiana). It's an interesting outlet where you can pick up anything from new cowboy boots to loose nuggets of turquoise; socks and beef jerky are also well represented. Stop off at one of the myriad food stands for

The Albuquerque Art Scene

When it comes to art, the Duke City may not have the buzz or the wealth that's concentrated farther north in Santa Fe, but it does have DIY energy, refreshing diversity, and a long history, thanks to the highly respected fine arts program at the University of New Mexico. On the first Friday of every month, the citywide **Artscrawl** (www.artscrawlabq.org) keeps galleries and shops open late in Nob Hill, Old Town, and downtown. The rest of the time, check out these arts spaces and galleries:

Exhibit/208 (208 Broadway SE, www.exhibit208.com, 10am-4pm Thurs.-Sat.): Work by full-time artists, some well-known in the state. Openings are usually the second Friday evening of the month.

- **516 Arts** (516 Central Ave. SW, 505/242-1445, www.516arts.org, noon-5pm Tues.-Sat.): Polished downtown space with numerous international artists.

- **Harwood Art Center** (1114 7th St., 505/242-6367, www.harwoodartcenter.org, 9am-5pm Mon.-Thurs., 9am-4pm Fri.): Classes, exhibits, and special events, all with a strong community connection.

- **Mariposa Gallery** (3500 Central Ave. SE, 505/268-6828, 11am-6pm Mon.-Sat., noon-5pm Sun.): In Nob Hill, long established (since 1974) and eclectic, with jewelry, fiber art, and other crafts.

- **Matrix Fine Art** (3812 Central Ave. SE, 505/268-8952, 10am-4pm Tues., 10am-6pm Wed.-Sun.): In east Nob Hill, showing only New Mexico artists, usually figurative.

- **Richard Levy Gallery** (514 Central Ave. SW, 505/766-9888, 11am-4pm Tues.-Sat.): Ed Ruscha or John Baldessari alongside emerging artists.

- **SCA Contemporary** (401 2nd Street SW, 505/228-3749, www.scacontemporary.com, noon-5pm Thurs.-Fri.): Located in a former restaurant, the site is in the early phases of an ambitious plan that will add to its modernist exhibition space several artists' studios, a second exhibition hall, and a fabrication space.

- **Tamarind Institute** (2500 Central Ave. SE, 505/277-3901, tamarind.unm.edu, 9am-5pm Mon.-Fri.): Long-established and nationally renowned lithography center; gallery on the second floor shows expert prints.

- **Tortuga Gallery** (901 Edith Blvd. SE, 505/369-1648, www.tortugagallery.org, hours vary): Music, poetry, and more, with a super-grassroots vibe.

a snack—refreshing aguas frescas (fruit juices, in flavors such as watermelon and tamarind) and Indian fry bread are the most popular. It allegedly starts at 7am, but most vendors get rolling around 9am and go till a little after 4pm.

Sports and Recreation

From the river basin up to mountain peaks, Albuquerque has plenty to keep you active in the outdoors for days on end. Late summer (after rains have started and fire danger is past) and fall are the best times to head to the higher elevations on the Sandia Mountains. Once the cooler weather sets in, the scrub-covered foothills and the bare, rocky West Mesa are more hospitable. The valley along the Rio Grande, running through the center of the city, is remarkably pleasant year-round: mild in winter and cool and shady in summer. As everywhere in the desert, always pack extra layers of clothing and plenty of water before you set out, and don't go charging up Sandia Peak (10,678 feet above sea level) your first day off the plane.

★ BALLOONING

For most people, the Balloon Fiesta is a spectator event, but the truth is you can go up, up, and away yourself just about any day of the year, thanks to the ideal conditions nearly always present around Albuquerque. A trip is admittedly an investment (and you have to wake up well before dawn for sunrise trips), but there's no other ride quite like it and the views can forever change how you see the city. One of the longest established operations is **Rainbow Ryders** (505/823-1111, www.rain-bowryders.com, $159 pp). Typically, you're up in the balloon for an hour or so, depending on wind conditions, and you get a champagne toast when you're back on solid ground.

HIKING

Between the West Mesa and the East Mountains, there are plenty of day hikes to choose from. The least strenuous is the *bosque* (the wooded area along the Rio Grande), where level paths lead through groves of cottonwoods, willows, and olive trees. The **Rio**

Grande Nature Center State Park (2901 Candelaria St. NW, 505/344-7240, www.rgnc. org, 8am-5pm daily, $3/car) is the best starting point for any walk around the area.

On the east side, the easiest approach to the mountains is to take the tram to **Sandia Peak** or drive up the east face of the mountain via scenic byway Highway 536, aka the Crest Road, to the **Sandia Crest Visitor Center** ($3/car). The 1.6-mile **Crest Trail** links the two points (tram and visitors center), with possible smaller loops in between. The views are fantastic, and the river-stone Kiwanis Cabin, a Civilian Conservation Corps project on a cliff edge, makes a nice picnic destination about halfway along.

In the fall, a hike in **Fourth of July Canyon,** in the Manzano Mountains east of the city, is a wonderful place to see the leaves changing color.

For a little elevation gain, head to the Sandia foothills, ideal in the winter but a little hot in the summertime. The best access is at **Elena Gallegos Picnic Area** (7am-9pm daily Apr.-Oct., 7am-7pm daily Nov.-Mar., $1 weekdays, $2 weekends), east of Tramway Boulevard and north of Academy, at the end of Simms Park Road.

The foothills are also the starting point for the popular but tough **La Luz Trail,** a 7.5-mile ascent to the Sandia Crest Visitor Center. The trail has a 12 percent grade at certain points, and passes through four climate zones (pack lots of layers) as you climb 3,200 vertical feet. Near the top, you can take a spur that leads north to the Sandia Crest observation point or continue on the main trail south to the ski area and the Sandia Peak Tramway, which you can take back down the mountain. Ideally, you'd have someone pick you up at the bottom, because the 2.5-mile trail from the tram back to the trailhead has no shade. (You might be tempted to take the tram up and hike down, but the steep descent can be deadly to

Birding on the Peak

In the dead of winter, **Sandia Peak** does not seem hospitable to life in any form, much less flocks of delicate-looking birds the size of your fist, fluffing around cheerfully in the frigid air. But that's precisely what you'll see if you visit right after a big snowfall. These are rosy finches, a contrary, cold-loving variety (sometimes called "refrigerator birds") that migrate from as far north as the Arctic tundra to the higher elevations of New Mexico, which must seem relatively tropical by comparison.

What's special about Sandia is that it draws all three species of **rosy finch,** which in turn draws dedicated birders looking to add the finches to their life lists, and it's one of the few places to see them that's close to a city and accessible by car. So, if you see the finches—they're midsize brown or black birds with pink bellies, rumps, and wings—you'll probably also spy some human finch fans. But they might not have time to talk, as it's not unheard-of for the most obsessive birders— those on their "big year," out to spot as many species as possible in precisely 365 days—to fly in to Albuquerque, drive to the crest, eyeball the finches, and drive right back to the airport again.

toes and knees.) The La Luz trailhead ($3/car) is at the far north end of Tramway Boulevard, just before the road turns west.

BIKING

Albuquerque maintains a great network of paved trails in the city, and the mountains and foothills have challenging dirt tracks. The most visitor-friendly bike store in town is **Routes** (404 San Felipe St. NW, 505/933-5667, www.routesrentals.com, 8am-7pm Mon.-Fri., 7am-7pm Sat.-Sun. Mar.-Oct., 9am-6pm Mon.-Fri., 8am-6pm Sat.-Sun. Nov.-Feb., $20/4 hours, $35/day), which rents city cruisers, mountain bikes, and more at its handy location in Old Town; pickup and drop-off from hotels is free. It also runs fun daylong **bike tours** along the Rio Grande (from $30), and rents snowshoes ($15/day) in the winter.

Road Biking

Recreational cyclists should look no farther than the river, where the **Paseo del Bosque,** a 16-mile-long, completely flat biking and jogging path, runs through the Rio Grande Valley State Park. The northern starting point is at **Alameda/Rio Grande Open Space** (7am-9pm daily Apr.-Oct., 7am-7pm daily Nov.-Mar.) on Alameda Boulevard. You can also reach the trail through the **Rio Grande Nature Center** (www.rgnc.org, 8am-5pm

daily, $3/car), at the end of Candelaria, and at several other major intersections along the way. For details on this and other bike trails in Albuquerque, download a map from the city's bike info page (www.cabq.gov/bike), or pick up a free copy at bike shops around town.

Corrales, in the far North Valley, is also good for an afternoon bike ride: The speed limit on the main street is low, and you can dip into smaller side streets and bike along the acequias. The excellent and now mobile **Stevie's Happy Bikes** (505/897-7900, call for hours and location) rents comfy cruisers ($25/day) and even tandems ($35/day), and can advise on the best routes on and around the river.

A popular tour is up to **Sandia Peak** via the Crest Road on the east side—you can park and ride from any point, but cyclists typically start somewhere along Highway 14 north of I-40, then ride up Highway 536, which winds 13.5 miles along increasingly steep switch-backs to the crest. The **New Mexico Touring Society** (www.nmts.org) lists descriptions of other routes and organizes group rides.

Mountain Biking

Mountain bikers can take the Sandia Peak Tramway to the **ski area,** then rent wheels to explore the 30 miles of wooded trails. Bikes aren't allowed on the tram, though, so if you have your own ride, you can drive around the east side of the mountain.

Also on the east side of the mountains, a whole network of trails leads off Highway 337 (south of I-25), through **Otero Canyon** and other routes through the juniper-studded Manzanos. Or stay in the city and ride the popular 9.9 single track **Foothills Trail** in the Elena Gallegos Open Space Park. For longer cruises in the area, explore the **Sandia Foothills Trails,** a network of dirt tracks all along the edge of the Northeast Heights. Locals built a small but fun BMX terrain park at **Embudo Canyon;** park at the end of Indian School Road.

SWIMMING

Beat the heat at the **Rio Grande Pool** (1410 Iron Ave. SW, 505/848-1397, noon-5pm daily June-mid-Aug., $2.50), Albuquerque's nicest public place to take a dip; the outdoor 25-meter pool is shaded by giant cottonwoods.

WINTER SPORTS

Sandia Peak Ski Area (505/242-9052, www. sandiapeak.com, $55 full-day lift ticket) is open mid-December-mid-March, though it often takes till about February for a good base to build up. The 10 main trails, serviced by

four lifts, are not dramatic, but they are good and long. The area is open daily in the holiday season, then Wednesday-Sunday for the rest of the winter.

Sandia Peak also has plenty of opportunities for cross-country skiing. Groomed trails start from **Capulin Springs Snow Play Area** (9:30am-3:30pm Fri.-Sun. in winter, $3/car), where there are also big hills for tubing and sledding. Look for the parking lot nine miles up Highway 536 to the crest. Farther up on the mountain, **10K Trail** is usually groomed for skiers, as is a service road heading south to the upper tramway terminal; the latter is wide and relatively level, good for beginners. For trail conditions, call or visit the Sandia **ranger station** (505/281-3304) on Highway 337 in Tijeras.

SPAS

Betty's Bath & Day Spa (1835 Candelaria Rd. NW, 505/341-3456, www.bettysbath.com) is the place to get pampered, whether with a massage and a facial or with an extended dip in one of two outdoor communal hot tubs. One is co-ed and the other for women only; both have access to dry saunas and cold plunges—a bargain at just $12. Private reservations are available most evenings.

Routes rents bikes in Old Town and runs city cycling tours.

Closer to downtown, **Albuquerque Baths** (1218 Broadway NE, 505/243-3721, www.abq-baths.com) has similar facilities, though only one communal tub, which is solar-heated; the sauna is done in Finnish cedar. The reasonable rates ($15/two hours) include the use of robes and sandals, and massages are available too.

SPECTATOR SPORTS

Minor-league baseball thrives in Albuquerque, apparently all because of some clever name: The so-so Dukes petered out a while back, but a fresh franchise, under the name of the **Albuquerque Isotopes,** has been drawing crowds since 2003. It's hard to judge whether the appeal is the cool **Isotopes Park** (1601 Avenida Cesar Chavez NE, 505/924-2255, www.albuquerquebaseball. com), the whoopee-cushion theme nights, or just the name, drawn from an episode of *The Simpsons.* Regardless, a summer night under the ballpark lights is undeniably pleasant; it helps that you can usually get good seats for $15.

Burqueños also go crazy for UNM Lobos **basketball,** packing the raucous University Arena, aka **The Pit** (Avenida Cesar Chavez at University Blvd., 505/925-5626, www.golo-bos.com).

Food

Albuquerque has a few dress-up establishments, but the real spirit of the city's cuisine is in its lower-rent spots where dedicated owners follow their individual visions. The more traditional New Mexican places tend to be open only for breakfast and lunch, so plan accordingly.

OLD TOWN

Aside from the few recommended here, the restaurants in the blocks immediately adjacent to the Old Town plaza are expensive and only so-so; better to walk another block or two for real New Mexican flavor, or drive a short way west on Central.

New Mexican

Look behind the magazine rack at ★ **Duran Central Pharmacy** (1815 Central Ave. NW, 505/247-4141, 9am-6:30pm Mon.-Tues., 9am-8pm Wed.-Sun., $9, cash only), and you'll find an old-fashioned lunch counter. Regulars pack this place at lunch for all the New Mexican staples: huevos rancheros, green-chile stew, and big enchilada plates.

Mexican

In a shady Old Town courtyard, **Backstreet Grill** (1919 Old Town Rd. NW, 505/842-5434, 11am-9pm daily, $12) is a great place to rest your tourist feet and enjoy a New Mexican craft beer, and maybe a bowl of guacamole. For a full meal, though, you're better off elsewhere.

Cafés

Inside the Albuquerque Museum, **Slate Street Café** (2000 Mountain Rd. NW, 505/243-2220, 10am-2:30pm Tues.-Fri. and Sun., 10am-4pm Sat., $8-14) is great for coffee and cupcakes, as well as more substantial breakfast and lunch entrées, such as a seared salmon club with applewood bacon. Its larger, original location is at 515 Slate Ave. NW (505/243-2210).

A 10-minute walk from Old Town, **Golden Crown Panaderia** (1103 Mountain Rd. NW, 505/243-2424, 7am-8pm Tues.-Sat., 10am-8pm Sun., $4-16) is a real neighborhood hangout that's so much more than a bakery. Famous for its green-chile bread and *bizcochitos* (the anise-laced state cookie), it also does pizza with blue-corn or green-chile crust, to take away or to eat at the picnic tables out back. Wash it down with a coffee milkshake.

Diner

Built on the bones of an old fast-food joint, **Central Grill** (2056 Central Ave. SW, 505/554-1424, 6:30am-4pm Mon.-Sat., 6:30am-3pm Sun., $7) still does quick food, but with a fresher, more homemade feel. Like a good diner should, it serves breakfast all day, and real maple syrup is an option. Its daily special plate is usually a solid deal, with a main like barbecue chicken plus sides and a drink for around $9.

Fresh and Local

Founded in Santa Fe, **Vinaigrette** (1828 Central Ave. SW, 505/842-5507, 11am-9pm daily, $9-18) is an excellent "salad bistro" with more substantial plates than you might imagine—its apple-cheddar chop with arugula is especially satisfying and it has sandwiches such as a Reuben and turkey melt. It's a welcome spot of healthy eating around Old Town.

Steak

With a brown, windowless cinderblock facade and a package-liquor store in the front, **Monte Carlo Steakhouse** (3916 Central Ave. SW, 505/831-2444, 11am-10pm Mon.-Sat., $9-29) doesn't do itself any favors winning over new customers. That said, it's a wondrous time machine, lined with vintage Naugahyde booths and serving good, hearty food, with scant care for calorie counts. The prime-rib special Thursday-Saturday, a softball-size green-chile cheeseburger, and marinated pork kebab all come with delicious hand-cut fries. Greek ownership means you get a tangy feta dressing on your salad and baklava for dessert. And even though there's a full bar, you're still welcome to buy wine from the package store up front and have it with your dinner, for a nominal markup.

Italian

It's not necessarily a destination from elsewhere in the city, but **Old Town Pizza Parlor** (108 Rio Grande Blvd. NW, 505/999-1949, 11am-9pm Mon.-Sat., 11am-8pm Sun., $9-15) is an unpretentious, kid-friendly place to eat in the relative wasteland of Old Town, with generously topped pizzas, ultra-creamy pastas, dense calzones, and cheesy garlic fingers. The back patio is a welcomed bonus.

DOWNTOWN

While there's no shortage of bars in this area, there's not exactly a huge selection of places when it comes to finding a sit-down meal; thankfully, there are a few solid options.

New Mexican

Even though it's in the middle of Albuquerque's main business district, ★ **Cecilia's Café** (230 6th St. SW, 505/243-7070, 7am-2pm Mon.-Fri., 7:30am-2pm Sat.-Sun., $8-12) feels more like a living room than a restaurant. Maybe it's the woodstove in the corner—as well as the personal attention from Cecilia and her daughters and the food that's clearly made with care. The rich, dark-red chile really shines, elevating dishes such as a chorizo burrito, chicken enchiladas, and a sopaipilla burger.

Cafés

Deep Space Coffee (504 Central Ave. SW, 505/322-2812, 8am-8pm daily, $3) makes no bones about its dedication to serving seriously good coffee; its excellent hometown espresso blend makes this abundantly clear. It's a bright space, featuring works by local artists.

Breakfast and lunch are served throughout the day at the inviting **Café Laurel** (1433 Central Ave. NW, 505/259-2331, 8am-3pm Tues.-Fri., Sat.-Sun. 9am-2pm, $7-9), where you can choose from a long list of mouthwatering sandwiches, quiches, and salads; the "Burque Turkey"—roast turkey, Swiss cheese, avocado mash, and green chile on grilled sourdough is divine.

Fresh and Local

Past the railroad tracks in EDo (East Downtown), ★ **The Grove** (600 Central Ave. SE, 505/248-9800, 7am-4pm Tues.-Sat., 8am-3pm Sun., $6.25-13.50) complements its local-organic menu with big front windows facing

Green-chile stew is on the menu at The Frontier.

fraîche-chive dip for your crusts—it's the upscale version of the ranch dressing that's more commonly offered. There's often a beer-and-pizza combo special as well.

Spanish

Chef James Campbell Caruso made his name in Santa Fe as a maestro of Spanish cuisine. His Albuquerque outpost, **Más Tapas y Vino** (125 2nd St. NW, 505/923-9080, 6am-3pm and 5pm-9:30pm Sun.-Thurs., 6am-3pm and 5pm-10pm Fri.-Sat., $6-15 tapas, $26-39 mains), in the Hotel Andaluz, shows off many of his best dishes, but it's not quite as chummy as his other restaurants. If you're not also visiting Santa Fe and want a creative bite of Iberian goodness, including grilled octopus, or vegetarian paella, though, consider this a possible special-occasion meal. It also has happy hour from 4pm to 6pm daily.

THE UNIVERSITY AND NOB HILL

Thanks to the large student population, this area has several great and varied spots to grab a cheap bite; Nob Hill has some upscale options too.

New Mexican

You haven't been to Albuquerque unless you've been to ★ **The Frontier** (2400 Central Ave. SE, 505/266-0550, 5am-1am daily, $5-10), across from UNM. Everyone in the city passes through its doors at some point in their lives, so all you have to do is pick a seat in one of the five Western-themed rooms (Hmm, under the big portrait of John Wayne? Or maybe one of the smaller ones?) and watch the characters file in. You'll want some food, of course: a green-chile-smothered breakfast burrito filled with crispy hash browns, or a hamburger, or one of the signature cinnamon rolls, a deadly amalgam of flour, sugar, and some addictive drug that compels you to eat them despite all common sense.

Near the university, **El Patio** (142 Harvard Dr. SE, 505/268-4245, 8am-9pm Mon.-Thurs., 8am-9:30pm Fri.-Sat., 11am-9pm Sun., $8-15)

Central and a screened-in patio. The chalkboard menu features creative salads (mixed greens, roasted golden beets, asparagus, and almonds is one combo) as well as sandwiches and cupcakes; breakfast, with farm-fresh eggs and homemade English muffins, is served all day.

There are a number of **farmers markets** throughout the city; one of the largest is downtown at Robinson Park on Central Avenue at 8th Street (7am-noon Sat. May-Aug., 8am-1pm Sept.-Nov.). For other markets around the city, visit www.farmersmarketsnm.org.

Italian

A popular hangout for urban pioneers in the EDo neighborhood, ★ **Farina Pizzeria** (510 Central Ave. SE, 505/243-0130, 11am-9pm Mon., 11am-10pm Tues.-Fri., noon-10pm Sat., 5pm-9pm Sun., $8-16) has exposed brick walls and a casual vibe. The pies come out of the wood-fired oven suitably crisp-chewy and topped with seasonal veggies. Make sure you get a cup of the Gorgonzola-crème is the kind of old-reliable place that ex-locals get misty-eyed about after they've moved away. The green-chile-and-chicken enchiladas are high on many citywide-favorites lists and the Sunrise Burger—a hamburger with egg and bacon—makes a great case for kicking off your day with a large meat patty. It doesn't hurt that the setting, in an old bungalow with a shady outdoor space, feels like an extension of someone's home kitchen. The menu is more vegetarian-friendly than most New Mexican joints.

Cafés

Step in to **Flying Star Café** (3416 Central Ave. SE, 505/255-6633, 7am-9:30pm Sun.-Mon., 7am-10pm Tues.-Thurs., 7am-11pm Fri.-Sat., $11), and you'll likely be mesmerized by the pastry case, packed with triple-ginger cookies, lemon-blueberry cheesecake, and fat éclairs. But try to look up to appreciate the far-reaching menu: Asian noodles, hot and cold sandwiches, mac-and-cheese, and enchiladas sit alongside salads and shrimp tacos. The food isn't always quite as great as it looks, but with speedy service and locations all over town, it's a handy place to zip in or to lounge around (Wi-Fi is free).

Great single-source coffee, attentive baristas, and a smartly designed space give the Nob Hill institution ★ **Humble Coffee** (4200 Lomas Blvd. NE, 505/289-9909, 6am-6pm Mon.-Fri., 7am-6pm Sat.-Sun.) plenty of reasons to boast—the selection of fresh pastries and savory breakfast burritos only add to its considerable appeal.

Pick up goods for a picnic at **La Montañita Co-Op** (3500 Central Ave. SE, 505/265-4631, 7am-10pm Mon.-Sat., 8am-10pm Sun.), where quinoa salads and stuffed grape leaves are all the rage; look in the dairy section for "sampler" pieces of locally made cheese. There's a snacks-only operation in the **UNM Bookstore** (2301 Central Ave. NE, 505/277-9586, 7am-6pm Mon.-Fri., 10am-4pm Sat.), across from The Frontier.

Waffles sweet or savory are the thing at **Tia B's La Waffleria** (3710 Campus Blvd. NE,

505/492-2007, 8am-2pm daily, $8-10.50), set in a funky old house with front and back patios. Of course, you can get a blue-corn waffle with eggs and good hot chile—the adventurous can build their own, too.

Asian

The food at **Street Food Asia** (3422 Central Ave. SE, 505/260-0088, 11am-9pm Sun.-Thurs., 11am-10pm Fri.-Sat., $11-15.50) may not be as mind-blowing as it is in Asia, but there's something about its interior, with various cooking stations and lots of plastic, that does conjure a Bangkok mall food court. You can order noodles and other staples prepared in Thai, Vietnamese, Malaysian, and other styles; an authentic shaved-ice-and-bean dessert often comes free.

French

Sleek and modern **Frenchish** (3509 Central Ave. NE, 505/433-5911, 5pm-9pm Tues.-Sat., $18-32) has quickly built a reputation for serving French classics that look as good as they taste, and their personal touches shine on dishes such as a coffee-marinated beef tournedoes. The menu's not extensive and all the better for its focus. The three-course prix-fixe with a four-ounce filet is a bargain for $25.

A cozy restaurant with ample old-world charm, **P'tit Louis** (3218 Silver Ave. NE, 505/314-1110, 5:30pm-10pm Tues.-Wed., 11am-2:30pm and 5:30pm-10pm, Thurs.-Sat., 11am-2:30pm Sun.) serves familiar French fare such as steamed mussels, steak frites, and onion soup. There's little in the way of surprises, but the execution is first-rate and the atmosphere can't be beat. Don't leave without trying the perfectly executed crème brûlée, sure to give your meal a blissful closure.

Latin American

Guava Tree Café (118 Richmond Dr. SE, 505/990-2599, 11am-4pm Mon.-Sat., 11am-3pm Sun., $4.75-12.50) is a cheerful place serving succulent Cubano sandwiches, as well as pan-Central-American treats such as arepas, plus tropical fruit juices. It's very vegetarian-friendly, and the daily set lunch ($12.50) is good for bigger appetites.

NORTH VALLEY
New Mexican

For New Mexican food with a heavier American Indian influence, hit the **Pueblo Harvest Café** (2401 12th St. NW, 505/724-3510, 7am-9pm Mon. Sat., 7am-4pm Sun., $9-26), at the Indian Pueblo Cultural Center. The menu has standard burgers and fries, but specialties such as a buffalo meat loaf with a mango chipotle glaze and a mutton stew are rich and earthy and hard to find elsewhere. Breakfast is also good, with blue-corn chicken and waffles and a flavorful eggs Benedict among the standouts. There's live music Friday and Saturday evenings, as well as Sunday around noon.

★ **Mary & Tito's Café** (2711 4th St. NW, 505/344-6266, 9am-6pm Mon.-Thurs., 9am-8pm Fri.-Sat., $6-12) is *the* place to go for *carne adovada*, the dish of tender pork braised in red chile, particularly good in what the café calls a Mexican turnover (a stuffed sopaipilla). The meat is flavorful enough to stand alone, but the fruity, bright-red-chile sauce, flecked with seeds, is so good you'll want to put it on everything. This place is such a local icon, seemingly untouched since the 1980s (note the dusty-rose vinyl seats), it won a James Beard America's Classics award. Sadly, both Mary and Tito have passed on now, leaving the place ripe for a decline in standards; so far, though, it is holding strong.

Out in Corrales, dependable **Perea's Tijuana Bar and Restaurant** (4590 Corrales Rd., 505/898-2442, 11am-2pm Mon.-Sat., $7) is open only for lunch, but it's worth scheduling around if you know you'll be out this way. Everything's home-cooked, from Frito pie to *carne adovada*.

Cafés

There are two branches of **Flying Star** up this way: one in Los Ranchos (4026 Rio Grande Blvd. NW, 505/344-6714, 6:30am-9pm Mon.-Sat., 7am-9pm Sun., $11) and another in Corrales (10700 Corrales Rd., 505/938-4717, 6:30am-9:30pm Sun.-Thurs., 6:30am-10pm Fri.-Sat., $11).

La Montañita Co-Op (2400 Rio Grande Blvd. NW, 505/242-8800, 7am-10pm daily) also has a branch here, good for picnic goodies.

Fresh and Local

The restaurant at Los Poblanos Historic Inn, ★ **Campo** (4803 Rio Grande Blvd. NW, 505/344-9297, 5pm-9pm Wed.-Sun., $26), serves flawless food, a bit Mediterranean in style, but undeniably New Mexican in ingredients like heirloom beans. The short menu changes each night, based on available produce. Book well ahead—hotel guests get priority, so tables fill up fast.

Firmly ensconced as one of the city best and most inventive restaurants, ★ **Fork & Fig** (6904 Menaul Blvd. NE, 505/881-5293, 11am-9pm Mon.-Thurs., 11am-10pm Fri.-Sat.) was founded by Josh Kennon, a Le Cordon Bleu-trained chef from Deming, a few hours south of the city. His background and New Mexican heritage are reflected in unpretentious and irresistible sandwiches, burgers, salads, and wraps, such as The Fig, a burger with truffle fig aioli, bacon, and carmelized Swiss cheese, and a full-flavored Reuben with green-chile slaw. The atmosphere is industrial and modern, yet casual; reserve ahead if possible, as the space is compact and the word has long been out.

Featuring local and organic ingredients, **Seasonal Palate** (7600 Jefferson St. NE #2, 505/369-1046, 7:30am-2:30pm Mon.-Fri., $6.75-11) is a sunny bistro with a concise menu of refreshing salads, sandwiches, and soups. The kale super salad with shrimp is a steal at $9.50, while the veggie burger on a pretzel bun will tempt carnivores. For dessert, the homemade double-chocolate brownies are far too decadent to pass up.

Indian

Venerable **Annapurna's** (5939 4th St. NW, 505/254-2424, 8am-9pm Mon.-Sat.,

10am-8pm Sun., $6.25-13) is for some the city's de facto vegetarian option, partly due to its three branches, but mostly because of its extensive menu of meat-free dishes, such as the Yogi Bowl—veggies with rice or quinoa, a *dosa* crepe, and yogurt or chutney sauce.

ALBUQUERQUE METRO AREA

Great places to eat are scattered all over the city, often in unlikely looking strip malls. These places are worth making a trip for, or will provide a pick-me-up when you're far afield.

New Mexican

Cruise down by the rail yards south of downtown to find **El Modelo** (1715 2nd St. SW, 505/242-1843, 7am-7pm daily, $7), a local go-to for a hangover-curing chicharrón burrito, chile-smothered spareribs, or tamales for the whole family—you can order a single tamale or a whole platter of food. Because it's really a front for a tortilla factory, the flour tortillas are also particularly tender. If the weather's nice, grab a seat at a picnic table outside and watch the freight trains go by.

Just two blocks from the National Hispanic Cultural Center, popular **Barelas Coffee House** (1502 4th St. SW, 505/843-7577, 7:30am-3pm Mon.-Fri., 7:30am-2:30pm Sat., $7) is potentially confusing to the first-timer: The attraction is not coffee, but chile—especially the red, which infuses hearty, timeless New Mexican standards like posole, chicharrones, and menudo. The restaurant occupies

several storefronts, and even then, there's often a line out the door at lunchtime. But it's worth the wait—this is timeless food.

Fresh and Local

One-stop noshing can be done at **Green Jeans Farmery** (3600 Cutler Ave. NE, www.greenjeansfarmery.com), a kind of outdoor food court and general hangout spot built from shipping containers. Pick from tacos, big sandwiches, artisanal pizza, espresso, and an outpost of Santa Fe Brewing. It draws a nice cross section of the city's denizens.

Asian

Can't decide what kind of food you're craving? Cruise the aisles of **Talin Market World Food Fare** (88 Louisiana Blvd. SE, 505/268-0206, 8:30am-8pm Mon.-Sat., 9am-7pm Sun.), a megamarket near the fairgrounds that's stocked with items from Bombay to the United Kingdom. Its Asian stock is the largest, though, and you can get a variety of hot Laotian, Korean, and Filipino lunch items from the small cafeteria section in one corner and sweets such as pumpkin custard from the bakery. There's also a bubble-tea joint next door, and the parking lot draws a few food trucks.

Just across the parking lot from Talin is the excellent Vietnamese café **Coda Bakery** (230-C Louisiana Blvd. SE, 505/232-0085, 9am-7pm Mon.-Sat., $5), which specializes in banh mi sandwiches (try the peppery meatball) and also serves chewy-sweet coconut waffles and other treats.

Accommodations

Because Albuquerque isn't quite a tourist mecca, you can find some great-value hotels; you'll pay substantially less here than you would in Santa Fe for similar amenities, for example. The only time you'll need to book in advance is early October, during Balloon Fiesta (when prices are usually a bit higher).

UNDER $100

Funky and affordable, the **Route 66 Hostel** (1012 Central Ave. SW, 505/247-1813, www. route66hostel.com) is in a century-old house midway between downtown and Old Town and has been offering bargain accommodations since 1978. It's hardly modern and minimalist, but it's clean enough. Upstairs, along creaky-wood hallways, are private rooms ($25-35) with various configurations. Downstairs and in the basement area are single-sex dorms ($25 pp). Guests have run of the kitchen, and there's a laundry room and a place to lounge. The most useful city bus lines run right out front. Be sure to call and confirm before you arrive, as the front desk isn't always staffed.

The Hotel Blue (717 Central Ave. NW, 877/878-4868, www.thehotelblue.com, $69 s, $79 d) offers a solid value downtown. The rooms in this 1960s block are a slightly odd mix of cheesy motel decor (gold quilted bedspreads) and bachelor-pad flair (a gas "fireplace"), and the windows don't open. But the Tempur-Pedic beds are undeniably comfortable, and the low rates include breakfast, parking, and a shuttle to the airport. There's also a decent-size outdoor pool, open in summer. Request a room on the northeast side for a mountain view.

Central Avenue is dotted with motels, many built in Route 66's heyday. Almost all of them are unsavory, except for ★ **Monterey Non-Smokers Motel** (2402 Central Ave. SW, 505/243-3554, www.non-smokersmotel.com, $79 s, $85 d), which is as practical as its name implies. The place doesn't really capitalize on 1950s kitsch—it just offers meticulously clean, good-value rooms bereft of frills or flair. One large family suite has two beds and a foldout sofa. The outdoor pool is a treat, the laundry facilities

Sandia Peak Inn

are a nice bonus, and the location near Old Town is convenient.

A fully renovated motel on the west side, just over the river from Old Town, ★ **Sandia Peak Inn** (4614 Central Ave. SW, 505/831-5036, www.sandiapeakinnmotel.com, $62 s, $75 d) is named not for its proximity to the mountain, but its view of it. It's certainly the best value in this category, offering large, spotless rooms, all with bathtubs, fridges, microwaves, and huge TVs. Continental breakfast is included in the rate, and the proprietors are positively sunny. There's a small indoor pool and free Wi-Fi throughout.

On the north side of town, **Nativo Lodge** (6000 Pan American Fwy. NE, 505/798-4300, www.nativolodge.com, $89 d) is convenient for the Balloon Fiesta, an early start to Santa Fe, or a cheap off-airport rental-car pickup, as a Hertz office is within walking distance. The price is great for this level of comfort and style, with some rooms designed by local American Indian artists. Request a room in the back so you're not overlooking I-25.

$100-150

The heart of **Cinnamon Morning** (2700 Rio Grande Blvd. NW, 505/345-3541, www.cinnamonmorning.com, $125 s), in the North Valley, about a mile north of Old Town, is its lavish outdoor kitchen, with a huge round dining table and a fireplace to encourage lounging on nippier nights. Rooms are simply furnished, with minimalist Southwestern detail—choose from three smaller rooms in the main house, each with a private bath, or, across the garden, a two-bedroom guesthouse ($249) and a casita ($159) with a private patio and a kitchenette.

The exceptionally tasteful ★ **Downtown Historic Bed & Breakfasts of Albuquerque** (207 High St. NE, 505/842-0223, www.albuquerquebedandbreakfasts.com, $109 d) occupies two neighboring old houses on the east side of downtown, walking distance to good restaurants on Central in the EDo (East Downtown) stretch. Heritage House has more of a Victorian feel, while Spy House has a sparer, 1940s look—but both are nicely clutter-free. Two outbuildings are private suites.

The stately and very reasonably priced ★ **Bottger Mansion** (110 San Felipe St. NW, 505/243-3639, www.bottger.com, $125 d) is smack in the middle of Old Town, making this an excellent central choice. The seven themed rooms are nicely appointed, and most are fairly spacious and include a queen- or

Bottger Mansion

king-size bed. Breakfasts are generous, and the owners are quick to provide insight into area attractions.

Set in the original AT&SF railroad hospital and sporting a storied past, the stylishly **Parq Central** (806 Central Ave. SE, 505/242-0040, www.hotelparqcentral.com, $149 d), opened in late 2010. The rooms are a bit small but feel light and airy thanks to big windows and gray and white furnishings, with retro chrome fixtures and honeycomb tiles in the bath. The hospital vibe is largely eradicated, though whimsical vitrines in the halls conjure old-time medical treatments, and the rooftop bar sports a gurney. Perks include free parking, a decent continental breakfast, and an airport shuttle.

$150-250

At Albuquerque's nicest place to stay, you don't actually feel like you're anywhere near the city. ★ **Los Poblanos Historic Inn** (4803 Rio Grande Blvd. NW, 505/344-9297, www.lospoblanos.com, $210 d) sits on 25 acres, the largest remaining plot of land in the city, and the rooms are tucked into various corners of a sprawling rancho built in the 1930s by John Gaw Meem and beautifully maintained and preserved—even the huge, old kitchen ranges are still in place, as are murals by Taos artist Gustave Baumann and frescoes by Peter Hurd. In the main house, the guest rooms are set around a central patio and retain their old wood floors and heavy viga ceilings. Newer, larger rooms have been added and fit in flawlessly—deluxe rooms have a very light Southwest touch, while the farm suites have a whitewashed rustic aesthetic, accented by prints and fabrics by modernist designer Alexander Girard, of the folk-art museum in Santa Fe. There's also a saltwater pool and a gym, as well as extensive gardens. The included breakfast is exceptional, as is dinner at the onsite restaurant.

A beautiful relic of early 20th-century travel, ★ **Hotel Andaluz** (125 2nd St. NW, 505/242-9090, www.hotelandaluz.com, $169 d) was first opened in 1939 by New Mexico-raised hotelier Conrad Hilton. It received a massive overhaul in 2009, keeping all the old wood and murals but updating the core to be fully environmentally friendly, from solar hot-water heaters to a composting program. The neutral-palette rooms are soothing and well designed, with a little Moorish flair in the curvy door outlines. The place is worth a visit for the lobby alone; check out the exhibits from local museums on the 2nd-floor mezzanine.

North of the city, on Santa Ana Pueblo land, **Hyatt Regency Tamaya** (1300 Tuyuna Tr., Santa Ana Pueblo, 505/867-1234, www.hyattregencytamaya.com, $207 d) is a pretty resort. Rooms aren't always maintained as well as they could be, but even the standard ones are quite large, with either terraces or balconies. Three outdoor heated swimming pools and a full spa offer relaxation; the more active can play golf or tennis, take an archery class, or attend an evening storytelling program with a pueblo member.

Outside Albuquerque

Albuquerque is encircled by some of the state's top attractions, many of which are just 45 minutes away. To the west, on land that looks like a movie backdrop, stands **Acoma**, an ancient pueblo that seems to have emerged out of the tall mesa on which it's built. Southeast of the city, a winding mountain road brings you to the ruined **Salinas Pueblo Missions,** intriguing remnants of early Conquest history. To the east off I-40 is the start of one of three routes to Santa Fe, the **Turquoise Trail,** which leads through proudly independent communities still exhibiting vestiges of New Mexico's mining past. An equally scenic route north is the much more circuitous **Jemez Mountain Trail,** which passes a dramatic landscape marked by red rocks and hot springs. The most direct route north, on I-25, brings you to the windswept region known as **Kasha-Katuwe Tent Rocks National Monument.**

WEST TO ACOMA

I-40 climbs the West Mesa out of Albuquerque and heads dead straight across a plateau lined with flat mesas—archetypal Southwest scenery. Perched on top of one of these mesas is the ancient **Acoma Pueblo,** an unforgettable village that has endured for nearly a thousand years.

Laguna Pueblo

About 18 miles west of Albuquerque, I-40 crosses the border onto the 45 square miles of **Laguna Pueblo** (505/552-6654, www.lagunapueblo.org), on which 7,000 Keresan-speaking Ka-waikah (Lake People) live in six villages. From the highway, the only impression you get of Laguna is its Dancing Eagle Casino, but if you have time, get off at exit 114 to visit the **San José Mission Church.** Established in 1699 when the Laguna people requested a priest (unlike any other pueblo), it stands out for its stark white stucco coating,

but this is a relatively recent addition, following a 19th-century renovation. It was mudded and whitewashed every year until the 1950s, when the boom in uranium mining in the area left no time for this maintenance; it's now sealed with stucco.

Inside, between a packed-earth floor and a finely wrought wood ceiling, the late-18th-century altar screen commands the room. It's the work of the so-called Laguna Santero, an unidentified painter who made the innovation of placing icons inside a crowded field of decorative borders and carved and painted columns, creating a work of explosively colorful folk art that was copied elsewhere in the region in subsequent decades.

If you're lucky, **Alfred Pino,** a local artist and informal guide, will be hanging around the church to offer you a personal tour and explanation of the symbols on the altar and the painted elk hides on the walls, in exchange for a tip and donation to the church. The doors are usually open 9am to 3pm weekdays (after a 7am Mass), but the church can be open later and on weekends if Alfred's around.

Each of the six villages of Laguna celebrates its own feast day, and then the whole pueblo turns out at the church September 19 for the Feast of San José, one of the bigger pueblo events in the Albuquerque area.

TOP EXPERIENCE

★ ACOMA PUEBLO

On the road to Acoma, you may feel as though you've crossed through a pass into a Southwestern Shangri-la, for none of this great basin is visible from the highway. Down in the valley, the route runs directly toward a flat-topped rock that juts up like a tooth.

Atop the rock is the original **Acoma Pueblo,** the village known as **Sky City.** The community covers about 70 acres and is built largely of pale, sun-bleached adobe, as it has

Outside Albuquerque

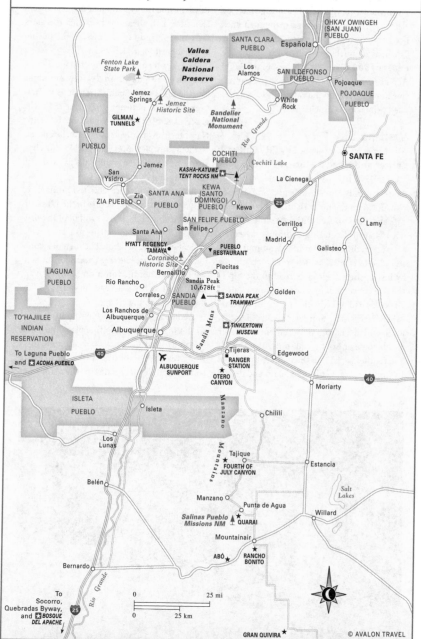

OHKAY OWINGEH (SAN JUAN) PUEBLO

SANTA CLARA PUEBLO

Española

SAN ILDEFONSO PUEBLO

Pojoaque

POJOAQUE PUEBLO

Valles Caldera National Preserve

Los Alamos

White Rock

Fenton Lake State Park

Jemez Springs

Jemez Historic Site

Bandelier National Monument

Rio Grande

GILMAN TUNNELS ★

JEMEZ PUEBLO

Jemez

COCHITI PUEBLO

Cochiti Lake

SANTA FE

La Cienega

San Ysidro

Zia

KASHA-KATUWE TENT ROCKS NM

ZIA PUEBLO

SANTA ANA PUEBLO

KEWA (SANTO DOMINGO) PUEBLO

Kewa

25

Lamy

Santa Ana

San Felipe

SAN FELIPE PUEBLO

Cerrillos

Madrid

Galisteo

HYATT REGENCY TAMAYA

PUEBLO RESTAURANT

Coronado Historic Site

Bernalillo

Placitas

Rio Rancho

Sandia Peak 10,678ft

SANDIA PEAK TRAMWAY

Golden

LAGUNA PUEBLO

Corrales

SANDIA PUEBLO

Los Ranchos de Albuquerque

TO'HAJIILEE INDIAN RESERVATION

Albuquerque

Sandia Mtns

TINKERTOWN MUSEUM

To Laguna Pueblo and ACOMA PUEBLO

40

ALBUQUERQUE SUNPORT

Tijeras

RANGER STATION

Edgewood

OTERO CANYON

40

Moriarty

ISLETA PUEBLO

Isleta

Manzano Mountains

Chililí

Los Lunas

Tajique

FOURTH OF JULY CANYON ★

Estancia

Belén

Salt Lakes

Manzano

Punta de Agua

Willard

Salinas Pueblo Missions NM

QUARAI ★

Mountainair

ABÓ ★

RANCHO BONITO ★

Bernardo

Rio Grande

To Socorro, Quebradas Byway, and BOSQUE DEL APACHE

25

0 ———— 25 mi
0 ———— 25 km

GRAN QUIVIRA ★

© AVALON TRAVEL

been since at least AD 1100. Only a hundred or so people live on the mesa top year-round, given the hardships of no running water or electricity. But many families maintain homes here, and the place is thronged on September 2, when the pueblo members gather for the **Feast of San Esteban.** The rest of the 2,800 Acoma (People of the White Rock, in their native Keresan) live on the valley floor, which is used primarily as ranchland.

Visiting Sky City

All visitors must stop at the **Sky City Cultural Center and Haak'u Museum** (Indian Rte. 23, 800/747-0181, www.acomaskycity.org, 8am-5pm daily Mar.-Oct., 9am-5pm Fri.-Sun. Nov.-Feb.) on the main road, which houses a café and shop stocked with local crafts, along with beautiful rotating exhibits on Acoma art and tradition. From here, you must join a guided tour ($25), which transports groups by bus to the village. The road to the top is the one concession to modernity; previously, all goods had to be hauled up the near-vertical cliff faces. The tour lasts about 1.5 hours, after which visitors may return by bus or climb down one of the old trails, using hand-and footholds dug into the rock centuries ago. In summer, tours start at 8:30am and depart

about every hour, with the last one going at 3:30pm. In the winter, the first tour begins at 10:15am, and they go about hourly until 3pm. Definitely call ahead to check that the tours are running and verify times, as the pueblo closes to visitors periodically.

The centerpiece of the village is the **Church of San Esteban del Rey,** one of the most iconic of the Spanish missions in New Mexico. Built between 1629 and 1640, the graceful, simple structure has been inspiring New Mexican architects ever since. Its interior is, like many New Mexican pueblo churches, spare and simple, the white walls painted with rainbows and corn.

As much as it represents the pinnacle of Hispano-Indian architecture in the 17th century, the church is also a symbol of the brutality of Spanish colonialism, as it rose in the typical way: forced labor. The men of Acoma felled and carried the tree trunks for the ceiling beams from the forest on Mount Taylor, more than 25 miles across the valley, and up the cliff face to the village.

Acoma is well known for its pottery, easily distinguished by the fine black lines that sweep around the curves of often creamy-white vessels. On the best works, the lines are so fine and densely painted, they shimmer

Acoma Pueblo

almost like a moiré. The clay particular to this area can be worked so thin that the finest pots will hum or ring when tapped. Throughout the tour, there are several opportunities to buy pieces. This can feel slightly pressured, but in many cases, you have the privilege of buying work directly from the artisan who created it.

Food and Accommodations

The cultural center contains the **Y'aak'a Café** (9am-3pm daily., $8), which serves earthy local dishes like lamb stew, Indian fry bread, and corn roasted in a traditional *horno* oven—as well as Starbucks coffee. Acoma Pueblo operates the small-scale **Sky City Casino & Hotel** (888/759-2489, www.skycity.com, $89 d), also at exit 102. Its rooms are perfectly clean and functional, and there's a little pool.

Getting There

Take exit 102 off I-40 (about 55 miles west of downtown Albuquerque), and follow signs south to Sky City—this drive, along Indian Service Route 38, is the best signposted and offers the most dramatic views of the valley around Acoma. Allow about 1.5 hours for the drive out, and an additional 2 hours for the tour. Leaving Acoma, to avoid backtracking, you can take Indian Service Route 23, from behind the cultural center, northeast back to I-40.

SALINAS PUEBLO MISSIONS NATIONAL MONUMENT

The **Salinas Pueblo Missions** are a trio of ruined pueblos (**Quarai, Gran Quivira,** and **Abó**) southeast of Albuquerque, on the plains on the far side of the Manzano Mountains. The eerily affecting foundations and frames of the mission churches, built by the pueblo residents under pressure from Franciscan brothers in the early years of the Conquest, stand starkly amid the other remnants of nearby buildings. The drive here also passes one of the area's most beautiful fall hiking spots, a few very old Hispano villages, and the little town of Mountainair.

Allow the better part of a day for a leisurely drive. The whole loop route, starting and ending in Albuquerque, is about 200 miles, and straight driving time is about four hours. From Albuquerque, take I-40 east to exit 179, to the village of Tijeras (Scissors, for the way the canyons meet here), established in the 1850s. Turn south on Highway 337.

Tijeras

Kick your tour off right with a stop for breakfast at **Roots Farm Café** (11784 Hwy. 337, 505/900-4118, 7am-4pm Mon., Wed.-Fri., 8am-4pm Sat.-Sun., $6), a cozy cabin space run by a couple who also own a farm up the road. In high season, their produce shapes a menu that often changes daily. The coffee is exceptionally good.

Fourth of July Canyon

After you pass through the Spanish land grant of Chililí, Highway 337 runs into Highway 55—make a right and head to Tajique, then turn onto Forest Road 55 to reach **Fourth of July Canyon.** The area in the foothills of the Manzanos, seven miles down the dirt road, is a destination in late September and early October, when the red maples and oak trees turn every shade of pink, crimson, and orange imaginable. (Surprisingly, the place got its name not for this fireworks-like show of colors, but for the date an Anglo explorer happened across it in 1906.) The canyon is also pretty in late summer, when the rains bring wildflowers. You can explore along the short **Spring Loop Trail** or **Crimson Maple Trail,** or really get into the woods on **Fourth of July Trail** (no. 173), which wanders into the canyon 1.8 miles and connects with **Albuquerque Trail** (no. 78) to form a 4.4-mile loop.

Technically, Forest Road 55 continues on to rejoin Highway 55 farther south, but after the Fourth of July campground, the road is not always maintained and can be very rough going. It's wiser to backtrack rather than carry on, especially if you're in a rental car.

Quarai

The first ruins you reach are those at **Quarai** (505/847-2290, www.nps.gov/sapu, 9am-6pm daily June-Aug., 9am-5pm daily Sept.-May, free), a pueblo inhabited in the 14th-17th centuries. Like the other two Salinas pueblos, Quarai was a hardscrabble place with no natural source of water and very little food, though it did act as a trading outpost for salt, brought from small salt lakes (*salinas*) farther east. When the Franciscans arrived, they put more than the usual strain on this community. The 400 or so Tiwa speakers nonetheless were pressed to build a grand sandstone-and-adobe mission, the most impressive of the ones at these pueblos.

The priests also found themselves at odds with the Spanish governors, who helped protect them but undermined their conversion work by encouraging ceremonial dances. At the same time, raids by Apaches increased because any crop surplus no longer went to them in trade, but to the Spanish. *And* there were terrible famines 1663-1670. No wonder, then, the place was abandoned even before the Pueblo Revolt of 1680. Only the mission has been excavated; the surrounding hillocks are all pueblo structures.

Mountainair

Highway 55 meets U.S. 60 in the village of **Mountainair,** once known as the Pinto Bean Capital of the World. It's less booming now, but you can still pick up a pound of local beans at the grocery store on the main road.

You'll find the **Salinas Pueblo Missions Visitors Center** (505/847-2585, www.nps.gov/sapu, 8am-5pm daily) on U.S. 60, west of the intersection—though it offers not much more information than what's available at the small but detailed museums at each site. The **Mountainair ranger station** (505/847-2990, 8am-noon and 12:30pm-4:30pm Mon.-Fri.) is here as well; coming from the north, follow signs west off Highway 55 before you reach the U.S. 60 intersection.

Mountainair is also home to the weird architectural treasure that is the **Shaffer Hotel** (103 Main St.), a 1923 Pueblo Deco confection with a folk-art twist, built by one Clem "Pop" Shaffer, who had a way with cast concrete—look for his name in the wall enclosing the little garden. (Similar stonework of his can also be spotted in the garden at Los Poblanos in Albuquerque.) The place is closed these days, but talk lingers of it reopening; if it does, peek in the hotel dining room to admire the ceiling, Shaffer's masterpiece of carved and painted turtles, snakes, and other critters.

For food, stop at bustling **Alpine Alley** (210 N. Summit Ave., 505/847-2478, 6am-2pm Mon.-Fri., 8am-2pm Sat., $8), just north of the main intersection on Highway 55. The menu features freshly baked treats, tasty soups, and creative sandwiches; many of the items were inspired by the regular crew that settles in at the café for long periods.

Gran Quivira

South from Mountainair 26 miles lies Gran Quivira—a bit of a drive, and you'll have to backtrack. On the way, about one mile south of town, you'll pass another Pop Shaffer creation, **Rancho Bonito,** his actual home. As it's private property, you can't go poking around, but from the road you can see a bit of the little log cabin painted in black, red, white, and blue. (If you happen to be in Mountainair in May for its art tour, the house is open then.)

Where Highway 55 makes a sharp turn east, **Gran Quivira** (505/847-2770, www.nps.gov/sapu, 9am-6pm daily June-Aug., 9am-5pm daily Sept.-May, free) looks different from the other two Salinas pueblos because it is built of gray San Andres limestone slab and finished with plaster that was painted with symbols. It's the largest of the three, and once was home to an estimated population of 1,500-2,000. The array of feathers and pottery styles found here indicate the community was devoted to trade. Like the people of Abó, the residents spoke Tompiro, and the Spanish dubbed them Los Rayados, for the striped decorations they wore on their faces. They appear to have outwardly accepted the Franciscan mission after the first sermon was preached here in 1627. But they took their own religion literally underground, building hidden kivas underneath the residential structures even as they toiled on two successive missions ordered by the Catholics. Nonetheless, the place was deserted by 1671, after more than onethird of the population had starved to death.

Abó

From Gran Quivira, drive back the way you came and turn west on U.S. 60 in Mountainair to reach **Abó** (505/847-2400, www.nps.gov/sapu, 9am-6pm daily June-Aug., 9am-5pm daily Sept.-May, free), nine miles on. This was the first pueblo the Franciscans visited, in 1622; the mission here, constructed over more than 60 years, shows details such as old wood stairs leading to the choir loft. (The Franciscans were so dedicated to re-creating the Catholic church experience here in the desert that they brought in portable pipe organs and trained their converts to sing.)

Abó is also notable for the placement of its kiva, right in the center of the *convento* (the compound adjoining the mission) and apparently dating from the same period. This suggests that the local populace came to some agreement with the priests, though no archaeologist or historian has been able to find proof

of this. The excellent condition of all of these ruins is due in part to the efforts of the family that owned the land from the mid-19th century. One member, Federico Sisneros, is buried near the mission, at his request.

From Abó, continue west through the mountain pass, then down into the long, flat Rio Grande Valley on U.S. 60. It runs straight into I-25 at Bernardo, but if you're heading back to Albuquerque, you can take Highway 47 northwest to Belén, about 25 miles closer to the city.

★ BOSQUE DEL APACHE

Bosque del Apache National Wildlife Refuge, 57,000 acres of wetlands along the river, is the site of a winter sojourn for some 15,000 giant sandhill cranes and hundreds of other migratory species. It's one of the country's top birding destinations as a result, but you don't need an ability to differentiate a great blue heron from a little blue heron to appreciate the spectacle of thousands of birds rising in unison at sunrise. It's a straight shot south on I-25, a little less than 100 miles. (To continue from Abó, head west on U.S. 60 to the interstate.) The **visitors center** (575/835-1828, www.friendsofthebosque.org, 8am-4pm Mon.-Fri., 8am-4:30pm Sat.-Sun.) hands out

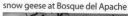
snow geese at Bosque del Apache

bird lists and maps; a **loop drive** ($5/car) through the wetlands opens one hour before sunrise and closes an hour after dark. The so-called Flight Deck adjacent to the Bosque's main pool is the place to be at dawn; arrive at least 30 minutes before sunrise to ensure an unobstructed view of massive flocks of snow geese taking flight.

Food and Accommodations

San Antonio, the nearest town, is notable for its green-chile cheeseburgers, especially at the legendary **Owl Bar & Café** (U.S. 380, 575/835-9946, 8am-9pm Mon.-Sat., $6-12), untouched by time—though rival **Buckhorn Burgers** (U.S. 380, 575/835-4423, 11am-7:50pm Mon.-Fri., 11am-2:45pm Sat., $6), just across the street, is solid too for similar fare.

You can stay overnight—either in San Antonio at **Casa Blanca B&B** (13 Montoya St., 575/835-3027, www.casablancabedandbreakfast.com, $90 d), or just north on I-25 in **Socorro,** at **America's Best Value Inn** (1009 N. California St., 575/835-0276, $57 d), which has a few chips in its furniture but is otherwise well-kept. Recommended dining here includes brewpub **Socorro Springs** (1012 N. California St., 575/838-0650, 11am-10pm daily, $12), all-night diner **El Camino** (707 N. California St., 575/835-1180, 24 hours, $6), **Mountain Coffeehouse** (110 Manzanares St., 575/838-0809, 7am-8pm daily), just off the plaza, and, on the plaza, the old-style **Capitol Bar** (575/835-1193, noon-2am Mon.-Sat., noon-midnight Sun.).

Quebradas Backcountry Byway

To vary the drive back to Albuquerque, take the **Quebradas Backcountry Byway,** a 24-mile dirt road with little traffic that runs in a jagged arc from U.S. 380 up to I-25 north of Socorro, cutting through arroyos and rainbow-striped hills. It adds about two hours to the drive. From the Owl, head east on U.S. 380 for just over 10 miles; then turn north on County Road A-129, the beginning of the byway.

THE TURQUOISE TRAIL

This scenic back route to Santa Fe, along the east side of the Sandias and up across high plateaus, revisits New Mexico's mining history as it passes through a series of former ghost towns. From Albuquerque, it's about 70 miles and can be driven straight through in 1.5 hours.

Take I-40 east from Albuquerque to exit 175. For hiking maps of the area, bear right to go into the village of Tijeras and the **Sandia ranger station** (11776 Hwy. 337, 505/281-3304), and to gas up if you need it—it's one of the last stops until close to Santa Fe. Go left to continue directly to the junction with Highway 14, the beginning of the Turquoise Trail.

East Mountains

The four-lane road heads north through alternating communities of old Spanish land grants and modern subdivisions collectively referred to as the East Mountains. Despite a few strip malls, the area still has a distinct identity from the city; one hub of mountain culture is the **Burger Boy** in the community of Cedar Crest (12023 Hwy. 14, 505/281-3949, 8am-7pm Mon. and Wed.-Sat., 8am-4pm Sun., $8). Its green-chile cheeseburger can hold its own against the state's best, plus the restaurant offers a range of breakfast and lunch specials. Don't miss the paintings, inside and out, of founding owner Green Chili Bill, by Ross Ward.

In Sandia Park is a large triangle intersection—to the left is Highway 536, the so-called **Crest Road** up to Sandia Peak, a beautiful winding drive through steadily thinning forests until you reach the exposed top of the mountain, more than 10,000 feet above sea level and more than 5,500 feet above the center of Albuquerque. At the peak is the Sandia Crest Visitor Center ($3/car), and the 1.6-mile Crest Trail along the rim.

★ Tinkertown Museum

Just 1.5 miles up the Crest Road is **Tinkertown Museum** (121 Sandia Crest

The Turquoise Trail

SANTA FE

Eldorado

La Cienega

COWBOY CHURCH

"OLD MAIN" STATE PENITENTIARY ★

Lamy

SAN MARCOS CAFÉ

Cerrillos Hills State Park

Galisteo

BROKEN SADDLE

BLACK BIRD SALOON

Cerrillos

JAVA JUNCTION/ THE HOLLAR

Madrid ★ OLD COAL TOWN MUSEUM/ MINE SHAFT TAVERN

0   4 mi

0   4 km

Golden   HENDERSON STORE

Sandia   Mountains

Cedar Grove

Sandia Peak

TINKERTOWN MUSEUM

San Antonito   FROST RD.

Cedar Crest

BURGER BOY

TRAMWAY BLVD

Tijeras   SANDIA RANGER STATION

ALBUQUERQUE

© AVALON TRAVEL

Rd., 505/281-5233, www.tinkertown.com, 9am-6pm daily Apr.-Oct., $3.75), a temple to the efficient use of downtime. Artist **Ross Ward,** a certified circus-model builder and sign painter who learned his trade making banners for carnivals, was also a master whittler and creative engineer who built, over 40 years, thousands of miniature figures and dioramas out of wood, clay, and found objects. Some of the scenes are even animated with tiny pulleys and levers: A man with a cleaver chases chickens in a circle; circus performers soar; the blacksmith's bellows huff and puff.

Much of the building is Ward's creation as well—undulating walls made of bottles and studded with odd collectibles, for instance. The museum, ever bulging at its seams, even took over a neighbor's 35-foot wooden boat. Ward died in 2002; his family keeps up the museum, and even though it's no longer growing as it used to, it remains a remarkable piece of pure American folk art.

Golden

Back on Highway 14, continue north through rolling hills and ever-broader skies. After 15 miles, you reach the all-but-gone town of **Golden,** site of the first gold strike west of the Mississippi, in 1825. All that's left now is a handful of homes, an attractive adobe church, and **Henderson Store** (10am-3:30pm Tues.-Sat.), open since 1918. It's largely given over to Indian jewelry and pottery, and antique trinkets line the upper shelves. The house across the road, bedecked with thousands of colored bottles, is worth a quick look.

Madrid

Thirteen miles beyond Golden, and about midway along the drive, **Madrid** (pronounced MAD-rid) is a ghost town back from the dead. Built by the Albuquerque & Cerrillos Coal Co. in 1906, it once housed 4,000 people, but by the end of World War II, when natural gas became the norm, it was deserted. By the late 1970s, a few of the swaybacked wood houses were squatted by hippies willing to live where indoor plumbing was barely available.

Over the decades, Madrid was slowly reborn. Portable toilets are still more common than flush models, but the arts scene has flourished, and a real sense of community pervades the main street, which is lined with galleries and pretty painted bungalows. In 2006, the village was the setting for the John Travolta film *Wild Hogs*, and the set-piece café built for the production (now a souvenir shop) has become a minor pilgrimage site for bikers. While you're in the area, tune in to local radio station KMRD, 96.9 FM.

You can learn more about Madrid's history at the **Old Coal Town Museum** (2846 Hwy. 14, 505/473-0743, www.themineshafttavern. com, hours vary Sat.-Sun., $5), where you can wander among sinister-looking machine parts and old locomotives. You'll feel the "ghost" in "ghost town" here, though current renovations might give the place a bit more life.

FOOD AND ACCOMMODATIONS

The **Mine Shaft Tavern** (2846 Hwy. 14, 505/473-0743, www.themineshafttavern. com, 11:30am-7:30pm Sun.-Thurs., 11:30am-9pm Fri.-Sat., $8-15) is a vibrant remnant of Madrid's company-town days, where you can belly up to a 40-foot-long pine-pole bar.

Above it are murals by local artist Ross Ward, who built the Tinkertown Museum in Sandia Park. "It is better to drink than to work," reads the Latin inscription interwoven among the mural panels, and certainly everyone in the bar, from long-distance bikers to gallery-hoppers, is living by those encouraging words. It serves solidly satisfying "New Mexico roadhouse cuisine," though that belies its winning entry in Santa Fe's Green Chile Cheeseburger Smackdown a few years back—the aptly named Mad Chile Burger. It is, as the name suggests, not for those with delicate palates.

For morning coffee and local gossip, hit **Java Junction** (2855 Hwy. 14, 505/438-2772, www.java-junction.com, 7:30am-close daily), which also rents a **suite** on its second floor ($129 d).

For more substance, head straight to ★ **The Hollar** (Hwy. 14, 505/471-4821, 11am-9pm daily May-Sept., 11am-7pm Mon.-Wed., 11am-9pm Thurs.-Sun. Oct.-Apr., $9-16), which does excellent Southern standards such as shrimp po'boys and fried okra and several New Mexican dishes, too. The green tomatoes and goat cheese are both local—and there's a dedicated menu for dogs. The outside patio makes for a great place to linger in summer.

Tinkertown Museum

Cerrillos

Though the source of turquoise that has been traced to Chaco Canyon, Spain, and Chichén Itzá in Mexico's Yucatán Peninsula, **Cerrillos** hasn't been gallery-fied the way Madrid, its neighbor down the road, has—even if many residents are wealthy escapees from Santa Fe. Representing old-time Cerrillos is the combo petting zoo-trading post **Casa Grande** (17 Waldo St, 505/438-3008, erratic hours, $2), with some llamas and goats, plus turquoise nuggets and taxidermied jackalopes, and the barest ghost of a bar, **Mary's** (15-A First St.), filled with cats and serving primarily as the package liquor store. New-look Cerrillos is next door at **Cerrillos Station** (15-B First St., 505/474-9326), a rather swank shop, gallery, dance studio, and spa. Opposite Mary's is Cerrillos's liveliest and newest joint, the ★ **Black Bird Saloon** (29 Main St., 505/438-1821, 10am-7pm Wed.-Sat., Sun. 10am-3pm, $9-15). Friendly and oozing a rustic Wild West vibe, the saloon offers plenty of local brews to wash down creative dishes such as lamb meatballs with a green onion yogurt sauce and an elk burger with blueberry mustard.

For some of the smoothest horseback rides around, visit the long-running **Broken Saddle Riding Co.** (505/424-7774, www.brokensaddle.com, $85 for two hours) on the edge of **Cerrillos Hills State Park** (head north across the railroad tracks, www.nmparks.com, $5/car), which has more than 1,000 acres of rolling hills and narrow canyons that are also ideal for hiking and mountain biking.

North to Santa Fe

After ascending from the canyons around Cerrillos onto a high plateau (look out for pronghorn), you're on the home stretch to Santa Fe—but you'll pass one more dining option, the **San Marcos Café** (3877 Hwy. 14, 505/471-9298, 8am-2pm daily, $10), which shares space with a working feed store where chickens and the occasional peacock scratch in the yard. Hearty meals are served in a country-style dining room (complete with potbellied stove); breakfast customarily starts with fresh cinnamon buns and from there can include homemade chicken sausage and a variety of egg dishes.

Five miles farther, off the west side of the road, is the **"Old Main" State Penitentiary** (4337 Hwy. 14, www.corrections.state.nm.us), site of a vicious riot in 1980 that is still counted as one of the worst in American history. The state corrections department offers

the former ghost town of Madrid

surprisingly detailed and thought-provoking **tours** ($15) of the old facility on Saturday in summer and early fall.

If you're heading into central Santa Fe, look for the on-ramp to I-25 (signs point to Las Vegas), then go north to the Old Pecos Trail exit. This is faster and prettier than continuing straight in on Highway 14, which turns into Cerrillos Road, a particularly slow and non-scenic route to the plaza.

THE JEMEZ MOUNTAIN TRAIL

Beginning just northwest of Albuquerque, the **Jemez** (HAY-mez) **Mountain Trail** is a beautiful drive through Jemez Indian Reservation, the Santa Fe National Forest, and the **Valles Caldera National Preserve.** It's the least direct way of getting to Santa Fe—from Albuquerque, it covers about 140 miles, and you wind up near Los Alamos and must backtrack a bit south to reach the city. But anyone in search of natural beauty will want to set aside a full day for the trip, or plan an overnight in **Jemez Springs,** especially in the fall, when the aspen leaves are gold against the red rocks.

The drive begins on U.S. 550, northwest out of the satellite town of Bernalillo, just west of I-25. (Stop here for gas, if necessary—stations are few on this route.) At the village of San Ysidro, bear right onto Highway 4, which forms the major part of the route north.

Jemez Pueblo

This community of some 1,800 tribal members was settled in the late 13th century, and Highway 4 runs through the middle of the 89,000 acres it still maintains. Before the Spanish arrived, the Hemish (literally, "the people," and which the Spanish spelled *Jemez*) had established more than 10 large villages in the area. **Jemez Pueblo** is quite conservative and closed to outsiders except for holidays. Because Jemez absorbed members of Pecos Pueblo in 1838, it celebrates two feast days, San Diego (November 12) and San Persingula (August 2), as well as Pueblo Independence Day (August 10), commemorating the Pueblo Revolt of 1680. It's also the only remaining pueblo where residents speak the Towa language, the rarest of the related New Mexico languages (Tewa and Tiwa are the other two).

The pueblo operates the **Walatowa Visitor Center** (575/834-7235, www.jemezpueblo.com, 8am-5pm daily Apr.-Dec., 10am-4pm Wed.-Sun. Jan.-Mar.), about five miles north of San Ysidro. You might miss it if you're gawking off the east side of the road at the vivid red sandstone cliffs at the mouth of the **San Diego Canyon.** April-October, another, tastier distraction is the Indian fry bread and enchiladas sold by roadside vendors. The center has exhibits about the local geology and the people of Jemez and doubles as a ranger station, dispensing maps and advice on outdoor recreation farther up the road. You can take a one-mile guided hike ($5) up into the red rocks; it's a good idea to call ahead and arrange a time.

Gilman Tunnels

Blasted in the 1920s for a spur of a logging railroad, the two narrow **Gilman Tunnels** over scenic Highway 485 make a good excuse to drive up this narrow road and through a dramatic canyon. Look for the turn left (west) off Highway 4, a couple of miles after the Walatowa Visitor Center, after mile marker 9; the tunnels are about five miles along. After the tunnels, the road turns to dirt and heads into the national forest. (Sturdy vehicles can make a big loop around via Fenton Lake, rejoining Highway 4 north of Jemez Springs.)

Jemez Springs

A funky old resort town where hippies and Jemez Pueblo residents meet, **Jemez Springs** is a handful of little clapboard buildings tucked in the narrow valley along the road. As the most convenient place to indulge in the area's springs, which have inspired tales of miraculous healing since the 1870s, the town makes for a nice afternoon pause or an overnight getaway. **Giggling Springs** (Hwy. 4, 575/829-9175, www.gigglingsprings.com,

11am-sunset Mon. and Wed.-Sun., $25/one hour, $40/two hours, $100/day) has a spring-fed pool enclosed in an attractively land-scaped flagstone area right near the Jemez River; reserve ahead, as occupancy is capped at 10. The **Jemez Springs Bath House** (Hwy. 4, 575/829-3303, www.jemezsprings-bathhouse.com, 10am-6pm Mon.-Tues. and Thurs.-Sat., 10am-5pm Sun., $18/50 min-utes), in one of the original historic build-ings, is operated by the village. (The source is in a gazebo next door—check out the min-eral buildup!) Here, the springs have been di-verted into eight concrete soaking tubs—a bit austere, but with a cool historic vibe. Reserve ahead here too; massages and other spa treat-ments are available. The most natural springs (expect some algae) are on the riverside at the **Bodhi Manda Zen Center** (Hwy. 4, 575/829-3854, www.bmzc.org, $10 donation); payment is cash only and on the honor system.

If you're planning to explore the wilder-ness and missed the Walatowa Visitor Center at Jemez Pueblo, you can stop at the **Jemez Ranger District office** (Hwy. 4, 575/829-3535, 8am-4:30pm Mon.-Fri.) for info; it's on the north edge of town.

FOOD AND ACCOMMODATIONS

The **Bodhi Manda Zen Center** (Hwy. 4, 575/829-3854, www.bmzc.org) has its own hot pools, rents bare-bones rooms ($70 pp), and offers vegetarian meals to guests. Another bargain place to stay, with a few more ame-nities, is the **Laughing Lizard Inn** (Hwy. 4, 575/829-3108, www.thelaughinglizard. com, $75 d, $110 suite); its four simple but pretty rooms, plus one suite, opening onto a long porch. Just across the street, **Jemez Mountain Inn** (Hwy. 4, 575/829-3926, www. jemezmtninn.com, $85 d) is slightly plusher, and its rooms a bit quieter, as they're back from the road. Hot springs are within easy walking distance.

Next door to the Laughing Lizard, ★ **Highway 4 Coffee** (17478 Hwy. 4, 575/829-4655, 8am-3pm Mon., Tues., and Thurs., 8am-11am Wed., 8am-4pm Fri. and Sun., 8am-7pm Sat., $6-11) has a great se-lection of pastries and hearty homemade lunches—there's plenty of coffee too, of course. For dinner, the only place open all the time is **Los Ojos Restaurant & Saloon** (17596 Hwy. 4, 575/829-3547, 11am-mid-night Mon.-Fri., 8am-midnight Sat.-Sun., $10), where horseshoes double as window grills, tree trunks act as bar stools, and the

Light Among the Ruins at the Jemez Historic Site

atmosphere hasn't changed in decades. Burgers and the green-chile stew are the way to go. The kitchen shuts around 9pm, and bar closing time can come earlier if business is slow, so call ahead in the evenings.

Jemez Historic Site

Just north of Jemez Springs, you pass the **Jemez Historic Site** (Hwy. 4, 575/829-3530, 8:30am-5pm Wed.-Sun., $5), a set of ruins where ancestors of the present Jemez people settled more than 700 years ago and apparently lived until 1694 or so, when Diego de Vargas returned after the Pueblo Revolt. The old pueblo, named Giusewa, has almost entirely dissolved; as at the Salinas Pueblo Missions south of Albuquerque, the attraction is the Franciscan convent and church. Built starting around 1620, it has been partially reconstructed, enough to show how the architecture—a floor that sloped up to the altar, a unique octagonal bell tower—created maximum awe in the local populace. If you pay $7 admission, you can also visit **Coronado State Monument,** on the north edge of Albuquerque, on the same or next day. If you're in the area in early to mid-December, check to see the date for the **Light Among the Ruins,** during which hundreds of farolitos are lit at the site and traditional Native American dances take place in front of a bonfire.

A couple of curves in the highway past the monument, you reach the rocks of **Soda Dam** off the right side of the road. The pale, bulbous mineral accretions that have developed around this spring resemble nothing so much as the top of a root beer float, with a waterfall crashing through the middle. You can't really get in the water here, but it's a good photo op.

Hot Springs

Outside Jemez Springs, you pass two other opportunities to soak in hot water. Five miles north, where the red rocks of the canyon have given way to steely-gray stone and Battleship Rock looms above the road, is the start of the East Fork Trail (no. 137)—there's a dedicated

The Interstate to Santa Fe

© AVALON TRAVEL

parking lot just north of the picnic area. From here, the hike up the trail to **McCauley Warm Springs** is a bit more than two miles, mostly uphill; follow the trail until it meets a small stream flowing down from your left (north), then walk up the creek about 0.25 mile to the spring, which has been diverted so it flows into a series of pools, only 85°F at most points. (You can also reach the springs from the other direction along East Fork Trail, parking at Jemez Falls, farther north on Highway 4; from here, the hike is downhill—but of course a slog back up.)

More accessible are **Spence Hot Springs,** about two miles north of Battleship Rock, between mile markers 24 and 25. Look for a loop parking area on the east side of the road (if it's full, there is another lot a short way north along the highway). The 0.5-mile trail down to the river is wide and well tended, but then it's a bit more strenuous heading up the steep hillside to two sets of 100°F pools with milky-blue mineral water.

Hiking

Several trails run through the Jemez, but damage from the 2011 Las Conchas Fire has made some less scenic. Portions of **East Fork Trail** (no. 137) are still quite nice, however.

The route runs between Battleship Rock (on the southwest end) and Las Conchas (on the northeast end), crossing Highway 4 at a convenient midpoint. If you head south from the highway parking area (about 3 miles after a hairpin turn southeast), you reach Jemez Falls after 1 mile, then gradually descend to Battleship Rock in about 6 miles, passing McCauley Springs on the way. Heading north from the highway is fine too, following a stream through a pine forest, though near the end of 4.5 miles, you approach the burned area.

THE INTERSTATE TO SANTA FE

The most direct route north from Albuquerque to Santa Fe is along I-25, a one-hour drive without stops. The road, which passes through the broad valley between the Sandia and Jemez mountain ranges, is not as scenic as the more meandering routes, but it does cross wide swaths of the undeveloped pueblo lands of Sandia, San Felipe, and Kewa (formerly Santo Domingo).

Kewa (Santo Domingo)

The pueblo of **Kewa** (505/465-2214, www.santodomingotribe.org) is a short drive from

the windswept spires of Kasha-Katuwe Tent Rocks National Monument

exit 259, via Highway 22. Formerly known as Santo Domingo, this Keresan-speaking community of 2,500 people has been here since the 1200s. If you're going to Kasha-Katuwe Tent Rocks anyway, you'll pass a freshly repainted old-time curio stand, the **Santo Domingo Trading Post** (by the Rail Runner station stop). Then it's worth a short detour west on Indian Service Route 88, to the center of the pueblo, to see the whitewashed village church, its facade adorned with two large horses. Set against the red earth here, it's a vivid image—but remember, no photography is allowed on pueblo land.

To continue to Kasha-Katuwe Tent Rocks, backtrack to Highway 22; the Indian service route to Cochiti does not go through.

★ Kasha-Katuwe Tent Rocks National Monument

A bit west of I-25, **Kasha-Katuwe Tent Rocks National Monument** (Forest Rd. 266, 505/331-6259, 7am-7pm daily mid-Mar.-Oct., 8am-5pm daily Nov.-mid-Mar., $5/car) is one of the region's most striking natural phenomena. The wind-whittled clusters of volcanic pumice and tuff do indeed resemble enormous tepees, some up to 90 feet tall. To reach the area, continue past Kewa Pueblo and head northwest toward Cochiti Pueblo on Highway 22. After about 15 miles, turn south in front of Cochiti Dam. In less than two miles, in the middle of the pueblo, turn right on Indian Service Route 92.

From the monument parking area, you have the choice of two short trails: An easy, relatively flat loop runs up to the base of the rocks, passing a small cave, while a longer option runs 1.5 miles into a narrow canyon where the rock towers loom up dramatically on either side. The latter trail is level at first, but the last stretch is steep and requires a little clambering. Even if you just want to take a quick peek and don't intend to hike, don't come too late in the day: The gates (close to the junction with Highway 22) are locked one hour before official closing time.

To get back to the freeway without backtracking, continue northeast on Highway 22, which makes a sharp turn at the base of Cochiti Dam (turn left, or north, and you'll reach **Cochiti Lake,** a popular summer destination for boaters). Follow Highway 22 back southeast, then take Highway 16 to rejoin the interstate at exit 264.

Food

At exit 252, hop off for a meal at the ★ **Pueblo Restaurant** (26 Hagen Rd., 505/867-4706, 6am-9pm daily, $8), alongside the San Felipe gas station and past a short hall of dinging slot machines. Its broad diner menu offers spaghetti and meatballs as well as New Mexican favorites. The pueblo dishes, such as posole with extra-thick tortillas, are excellent. Dig in alongside pueblo residents, day-trippers, and long-haul truckers.

Information and Services

TOURIST INFORMATION

The **Albuquerque Convention and Visitors Bureau** (800/284-2282, www. visitalbuquerque.org) offers the most detailed information on the city, maintaining a kiosk on the Old Town plaza in the summer and a desk at the airport near the baggage claim (9:30am-8pm daily). The **City of Albuquerque** website (www.cabq.gov) is very well organized, with all the essentials about city-run attractions and services.

Books and Maps

In the North Valley, **Bookworks** (4022 Rio Grande Blvd. NW, 505/344-8139, 9am-8pm Mon.-Sat., 9am-7pm Sun.) has a large stock of New Mexico-related work as well as plenty of other titles, all recommended with the personal care of the staff.

The **University of New Mexico Bookstore** (2301 Central Ave. NE, 505/277-5451, 8am-6pm Mon.-Fri., 11am-4pm Sat.) maintains a good stock of travel titles and maps, along with state history tomes and the like. In summer, it closes an hour earlier on weekdays.

Local Media

The *Albuquerque Journal* (www.abqjournal.com) publishes cultural-events listings in the Friday entertainment supplement. On Wednesday, pick up the new issue of the free weekly *Alibi* (www.alibi.com), which will give you a hipper, more critical outlook on city goings-on, from art openings to city council debates. The free *Local Flavor* (www.localflavormagazine.com) covers food topics.

Radio

KUNM (89.9 FM) is the university's radio station, delivering eclectic music, news from NPR and PRI, and local-interest shows, such as *Singing Wire,* where you'll hear traditional Native American music as well as pop anthems like Keith Secola's oft-requested "NDN Kars" and the Black Lodge Singers chanting the Mighty Mouse theme song.

KANW (89.1 FM) is a project of Albuquerque Public Schools, with an emphasis on New Mexican music, particularly mariachi and other music in Spanish. It also hosts a Saturday-night old-time-country show, and the most popular NPR programs.

SERVICES
Banks

Banks are plentiful, and grocery stores and pharmacies increasingly have ATMs inside. Downtown, look for **New Mexico Bank & Trust** (320 Gold Ave. SW, 505/830-8100, 9am-4pm Mon.-Thurs., 9am-5pm Fri.). In Nob Hill, **Wells Fargo** (3022 Central Ave. SE, 505/255-4372, 9am-5pm Mon.-Thurs., 9am-6pm Fri., 9am-1pm Sat.) is on Central at Dartmouth. Both have 24-hour ATMs.

Post Offices

Most convenient for visitors are the **Old Town Plaza Station** (303 Romero St. NW, 505/242-5927, 11am-4pm Mon.-Fri., noon-3pm Sat.), **Downtown Station** (201 5th St. SW, 505/346-1256, 9am-4:30pm Mon.-Fri.), and an office near **UNM** (115 Cornell Dr. SE, 505/346-0923, 8am-5pm Mon.-Fri.).

Internet

City-maintained **wireless hotspots** are listed at www.cabq.gov/wifi; many businesses around town also provide service.

Getting There and Around

AIR

Albuquerque International Sunport (ABQ, 505/244-7700, www.cabq.gov/airport) is a pleasant single-terminal airport served by all major U.S. airlines. It's on the south side of the city, just east of I-25, about four miles from downtown. It has free wireless Internet access. Near baggage claim is an info desk maintained by the convention and visitors bureau.

Transit from the airport includes **bus Route 50** ($1), which runs to the Alvarado Transportation Center downtown every half hour 7am-8pm, and on Saturday every hour and 10 minutes 9:45am-6:50pm; there is no Sunday service. The ride takes about 25 minutes.

Less frequent, but free, the **Airport Connection shuttle** (aka city bus Route 250) runs weekdays only (9:10am, 4:01pm, 5:09pm, and 6:10pm) to the downtown Alvarado Transportation Center (Central and 1st St.). The schedule is timed to meet the Rail Runner train to Santa Fe, departing about 30 minutes later. Another free weekday bus (Route 222) runs to the Bernalillo Rail Runner stop, though this is less convenient for visitors. Verify online at www.riometro.org, as the train schedule can change.

TRAIN

Amtrak (800/872-7245, www.amtrak.com) runs the Southwest Chief through Albuquerque. It arrives daily in the afternoon from Chicago and Los Angeles. The depot shares space with the Greyhound terminal, downtown on 1st Street, south of Central Avenue and the Alvarado Transportation Center.

The **Rail Runner** (866/795-7245, www.riometro.org) connects downtown Santa Fe with Albuquerque and continues as far south as Belén. The main stop in Albuquerque is downtown, at the Alvarado Transportation Center, at Central and 1st Street. If the not-so-frequent schedule fits yours, it's fantastic service to or from Santa Fe, but within Albuquerque, the system doesn't go anywhere visitors typically go. If you ride, keep your ticket—you get a free transfer from the train to any city bus.

BUS

Greyhound (800/231-2222, www.greyhound.com) runs buses from all major points east, west, north, and south, though departures are not frequent. The **bus station** (320 1st St. SW, 505/243-4435) is downtown, just south of Central Avenue. Cheaper *and* nicer are the bus services that cater to Mexicans traveling across the Southwest and into Mexico, though they offer service only to Las Cruces and Denver; **El Paso-Los Angeles Limousine Express** (2901 Pan American Fwy. NE, 505/247-8036, www.eplalimo.com) is the biggest operator, running since 1966.

With the city bus system, **ABQ Ride** (505/243-7433, www.cabq.gov/transit), it's possible to reach all the major sights along Central Avenue, but you can't get to the Sandia Peak Tramway or anywhere in the East Mountains. The most tourist-friendly bus line is Route 66 (of course), along Central Avenue, linking Old Town, downtown, and Nob Hill; service runs until a bit past 1am on summer weekends. The double-length red **Rapid Ride** buses (Route 766) follow the same route but stop at only the most popular stops. The fare for all buses, regardless of trip length, is $1 (coins or bills; no change given); passes are available for one ($2), two ($4), and three ($6) days and can be purchased on the bus. The D-Ride bus is a free loop-route bus around downtown that runs weekdays 6:30am-5:30pm.

CAR

From Santa Fe, Albuquerque is 60 miles (one hour) south on I-25; from Las Cruces, it is 225 miles (a little more than three hours) north on I-25. From Denver, the drive takes about 6.5 hours (445 miles); Phoenix is about the same distance west on I-40.

All the major car-rental companies are in a single complex adjacent to the airport, connected by shuttle bus. **Hertz** and **Enterprise** offer service at the Amtrak depot (really, just a refund for the cab ride to the airport offices). Hertz's two other city locations are usually less expensive because you bypass the airport service fee; if you're renting for more than a week, the savings can offset the cab fare. The prominent ride-sharing companies **Uber** (www.uber.com) and **Lyft** (www.lyft.com) both operate in Albuquerque.

BIKE

Albuquerque's **bike-route system** (www.cabq.gov/bike) is reasonably well developed, the terrain is flat, and the sun is usually shining. Rent bikes from **Routes** (404 San Felipe St. NW, 505/933-5667, www.routesrentals.com, 8am-7pm Mon.-Fri., 7am-7pm Sat.-Sun. Mar.-Oct., 9am-6pm Mon.-Fri., 8am-6pm Sat.-Sun. Nov.-Feb., $15/hour, $35/day). You can also try the **bike-sharing program** (www.zagster.com/abq, $3/1.5 hours) that covers downtown and Old Town. If you think you might use the bikes more than one day, applying for the monthly pass ($15) may be a better deal.

Background

The Landscape 218

Plants and Animals 220

History 224

Government and Economy 228

Local Culture 229

The Arts 232

The Landscape

Santa Fe, Taos, and Albuquerque are located in the high desert, and though the adjectives commonly used to describe the landscape—stark, unforgiving, rugged—are all true, they fall short of capturing its essence. Marked by jagged mountains, endless and impossibly blue skies, and flora that endures against all odds, the land has a primal beauty that can impact you to your core. The sheer vastness of the landscape is intoxicating, a feeling that is only enhanced by relatively compact population centers. When you get out on a hiking trail, chances are you won't be fighting the crowds to do so.

GEOGRAPHY AND GEOLOGY

Much of New Mexico's landscape is the product of volcanic activity that ceased (at least for now) around the year AD 500. The main mountain ranges, which form part of the **Continental Divide,** are relatively young, pushed up in the Eocene era 55 million-34 million years ago, when shock waves from the collision of the North American plate and the Farallon plate caused the continent to heave.

Just a few million years later, the **Rio Grande Rift**—one of the biggest rift valleys in the world—formed, as eras' worth of accumulated rock was pulled apart by shifting faults, leaving the perfect path for the Rio Grande when it began to flow about three million years ago. The water carved deep canyons, such as the 800-foot-deep gorge west of Taos. These canyons are perfect slices of geologic time, layers of limestone, sandstone, clay, and lava neatly stacked up.

A million years ago, a volcano's violent eruption and subsequent collapse created the huge **Valles Caldera,** and the jagged edges of the crater have barely softened in the intervening time. Only 1,500 years ago, in the Tularosa basin, molten lava hardened into black badlands. One tangible benefit of the state's volcanic activity is the numerous hot springs, especially in the young Jemez Mountains (15 million years old).

Beneath all this is evidence of a more stable time. For some four billion years, the land was completely underwater, then spent hundreds of millions of years supporting prehistoric sea life—hence the marine fossils found at the top of the Sandia Mountains, 10,000 feet above the current sea level. Dinosaurs, too, flourished for a time. One of the first, the nimble meat-eater *Coelophysis,* lived during the Triassic period around Abiquiu, but all of them were apparently killed at once, perhaps by a flash flood. Another product of the dinosaur age (specifically, the Jurassic) was the lurid red, pink, and orange sandstone. It began as a vast desert, then petrified into the very symbol of the American Southwest, and is visible around Abiquiu as well as Jemez Pueblo.

CLIMATE

For the most part, altitude determines the climate in New Mexico, where central Albuquerque, in the river valley, can be crisp and cloudless while Sandia Peak, 20 miles away and almost 5,000 feet up, is caught in a blinding snowstorm. (Yes, it snows plenty in New Mexico.) Nowhere, though, is it a particularly gentle climate; expect sudden and often extreme changes in weather patterns and temperatures.

At the lower elevations, winter is cold—days usually between 40°F and 55°F—but rarely cloudy, with a few snowstorms that never add up to as much moisture as people

---

Previous: winter scene near Chama; snow goose at Bosque del Apache.

hope. Come spring, the number of wildflowers that dot the hills is a direct reflection of the previous winter's precipitation. The higher the elevation, the later the spring: At 8,500 feet, snow could still be on the ground in May. Little rain falls in May and June, typically the hottest and windiest months of the year, with temperatures climbing into the 90s—though it can still drop to the 50s at night.

By early or mid-July, the so-called monsoon season brings heavy, refreshing downpours and thunderstorms nearly every afternoon for a couple of months. If you're out hiking in this season, steer clear of narrow canyons and arroyos during and after rains, as they can fill with powerful, deadly flash floods in a matter of minutes. Summer nights are rarely too warm.

September, October, and November are again dry, with the temperature dipping lower each month. Snow can often start falling in late October or November, although in recent years, overall winter precipitation has been low, so it takes months for a good base layer to build up at the ski areas—less so at the Taos Ski Valley.

ENVIRONMENTAL ISSUES

For thousands of years, New Mexicans have faced a water shortage. In prehistoric times, farming in the river valley was relatively easy, if subject to flooding. But at higher elevations, mountain streams had to be channeled into irrigation ditches. This system was perfected by Spanish settlers, who called their ditches acequias, a word they'd learned from the Arabs (*as-saqiya*), who used the system to cultivate the Iberian Peninsula.

Today, as an ever-growing population demands more amenities, traditional ways of managing water have given way to more complex legal wranglings and outright hostility (*No chingen con nuestra agua*—Don't f - - k with our water—reads a bumper sticker on some trucks in northern New Mexico). Some 49 billion gallons are pumped out of the middle Rio Grande aquifer every year, and only a portion of that is replenished through mountain runoff. Albuquerque started using filtered river water in late 2008. "Smart growth" gets lip service in city council meetings, although construction continues apace on Albuquerque's arid West Mesa. Neohomesteaders install cisterns to catch rain, as well as systems to reuse gray water, but these features are still far from standard.

Years of relative drought can make tinderboxes of the forests. In a few weeks in the summer of 2012, for instance, the Whitewater-Baldy fire in the Gila National Forest burned almost 300,000 acres, the largest recorded fire in New Mexico history (almost double the scale of the previous record-setter, the Las Conchas fire, near Los Alamos the year before).

Visitors to New Mexico can help by following local environmental policies: Take scrupulous care with fire in the wilderness (no campfires, of course), and follow drought measures such as keeping showers short. Golfers may want to consider curtailing their play here. New courses, improbably, have been installed at every new casino resort and high-end residential development, despite the fact that they're significant draws on the water table.

Leave No Trace

So as not to upset the rather precarious environmental balance in much of New Mexico, you should internalize the ethic of "leave no trace"—even on a short stroll. Let the phrase first guide your trip in the **planning** stages, when you equip yourself with good maps and GPS tools or a compass, to avoid relying on rock cairns or blazes. Backpackers should repackage food and other items to minimize the waste to pack out. And everyone should try to keep group size under six people; pets should be kept on a leash and in designated areas.

On the trail, resist the urge to cut across switchbacks. Stick to the center of the trail, even if it has been widened by others trying to avoid mud. Be quiet, to avoid disturbing wildlife and other hikers. Leave what you find, whether plants, rocks, or potsherds.

Camp only where others have, in durable areas, at least 200 feet from water sources; dig cat holes 200 feet away too. Pack out your toilet paper and other personal waste, and scatter dishwater and toothpaste. Safeguard food in "bear bags" hung at least 15 feet off the ground. Campfires are typically banned in New Mexico—please honor this policy, and keep a close eye on camp stoves. Pack out all cigarette butts.

Day hikers should also maintain a strict policy regarding litter. Tossing an orange peel, apple core, or other biodegradable item along the trail may not cause an environmental disaster, but it intrudes on the natural solitude of New Mexico's wilderness and could encourage other hikers to litter as well.

For more information, contact **Leave No Trace** (http://lnt.org).

Plants and Animals

Just as humans have managed to eke a life out of New Mexico, so have plants and animals—and a rather large variety of them. The state supports the fourth most diverse array of wildlife in the country.

PLANTS

Although much of the plant growth in New Mexico is nominally evergreen, the landscape skews toward brown until you get up to the wetter alpine elevations.

Vegetation Zones

Below 4,500 feet, New Mexico's **Lower Sonoran** zone, in the river valleys in the southern part of the state, is dotted with cactus, yucca, and scrubby creosote bushes. The **Upper Sonoran** zone, covering the areas between 4,500 and 7,000 feet, is the largest vegetation zone in the state and includes the high plains in the northeast and most of Albuquerque and Santa Fe, where the Sandia

and Sangre de Cristo foothills are covered with juniper and piñon trees. The **Transition** zone, 7,000-8,500 feet, sees a few more stately trees, such as ponderosa pine, and the state's more colorful wildflowers: orange Indian paintbrush, bright-red penstemon, purple lupine. Above 8,500 feet, the **Mixed Conifer** zone harbors that sort of tree, along with clusters of aspens. The **Subalpine** zone, starting at 9,500 feet, is home to Engelmann spruce and bristlecone pine, while 11,500 feet marks the tree line in most places and the beginning of the **Alpine** zone, where almost no greenery survives. At 11,973 feet, the top of Sierra Blanca, near Ruidoso, is the southernmost example of this zone in the United States.

Trees and Grasses

Trees are the clearest marker of elevation. In low areas, you'll see almost no trees, only assorted cacti, such as the common **cane cholla;** the spiky **yucca** plant, which produces towering stalks of blooms in May; and the humble **tumbleweed.** Along the Rio Grande and the Pecos River, thirsty **cottonwoods** provide dense shade; the biggest trees, with their gnarled, branching trunks, are centuries old. In spring, their cotton fills the air—hell for the allergic, but the source of a distinctive spicy fragrance—and in fall, their leaves turn pure yellow. Willow and olive are also common.

Everywhere in the foothills grows **piñon** (also spelled "pinyon"), the scrubby state tree that's slow-growing and drought-resistant, evolved to endure the New Mexican climate. When burned, its wood produces the scent of a New Mexico winter night, and its cones yield tasty nuts. Alongside piñon is **shaggy-bark juniper,** identifiable by its loose strips of bark, sprays of soft needles, and branches that look twisted by the wind. In season, it's studded with purple-gray berries—another treat for foraging humans and animals alike. At ground level in the foothills, also look for clumps of sagebrush and bear grass, which blooms in huge, creamy tufts at the ends of stalks up to six feet tall.

Up in the mountains, the trees are a bit taller. Here you'll find the towering **ponderosa pine,** with its thick, almost crusty chunks of reddish-black bark; the crevices smell distinctly of vanilla. At slightly higher elevations, dense stands of **aspens** provide a rare spot of fall color in the evergreen forests. The combination of their golden leaves and white bark creates a particularly magical glow, especially in the mountains near Santa Fe. The highest mountain areas are home to a number of dense-needled hardy pines, such as blue-green **Engelmann spruce, corkbark fir, bristlecone pines,** and **subalpine fir,** with its sleek, rounded pinecones. Hike your way up to stands of these, which are tall but with sparse branches, and you'll know you're close to the peak.

ANIMALS

As with plants, what you see depends on whether you're down in the desert or up on the mountain slopes. And you'll have to look carefully, because a lot of the animals that have survived here this long are the sort that blend in with their surroundings—which means there are a lot of brown critters.

Mammals

In the open, flat areas (and sometimes in the occasional vacant urban lot), look for **prairie dogs,** which live in huge underground

conifers high in the Sangre de Cristo Mountains

warrens. When you're camping, the first creatures you'll meet are **squirrels** and **chipmunks**—at higher elevations, look out for Abert's squirrel, with its tufted ears and extra-fluffy tail.

On the plains, you may see **pronghorns** (often called pronghorn antelope, though they are not related to true antelope) springing through the grasses, while long-eared **mule deer** flourish in mountain forests, such as the Pecos Wilderness. Herds of **elk** live in the high valleys; Rocky Mountain elk are common, thanks to an aggressive reintroduction effort in the early 20th century to make up for overhunting. A group of the largest variety, Roosevelt elk, whose fanlike antlers are the stuff of dreams for trophy hunters, roams in Valles Caldera. **Bighorn sheep** live in the mountains around Taos and in the Gila Wilderness.

Taos is also a hot spot for **North American river otters,** which were reintroduced in Taos Pueblo starting in 2008—after their absence from the whole state for some 55 years. The small aquatic mammals seem to be flourishing and can now be spotted in the Rio Grande and tributaries, from the Colorado border to Cochiti Dam.

Long-haunched, clever, and highly adaptable, **coyotes** roam in a variety of habitats and elevations; they're not shy about nosing around backyards either. At night, their eerie howls are heard in and around some cities and towns. **Black bears** inhabit forests at higher elevations—and occasionally are spotted in Santa Fe and Los Alamos—though their name is misleading—they can be brown, cinnamon-red, or even nearly blond. (Smokey Bear, the mascot of the National Forest Service, was from New Mexico, a cub rescued from a forest fire in the southern town of Capitan.) Drought often drives the omnivorous beasts into suburban trash cans to forage, with tragic results for both people and the animals. Campers are strongly urged to pack food in bear-proof canisters.

Birds

New Mexico's state bird is the elusive **roadrunner:** It grows up to two feet long, nests in the ground, feeds on insects and even rattlesnakes, and has feet specially adapted to racing on sandy ground. It can be spotted at lower desert elevations. Blue-and-black **Steller's jays** and raucous all-blue **piñon jays** are common in the foothills and farther up in the mountains, where you can also see **bluebirds, black-masked mountain**

chipmunk in the Taos Ski Valley

chickadees, and Clark's nutcrackers, which hoard great stashes of piñon nuts for winter. Also look around for woodpeckers, including the three-toed variety, which live at higher elevations. On the highest peaks are white-tailed ptarmigans, which blend in with their snowy environment. But you can't miss the yellow-and-red western tanager, a vivid shot of tropical delight in the Transition zone forests.

In late summer, keep an eye out for tiny, red-throated rufous hummingbirds on their way to Mexico for the winter, along with hundreds of other birds that use the center of the state as a migratory corridor. The Sandia Mountains and the Las Vegas National Wildlife Refuge, among other spots, are on the flight path for red-tailed hawks, eagles, and other raptors, especially numerous in the springtime.

With more than 450 species spotted in New Mexico, this list is only scraping the surface. If you're a dedicated birder, first contact the Randall Davey Audubon Center in Santa Fe, which leads bird walks, or the Rio Grande Nature Center in Albuquerque. Bosque del Apache National Wildlife Refuge, south of Albuquerque, is a must in the winter when thousands of sandhill cranes—and even the occasional rare whooping crane—rest in the wetlands. Jim West of WingsWest Birding (800/583-6928, www.wingswestnm.com) is a reputable guide who has been leading groups around New Mexico since 1996.

Fish

Trout is the major endemic fish, found in the cold waters of the Rio Grande as well as the San Juan, Chama, and Pecos Rivers and the streams of the Valles Caldera. The cutthroat is particularly beloved in New Mexico—the only variety of trout originally found on the eastern side of the Continental Divide. (The more aggressive rainbow and brown trout are interlopers.) The Rio Grande cutthroat, the official state fish, is now quite uncommon. Another local fish in jeopardy is the Rio Grande silvery minnow, listed as endangered since 1994. The last of the Rio Grande's five native fish, it's in such a dire state that biologists have scooped them out of the water individually during dry spells and taken them to the Albuquerque aquarium for safekeeping.

Reptiles

One can't step foot in the desert without thinking of rattlesnakes, and New Mexico has plenty of them, usually hidden away under rocks and brush, but very occasionally sunning themselves in full view. The predominant species in the Rio Grande Valley, the Western diamondback, can grow to be seven feet long. Although its venom is relatively weak, it has an impressive striking distance of almost three feet. Around Taos and Santa Fe, the main species is the prairie rattlesnake, which is only four feet long at most; the threatened New Mexico ridgenose is only about two feet long. The snakes you're more likely to encounter, however, are bull snakes. Though often mistaken for rattlesnakes due to similar size and colorings, they're not venomous.

More benign cold-blooded critters include lizards, such as the short-horned lizard (aka horny toad), a miniature dinosaur, in effect, about as big as your palm. Look for it in the desert and the scrubby foothills.

Insects and Arachnids

Because it's so dry, New Mexico isn't teeming with bugs. The ones that are there, however, can be off-putting, particularly if you chance upon the springtime tarantula migration, usually in May around Albuquerque. It's not a true seasonal relocation, just the time when males come out of their dens to prowl for mates. The fist-size spiders move hundreds at a time, and occasionally back roads are closed to let them pass. If you'll be camping in the desert in the spring, ask the ranger's office about the status. Though they're big and hairy, they're not venomous.

Scorpions, though, can be more dangerous, if very rarely deadly. In the southern desert areas, the most common variety is the bark scorpion, which nestles in rock crevices and woodpiles and can find its way into your shoes or the bottom of your sleeping bag. Its sting can cause anything from severe pain to difficulty breathing and should be treated with antivenin as soon as possible. Hard-shelled, segmented **desert centipedes** are another local creepy-crawly; they're often out at night and can grow up to nine inches long.

History

The historical and cultural continuity in New Mexico is remarkable. The state has been transformed from ice-age hunting ground to home of the atom bomb and a spaceport, but many of its inhabitants claim roots that stretch back hundreds, even thousands, of years.

ANCIENT AND ARCHAIC CIVILIZATION

New Mexico was one of the first places to harbor humans after the end of the last **ice age.** Archaeological findings indicate that some 12,000 years ago, people were hunting mastodons and other big game across the state. Mammoth bones, arrowheads, and the remains of campfires have been found in the Sandia Mountains east of Albuquerque; Folsom, in northeastern New Mexico; and Clovis, in the south. Sometime between 8000 and 5000 BC, these bands of hunters formed a small temporary settlement just north of Albuquerque, but it was not enough to stave off the decline of that ancient culture, as climatic shifts caused the big game to die off. Nomadic hunter-gatherers, seeking out smaller animals as well as seeds and nuts, did better in the new land, and by 1000 BC, they had established communities built around clusters of pit houses—sunken, log-covered rooms dug into the earth.

Along with this new form of shelter came an equally important advance in food: Mexican people gave corn kernels (maize) and lessons in agriculture to their neighbors, the **Mogollon,** who occupied southern New Mexico and Arizona. By AD 400, the Mogollon had begun growing squash and beans as well and had established concentrated communities all around the southern Rio Grande basin. This culture, dubbed the Basketmakers by archaeologists, also developed its own pottery, another skill learned from the indigenous people of Mexico. So, when the Mogollon made contact with the Ancestral Puebloans (also known as the Anasazi) in the northern part of the state, they had plenty to share.

THE PUEBLOS

The year 700 marks the beginning of what archaeologists call the **Pueblo I** phase, when disparate groups began to form larger communities in the upland areas on either side of the northern Rio Grande. Pit houses were still in use, but aboveground buildings of clay and sticks were erected alongside them. Increasingly, the pit houses were sacred spaces, chambers in which religious ceremonies were carried out; these are now known as kivas and are still an integral part of pueblo life.

The **Pueblo II** era began in 850 and is distinguished by the rise of Pueblo Bonito in Chaco Canyon, northwest of Santa Fe, into a full-scale city and perhaps capital of a small state. It was home to an estimated 1,500 people ruled by a religious elite. But Chaco abruptly began to crumble around 1150, perhaps due to drought, famine, or warfare. This shift marked the **Pueblo III** period, when the people who were to become today's Puebloans began building their easily defended cliff dwellings—most famously in the Four Corners area, at Mesa Verde in present-day Colorado, but also farther south, on the Pajarito Plateau in what's now Bandelier National Monument, and in Puyé, on Santa Clara Pueblo land. A drought at the end of the 13th century cleared out the Four Corners at the start of the **Pueblo IV** era, provoking the population to consolidate along the Rio Grande in clusters of sometimes more than a thousand interconnected rooms. These communities dotted the riverbank, drawing their sustenance both from the river water and from the mountains behind them.

THE SPANISH ARRIVE

These settlements were what the Spanish explorer **Francisco Vásquez de Coronado** and his crew saw when they first ventured into the area in 1540. Their Spanish word for the villages, *pueblos*, stuck and is still the name for both the places and the people who live in them. Coronado wasn't impressed, however, because the pueblos were made out of mud, not gold as he had been hoping. So, after two years and a couple of skirmishes with the natives, the team turned around and headed back to Mexico City.

It took another 50 years for the Spanish to muster more interest in the area. This time, in 1598, **Don Juan de Oñate** led a small group of Spanish families to settle on the banks of the Rio Grande, at a place they called San Gabriel, near Ohkay Owingeh (which they called San Juan Pueblo). About a decade later, the settlers moved away from their American Indian neighbors, to the new village of Santa Fe. The territory's third governor, Don Pedro de Peralta, made it the official capital of the territory of Nuevo México, which in those days stretched far into what is now Colorado and Arizona.

This time the colonists, mostly farmers, were motivated not so much by hopes of striking it rich but simply of making a living. Moreover, they were inspired by Catholic zeal, and Franciscan missionaries accompanied them to promote the faith among the Puebloans. It was partly these missionaries and their ruthless oppression of the native religion that drove the Indians to organize

the **Pueblo Revolt** of 1680. The Franciscans' "conversion" strategy involved public executions of the pueblos' medicine men, among other violent assaults on local traditions. But the Spanish colonists were no help either. In their desperation to squeeze wealth out of the hard land, they exploited the only resource they had, the slave labor of the Indians, who were either conscripts or stolen from their families. (The Indians did some poaching from Spanish families too, creating a violent sort of cultural exchange program.)

The leader of the Pueblo Revolt was a man named Popé (also spelled Po'pay), from San Juan Pueblo. Using Taos Pueblo as his base, he traveled to the other communities, secretly meeting with leaders to plan a united insurrection. Historians theorize he may have used Spanish to communicate with other Puebloans who did not speak his native Tewa, and he distributed among the conspirators lengths of knotted rope with which to count down the days to the insurrection. Although the Spanish captured a few of the rope-bearing messengers (Isleta Pueblo may never have gotten the message, which could explain its being the only pueblo not to participate), they could not avert the bloodshed. The Puebloan warriors killed families and missionaries, burned crops, and toppled churches. Santa Fe was besieged, and its population of more than 1,000 finally evacuated in a pitiful retreat.

The Spanish stayed away for 12 years, but a new governor, **Diego de Vargas,** took it upon himself to reclaim the area. He managed to talk many pueblos into a peaceful surrender, meeting resistance only in Taos and Santa Fe, where a two-day fight was required to oust the Indians from the Palace of the Governors; in Taos, violence ground on for an additional four years. The Spanish strategy in the post-revolt era was softer, with more compromise between the Franciscans and their intended flock, and a fair amount of cultural and economic exchange. The threat of raiding Comanche, Apache, and Navajo also forced both sides to cooperate. Banding together for defense, they were finally able to drive the Comanche away, culminating in a 1778 battle with Chief Cuerno Verde (Green Horn). The decisive victory is celebrated in the ritual dance called Los Comanches, still performed in small villages by Hispanos and Puebloans alike.

The other bonding force was trade. The Spanish maintained the **Camino Real de Tierra Adentro** (Royal Road of the Interior), which linked Santa Fe with central Mexico—the route follows roughly the line carved by I-25 today. Caravans came through only every year or two, but the profit from furs, pottery, textiles, and other local goods was enough to keep both cultures afloat, if utterly dependent on the Spanish government.

MEXICAN INDEPENDENCE AND THE FIRST ANGLOS

Spain carefully guarded all of its trade routes in the New World, even in a relatively unprofitable territory like Nuevo México. The only outside trade permitted was through the Comancheros, a ragtag band who traded with Comanche and other Plains Indians, working well into what would later be Oklahoma and even up to North Dakota. The Spanish governor encouraged them because their tight relationship with the Comanche helped protect New Mexico and Texas against intruders.

Interlopers were not welcome. Only a few enterprising fur trappers, lone mountain men in search of beaver pelts, slipped in. Spy-explorer **Zebulon Pike** and his crew were captured (perhaps intentionally, so Pike could get more inside information) and detained in Santa Fe for a spell in 1807. But in 1821, Mexico declared independence from Spain, liberating the territory of Nuevo México along with it. One of the first acts of the new government was to open the borders to trade. Initially just a trickle of curious traders came down the rough track from St. Louis, Missouri, but soon a flood of commerce flowed along the increasingly rutted and broad **Santa Fe Trail,** making the territory's capital city a meeting place between Mexicans and Americans swapping furs, gold, cloth, and more.

THE MEXICAN-AMERICAN WAR AND AFTER

Pike's expedition gave the U.S. government new details about the locations of Spanish forts. Just as important, Pike, who returned not long after Lewis and Clark completed their march across the Louisiana Purchase, helped fuel the country's expansionist fervor. In the next few decades, **"manifest destiny"** became the phrase on every American's lips, and the government was eyeing the Southwest. It annexed Texas in 1845, but New Mexico, with its small population and meager resources, didn't figure heavily in the short-lived war that followed. The Mexican governor surrendered peacefully to General Stephen Watts Kearny when he arrived in Santa Fe in 1846. In Taos, the transition was not accepted so readily, as Hispano business leaders and Taos Pueblo Indians instigated a brief but violent uprising, in which the first American governor, Charles Bent, was beheaded.

During the **Civil War,** New Mexico was in the way of a Texan Confederate strategy to secure the Southwest, but the rebels were thwarted in 1862 at the Battle of Glorieta Pass. The territory stayed in the hands of the Union until the end of the war, and people were more concerned with the local, increasingly brutal skirmishes caused by the arrival in Santa Fe of Bishop Jean-Baptiste Lamy, a tyrannical—or at least very thoughtless—Frenchman who tried to impose a European vision of the Catholic Church on a populace that had been beyond centralized control for centuries.

Even more significant to New Mexico's development was the arrival of the **railroad** in 1880, as it was laid through Raton Pass, near Santa Fe, and close to Albuquerque. Virtually overnight, strange goods and even stranger people came pouring into one of the remoter frontier outposts of the United States. Anglo influence was suddenly everywhere, in the form of new architecture (red brick was an Eastern affectation) and new business. Albuquerque, almost directly on the new railway tracks, boomed, while Santa Fe's fortunes slumped and Taos all but withered away, having peaked back in the late days of the Camino Real.

But while wheeler-dealers were setting up shop in central New Mexico, some more intrepid souls were poking around in the less-connected areas farther north. These tourists were artists who valued New Mexico not for its commercial potential but for its dramatic landscapes and exotic populace who seemed untouched by American ways. From the early 20th century on, Santa Fe and Taos were cultivated as art colonies, a function they still fulfill today.

FROM STATEHOOD TO WORLD WAR II

Based on its burgeoning economy, New Mexico became the 47th state in the union in 1912, effectively marking the end of the frontier period, a phase of violence, uncertainty, and isolation that lasted about 300 years—longer here than anywhere else in the United States. In addition to the painters and writers flocking to the new state, another group of migrants arrived: tuberculosis (TB) patients. Soon the state was known as a health retreat, and countless people did stints in its dry air to treat their ailing lungs.

One of these patients was J. Robert Oppenheimer, whose mild case of TB got him packed off to a camp near Pecos for a year after high school. He loved northern New Mexico and got to know some of its more hidden pockets. So, when the U.S. Army asked him if he had an idea where it should establish a secret base for the **Manhattan Project,** he knew just the place: a little camp high on a plateau above Santa Fe, named Los Alamos. This was the birthplace of the atomic bomb, or A-bomb, a weird, close-knit community of the country's greatest scientific minds (and biggest egos), working in utter secrecy. Only after the bomb was tested in the desert far to the south and Fat Man and Little Boy were dropped over Japan was the mysterious camp's mission revealed.

CONTEMPORARY HISTORY

The A-bomb ushered New Mexico into the modern era. Not only was it world-changing technology, but it also boosted the local economy. High-paying support staff jobs at Los Alamos and Kirtland Air Force Base in Albuquerque pulled some of the population away from subsistence farming and into a life that involved cars and electricity. But even so, the character of the state remained conservative and closed, so when the 1960s rolled around and New Mexico's empty space looked like the promised land to hippies, the culture clash was fierce. Staunch Catholic farmers took potshots at their naked, hallucinogen-ingesting neighbors who fantasized about getting back to the land but had no clue how to do it. After a decade or so, though, only the hardiest of the commune-dwellers were left, and they'd mellowed a bit, while the locals had come to appreciate at least their enthusiasm. Even if the communes didn't last, hippie culture has proven remarkably persistent in New Mexico. Even today, distinctly straight Hispanos can be heard saying things like, "I was tripping out on that band, man," and the state still draws Rainbow Gatherings, would-be Buddhists, and alternative healers.

The end of the 20th century saw unprecedented growth in both Albuquerque and Santa Fe. As usual, Albuquerque got the practical-minded development, such as the Intel chip-manufacturing plant and the services headquarters for Gap Inc., while Santa Fe was almost felled by its own artiness, turned inside-out during a few frenzied years in the early 1990s when movie stars and other moneyed types bought up prime real estate. In just a matter of months, rents went up tenfold and houses started selling for more than $1 million. Santa Fe has yet to work out the imbalance between its creative forces, which did save the city from utter decline, and economic ones, though it implemented a living-wage law in 2009. The state's capital has drawn both praise and ire for standing firm in its stance as a sanctuary city, even in the face of possible cuts in federal funding as a result.

Meanwhile, Taos has grown slowly but steadily, as have the pueblos, thanks to the legalization of gambling on their lands, but all of these communities retain an air of old New Mexico, where the frontier flavor and solitude can still be felt.

Government and Economy

New Mexico doesn't look so good on paper—in national rankings of income, education, and more, it often ranks 49th or 50th. "New Mexico is a third-world country" is a common quip, at least among an older generation that has seen a lifetime of nepotism and incompetence in government. But these issues have also inspired a good deal of activist sentiment, and politics are lively.

GOVERNMENT

New Mexico's political scene is as diverse as its population, though the cities tend to vote Democrat. Still, Republican Susana Martinez became New Mexico's first woman governor in 2010 (her opponent was also a woman, incidentally), and was reelected in 2014. In the 2016 presidential election, counties skewed extremely red or blue; former governor and Libertarian Gary Johnson took over 9 percent of the vote, his highest stake in the nation.

New Mexico is notable for its equitable Hispanic representation in every level of government, including the state legislature, where it consistently matches the state Hispanic population, just under 50 percent. This has helped keep the immigration debate at a relatively polite pitch—unlike in neighboring Arizona and Texas, where the Hispanic population is underrepresented in the government.

Each American Indian pueblo (as well as Navajo, Zuni, and Apache lands elsewhere in the state) acts as a sovereign nation, with its own laws, tax regulations, police forces, and government. Indians vote in U.S. and state elections, while in the pueblos, most domestic issues are decided by a tribal governor, a war chief, and a few other officials elected by a consensus of men in the kiva.

The Navajo Nation, with more than 250,000 people to manage, as well as a substantial cache of natural resources, does practice direct democracy, open to both men and women. In its system, the reservation, which reaches into Arizona and Utah, is divided into "chapters," and their elected representatives participate in the Navajo Council, which convenes in the capital at Window Rock, Arizona. Since a reform in 1991, the Navajo system has had three branches, like the American one. In 2006, Lynda Lovejoy was the first woman to run for nation president; she ran again in 2010, losing by a small margin. The 2014 election brought up a different issue, when one candidate was disqualified for failing to demonstrate fluency in the Navajo language, a legal requirement for holding the position.

ECONOMY

In New Mexico, roughly 20 percent of the population lives below the poverty level, compared with national averages around 15 percent. It's also near the bottom in the number of high school and college graduates per capita. Statistics in the pueblos and reservations have historically been grimmer, with up to 50 percent unemployment in some areas—but this has changed due to casino-fueled development. The Navajo Nation has extensive landholdings, but with an infrastructure that's more 19th than 21st century, businesses seldom invest. The same could in fact be said for many of the rural sections of the state, on Indian land or not.

The unemployment rate, however, is

often lower than the national average, in part because Albuquerque continues to be a **manufacturing** center for computer chips, mattresses, specialty running shoes, and more. And the city where Microsoft was founded (Bill Gates and Paul Allen later moved back to Seattle, Washington, to be close to their families) does foster **technology** development. As well, the Sandia and Los Alamos **national laboratories** are the state's biggest employers—together they employ over 23,000 people. **Aerospace** manufacturing parks are growing outside Albuquerque and Las Cruces, including Spaceport America near Truth or Consequences.

Outside the cities, significant profits from coal, copper, oil, and natural gas—most in the southern part of the state, as well as in the northwest—keep the economy afloat. That's the big money, but the **agricultural** sector, from dairy cows in the south to apple orchards along the Rio Grande to beef jerky from the numerous cattle ranches, contributes a decent amount to the pot. And Santa Fe's **arts** sector shouldn't be overlooked—galleries post sales of $200 million every year, though they're criticized for sending much of that money right back to artists who live and work out of state. Thanks to sizable tax rebates (courtesy of the so-named Breaking Bad bill), the **film industry** has flourished. Albuquerque Studios is one of the largest production facilities in the country, while Santa Fe Studios has been the site of numbers film and TV productions in the relatively short time since it was founded.

Even if the economic situation isn't ideal, it's nothing New Mexicans aren't used to. Low income has been the norm for so long that a large segment of the population is, if not content with, at least adapted to eking out a living from very little (the median family income is only around $43,800, compared to the U.S. median of $52,250). In this respect, the state hasn't lost its frontier spirit at all.

Local Culture

New Mexico's 1.8 million people have typically been described as a tricultural mix of Indians, Spanish, and Anglos. That self-image has begun to expand as residents have delved deeper into history and seen that the story involves a few more threads.

DEMOGRAPHY

The labels of Indian, Spanish, and Anglo are used uniquely in New Mexico. First, **Indian:** This is still a common term, as "Native American" never fully caught on. You'll see "American Indian" in formal situations, but even the "American" part is a bit laughable, considering "America" wasn't so named until Christopher Columbus made his voyage west. "Indian" refers to a number of different peoples who do not share a common culture or language: Navajo on the west side of the state, Jicarilla and Mescalero Apache, and the Puebloans of the Rio Grande and west as far as Acoma and Zuni. "Pueblo" refers not to a particular tribe, but to a larger group of people who speak four distinct languages but are banded together by a common way of living. Typically, people will identify themselves by their particular tribe: Santa Clara, for instance, or Taos. With about 10.2 percent of the population claiming American Indian ancestry (nearly 10 times the national average, and second only to Alaska), traditions are still strong.

Spanish really means that: the people, primarily in northern New Mexico, whose ancestors were Spaniards, rather than the mestizos of Mexico. For many families, it's a point of pride similar to that of *Mayflower* descendants. Over the years, particularly during the 20th century, a steady influx of Mexican immigrants blurred racial distinctions a bit, but it also reinforced the use of Spanish as a daily language and inspired pride in the culture's music and other folkways. In some circles, the word **Hispano** is used to label New Mexico's distinct culture with centuries-old Iberian roots, which includes the **Basques,** who came here both during the conquest (Don Juan de Oñate, the first Spanish governor, was Basque) and in the early 20th century as sheepherders. The discovery of families of **crypto-Jews** (Spanish Jews who nominally converted to Catholicism but fled here to avoid the Inquisition) has added another fascinating layer to the Spanish story, along with the knowledge that many of the first Spanish explorers likely had Arab blood as well.

Anglo is the most imprecise term, as it can mean anyone who's not Spanish or Indian. Originally used to talk about traders of European descent who came to hunt and sell furs and trade on the Santa Fe Trail, it still refers to people who can't trace their roots back to the conquistadors or farther. If you're a Vietnamese immigrant, a Tibetan refugee, or an African American whose family settled a farm here after the Civil War, you could be, at least in jest, Anglo. (As of 2014, about 38.9 percent of the population was non-Hispanic Caucasian; Asians were only 1.7 percent, and African Americans made up 2.5 percent.) But all Anglo culture is shot through with Spanish and Indian influence, whether among the organic garlic farmers from California who rely on their acequias for water or the New Age seekers who do sweat lodge rituals.

Even with a liberal application of "Anglo," the tricultural arrangement is limiting, as it doesn't assign a place to contemporary immigrants from Mexico and other Latin American countries, and their numbers are growing steadily. It also doesn't acknowledge the strong Mexican American **Chicano** culture that's shared across the Southwest, from Los Angeles through Texas. The U.S. census form lumps both newer arrivals and old Spanish under "Hispanic"—a category (distinct from race) that made up 47.7 percent of the population in 2014, the highest in the country.

RELIGION

Four hundred years after the arrival of the Franciscan missionaries, New Mexico is still a heavily **Catholic** state—even KFC offers a Friday-night fish fry during Lent here. But the relative isolation of the territory produced some variances that have disturbed the Vatican. In both Indian and Spanish churches, the pageantry of medieval Christianity is preserved. Las Posadas, the reenactment of Mary and Joseph's search for lodging in Bethlehem, is a festive torch-lit tradition every December, and during the annual spring Holy Week pilgrimage to Chimayó, devoted groups stage the stations of the cross, complete with 100-pound wood beams and lots of fake blood.

The Pueblo Indians play on church-as-theater too: During Christmas Eve Mass, for instance, the service may come to an abrupt end as the priest is hustled off the pulpit by face-painted clowns making way for the parade of ceremonial dancers down the aisle. In both cultures, the Mexican Virgin of Guadalupe is highly revered, and a number of saints are honored as intercessors for all manner of dilemmas, from failing crops to false imprisonment.

Eastern religions have a noticeable presence in New Mexico as well, and even a bit of political clout. A community of primarily American-born converts to **Sikhism** in Española, for example, is a major donor to both parties. Santa Fe is home to a substantial number of **Buddhists,** both American converts and native Tibetan refugees who have relocated to this different mountainous land. Stupas can be found up and down the Rio Grande.

LANGUAGE

English is the predominant language, but **Spanish** is very commonly used—about 30 percent of the population speaks it regularly. Spanish-speakers in northern New Mexico were for centuries only the old

New Mexico's Penitentes

Most Hispano villages in northern New Mexico have a modest one-story building called a morada—the meeting place of **Los Hermanos Penitentes** (The Penitent Brothers), a lay Catholic fraternity with deep roots in medieval Spain and a history that has often put it at odds with the church.

The Penitentes developed in New Mexico in the early colonial era and were at the height of their influence during the so-called Secular Period (1790-1850), when the Franciscans had been pushed out by church leaders in Mexico but no new priests were sent to the territory. Members of the brotherhood cared for the ill, conducted funerals, and settled petty disputes and even elections. They maintained the spiritual and political welfare of their villages when there were no priests or central government to do so.

The Penitentes are best known for their intense religious rituals, which are rumored to still include self-flagellation, bloodletting, and mock crucifixion—activities that took place in public processions for centuries but were driven underground in the late 19th century following official church condemnation. The secrecy, along with sensational journalism by visitors from the East Coast, fueled gruesome rumors. For their crucifixion reenactments, it was said Penitentes used real nails, and the man drawn by lot to be the *Cristo* had a good chance of dying—though no eyewitness ever recorded the practice on paper. One well-documented ritual involves pulling *la carretera del muerte*, an oxcart filled with rocks and a wooden figure of Doña Sebastiana, Lady Death. Morbid imagery bred morbid curiosity: Photos in a *Harper's* magazine story from the early 1900s show Anglos looking on agog as Penitentes clad in white pants and black hoods whip themselves.

In 1947, after years of concerted lobbying (but not an official renunciation of its rituals), the Penitentes were again accepted into the fold of the Catholic Church. The *hermanos mayores* (head brothers) from all of the moradas convene annually in Santa Fe, and the group, which has an estimated 3,000 members, functions as a political and public-service club.

The rituals do continue, most visibly during Holy Week, when the group's devotion to the physical suffering of the human Jesus is at its keenest. The Penitentes reenact the stations of the cross and the crucifixion, and although ketchup is more prevalent than real blood and statues often stand in for the major players, the scenes are solemn and affectingly tragic. On some days during Holy Week, the morada is open to non-Penitentes—a rare chance for outsiders to see the meeting place of this secretive group.

Hispano families, communicating in a variant of Castilian with a distinct vocabulary that developed in isolation. This "Quixotic" dialect changed little until the early 1900s, when immigrants arrived from Mexico and elsewhere in Latin America. For much of the 20th century, English was the only permissible classroom language, although many school districts required Spanish as a foreign language. Since the 1990s, education policy has shifted to include bilingual classrooms.

Additionally, you'll occasionally hear Indians speaking their respective languages. Of the four main Pueblo tongues, **Tewa, Tiwa,** and **Towa** are part of the Tanoan family of languages, which are also spoken by Plains Indians. They are related but mutually unintelligible, roughly equivalent to, say, French, Spanish, and Italian. Tewa is the most widely spoken, used in all of the pueblos just north of Santa Fe: Ohkay Owingeh, San Ildefonso, Santa Clara, Pojoaque, Tesuque, and Nambé. Four pueblos speak Tiwa—Taos and Picurís share one dialect, while Isleta and Sandia, in an odd pocket near Albuquerque, speak a different dialect. Towa is now spoken only at Jemez Pueblo. Part of the greater Athabaskan family, the **Navajo** and **Apache** languages are related to but distinct from one another.

Keresan (spoken in Laguna, Acoma, Cochiti, Kewa, San Felipe, Santa Ana, and Zia) and **Zuni** (spoken only at that pueblo) are what linguists call "isolates." Like

Basque, they are not connected to neighboring languages, nor to any other language. Additionally, each Keresan-speaking pueblo has developed its own dialect, so immediately adjacent communities can understand each other, but those farthest apart cannot.

One interesting characteristic of the Pueblo languages is that they have remained relatively pure. Tewa vocabulary, for instance, is still less than 5 percent loan words, despite centuries of Spanish and English influence. This is probably due to the way speakers have long been forced to compartmentalize, using Tewa for conversation at home and switching to English or Spanish for business and trade. For centuries, the Franciscan priests, then the U.S. government, attempted to stamp out Native American languages. Following the Civil War, Puebloan children were moved forcibly to boarding schools, where they were given Anglo names and permitted to speak only English, a policy that continued for decades.

Only in 1990, with the passage of the **Native American Languages Act,** were American Indian languages officially permitted in government-funded schools—indeed, they are now recognized as a unique element of this country's culture and encouraged. In Taos, where the Tiwa language is a ritual secret that outsiders are not permitted to learn, one public school has Tiwa classes for younger students, open only to tribe members and taught by approved teachers; as an added measure against the language being recorded, the classroom has no chalkboard. Less-formal instruction within the pueblos as well as on the Navajo Nation has also helped the Indian languages enjoy a renaissance.

The Arts

New Mexico is a hotbed of creativity, from Santa Fe's burgeoning contemporary art scene to traditional Spanish folk artists working in remote villages, using the same tools their great-grandfathers did, to whole American Indian villages, such as Acoma Pueblo, devoted to the production of distinctive pottery. Here's what to look for in the more traditional arenas of pottery, weaving, jewelry, and wood carving.

POTTERY

New Mexico's pottery tradition thrives, drawing on millennia of craftsmanship. About 2,000 years ago, the **Mogollon** people in the southern part of the state began making simple pots of brown coiled clay. A thousand years later, the craft had developed into the beautiful black-on-white symmetry of the **Mimbres** people. Later, each of the pueblos developed its own style.

By the 20th century, some traditions had died out, but almost all felt some kind of renaissance following the work of San Ildefonso potter **María Martinez** in the first half of the 20th century. Along with her husband, Julian, Martinez revived a long-lost style of lustrous black pottery with subtle matte decoration. The elegant pieces, which looked at once innovative and traditional, inspired Anglo collectors (who saw the couple's work at the 1934 Chicago World's Fair, among other places) as well as local potters. Today, many artists make their livings with clay.

The various tribal styles are distinguished by their base clay, the "slip" (the clay-and-water finish), and their shape. Taos and Picurís pueblos, for instance, are surrounded by beds of micaceous clay, which lends pots a subtle glitter. (It also helps them withstand heat well; they're renowned for cooking beans.) Acoma specializes in intricate black designs painted on thin white clay. Pottery from Ohkay Owingeh (formerly San Juan) is typically reddish-brown with incised symbols. And Santa Clara developed the "wedding jar," a double-neck design with a handle. If a particular style catches your eye in city galleries, then you can

Luminarias or *Farolitos*?

luminarias in Santa Fe ... where most people would call them *farolitos*

The cultural differences between Santa Fe and Albuquerque don't apply just to the number of art galleries per square block and whether you eat posole or rice with your enchiladas. Every Christmas, a debate rears its head: What do you call a paper bag with a bit of sand in the bottom and a votive candle inside? These traditional holiday decorations, which line driveways and flat adobe rooftops in the last weeks of December, are commonly known as luminarias in Albuquerque and most towns to the south, and as *farolitos* in Santa Fe and all the villages to the north.

To complicate matters, another holiday tradition in Santa Fe and other northern towns is to light small bonfires of piñon logs in front of houses. And Santa Feans call these little stacks of wood ... luminarias. *Farolitos*, they argue, are literally "little lanterns," an accurate description of the glowing paper bags—and under this logic, use of the term *farolito* has spread a bit in Albuquerque, at least among people who weren't raised saying luminaria from birth.

Albuquerqueans do have Webster's on their side, however; the dictionary concurs that luminarias are paper-bag lanterns and notes the tradition comes from Mexico, where the bags are often colored and pricked with holes. Because this author's loyalties are to Santa Fe—and the city does have a hugely popular annual event named after them—the argument is settled, at least in these pages: *Farolito* it is.

visit the specific pueblo, where you may be able to buy directly from the artisan and perhaps see where the piece was made.

TEXTILES

After pottery, **weaving** is probably the state's most widespread craft. Historically, Indian and Spanish weaving styles were separate, but they have merged over the centuries to create some patterns and styles unique to the Rio Grande Valley. The first Spanish explorers marveled at the Navajo cotton blankets, woven in whole panels on wide looms; Spaniards had been working with narrow looms and stitching two panels together. Spanish weavers introduced the hardy Churro sheep, with its rough wool that was good for hand-spinning, as well as new dyes, such as indigo (although the blue-tinted rugs are often called **Moki** rugs, using a Navajo word).

In the early 1800s, in an attempt to make a better product for trade, the Spanish government sent Mexican artists north to work with local weavers. Out of this meeting came the distinctive **Saltillo** styles (named for the region the Mexican teachers came from), such as the running-leaf pattern, which Rio Grande weavers alternated with solid-color stripes. In the 1880s, New Mexican artisans first saw quilts from the eastern United States, and they adapted the eight-pointed star to their wool rugs. Another popular motif from the 19th century is a zigzag pattern that resembles lightning.

One item that shows up in antiques shops is the **Chimayó blanket,** an invention of the tourist age in the early 20th century, when Anglo traders encouraged local Hispano weavers to make an affordable souvenir to sell to visitors looking for "Indian" blankets. They're handsome, single-width rugs with a strong central motif, perhaps the iconic Southwestern-look rug.

Also look for *colcha* work, a Spanish style in which a loose-weave rug is decorated with wool embroidery. It was revived in the 1930s by Mormons, and you will occasionally see beautiful examples from this period in collectors' shops. Contemporary weaving can draw on any and all of these innovations and is practiced just as often by a young Anglo as a Hispano grandmother. A strong small-batch wool industry in New Mexico helps the scene tremendously—expect to see vivid color-block contemporary pieces alongside the more traditional patterns.

JEWELRY

Despite a long native tradition, the familiar forms of jewelry seen today date only from the mid-19th century, when the Navajo of western New Mexico pioneered silversmithing (it's thought they learned it during their internment at Fort Sumner) and taught it to the Pueblo Indians. The most iconic piece of Southwestern jewelry, a signature Navajo design, is the turquoise-and-silver **squash-blossom necklace,** a large crescent pendant decorated with flowerlike silver beads. Actually derived from Spanish pomegranate

decorations, rather than native plant imagery, it's seen in every Southwest jewelry store.

Look also for shell-shaped **concha belts** (also spelled "concho"), silver "shells" linked together or strung on a leather belt, and the San Felipe specialty, **heishi,** tiny disks made of shell and threaded to make a rope-like strand. The Zuni carve small animal **fetishes**—bears, birds, and more—often strung on necklaces with heishi. In addition to turquoise, opals are a popular decorative stone, along with brick-red coral, lapis lazuli, and black jet and marble. Whatever you buy, the gallery or artisan should supply you with a written receipt of its components—which stones, the grade of silver, and so forth.

Turquoise

Although New Mexico's turquoise is all mined out, the stone is still an essential part of local jewelry-making; most of it is imported from mines in China. It is available in shades from lime-green to pure sky-blue, and much of it has been subjected to various processes to make it stabler and more versatile, which affects the price.

Rare gem-grade turquoise is the top of the line—a high-quality piece with complex spiderwebbing from now-empty mines like Lander or Lone Mountain can cost $350 per carat. "Gem-grade" applies only to **natural stones** (those that have not been chemically treated in any way) and is based on the piece's luster, hardness, and matrix, the term for the web of dark veins running through it, which you should be able to feel in any natural turquoise, regardless of grade. Highest-quality stones from still-functioning mines in China or Tibet will cost significantly less ($10-20 per carat) but will be of the same quality as some premium American stones. Slightly less splendid natural stones are graded jewelry-quality, high-quality, or investment-quality—but they are not quite hard enough to guarantee they will not change color over decades. They cost $2-5 per carat. For any natural stone, the seller must provide you with a written certificate of its status.

Because good natural turquoise is increasingly difficult to come by and turquoise is such an unreliable stone, various treatments are a common and acceptable way of making a great deal of the stuff usable. **Treated turquoise** refers to any stone that has added resins, waxes, or other foreign elements. A certain proprietary treatment, **enhanced turquoise,** also called "Zachary process turquoise," is usually applied to medium-grade or higher stones.

Turquoise that has been **stabilized,** or submerged in epoxy resin to harden it and deepen the color, makes up the bulk of the market. Because it's less expensive, it allows for a little waste in the carving process, and good-quality stabilized turquoise is often found in expensive jewelry with elaborate inlay. Average-quality stabilized stone, the next grade down, is used by perhaps 70 percent of American Indian artisans—it can stand up to being carved and is very well priced. Though it ranks relatively low in the range of turquoise available, it produces an attractive piece of jewelry—perhaps not with the elaborate spiderwebbing of a rare piece, but with an overall good color and luster.

Below this are low-quality stabilized stones that have been artificially colored (often called "color shot," or, more confusingly, "color stabilized"). **"Synthetic"** stones are actually real turquoise—small chunks mixed with a binding powder of ground turquoise or pyrite, then pressed into shapes and cut. The result is surprisingly attractive, with natural spiderwebbing, but it should be clearly labeled as synthetic. And of course there is the turquoise that isn't at all—plastic stuff that can be quite convincing.

Aside from the synthetic stuff, don't worry too much about getting "bad" or "cheap" turquoise—because each stone is different, the more important thing is to find a piece that's attractive to you and is priced to reflect its quality. Just remember that the words "genuine," "authentic," or "pure" have no real meaning—only "natural" is legally defined. Likewise, the phrase **"authentic Indian handmade"** is a legal one—any variation on this wording (such as "Indian crafted") is likely some kind of ruse. Shopping in New Mexico provides many opportunities to buy direct from the artisan—under the portal at the Palace of the Governors in Santa Fe, for instance. Otherwise, just avoid shopping in too-good-to-be-true stores that are perpetually "going out of business" or "in liquidation."

WOOD AND TINWORK

When Spanish colonists arrived in New Mexico, they had few resources, little money, and only the most basic tools. A group of settlers would typically include one carpenter, whose skills helped fill everyone's houses with heavy wood **furniture** (still made today). But the carpenter also helped the group to worship—for chief among the wood-carvers was (and is) the *santero* or *santera,* who carves images of saints. These so-called **santos** can be either flat (retablos) or three-dimensional (bultos) and are typically painted in lively colors, though some outstanding work has been produced in plain, unpainted wood.

Santo styles have shown remarkable continuity over the centuries. The most notable break from tradition was by Patrocinio Barela, whose WPA-sponsored work in the 1930s was almost fluid, utilizing the natural curves and grains of the wood. His sons and grandsons practice the art today. For centuries, the piousness of the *santero* was valued at least as much as his skill in carving, though many contemporary carvers do their work for a large market of avid collectors. One popular figure is San Isidro, patron saint of farmers, from 12th-century Spain.

Look also for **straw marquetry,** another product of hard times in the colonial period, in which tiny fibers of "poor man's gold" replaced precious metals as inlay to make elaborate geometric designs on dark wood. Tinwork is another ubiquitous craft, found in inexpensive votive-candle holders as well as elaborately punched and engraved mirror frames and chandeliers.

Essentials

Transportation.................. 237
Food and Accommodations.... 239
Travel Tips...................... 242
Health and Safety.............. 246

Transportation

GETTING THERE
Air
Albuquerque International Sunport
(ABQ; 505/244-7700, www.cabq.gov/airport) is the main access point to the region. It's served by the three major domestic carriers, plus Southwest Airlines, Alaska Airlines, Allegiant Air, and JetBlue. Fares fluctuate on the same schedule as the rest of the country, with higher rates in summer and over holidays; in the winter, it's wise to choose a connection through a more temperate hub, such as Dallas/Fort Worth (American) or Salt Lake City (Delta).

Small **Santa Fe Municipal Airport** (SAF; 121 Aviation Dr.; 505/955-2900, www.santafenm.gov/airport), west of the city, receives direct flights from Dallas and Phoenix with American Eagle, and from Denver with United.

Train
Amtrak (800/872-7245, www.amtrak.com) runs the Southwest Chief daily between Chicago and Los Angeles, stopping in **Lamy** (18 miles from Santa Fe) and **Albuquerque.**

Arriving in Albuquerque, you're in the middle of downtown, in a depot shared with Greyhound. There are lockers here (occasionally full), and city buses are available just up the block. Lamy (the stop nearest Santa Fe) is no more than a depot—though it is a dramatic and wild-feeling place to get off the train. Amtrak provides an awkwardly timed shuttle service to Santa Fe hotels (passengers arriving on eastbound trains must wait for passengers from the westbound train, an hour later). From Chicago, Amtrak pads its schedule heavily between Lamy and Albuquerque—so if the train is running behind, you'll be late

arriving in Lamy but generally will still get to Albuquerque on schedule.

Bus
Greyhound (800/231-2222, www.greyhound.com) connects New Mexico with adjacent states and Mexico. Routes run roughly along I-40 and I-25, with little service to outlying areas. If you're coming from elsewhere in the Southwest, you may want to investigate **El Paso-Los Angeles Limousine Express** (915/532-4061 in El Paso, 626/442-1945 in Los Angeles, 505/247-8036 in Albuquerque, www.eplalimo.com), a long-established operator that originally served the Mexican immigrant population—it connects Denver and Albuquerque.

Car
Conveniently, New Mexico is crisscrossed by interstates: **I-40** and **I-10** run east-west, and **I-25** cuts roughly down the center, north-south. Denver to Santa Fe is 450 miles, about a 6-hour drive; add another hour to reach Albuquerque. El Paso, Texas, to Albuquerque is 275 miles, about 4 hours. Coming from Flagstaff, Arizona, Albuquerque is 325 miles along I-40, about 4.5 hours; from Amarillo, Texas, it's just slightly less distance in the other direction.

Southwest road-trippers often combine New Mexico with southwestern Colorado, in which case **U.S. 550** makes a good route south from Durango, and **U.S. 84** runs from Pagosa Springs. From Tucson, Arizona, a nice route into New Mexico is to cut north off I-10 at Lordsburg, following Highway 90 to Silver City and winding through the mountains northeast to reach I-25 to Albuquerque.

GETTING AROUND

This guide covers a relatively small area—about 200 miles from north to south. Within Albuquerque and Santa Fe, you can often get around by walking, biking, or public transportation, but count on having a car for at least a portion of your trip.

If you're visiting just Albuquerque or Santa Fe, you can get around on foot and public transportation—easily in Santa Fe, and with a little planning in Albuquerque. A commuter rail line links the two cities, with handy stops in each downtown area. Parking in downtown Santa Fe can be expensive and difficult, so it's best to rent a car only for day trips out of the city. Taos, however, has only minimal bus service, so a car will make things much easier.

Bus

Between Santa Fe and Taos (and communities around and in between, including the pueblos), the **North Central Regional Transit District** (866/206-0754, www.ncrtd.org) offers commuter bus service. It's not very frequent, but it's free, and it covers a lot of area, making it an option for the hard-core no-car traveler.

Greyhound (800/231-2222, www.greyhound.com) connects Albuquerque with Santa Fe and Las Cruces, as well as a few other midsize towns.

Train

The **Rail Runner** (866/795-7245, www.riometro.org) commuter train connects Belén, Albuquerque, and Santa Fe, with convenient downtown stations, making a car-free visit quite feasible, or even a day trip. The train passes through odd pockets of Albuquerque and stunning, untouched pueblo lands. Tickets are based on a zone system; the 90-minute ride between downtown Albuquerque and Santa Fe costs $9, or $10 for a day pass. (Kids: Listen for the "meep-meep!" warning as the doors close!)

Car

Driving New Mexico's scenic byways is definitely one of the pleasures of traveling here. On the other hand, parking in Santa Fe can be unpleasant, or at least expensive—and you can get around the center of town very easily on foot. So, ideally, you would rent a car only for the days you plan to go out of the city. Central Taos is small, but sights are spread out on the fringes, and only the most dedicated can manage without a car. In Albuquerque, you can live without a car for a few days, but it requires planning and rules out a few of the sights. All of the major car-rental chains are at Albuquerque's airport, in a single building; see the respective city chapters for other rental companies and offices.

All but a few roads are passable year-round. You won't need four-wheel drive, but be prepared in winter for ice and snow anywhere other than central Albuquerque. Plan on an hour's drive from Albuquerque to Santa Fe via I-25, and an hour and a half from Santa Fe to Taos via the low road.

Bike

With beautiful vistas, often deserted roads, and a strong community of both road cyclists and mountain bikers, northern New Mexico can be a great place to get around on two wheels, as long as it's not your main form of transport. Whether you'll be riding your own bike or renting one here, always pack a patch kit, and consider installing tire liners. Goathead thorns and broken glass are particular scourges of the highway shoulder.

Central Albuquerque and Santa Fe are both manageable by bicycle, with separate lanes in many cases. Taos is less accommodating, and traffic on the main road through town can be unpleasantly heavy and fast. But both the Rail Runner and the Taos Express bus service accommodate bicycles, so it's possible to take your wheels with you from town to town.

Food and Accommodations

FOOD

New Mexicans love their food so much, they have been known to enshrine it on lottery tickets, with scratch cards named Chile Cash, Chips and Salsa, and Sopaipilla Dough (promising "lots of honey and plenty of money"). The state cuisine is a distinctive culinary tradition that shouldn't be confused with Tex-Mex, Californian Mex, or south-of-the-border Mexican—even though most locals will say they're going out for "Mexican" when they mean they want a bowl of purely *New* Mexican green-chile stew. (But if you're eating mole or ceviche, that's *"Mexican* Mexican," and you can get more of it the farther south you drive.) New Mexican cuisine doesn't typically do bean-and-meat chile, certainly not mango-flavored anything, and only rarely guacamole—you can get it, but avocados are expensive here.

All Chile, All the Time

The cuisine's distinguishing element is the **New Mexico chile pepper.** The best-known variety is the Hatch chile, named for the southern New Mexican town that's the center of the industry. In the north, Chimayó is another big chile-producing town, with its own heirloom strain, usually picked red.

When the chile is picked green, it is roasted and peeled, then used whole to make chiles rellenos (stuffed with cheese and fried in batter), or cut into chunks and cooked in sauces or used as the base of a meaty green-chile stew. In northern New Mexico, that sauce is pure chile, maybe thinned with chicken broth; in some towns in the southern part of the state, it's more like a green-chile cream gravy, often with a base of cream-of-mushroom soup.

When the New Mexico chile is left to ripen, then dried in the sun, it turns dark red and leathery. These dry red chiles are stored whole, in long chains called *ristras*, or ground into flakes (*chile caribe*) or finer powder to be the base of a sauce or marinade. The heartiest red-chile dish is *carne adovada*, chunks of pork shoulder stewed with pure red sauce.

Most other items—enchiladas, burritos, and eggs (huevos rancheros), to name a few—can be ordered with either variety of chile, so a standard query in restaurants (and now enshrined as the official state question) is "Red or green?" You can have both, splitting the plate half-and-half, a style many people call "Christmas," though old-timers still call it "Mexican flag."

The chile is often coupled with the traditional Native American triad of **corn, squash,** and **beans.** The beans are typically brown, meaty pintos, served whole in a stew or mashed up and "refried" (not actually fried twice—the term is a mistranslation of the Spanish *refrito,* which means "really fried"). Corn takes the form of tortillas as well as hulled kernels of hominy, called posole here and often cooked into a stew with chile, oregano, and meat. Ground corn paste (masa) is whipped with lard (or Crisco, if you're "healthy") and wrapped around a meaty filling, then tied in a corn husk and steamed to make a **tamale.** Squash comes in a common side dish called *calabacitas,* sautéed with onions and a touch of green chile. Spanish settlers brought lamb, which finds its way into tacos and stews.

American Indian cuisine isn't so distinct from what everyone else eats—its one major element is **fry bread,** a round of deep-fried dough served with honey or filled with ground meat, cheese, and lettuce to make an "Indian taco"; a "Navajo taco" often uses shredded lamb or mutton in place of ground beef. Bread baked in a traditional domed adobe *horno* oven is also popular, and the Zuni make a distinctive sourdough this way. In pueblos and on the reservations, you'll see these mud ovens in most yards. Game meat, such as deer, is also a major component of

Red-Chile Sauce

Use only freshly ground New Mexico red chile for this sauce—not the chile powder sold in most grocery stores. The sauce will keep in the refrigerator for a month, and you can use it to top eggs or steaks, or devote the whole batch to a tray of enchiladas. (If you're doing the latter, you'll want to keep the sauce relatively thin, so you can easily coat the tortillas with sauce before filling them.) The flavor is best if it is prepared ahead and left to sit overnight.

Yield: 2 cups
½ c. New Mexico red chile powder
½ tsp. ground cumin (optional)
1 tsp. ground coriander (optional)
2 Tbsp. all-purpose flour
2 Tbsp. lard (or vegetable oil)
2 or 3 cloves garlic, crushed or minced
2 c. chicken stock or water
1 tsp. dried oregano (optional)

Measure the chile, cumin, coriander, and flour into a heavy-bottomed saucepan and place over medium-high heat. Stir continuously until the spices are just fragrant and the flour has darkened slightly. Remove the chile-flour mix to a small bowl. Heat the lard or oil in the pan, and add the garlic. Stir until fragrant. Then stir the chile-flour mix into the oil-garlic mixture—you will have a very coarse paste. Stirring constantly, slowly add half of the stock or water. Continue stirring, and the mixture will thicken and become velvety. Add the remaining stock or water and the oregano, mix well, turn heat to low, and let sauce simmer for about 20 minutes, until it is somewhat reduced and thickened to your liking. If the mixture becomes too thick, simply add more water.

American Indian cooking, though you'll rarely see it in restaurants.

Green chile makes its way into standard American fare as well. It's a popular pizza topping (great with pepperoni or ham), and the **green-chile cheeseburger** is a top choice everywhere. Also look out for **breakfast burritos,** big flour tortillas filled with scrambled eggs, hash browns, and some kind of meat—bacon, crumbled sausage, or sometimes Mexican chorizo, a spicy pork sausage. Some places sell them as to-go food, wrapped in foil with green chile added to the mix. At sit-down places, you get the whole construction smothered in either red or green chile.

Sopaipillas are another New Mexican specialty. They're palm-sized pillows of deep-fried dough, used to mop up chile and beans during the main meal, then slathered with honey for dessert. In a disturbing trend, some restaurants now offer a honey-flavored corn syrup, because it's cheaper and doesn't crystallize—if you encounter this, complain at top volume.

Bizcochitos, little anise-laced cookies, are the state's official sweet treat. Wash it all down with a **margarita,** which purists insist should involve only lime, tequila, and triple sec and be served on the rocks in a salt-rimmed glass. (Restaurants with only a beer-and-wine license often offer an agave-wine margarita—decent flavor, but pretty weak.)

How to Take the Heat

When your server plunks down a heavy white ceramic plate covered in chile and melted cheese, the words "this plate is very hot" cover only half of the story. Every year the harvest varies a bit, and the chile can be mild or so spicy as to blister lips and produce a dizzying (and addictive) endorphin rush. Locals look back on particularly incendiary seasons with that mixture of awe, fear, and longing that junkies reserve for their best scores. In general, green chile tends to be hotter than red, but it's best to ask your server what to expect—some restaurants specialize in one or the other.

You can protect yourself against chile heat by ordering a side of sour cream with your enchiladas or burrito—although be warned that many consider this a "Texan" affectation, and you may be derided by your fellow diners. Locals usually just reach for a **sopaipilla,** the starch from which can absorb some of the chile oils. Don't gulp down water, which only spreads the searing oils around your mouth. Beer is a marginal improvement, and margaritas are at least distracting.

Fine Dining and Wine
While there are plenty of time-warp diners and mom-and-pop hole-in-the-wall joints in New Mexico, dining can also be very sophisticated, keeping pace with the national trend toward local and organic produce. This movement hasn't been such a huge leap here: Many small family farms didn't have to "go organic," because they were never very industrialized in the first place. At white-tablecloth places, Southwestern fusion is still common, with chile working its way into foie gras appetizers and even high-concept desserts.

The fine dining scene is enhanced by a burgeoning wine industry, initiated by Spanish settlers in the 17th century but enjoying a resurgence since the 1980s. Gruet Winery in Albuquerque is the best-known New Mexico producer, especially for its excellent sparkling wine. This makes for a nice little perk of New Mexico dining: You can get inexpensive bubbly by the glass almost everywhere. The **New Mexico Wine Growers Association** (www. nmwine.com) has information on more wineries, and you can read more about the high-end and organic food scene in *Local Flavor* (www.localflavormagazine.com), a monthly tabloid, and the bimonthly *Edible Santa Fe* (www.ediblesantafe.com).

Vegetarian Food
New Mexican food isn't meat-centric, but strict vegetarians will have to be vigilant, as

many chile dishes are traditionally made with beef or chicken stock as well as lard for flavoring. The closer you get to Texas, the more likely it is that red chile sauce will contain bits of meat. Decades of hippie influence, though, have resulted in many menus stating clearly whether the chile is meatless. Some restaurants have an unreconstructed 1970s worldview, with alfalfa sprouts and squash casseroles galore.

ACCOMMODATIONS
Throughout this guide, distinctive choices—bed-and-breakfasts, lodges, and small, independently owned hotels and motels—are emphasized over chain options as much as possible. Just because the chains are not listed doesn't mean they're not available—and in many small towns, they're the only solid option.

The prices listed are the official high-season rack rates—that is, what you'd pay if you just walked in off the street, with no discounts; tax is not included. Most often, the numbers are the least expensive room for one person in one bed (a single, abbreviated *s*) and two people in two beds (a double, abbreviated *d*). **High season** is usually June-August. **Ski season** is January-March; prices in Taos and Santa Fe don't completely bottom out—but they are still cheaper than summer. Expect higher rates the week following Christmas and during special events, such as Indian Market in Santa Fe and Balloon Fiesta in Albuquerque, but overall you will be able to secure lower rates than those listed simply by looking online or calling the hotel directly.

Note that while many hotels tout their swimming pools, they are often forced to leave them empty due to water restrictions imposed during droughts. If you've booked at a hotel specifically for the pool, call to check the status before your trip, so you don't wind up paying a premium for a service you can't use. Santa Fe is the strictest area in the state, and it also limits hotels to changing towels and bed linens only every four days during your visit.

Travel Tips

WHAT TO PACK

The contents of your suitcase will be determined largely by the time of year, but be prepared for a **wide range of temperatures**—with a variety of layers—whenever you visit. Many people wrongly assume that New Mexico's desert setting means heat all day, all year round. In fact, due to the altitude, you may encounter severe cold. Winter temperatures can dip well below freezing even in the relatively low elevations of central Albuquerque, though it sees little snow. If you think you'll attend pueblo ceremonial dances during the winter, pack mittens, long underwear, double-thick wool socks, and a hat with earflaps—there will be a lot of standing around outside.

Spring is mud season—if you hike or head to rural areas during this time, save a clean pair of shoes for around town. Summers are hot by day (July's average temperature is 92°F), but as soon as the sun dips below the horizon, the temperature can drop up to 30°F, especially outside of city centers; always keep a sweater on hand. Brief afternoon **"monsoons"** in July and August sometimes warrant an umbrella or rain slicker. In the strong sun, you'll be more comfortable if you cover up, in long-sleeved, light-colored shirts and pants in silk or cotton. In fact, you should guard against the sun any time of year, as the thin atmosphere at this altitude means you'll burn more quickly than you're used to. You should never be without **sunglasses,** heavy-duty **sunscreen,** and a **brimmed hat.**

As for style, anything goes. If you'll be hobnobbing with Santa Fe's upper echelon, you might want to pack something dressy—the local formalwear for men is clean jeans, shined cowboy boots, and a bolo tie. Otherwise, though, New Mexicans are very casual. But note that when visiting churches and pueblos, it's respectful to not show excessive skin—women should avoid obvious cleavage and super-short skirts.

TOURIST INFORMATION

For pre-trip inspiration, the New Mexico Tourism Board publishes the monthly *New Mexico* magazine (www.nmmagazine.com), which does an excellent job covering both mainstream attractions and more obscure corners of the state.

Many smaller towns' chambers of commerce can also be extremely helpful.

If you plan to do a lot of hiking, you can order detailed topographical maps from the **National Forest Service** office in New Mexico (505/842-3292) or from the Bureau of Land Management's **Public Lands Information Center** (www.publiclands.org). Santa Fe's **Travel Bug** bookstore (839 Paseo de Peralta, 505/992-0418, 7:30am-5:30pm Mon.-Sat., 11am-4pm Sun.) also stocks maps, as do the **REI** stores in Santa Fe (500 Market St., 505/982-3557, 10am-8pm Mon.-Fri., 10am-7pm Sat., 11am-6pm Sun.) and Albuquerque (1550 Mercantile Ave. NE, 505/247-1191, 10am-9pm Mon.-Fri., 9am-7pm Sat., 11am-7pm Sun.).

TELEPHONE AND INTERNET

Albuquerque, Santa Fe, Los Alamos, Gallup, and Farmington use the area code 505, while the rest of the state's numbers start with 575.

For mobile phone reception, the corridor between Albuquerque and Santa Fe is fine, but in rural areas, phones on the GSM network (AT&T, T-Mobile) get very poor or no reception. Data service is equally spotty. If you'll be spending a lot of time outside of the cities or counting on your phone for emergencies, you might consider a CDMA phone (Verizon is best). Likewise, don't count on data service on your smartphone.

Internet access is widespread, though DSL

and other high-speed service is still not necessarily the norm, and thick adobe walls can be a hindrance for wireless signals. Rural areas still rely on satellite Internet, which can be poor in bad weather. In the cities, cafés often have hotspots, and the city of Albuquerque even maintains a few free ones in public spaces, such as the Old Town plaza.

TIME ZONE

New Mexico is in the **mountain time** zone, one hour ahead of the West Coast of the United States and two hours behind the East Coast. It's -7 GMT (Greenwich Mean Time) during the winter and -6 GMT in summer, when Daylight Saving Time is followed statewide.

Note that neighboring Arizona does not follow Daylight Saving Time, which can lead to confusion around the border.

CONDUCT AND CUSTOMS

New Mexico is a part of the United States, but it can sometimes feel quite foreign, particularly in the high mountain Spanish villages and in the Indian pueblos. Regardless, basic courtesy rules and, in smaller communities, modest dress are appreciated, especially at the older Catholic churches.

Some Pueblo Indians, as well as Navajo, find loud voices, direct eye contact, and firm handshakes off-putting and, by the same token, may not express themselves in the forthright way a lot of visitors are used to. Similarly, a subdued reaction doesn't necessarily mean a lack of enthusiasm.

New Mexico is not a wealthy state, and the gap between rich and poor can be wide. In general, people don't appreciate conspicuous displays of wealth, and it's doubly rude to flash cash, fancy gadgets, and jewelry in tiny villages and pueblos (and public cell-phone use is still considered tacky most places). Be thoughtful when taking photos, particularly of people's homes—always ask permission, and consider that some of the more "scenic" elements of New Mexico are also the products of poverty, which some people may not be proud to have captured on film.

You can help the local economy by favoring New Mexican-owned businesses, rather than chain operations, and buying directly from artisans wherever possible. In these situations, don't get too bent on bargaining. The item you're buying represents not just raw materials and hours of work, but a person's particular talent, skill, and heritage. Insisting on an extra-low price belittles not just the item, but the artisan as well.

Pueblo Etiquette

When visiting pueblos and reservations, remember that you are not at a tourist attraction—you are walking around someone's neighborhood. So peeking in windows and wandering off the suggested route isn't polite. If you want to take photos, you'll usually need a camera permit, for an additional fee. Always ask permission before taking photos of people, and ask parents, rather than children, for their consent. All pueblos ban alcohol.

Some pueblos are more welcoming than others. San Ildefonso, for instance, is open year-round, whereas Jemez is completely closed except for some feast days. So it's flawed logic to seek out the less-visited places or go in the off times in order to have a less "touristy" experience. In fact, the most rewarding time to visit *is* on a big feast day—you may not be the only tourist there, but you have a better chance of being invited into a local's home.

CLASSES AND VOLUNTEERING

From afternoon cooking workshops to intensives on adobe building techniques, the opportunities to learn in northern New Mexico are broad.

General Education

Look first into the art, music, and outdoors programs at **Ghost Ranch** (877/804-4678, www.ghostranch.org), the beautiful property in Abiquiu. Santa Fe and Albuquerque are both home to renowned alternative healing, herbal medicine, and massage schools—more than can be listed here. Visit **Natural Healers** (www.naturalhealers.com) for a current list.

Arts and Crafts

Taos in particular is a hotbed for art classes. **Fechin Art Workshops** (575/751-0647, www.fineartservices.info) are five-day live-in retreats that have been running for more than two decades; they are based in the Taos Ski Valley. The equally long-established **Taos Art School** (575/758-0350, www.taosartschool.org) focuses on landscape techniques, in six-day painting or photo workshops that include hiking and rafting options.

For crafts, Taos is also the place to be: **Weaving Southwest** (575/758-0433, www.weavingsouthwest.com) gives three-day workshops on Navajo frame looms. **Taos School of Metalsmithing and Lapidary Design** (575/758-0207, www.taosjewelryschool.com) covers a range of jewelry-making topics, starting with half-day sessions. Just north of Tierra Amarilla, in the tiny community of Los Ojos, the long-running **Río Grande Weaving School** (575/588-7231, www.tierrawools.com) offers five-day weaving workshops and three-day natural dye classes, among other classes.

The excellent **Santa Fe Photographic Workshops** (505/983-1400, www.santafeworkshops.com) gives nationally recognized photography classes in its campus in the Sangre de Cristo Mountains, just outside the city. Workshops range from three days onsite to longer field programs around New Mexico.

In Albuquerque, **Casa Flamenca** (505/247-0622, www.casaflamenca.org) teaches flamenco dance and classical Spanish guitar.

Cooking

Santa Fe School of Cooking (125 N. Guadalupe St., 505/983-4511, www.santafeschoolofcooking.com) holds day classes in contemporary Southwestern cuisine, as well as traditional Native American cooking and New Mexican standards; nice farmers market trips and restaurant walking tours are offered too.

In Arroyo Seco, **Cooking Studio Taos** (575/775-2665, www.cookingstudiotaos.com) offers classes on cooking a variety of cuisines—including New Mexican, Moroccan, and French—with acclaimed chef Christopher Maher.

Permaculture and Alternative Construction

In Albuquerque, **The Old School** (www.abqoldschool.com) teaches sustainable living skills such as canning, quilting, and building solar phone chargers. If you're interested in New Mexico's solar architecture movement, you can enroll in the month-long intensive **Earthship Academy** (575/751-0462, www.earthship.org), a crash course in building the off-the-grid rammed-earth houses that have their roots in Taos. The Earthship Biotecture organization also accepts volunteers. For more on local building styles, look into the semester-long classes in adobe construction at **Northern New Mexico College's** Española campus (575/747-2100, www.nnmc.edu).

INTERNATIONAL TRAVELERS

As for any destination in the United States, check before departure whether you'll need a **visa** to enter; most European nationals do not need one.

New Mexico uses the **U.S. dollar,** and currency exchange is available at most banks as well as in better hotels, though the rates in the latter case will not be as good. For the best rates and convenience, withdraw cash from your home account through **automatic teller machines** (ATMs); check first, though, what fee your home bank and the ATM's bank will charge you for the transaction, including any fee for a foreign-currency transaction.

Tipping is similar to elsewhere in the country: 15 percent to cab drivers, and 15-20 percent on restaurant bills. For larger groups, often restaurants will add 18 percent or so to the bill; this is suggested, and you may refuse it or write in a lower amount if service was poor. Add $1 or so per drink when ordered at the bar; $1 or $2 to staff who handle your luggage in hotels; and $3-5 per day to housekeeping in hotels—envelopes are often left in rooms for this purpose. **Bargaining** is acceptable only if you're dealing directly with an artisan, and even then, it is often politely deflected. But it doesn't hurt to ask, nicely, if the quoted price is the best possible one.

Electricity is 120 volts, with a two-prong, flat-head plug, the same as Canada and Mexico.

ACCESS FOR TRAVELERS WITH DISABILITIES

Wheelchair access can be frustrating in some historic properties and on the narrower sidewalks of Santa Fe and Taos, but in most other respects, travelers with disabilities should find problems no worse in New Mexico than elsewhere in the United States. Public buses are wheelchair accessible, an increasing number of hotels have Americans with Disabilities Act (ADA)-compliant rooms, and you can even get out in nature a bit on paved trails such as the Santa Fe Canyon Preserve loop and the Paseo del Bosque in Albuquerque.

If you'll be visiting a number of wilderness areas, consider the National Park Service's **Access Pass** (888/467-2757, www.nps.gov), a free lifetime pass that grants admission for the pass-holder and three adults to all national parks, national forests, and the like, as well as discounts on interpretive services, camping fees, fishing licenses, and more. Apply in person at any federally managed park or wilderness area; you must show medical documentation of blindness or permanent disability.

TRAVELING WITH CHILDREN

Though the specific prices are not listed in this guide, admission at major attractions is almost always lower for children than for adults. Your little ones will be welcome in most environments, the only exceptions being a few of the more formal restaurants in Santa Fe and Albuquerque. Kids are sure to be fascinated by ceremonial dances at the pueblos, but be prepared with distractions, because long waits are the norm. Prep children with information about American Indian culture, and brief them on the basic etiquette at dances, which applies to them as well as adults. Kids will also enjoy river rafting (relaxing "floats" along placid sections of the Rio Grande and Rio Chama are good for younger ones). For skiing, Taos Ski Valley has a very strong program of classes for youngsters.

SENIOR TRAVELERS

Senior discounts are available at most museums and other attractions.

The **America the Beautiful Senior Pass** ($80) is a lifetime pass for people 62 and older that grants free admission for the pass-holder and three additional adults to national parks, National Forest Service lands, and many other areas, as well as discounts on activities such as camping and boat launching. The pass can be purchased in person at any federally managed wilderness area, or online with an additional $10 processing fee; for more information, contact the **National Park Service** (888/467-2757, www.nps.gov).

If you're a New Mexico resident and anticipating doing a fair amount of camping in state parks during your visit to the region, consider picking up an **Annual Camping Permit** for seniors ($100). The pass can be purchased in person at any New Mexico State Park office. For more information, contact **New Mexico State Parks** (888/667-2757).

Road Scholar (800/454-5768, www.road-scholar.org) runs more than 20 reasonably priced group trips in northern New Mexico, from a five-day general introduction to Santa Fe history to more focused tours focusing on the history of crypto-Jews, for instance, or ancestral Puebloan culture.

GAY AND LESBIAN TRAVELERS

Gay marriage was legalized in New Mexico in late 2013, but Santa Fe has been one of the major gay capitals in the United States for decades, second only to San Francisco in the per-capita rates of same-sex coupledom. There are no designated "gay-borhoods" (unless you count Rainbow Vision Santa Fe, a retirement community) or even particular bar scenes. Instead, gay men and lesbian women are well integrated throughout town, running businesses and serving on the city council. The city's Pride parade is usually in late June, and is preceded by several big events.

Albuquerque also has a decent gay scene, especially if you want to go clubbing, which is not an option in quieter Santa Fe. As for smaller towns and pueblos, they're still significantly more conservative.

Gay culture in the state isn't all about cute shops and cabarets. One big event is the annual **Zia Regional Rodeo,** sponsored by the **New Mexico Gay Rodeo Association** (505/720-3749, www.nmgra.org). It takes place every summer (July or August), with all the standard rodeo events, plus goat dressing and a wild drag race.

Health and Safety

Visitors to New Mexico face several unique health concerns. First and foremost are the environmental hazards of **dehydration, sunburn,** and **altitude sickness.** The desert climate, glaring sun, and thinner atmosphere conspire to fry your skin and drain you of all moisture. (On the plus side, sweat evaporates immediately.) Apply SPF 30 sunscreen daily, even in winter, and try to drink at least a liter of water a day, whether you feel thirsty or not. (Request water in restaurants—it's usually brought only on demand, to cut down on waste.) By the time you start feeling thirsty, you're already seriously dehydrated and at risk of further bad effects: headaches, nausea, and dizziness, all of which can become full-blown, life-threatening **heatstroke** if left untreated. Heatstroke can happen even without serious exertion—just lack of water and very hot sun. So if you're feeling at all woozy or cranky (another common symptom), head for shade and sip a Gatorade or similar electrolyte-replacement drink.

Staying hydrated also staves off the effects of the high elevation, to which most visitors will not be acclimated. The mildest reaction to being 7,000 feet or more above sea level is lethargy or light-headedness—you will probably sleep long and soundly on your first night in New Mexico. Some people do have more severe reactions, such as a piercing headache or intense nausea, especially if they engage in strenuous physical activity. Unfortunately, there's no good way to judge how your body will react, so give yourself a few days to adjust, with a light schedule and plenty of time to sleep.

More obscure hazards include **West Nile virus** (wear a DEET-based insect repellent if you're down along the river in the summer); **hantavirus,** an extremely rare pulmonary ailment transmitted by rodents; and the even rarer **bubonic plague** (aka the Black Death), the very same disease that killed millions of Europeans in the Middle Ages. Luckily, only a case or two of the plague crops up every year, and it's easily treated if diagnosed early. **Lyme disease** is almost as rare, as deer ticks do not flourish in the mountains.

If you'll be spending a lot of time hiking or camping, take precautions against **giardiasis** and other waterborne ailments by boiling your water or treating it with iodine or a SteriPen (www.steripen.com), as even the clearest mountain waterways may have been tainted by cows upstream. **Snake** bites are also a hazard in the wild, so wear boots that cover your ankles, stay on trails, and keep your hands and feet out of odd holes and cracks between rocks. Only the Western diamondback rattlesnake is aggressive when disturbed; other snakes typically will not bite if you simply back away quietly.

General **outdoor safety rules** apply: Don't hike by yourself, always register with the ranger station when heading out overnight, and let friends know where you're going and when you'll be back. Pack a good topographical map and a compass or GPS device; people manage to get lost even when hiking in the foothills, and if you're at all dehydrated or dizzy from the altitude, any disorientation can be magnified to a disastrous degree. Also pack layers of clothing, and be prepared for cold snaps and snow at higher elevations, even in the summer.

CRIME AND DRUGS

Recreational drug use is not uncommon in New Mexico—generally in a relatively benign form, with marijuana fairly widespread. (Former governor and Republican presidential candidate Gary Johnson, though no longer a user himself, has been a strenuous advocate for its legalization.) But as in much of the rural United States, crystal methamphetamine is an epidemic, and some villages in northern New Mexico have also been devastated by heroin use, with overdose deaths at a rate several hundred times higher than the national average. None of this affects travelers, except that petty theft, especially in isolated areas such as trailheads, can be an issue. Always lock your car doors, and secure any valuables in the trunk. Don't leave anything enticing in view.

Drinking and driving is unfortunately still common, especially in rural areas; be particularly alert when driving at night. A distressing number of crosses along the roadside (*descansos*) mark the sites of fatal car accidents, many of which had alcohol involved.

Resources

Glossary

abierto: Spanish for "open"

acequia: irrigation ditch, specifically one regulated by the traditional Spanish method, maintained by a *mayordomo,* or "ditch boss," who oversees how much water each shareholder receives

adobe: building material of sun-dried bricks made of a mix of mud, sand, clay, and straw

arroyo: stream or dry gully where mountain runoff occasionally flows

asado: stew (usually pork) with red-chile sauce

atrio: churchyard between the boundary wall and the church entrance, usually used as a cemetery

bizcochito: anise-laced shortbread, traditionally made with lard

bosque: Spanish for "forest," specifically the cottonwoods and trees along a river

bulto: three-dimensional wood carving, typically of a saint

caldera: basin or crater formed by a collapsed volcano

canal: water drain from a flat roof; pl. *canales*

carne adovada: pork chunks marinated in red chile, then braised; meatier and dryer than *asado*

cerrado: Spanish for "closed"

chicharrón: fried pork skin, usually with a layer of meat still attached

chile: not to be confused with Texas chili, Cincinnati chili, or any other American concoction; refers to the fruit of the chile plant itself, eaten green (picked unripe and then roasted) or red (ripened and dried)

chimichanga: deep-fried burrito; allegedly invented in Arizona

colcha: style of blanket, in which loom-woven wool is embellished with long strands of wool embroidery

concha belt: belt made of stamped, carved silver medallions; concha is Spanish for "shell"; also, *concho*

convento: residential compound adjoining a mission church

enchilada: corn tortilla dipped in chile sauce, filled with cheese or meat, and topped with more chile; can be served either rolled or flat (stacked in layers)

farolito: in Santa Fe and Taos, a luminaria

GCCB: common abbreviation for green-chile cheeseburger

genízaro: during Spanish colonial times, a detribalized Indian (usually due to having been taken as a slave) who lived with Spaniards and followed Catholic tradition

gordita: a variation on the taco, with a thicker tortilla-like shell, sometimes deep-fried; these are a more traditionally Mexican dish (though in that case rarely fried) and are available only in the southern part of the state

heishi: fine disk-shaped beads carved from shells

horno: traditional dome-shaped adobe oven

jerga: Spanish-style wool blanket or rug, loosely woven and barely decorated, meant for daily use

kachina: ancestral spirit of the Pueblo people as well as the carved figurine representing the spirit; also spelled "katsina"

kiva: sacred ceremonial space in a pueblo, at least partially underground and entered by a hole in the ceiling

latillas: thin saplings cut and laid across vigas to make a solid ceiling

lowrider: elaborately painted and customized car with hydraulic lifts

luminaria: in Albuquerque, lantern made of a sand-filled paper bag with a votive candle set inside; in Santa Fe and Taos, refers to small bonfires lit during the Christmas season

menudo: tripe soup, said to be good for curing a hangover

morada: meeting space of the Penitente brotherhood

nicho: small niche in an adobe wall, usually meant to hold a santo

Penitente: member of a long-established Catholic brotherhood in northern New Mexico

petroglyph: rock carving

pictograph: painting on a rock surface

piñon: any of several fragrant varieties of pine tree that grow in New Mexico

portal: the covered sidewalk area in front of a traditional adobe structure; pl. *portales*

posole: stew of hulled corn (hominy), pork, and a little chile, either green or red

pueblo: Spanish for "village," referring to the various communities of American Indians settled in the Rio Grande Valley, as well as the larger land area owned by the community (preferable to the term "reservation"); also, capitalized, the people themselves, though they speak several different languages

rajas: rough-hewn slats laid over vigas to form a ceiling; also, strips of roasted chile

ramada: simple structure built of four sapling posts and topped with additional saplings laid flat to form a shade structure and a place to hang things to dry

reredos: altar screen, usually elaborately painted or carved with various portraits of Christ and the saints

retablo: flat portrait of a saint, painted or carved in low relief, usually on wood

ristra: string of dried red chiles

santero/santera: craftsperson who produces santos

santo: portrait of a saint, either flat (a *retablo*) or three-dimensional (a *bulto*)

sipapu: hole in the floor of a kiva, signifying the passage to the spirit world

sopaipilla: square of puffed fried dough, served with the main meal for wiping up sauces and with honey for dessert

tamale: corn husk filled with masa (hominy paste) and a dab of meat, vegetables, or cheese, then steamed; usually made in large quantities for holidays

terrón: building material of bricks cut out of sod and dried in the sun, similar to adobe, but less common

Tewa: language spoken by the majority of Pueblo Indians; others in the Rio Grande Valley speak Tiwa, Towa, and Keresan

torreón: round defensive tower built in Spanish colonial times

vato: cool Chicano, usually driving a lowrider

viga: ceiling beam made of a single tree trunk

zaguán: long central hallway

Suggested Reading

ART AND CULTURE

Clark, Willard. *Remembering Santa Fe.* Layton, UT: Gibbs Smith, 2004. A small hardback edition of selections from the Boston artist who stopped off in Santa Fe in 1928. He stayed to learn printmaking and produce this series of etchings depicting city life.

Gandert, Miguel. *Nuevo México Profundo: Rituals of an Indo-Hispanic Homeland.* Santa Fe: Museum of New Mexico Press, 2000. Like Enrique Lamadrid's work, but with a slightly broader scope. There's an attempt at scholarly analysis in the text, but it's really about the 130 beautiful photographs.

Lamadrid, Enrique. *Hermanitos Comanchitos: Indo-Hispano Rituals of Captivity and Redemption.* Albuquerque: University of New Mexico Press, 2003. Fascinating documentation, in descriptive prose and rich black-and-white photos, of the traditional Spanish dances of northern New Mexico, such as Los Comanches and Los Matachines.

Lummis, Charles F. *A Tramp Across the Continent.* Lincoln: University of Nebraska Press, 1982. In 1884, fledgling journalist Lummis decided to walk from Cincinnati, Ohio, to his new job in Los Angeles, California; this book chronicles his trip. The sections on New Mexico shine, and Lummis was so entranced that he later moved to the territory. He was the first to write stories about the Penitente brotherhood in the national press.

Myers, Joan. *Pie Town Woman: The Hard Life and Good Times of a New Mexico Homesteader.* Albuquerque: University of New Mexico Press, 2001. The biography of a woman captured in famous Farm Security Administration photos from 1940, this book also muses on the power of memory and photography.

Padilla, Carmella, and Juan Estevan Arellano. *Low 'n Slow: Lowriding in New Mexico.* Santa Fe: Museum of New Mexico Press, 2005. Lovingly lurid color photographs by Jack Parsons are the centerpiece of this book, which pays tribute to New Mexico's Latino car culture—an art form that has even landed a Chimayó lowrider in the Smithsonian.

Parhad, Elisa. *New Mexico: A Guide for the Eyes.* Los Angeles: EyeMuse Books, 2009. Informative short essays on the distinctive things you see in New Mexico and then wonder what the backstory is: concha belts, beat-up pickup trucks, blue sky. The richly illustrated book makes good pre-trip reading or a souvenir when you return.

Price, Roberta. *Across the Great Divide: A Photo Chronicle of the Counterculture.* Albuquerque: University of New Mexico Press, 2010. Documentary photographer Price "went native" with a Colorado commune in the 1960s and visited several groups in New Mexico. She also wrote the narrative *Huerfano: A Memoir of Life in the Counterculture* (Amherst: University of Massachusetts Press, 2004).

Price, V. B. *Albuquerque: A City at the End of the World.* Albuquerque: University of New Mexico Press, 2003. Journalist and poet Price writes a travel guide to New Mexico's biggest metropolis but disguises it as a discourse on urban theory, recommending his favorite spots in the context of the city's unique position and growth processes. Black-and-white photographs by Kirk Gittings highlight the stark landscape.

Robinson, Roxana. *Georgia O'Keeffe: A Life.* Lebanon, NH: University Press of New England, 1998. A strong and intimate biography, focusing on the celebrated painter's role as a protofeminist and her difficult relationships.

FOOD

Feucht, Andrea. *Food Lovers' Guide to Santa Fe, Albuquerque & Taos.* Guilford, CT: Globe Pequot, 2012. A good companion for adventurous eaters, with especially good coverage of Albuquerque's more obscure ethnic restaurants. The author maintains an updated website (www.foodloversnm.com).

Frank, Lois Ellen. *Foods of the Southwest Indian Nations.* Berkeley, CA: Ten Speed Press, 2002. Beautiful photographs are a highlight of this thorough documentation of a little-covered cuisine. They help make an ancient culinary tradition accessible and modern without subjecting it to a heavy-handed fusion treatment. For good reason, it earned a James Beard Award.

Kagel, Katharine. *Cooking with Café Pasqual's: Recipes from Santa Fe's Renowned Corner Cafe.* Berkeley, CA: Ten Speed Press, 2006. Re-create your best meals from the legendary restaurant that set the standard for Santa Fe fusion cooking. Chef Kagel is a charming contrarian too, which makes for great reading.

HISTORY

Childs, Craig. *House of Rain: Tracking a Vanished Civilization Across the American Southwest.* New York: Little, Brown, 2007. The story of the Ancestral Puebloans (Anasazi), as told by a curious naturalist, becomes less a solution to an archaeological puzzle than a meditation of why we romanticize "lost" civilizations. His more recent book, *Finders Keepers: A Tale of Archaeological Plunder and Possession* (Little, Brown, 2010), takes the drama to the academy, with tales of scholarly intrigue.

Egan, Timothy. *The Worst Hard Time: The Untold Story of Those Who Survived the Great American Dust Bowl.* New York: Mariner Books, 2006. The town of Clayton features a bit in the pages of this highly readable history that conveys the misery and environmental folly of the period.

Held, E. B. *A Spy's Guide to Santa Fe and Albuquerque.* Albuquerque: University of New Mexico Press, 2011. A former CIA agent reveals nefarious Cold War intrigue—fascinating details, if not so grippingly told.

Hordes, Stanley. *To the End of the Earth: A History of the Crypto-Jews of New Mexico.* New York: Columbia University Press, 2008. An exhaustive but intriguing account of the Jewish families who fled the Inquisition and lived in the Southwest as Catholic converts. The communities, some still practicing distinctly Jewish rituals, came to light only a few decades ago.

Horgan, Paul. *Great River.* Middletown, CT: Wesleyan University Press, 1991. Two enormous tomes (*Vol. 1: The Indians and Spain* and *Vol. 2: Mexico and the United States*) won the Pulitzer Prize for history. They're packed with drama, on a base of meticulous analysis of primary sources.

Martinez, Esther. *My Life in San Juan Pueblo.* Champaign: University of Illinois Press, 2004. Born in 1912, Martinez has a lot of stories to tell. This free-flowing book incorporates her memories with larger pueblo folklore, and a CD with recordings of some of her stories is included.

Poling-Kempes, Lesley. *Valley of Shining Stone: The Story of Abiquiu.* Tucson: University of Arizona Press, 1997. Georgia O'Keeffe fans will like the personal stories of those in her circle in the 1930s, while historians will appreciate the detailed, linear second half of the book, about the transformation of this remote valley into an artists' haven.

Sides, Hampton. *Blood and Thunder: An Epic of the American West.* New York: Doubleday, 2006. Working from the story of Kit Carson and the campaign against the Navajo, including the Long Walk, Sides tells the gripping story of the entire American West. He's an excellent storyteller, and the 480 pages flow by in a rush of land grabs, battles on horseback, and brutality on all sides.

Simmons, Marc. *New Mexico: An Interpretive History.* Albuquerque: University of New Mexico Press, 1988. The state's historian laureate presents an easy, concise overview of the major historical events. Also look into his more specialized titles, such as *The Last Conquistador: Juan de Oñate and the Settling of the Far Southwest* (Norman: University of Oklahoma Press, 1993).

Smith, Mike. *Towns of the Sandia Mountains.* Charleston, SC: Arcadia, 2006. This slim volume of vintage photographs and juicy stories in extended captions is about a very specific region, but it could tell the story of much of New Mexico in its shift to modernity.

Usner, Donald J. *Sabino's Map: Life in Chimayó's Old Plaza.* Santa Fe: Museum of New Mexico Press, 1995. A balanced and gracefully written history of the author's hometown, illustrated with fond photos of all the craggy-faced characters involved. Usner's follow-up, *Benigna's Chimayo: Cuentos from the Old Plaza* (Santa Fe: Museum of New Mexico Press, 2001) relates his grandmother's story of the village and her trove of folktales.

LITERATURE AND MEMOIR

Anaya, Rudolfo. *Bless Me, Ultima.* New York: Warner, 1994. Anaya's story of a young boy coming of age in New Mexico in the 1940s is beautifully told. The book, first published in 1973, launched Anaya into his role as Chicano literary hero; his later books, such as *Alburquerque* (1992), are not quite so touching, but they have a lot of historical and ethnic detail.

Blume, Judy. *Tiger Eyes.* New York: Delacorte, 2010. A young girl with family troubles relocates to Los Alamos, giving a great teen's-eye view on the landscape of New Mexico.

Connors, Philip. *Fire Season: Field Notes from a Wilderness Lookout.* New York: Ecco, 2012. In the tradition of Edward Abbey, this memoir recounts life in a remote fire tower in the Gila Wilderness.

Goodman, Tanya Ward. *Leaving Tinkertown.* Albuquerque: University of New Mexico Press, 2013. A poignant memoir of growing up in the wondrous folk-art assemblage outside Albuquerque. The author's father, Ross Ward, died of early onset Alzheimer's disease, and this book logs that medical tale, unflinchingly, alongside the larger-than-life artist's own story.

Hillerman, Tony. *Skinwalkers.* New York: HarperTorch, 1990. Hillerman's breakout detective novel, set on the Navajo Nation, weaves a fascinating amount of lore into the plot—which comes in handy when Tribal Affairs police Joe Leaphorn and Jim Chee investigate homicides. Hillerman spun Leaphorn and Chee into a successful franchise, and all of the books show the same cultural depth.

Pillsbury, Dorothy. *Roots in Adobe.* Santa Fe: Lightning Tree Press, 1983. Pillsbury's charming stories capture the strangeness and warmth of Santa Fe culture in the 1940s. The author tells hilarious stories of settling into her little home and the characters she meets.

Quade, Kirstin Valdez. *Night at the Fiestas.* New York: W. W. Norton, 2015. Quade, who grew up in New Mexico, sets many of the short stories in this collection in tiny Hispano towns, amid the most intense belief and ritual. A great mix of cultural detail and poignant characters.

Silko, Leslie Marmon. *Ceremony.* New York: Penguin, 1988. Silko's classic novel about the impact of the atomic bomb on Native Americans' worldview (and that of all Americans) is brutal, beautiful, and bleak.

NATURE AND THE ENVIRONMENT

Coltrin, Mike. *Sandia Mountain Hiking Guide.* Albuquerque: University of New Mexico Press, 2005. A print version of Coltrin's meticulously maintained website (www.sandiahiking.com), with thorough trail descriptions, GPS coordinates, and a foldout map of the east and west slopes of the mountain.

Julyan, Robert, and Mary Stuever, eds. *Field Guide to the Sandia Mountains.* Albuquerque: University of New Mexico Press, 2005. A thorough guide illustrated with color photographs, detailing birds, animals, plants, even insects of the Sandias. Most of it applies to the Santa Fe area too.

Kricher, John. *A Field Guide to Rocky Mountain and Southwest Forests.* New York: Houghton Mifflin Harcourt, 2003. A Peterson Field Guide, covering both flora and fauna: trees, birds, mammals, you name it. It's illustrated with both color photos and drawings. It's not encyclopedic, but it's a great basic reference. Peterson guides are also available for narrower categories such as reptiles and amphibians or butterflies.

McFarland, Casey, and S. David Scott. *Bird Feathers: A Guide to North American*

Species. Mechanicsburg, PA: Stackpole Books, 2010. While not New Mexico-specific, it is the only guide of its kind, and its authors grew up in the state and know the birdlife well. Great for serious birders and curious hikers, with detailed photographs.

Nichols, John. *On the Mesa.* Layton, Utah: Gibbs Smith, 2005. Best known for his comic novel *The Milagro Beanfield War,* Nichols here writes some visionary nonfiction about traditional life and the environment near his home in Taos.

Price, V. B. *The Orphaned Land: New Mexico's Environment Since the Manhattan Project.* Albuquerque: University of New Mexico Press, 2011. Journalist Price examines New Mexico's droughts and other trials—in the same vein as Reisner's *Cadillac Desert.*

Reisner, Marc. *Cadillac Desert: The American West and Its Disappearing Water.* New York: Penguin, 1993. Not specifically about New Mexico, but an excellent analysis of the Southwest's water shortage and how the U.S. government's dam-building projects exacerbated it. Apocalyptic, sarcastic, and totally compelling.

Sibley, David Allen. *The Sibley Field Guide to Birds of Western North America.* New York: Knopf, 2003. The New Mexican birder's book of choice, with 810 species listed, about 4,600 color illustrations, and a handy compact format. Generally, it beats out Peterson's otherwise respectable series.

Tekiela, Stan. *Birds of New Mexico: Field Guide.* Cambridge, MN: Adventure Publications, 2003. A great book for beginning birders or curious visitors, with 140 of the state's most common species listed, many illustrated with photographs.

Internet Resources

TRAVEL INFORMATION

Albuquerque Convention and Visitors Bureau
www.visitalbuquerque.org
The official intro to the city and surrounding areas, with events listings as well as hotel-booking services.

ExploreNM
Explorenm.com
A barebones repository of user reviews of hikes and campgrounds around New Mexico.

Four Corners Geotourism
www.fourcornersgeotourism.com
A directory of sustainable tourism, sponsored by *National Geographic*.

Hiking in the Sandia Mountains
www.sandiahiking.com
Mike Coltrin hiked every trail in the Sandias over the course of a year, covering about 250 miles. He detailed each hike, complete with GPS references, here.

New Mexico Board of Tourism
www.newmexico.org
The best of the official sites, this one has thorough maps and suggested itineraries.

Public Lands Information Center
publiclands.org
Buy U.S. Geological Survey, U.S. Forest Service, and other topographical maps online from the Bureau of Land Management's well-organized website. Good stock of nature guides and other travel books too.

Rio Grande Chapter of the Sierra Club
www.riograndesierraclub.org
Events calendar with group hikes—mostly around Santa Fe—and an excellent resource of public lands issues.

Taos Vacation Guide
www.taos.org
A thorough directory and events listings.

Tourism Santa Fe
www.santafe.org
Near-exhaustive listings of tourist attractions and services on this slickly produced site.

NEWS AND CULTURE

Albuquerque Journal
www.abqjournal.com
The state's largest newspaper is available free online after answering survey questions.

Alibi
www.alibi.com
This free weekly has been cracking wise since 1992, taking a critical look at politics and culture. Its annual "Best of Burque" guide is usually reliable.

Chasing Santa Fe
www.chasingsantafe.blogspot.com
The glamorous Santa Fe lifestyle, lovingly documented: local chefs, new shops, and fashion spotting.

Duke City Fix
www.dukecityfix.com
This Albuquerque-centric discussion forum covers everything from politics to gossip about the restaurant scene.

Santa Fe New Mexican
www.santafenewmexican.com
Santa Fe's main newspaper. The gossip column *El Mitote* documents celebs in Santa Fe, and the Roundhouse Roundup does roughly the same—but with politicians.

Santa Fe Reporter
www.sfreporter.com
Santa Fe's free weekly is politically sharp and often funny. Get opinionated reviews and news analysis here.

Smithsonian Folkways
www.folkways.si.edu
Prep for your road trip at this enormous online music archive, which has a number of traditional treasures from the state, including the excellent *Music of New Mexico: Hispanic Traditions* and *New Mexico: Native American Traditions.*

Taos News
www.taosnews.com
The town paper is a weekly, but its website has daily updates and an events calendar.

SPECIALIZED GUIDES
Birding Trail
wildlife.state.nm.us
A map and road signs for feathered friends.

Brewery Trail
www.nmbeer.org
Features a downloadable map to breweries across the state.

Clay Arts Trail
www.claytrail.org
A guide to the "creative economy of clay" in the southwest corner of the state.

Fiber Arts Trails
www.nmfiberarts.org
Three routes around this wool-loving state.

Film Trails
www.newmexico.org
Filming locations for more than a dozen films, plus *Breaking Bad.*

Green Chile Cheeseburger Trail
www.newmexico.org
Between this and a breakfast burrito trail, you'll never go hungry again.

Space Trail
www.nmspacemuseum.org
Locations where rockets were launched.

Index

A

Abiquiu: 94-98
Abiquiu Lake: 96
Abó: 205
ABQ BioPark: 167-168
ABQ Trolley Co.: 26, 166-167, 169
accommodations: 241
Acoma Pueblo (Sky City): 28, 200, 202-203
Adobe Bar: 21, 128
Adobe Theater: 182
air travel: 237
Alameda/Rio Grande Open Space: 189
Albuquerque: 23, 161-216; maps 164, 167, 172, 175, 201
Albuquerque International Balloon Fiesta: 180, 184
Albuquerque International Sunsport (ABQ) airport: 25, 215
Albuquerque Isotopes (baseball): 191
Albuquerque Little Theatre: 182
Albuquerque Museum of Art and History: 168
Albuquerque Trail: 203
Alcove House Trail: 89
Alley Cantina: 25, 128
American Indian heritage: 27-28
American International Rattlesnake Museum: 168
Anderson Abruzzo Albuquerque International Balloon Museum (BaMu): 179
Angel Fire: 152-153
Angel Fire Bike Park: 152
animals: 221-224
Apothecary Lounge: 26, 181
aquarium: 167
architecture (Santa Fe): 49
Arroyo Seco: 126
Arroyo Seco Fourth of July Parade: 129
arts: 22, 232-235
ArtsCrawl: 187
Aspen Vista: 29, 63
Atalaya Mountain: 63
ATMs: 244
auto travel: 237, 238

B

ballooning: 24, 180, 184, 188
Bandelier National Monument: 21, 27, 88-90
Bang Bite: 30, 70
bargaining: 245
Bart Prince House: 175
Bathtub Row Brewing Co-Op: 88
Battle of Glorieta Pass: 79

beer/breweries: Albuquerque 182; Santa Fe 52, 56, 88, 92; Taos 128, 150
Bicentennial Pool: 67
bicycling: general discussion 238; Albuquerque 168, 189; Santa Fe 56, 63-65; Taos 134, 152; see also mountain biking
Big Arsenic Trail: 158
birds/bird-watching: general discussion 222-223; Albuquerque 176, 189, 205-206; Taos 158
Blackout Theatre: 183
Blackrock Springs: 136
Blue Heron Brewing Company: 92
boating: Albuquerque 214; Taos 148
Bobcat Pass: 156
Boca Negra Canyon: 178
Bode's: 94
Bodhi Manda Zen Center: 211
Boese Brothers: 182
Bond House Museum: 91
Bosque del Apache: 205-206
botanical gardens/arboretums: Albuquerque 167; Santa Fe 49
Bouche Bistro: 21, 70
Box Canyon: 96
Box Performance Space: 182
Bradbury Science Museum: 85, 87
Breaking Bad tour: 169
Brew House: 150
Burger Stand, The: 25, 138
Burning of Zozobra: 56, 57
bus travel: 237, 238

C

Café Fina: 25, 75
Café Pasqual's: 30, 68
Camel Rock: 82
Camino del Monte Sol: 45-46
camping: Santa Fe 81, 90, 96, 98; Taos 148, 154, 155, 158
Campo: 30, 195
Canteen Brewhouse: 182
Canyon Rim Trail: 87
Canyon Road: 21, 24, 44-46; map 45
Capilla de Nuestra Señora de Guadalupe: 168, 170
Capulin Springs Snow Play Area: 190
Carson National Forest: 136
car travel: 237, 238
Casa Flamenca: 184
Casa Grande: 209
Casa San Ysidro: 177

Castillo Gallery: 102
Cathedral Basilica of St. Francis of Assisi: 40-41
Cave Creek Trail: 81
cell phones: 242
Cell Theatre: 182
Center for Contemporary Arts: 50
ceremonial dances: general discussion 130; Albuquerque 185; Santa Fe 83; Taos 131
Cerrillos: 23, 209
Chama: 149-151
Chatter Sunday: 183
children, Santa Fe activities for: 60
children, traveling with: 245
Chimayó: 21, 100-102, 103
Chimayó Museum: 101
Chimayó Trading Post: 91-92
Chimney Rock: 96
Christ in the Desert Monastery: 97
churches/temples: Albuquerque 168, 170, 171, 176, 200, 202, 207; Santa Fe 40-41, 42-43, 46, 92, 95, 97, 103, 104; Taos 121-122, 123-124, 126, 158
Church of San Esteban del Rey: 202
Cimarron: 155
classes: 243-244
Classical Gas Museum: 98
climate: 218-219
climbing: Santa Fe 65; Taos 135
Cochiti Lake: 214
Columbine Trail: 156
communes: 127
conduct and customs: 243
Córdova: 102
Cordovas Handweaving Workshop, The: 103-104
Coronado Historic Site: 179-180
Coronado State Monument: 28, 212
Corrales: 176-177
Couse-Sharp Historic Site: 120
Cowgirl BBQ: 21, 29, 53, 72
Crest Road: 206
Crest Trail: 188
crime: 247
Crimson Maple Trail: 203
Cristo Rey Catholic Church: 46
Cross of the Martyrs: 44
Cumbres & Toltec Scenic Railroad: 149-150
currency: 244

D

Dale Ball Trails: 25, 64
Dar al Islam: 95
David Loughridge Learning Center: 50
demographics: 229-230
D. H. Lawrence Ranch: 22, 158-159
disabilities, travelers with: 245
Dixon: 99
Don Quixote Distillery: 82

Downtown Albuquerque: 171-174; map 172
Downtown Santa Fe: 36-44; map 38-39
drugs, illegal: 247
Duel Brewing: 52
Duke City Repertory Theatre: 183
Dulce: 151
Duran Central Pharmacy: 26, 186, 191

E

Eagle Nest: 154-155
Eagle Nest Lake State Park: 154
East Mountains: 206
Eastside (Santa Fe): 44-46; map 45
Echo Amphitheater: 97-98
economy: 228-229
educational opportunities: 243-244
Edward Sargent Wildlife Management Area: 150
E. L. Blumenschein Home: 22, 25, 115-116
electricity: 245
Elena Gallegos Picnic Area: 188
El Farol: 21, 53, 73
Elizabethtown: 155
El Meze: 25, 137
El Museo Cultural de Santa Fe: 47
El Parasol: 21, 92
El Prado: 124
El Rey Theater: 184
El Salto Falls: 133
El Vado Lake State Park: 146, 148
El Zaguán: 45
Embudo: 98-99
Embudo Canyon: 190
Enchanted Circle: 62, 152-159; map 153
Enchanted Circle Century Tour: 134, 155
Enchanted Circle Gateway Museum: 154-155
Enchanted Forest: 135, 156
environmental issues: 219, 220
Ernie Blake Snowsports School: 135
Eske's Brew Pub: 128
Española: 91-93; map 92
etiquette: 243
¡Explora!: 170

F

fall foliage: 62
Farina Pizzeria: 26, 193
farolitos: 233
fauna: 221-224
Feast of San Esteban: 202
Feast of San Geronimo: 130
Fiesta de Santa Fe: 56
Fiestas de Taos: 129
fish/fishing: general discussion 223; Albuquerque 168; Santa Fe 65-66; Taos 136, 148, 151, 152, 154, 155
flora: 220-221

Florence Hawley Ellis Museum of Anthropology: 96-97
food/restaurants: 30, 239-241
Foothills Trail: 190
Fort Marcy Recreation Complex: 67
Fourth of July Canyon: 62, 188, 203
Fourth of July Trail: 203
Frenchish: 26, 194
Frey Trail: 89
Frontier, The: 23, 29, 30, 193
Fuller Lodge Art Center: 85

G

gaming: 84
Gathering of Nations Powwow: 184
Gavilan Trail: 133
gay and lesbian travelers: 246
Genoveva Chavez Community Center: 67
geography: 218
geology: 218
Georgia O'Keeffe Home: 94-95
Georgia O'Keeffe Museum: 25, 43-44
Ghost Ranch: 22
Giggling Springs: 210
Gilman Tunnels: 210
¡Globalquerque!: 96-97, 98, 184
Go-Jii-Ya: 151
Golden: 207
golf: 66
government: 228
Governor Bent House and Museum: 116-117
Gran Quivira: 204-205
gratuities: 244-245
Greater World Earthship Development: 125-126
Green Chile Cheeseburger Smackdown: 56
Grove, The: 26, 169, 192
Gruet Winery: 180-181
Guadalupe: 46-47, 69-72
Gutiz: 23, 139

H

Hacienda de los Martinez: 121
Hamilton Mesa Trail: 81
Harry's Roadhouse: 25, 75
Harwood Museum of Art: 115
health and safety: 246-247
Heron Lake State Park: 148
High Road to Taos: 22, 25, 29, 65, 79, 100-105
Highway 3: 81
Highway 150: 126-127
Highway 475: 62
hiking: general discussion 28-29; Albuquerque 178, 188-189, 203, 209, 210, 213, 214; Santa Fe 61-63, 81, 87, 90-91, 96, 97, 105; Taos 125, 132-133, 148, 155, 156, 158

Historic Santa Fe Foundation: 45
history: 224-228
Holocaust and Intolerance Museum: 173
Hopper, Dennis: 123
Hopper, The: 182
horseback riding: Albuquerque 209; Santa Fe 81, 97; Taos 152, 156
hot-air ballooning: 24, 180, 184, 188
Hotel Andaluz: 26, 181, 199
Hotel La Fonda de Taos: 25, 113, 143
Hotel Santa Fe: 27, 84
hot springs: Albuquerque 212-213; Taos 136
House of Eternal Return: 21, 25, 50
hunting: 136, 151
Hyatt Regency Tamaya: 28, 199
Hyde Memorial State Park: 66

I

Il Vicino: 182
Indian Market, Santa Fe: 27, 56
Indian Pueblo Cultural Center: 26, 28, 175-176
Indigenous Fine Art Market: 56
Inn of the Governors: 24, 77
Inn on the Rio: 29, 143
International Folk Art Market: 56
international travelers: 244-245
Internet access: 242-243
Interstate 25 to Santa Fe: 213-214; map 212
Isleta Amphitheater: 184
Isotopes Park: 191
itineraries: 21-30
Izanami: 25, 29, 75

J

Jack's Creek Trail: 81
Jean Cocteau Cinema: 54, 55
Jemez Historic Site: 212
Jemez Mountain Trail: 28, 29, 210-213
Jemez Pueblo: 28, 210
Jemez Springs: 29, 210-213
Jemez Springs Bath House: 211
Jesus Nazareno Cemetery: 123
jewelry: 234-235
Jicarilla Apache Nation: 151
Joseph's: 21, 24, 30, 71
Jucarilla Cultural Center: 151
Juniper Campground: 89, 90

KL

Kasha-Katuwe Tent Rocks National Monument: 26, 29, 214
kayaking/canoeing: Albuquerque 168; Taos 148
Kelly's Brew Pub: 182
Kewa (Santo Domingo): 213-214
KiMo Theatre: 26, 173, 183

Kit Carson Home and Museum: 120-121
Kit Carson Park and Cemetery: 118-119
Kitchen Mesa Trail: 96
La Chiripada: 99
La Cumbre Brewing: 182
La Fonda: 24, 40, 78
Laguna Pueblo: 28, 200
La Junta: 134
La Junta Point: 158
Lake Peak: 63
La Loma Plaza: 116
La Luz Trail: 188
Lamy Railroad & History Museum: 51
language: 230-232
Lannan Foundation Gallery: 47
Lannan Foundation Lecture Series: 55
La Santísima Trinidad Church: 126
Las Trampas: 104
La Tierra Trails: 29, 64
Launchpad: 184
Leave No Trace: 220
Lensic Performing Arts Center: 53
lesbian and gay travelers: 246
Light Among the Ruins: 212
Little Arsenic Trail: 158
Little Beaver Roundup: 151
Long House: 89
Loretto Chapel: 21, 42
Los Alamos: 85-88; map 86
Los Alamos Historical Museum: 85
Los Alamos National Laboratory: 85
Los Alamos Nature Center: 87
Los Ojos: 146
Los Poblanos Historic Inn: 26, 199
Los Ranchos: 176
Love Apple, The: 21, 30, 138
Low Road to Taos: 25, 29, 79, 98-100
luminarias: 233

M

Mabel Dodge Luhan House: 22, 119-120
Madison Winery: 81
Madrid: 23, 26, 207-208
Main Loop Trail: 89
Manby Springs: 136
Marble Pub: 182
Marigold Parade: 185
Martin, George R. R.: 55
Mary & Tito's Café: 30, 195
Matanza: 182
Maxwell Museum of Anthropology: 174
McCauley Warm Springs: 213
Memorial Day Motorcycle Rally: 155
Meow Wolf Art Complex: 50, 55; see also House of
    Eternal Return
Mesa Vista Hall: 174

Mica Mine: 93
Michael's Kitchen: 23, 138
Millicent Rogers Museum: 25, 28, 124
Misión Museum: 91
mobile phones: 242
money: 244-245
Monte Verde Lake: 152
Mother Road Theatre Company: 183
Mountainair: 204
mountain biking: general discussion 28-29;
    Albuquerque 189-190, 209; Santa Fe 64-65, 91;
    Taos 134, 152, 156
Museum Hill: 27, 47-49
Museum of Contemporary Native Arts: 27, 41-42
Museum of Indian Arts & Culture: 27, 42, 47-48
Museum of International Folk Art: 25, 48
Museum of Natural History and Science: 170
Museum of Spanish Colonial Art: 47
museum pass: 36
Music on the Mesa: 129

N

National Hispanic Cultural Center: 177
National Museum of Nuclear Science & History:
    177
Native American heritage: 27-28
New Mexico Brewers Guild: 182
New Mexico Culture Pass: 36
New Mexico Green Chile Cheeseburger Trail: 30, 255
New Mexico History Museum: 37
New Mexico Museum of Art: 21, 25, 40
New Mexico National Guard Museum: 49-50
New Mexico State Capitol: 43
New Mexico State Fair: 184
Nob Hill: 23, 26, 174-175
Norski Trail: 66
Northside: 134
North Valley: 175-177
Nuestra Señora del Rosario de las Truchas Church:
    103

O

Occidental Life Building: 173
Ocho: 158
Ojo Caliente: 93-94
Old Coal Town Museum: 208
Old Fort Marcy Park: 44
"Old Man" State Penitentiary: 209
Old Martina's Hall: 25, 129, 140
Old San Ysidro Church: 176
Old Taos County Courthouse: 113
Old Town Albuquerque: 166-169, 170-171; map 167
Oo-oonah Art Center: 122
open-air bars: 53
Orilla Verde Recreation Area: 99

Orlando's: 21, 30, 137
Otero Canyon: 190
Outpost Performance Space: 184
Outside Bike & Brew: 56

P

packing tips: 242
Padre Antonio Martinez, statue of: 115
Pajarito Mountain: 87
Palace of the Governors: 21, 27, 36-37
Palacio de Marquesa: 25, 144
parks and gardens: Albuquerque 167; Santa Fe 46
Paseo del Bosque: 189
Pecos: 79-82
Pecos National Historical Park: 79-80
Pecos Pueblo: 79
Pecos Wilderness: 79, 81
Pecos Wilderness Area: 105
Pedernal: 96
Peñasco: 104-105
Peñasco Theatre: 105
Pescado Trail: 158
Petroglyph National Monument: 28, 178-179
phones: 242
Picurís Pueblo: 104
Piedras Marcadas Canyon: 178
Pilar: 99-100
Pilar Yacht Club: 99
Pioneer Creek Trail: 156
plane travel: 237
planning tips: 18-21
plants: 220-221
Platinum Chairlift: 156
Plaza Blanca: 95-96
Plaza Café: 24, 69
Plaza de Española: 91
Poeh Museum: 27, 82
Pojoaque: 82
politics: 228
Popejoy Hall: 183
Poshuouinge Ruin Trail: 94
Posi Trail: 93
Pot Creek Cultural Site: 105
pottery: 232-233
pueblo dances: general discussion 130; Albuquerque 185; Santa Fe 83; Taos 131
pueblo etiquette: 243
Pueblo Restaurant: 26, 214
Puyé Cliff Dwellings: 27, 82, 84

QR

Quarai: 204
Quebradas Backcountry Byway: 206
Questa: 157-158
Racecourse: 65, 134

rafting: Santa Fe 65, 99; Taos 125, 134-135, 148-149, 158
rail travel: 237, 238
Railyard: 21, 46-47, 69-72
Railyard Park: 46
Rancho Bonito: 204
Rancho de Chimayó: 30, 102
Rancho de las Golondrinas: 50-51
Randall Davey Audubon Center & Sanctuary: 62
Raven's Ridge: 63
Red Dot Trail: 87
Red River: 155-157
Red River Folk Festival: 155-156
Red River Nature Trail: 156
Red River Ski & Summer Area: 156
religion: 230
Rim Road: 126-127
Rim Vista Trail: 97
Rinconada Canyon: 178
Rio Chama: 65
Rio en Medio Trail: 29, 63
Rio Grande: 65
Rio Grande del Norte National Monument: 158
Rio Grande Gorge: 21, 29, 124-125, 134-135
Rio Grande Gorge Visitors Center: 99
Rio Grande Heritage Farm: 167
Rio Grande Nature Center: 189
Rio Grande Nature Center State Park: 176, 188
Rio Grande Pool: 190
Road to Chama: 146, 148-149
Rockin' 3M Chuckwagon Amphitheater: 156
Route 66: 176
Roy E. Disney Center for Performing Arts: 177, 183
Ruth Hall Museum of Paleontology: 97

S

safety: 246-247
Salinas Pueblo Missions National Monument: 28, 203-205
Salinas Pueblo Missions Visitors Center: 204
San Antonio Church: 158
Sandia Crest Visitor Center: 188
Sandia Foothills Trails: 190
Sandia Mountains: 62
Sandia Peak: 188, 189
Sandia Peak Ski Area: 190
Sandia Peak Tramway: 23, 177-178
San Diego Canyon: 210
San Felipe de Neri Church: 171
San Francisco de Asis Church: 23, 25, 121-122
San Geronimo Church: 123-124
San Ildefonso Pueblo: 27, 40, 82
San José de Gracia Church: 104
San José Mission Church: 200
San Lorenzo de Picurís Church: 104
San Miguel Chapel: 42-43

Santa Clara: 82, 84
Santa Cruz de la Cañada Church: 92
Santa Fe: 21, 29, 31-107; maps 34, 38-39, 45, 80
Santa Fe Bite: 30, 69
Santa Fe Botanical Garden: 49
Santa Fe Brewing Company: 52
Santa Fe Canyon Preserve: 25, 61-62
Santa Fe Century: 65
Santa Fe Chamber Music Festival: 54
Santa Fe Children's Museum: 50, 60
Santa Fe Climbing Center: 65
Santa Fe Fuego (baseball): 67
Santa Fe Indian Market: 27, 56
Santa Fe Opera: 54
Santa Fe Plaza: 36-37
Santa Fe Pro Musica: 54
Santa Fe Rail Trail: 29, 64
Santa Fe Wine and Chile Festival: 58
Santo Domingo: 213-214
Santo Domingo Trading Post: 214
Santo Niño de Atocha: 103
Santuario de Chimayó: 101
Santuario de Guadalupe: 46
scenic drives: general discussion 62; Albuquerque
    176-177, 306; Santa Fe 81; Taos 126
Second Street Brewery: 52
Secreto Lounge: 24, 53
senior travelers: 245
Shed, The: 21, 68
Sipapu: 105
SITE Santa Fe: 46-47
Ski Santa Fe: 66
Sky City (Acoma Pueblo): 28, 200, 202-203
Sky City Cultural Center and Haak'u Museum: 202
SMU in Taos: 129
Soda Dam: 212
Soldiers' Monument: 36
South Boundary Trail: 152
Southwest cuisine: 30, 239-241
Southwest Seminars Series: 55
Spanish Market: 56
spas: Albuquerque 190-191; Santa Fe 66-67
spectator sports: Albuquerque 191; Santa Fe 67
Spence Hot Springs: 213
Spring Harvest Festival: 146
Spring Loop Trail: 203
Stagecoach Foundation: 55
stand-up paddleboarding: 134, 152
state parks: Albuquerque 176, 188, 209; Santa Fe
    66, 81; Taos 146, 148, 154, 155
Stone Lake: 151
Storyteller, The: 129
Sugar's: 30, 99
Sun Mountain: 62-63
Sunshine Theater: 184

Taos: 21, 29, 108-160; maps 111, 114, 116, 147
Taos Art Museum at Fechin House: 22, 25, 118
Taos Box: 24, 65, 134
Taos Center for the Arts: 129
Taos Environmental Film Festival: 130
Taos Fall Arts Festival: 130
Taos Inn: 21, 117, 121
Taos Mesa Brewing: 29, 128
Taos Plaza: 113, 115-121; map 116
Taos Pueblo: 21, 25, 28, 122-124
Taos Pueblo Powwow: 129
Taos Shortz Film Fest: 130
Taos Ski Valley: 24, 25, 127, 133, 134, 135, 141-142,
    144-145
Taos treelighting ceremony: 130
Taos Wool Festival: 130
Telephone Museum: 174
telephones: 242
10K Trail: 190
Ten Thousand Waves: 25, 29, 66-67
Tesuque: 65, 82
Tesuque Glassworks: 22, 58
textiles: 233-234
Tia Sophia's: 21, 30, 69
Tierra Amarilla: 146, 148
Tijeras: 203
time zone: 243
Tingley Beach: 168
Tinkertown Museum: 23, 26, 206-207
tinwork: 235
tipping: 244-245
Tiwa Kitchen: 28, 140
tourist information: 242
Tractor Brewing: 182
train travel: 237, 238
transportation: 237-238
Tres Piedras: 146
Tricklock: 182
Truchas: 102-104
Tsankawi: 89
Turquoise Museum: 171
Turquoise Trail: 23, 24, 206-210; map 207
Tyuonyi: 89

UV

University Art Museum: 174
University of New Mexico: 174; map 175
UNM Lobos sports: 191
U.S. Highway 64: 124-126, 146, 148-149
Valle Grande Contact Station: 90
Valles Caldera National Preserve: 24, 29, 65, 90-
    91, 210
Valle Valdez: 126
Vietnam Veterans Memorial State Park: 154

Villanueva: 81
Vinaigrette: 30, 71
Violet Crown: 25, 53, 54
visas: 244
Vista Verde Trail: 99
Vivác: 99
Volcanoes Day Use Area: 178
volunteering: 244
Vortex Theatre: 182

WXYZ
Walatowa Visitor Center: 28, 210
waterfalls: Albuquerque 212; Santa Fe 63; Taos 133
water sports: Albuquerque 190; Santa Fe 67, 96, 99-100, see also specific activity
weather: 218-219
West Rim Trail: 29, 125, 134
Wheeler Peak Summit Trail: 133

Wheels Museum: 174
Wheelwright Museum of the American Indian: 27, 48-49
White Rock Rim Trail: 87
wildlife refuge: 205-206
wildlife/wildlife-watching: general discussion 221-224; Santa Fe 90; Taos 150, 158
Wild Rivers Recreation Area: 158
Williams Lake: 25, 133
wine/wineries: general discussion 241; Albuquerque 180-181; Santa Fe 58, 81, 99
Winsor Trail: 64
winter sports: Albuquerque 190; Santa Fe 66, 91; Taos 135-136, 156
woodwork: 235
Zimmerman Library: 174
zoo: 167
Zuly's: 21, 99

List of Maps

Front Map
Santa Fe, Taos & Albuquerque: 2–3

Discover Santa Fe, Taos & Albuquerque
chapter divisions map: 19

Santa Fe
Santa Fe: 34
Downtown Santa Fe: 38–39
Canyon Road and the Eastside: 45
Outside Santa Fe: 80
Los Alamos: 86
Española: 92

Taos
Taos Area: 111
Taos: 114
Taos Plaza: 116
Greater Taos: 147
The Enchanted Circle: 153

Albuquerque
Albuquerque: 164
Old Town Albuquerque: 167
Downtown Albuquerque: 172
University Area: 175
Outside Albuquerque: 201
The Turquoise Trail: 207
The Interstate to Santa Fe: 212

Photo Credits

Wander through the
Southwest and Texas
with Moon Travel Guides!

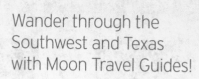

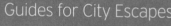

Guides for City Escapes

Trips South of the Border

MOON NATIONAL PARKS

ACADIA NATIONAL PARK

ARCHES & CANYONLANDS NATIONAL PARKS

BANFF NATIONAL PARK

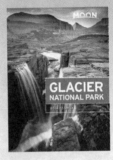

DEATH VALLEY NATIONAL PARK

GLACIER NATIONAL PARK

GRAND CANYON

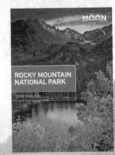

GREAT SMOKY MOUNTAINS NATIONAL PARK

MOUNT RUSHMORE & THE BLACK HILLS

ROCKY MOUNTAIN NATIONAL PARK

In these books:

- Full coverage of gateway cities and towns
- Itineraries from one day to multiple weeks
- Advice on where to stay (or camp) in and around the parks

Craft a personalized journey through the top National Parks in the U.S. and Canada with Moon Travel Guides.

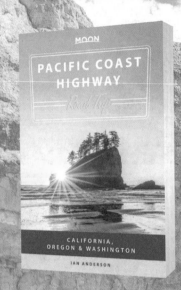

Road Trip USA

Criss-cross the country on America's classic two-lane highways with the newest edition of *Road Trip USA!*

Packed with over 125 detailed driving maps (covering more than 35,000 miles), colorful photos and illustrations of America both then and now, and mile-by-mile highlights

Advice on where to
sleep, eat, and explore

Detailed driving
directions including
mileage and
drive times

Itineraries for a
range of timelines

*Moon Travel Guides
are available from your
favorite bookseller.*

MOON
PACIFIC
NORTHWEST
Road Trip

SEATTLE, VANCOUVER, VICTORIA,
THE OLYMPIC PENINSULA, PORTLAND,
THE OREGON COAST & MOUNT RAINIER

ALLISON WILLIAMS

MOON
ROUTE 66
Road Trip

CANDACY TAYLOR

MOON
SOUTHWEST
Road Trip

LAS VEGAS, ZION & BRYCE, MONUMENT VALLEY,
SANTA FE & TAOS, AND THE GRAND CANYON

TIM HULL

MOON
VANCOUVER &
CANADIAN ROCKIES
Road Trip

VICTORIA, BANFF, JASPER, CALGARY,
THE OKANAGAN, WHISTLER &
THE SEA-TO-SKY HIGHWAY

CAROLYN B. HELLER

Join our travel community!
Share your adventures using **#travelwithmoon**

MOON.COM
@MOONGUIDES

MAP SYMBOLS

≋≋≋	Expressway	○	City/Town	✈	Airport	⚓	Golf Course
≋≋	Primary Road	◉	State Capital	✕	Airfield	🅿	Parking Area
≋	Secondary Road	⊛	National Capital	▲	Mountain	▰	Archaeological Site
‒ ‒ ‒	Unpaved Road	★	Point of Interest	✛	Unique Natural Feature	⛽	Church
———	Feature Trail	•	Accommodation				Gas Station
- - - -	Other Trail	▼	Restaurant/Bar	⟲	Waterfall	◯	Glacier
··········	Ferry	■	Other Location	▲	Park	▨	Mangrove
≋≋	Pedestrian Walkway			🚻	Trailhead	▨	Reef
▮▮▮▮	Stairs	Λ	Campground	⛷	Skiing Area	▭	Swamp

CONVERSION TABLES

$^\circ C = (^\circ F - 32) / 1.8$
$^\circ F = (^\circ C \times 1.8) + 32$
1 inch = 2.54 centimeters (cm)
1 foot = 0.304 meters (m)
1 yard = 0.914 meters
1 mile = 1.6093 kilometers (km)
1 km = 0.6214 miles
1 fathom = 1.8288 m
1 chain = 20.1168 m
1 furlong = 201.168 m
1 acre = 0.4047 hectares
1 sq km = 100 hectares
1 sq mile = 2.59 square km
1 ounce = 28.35 grams
1 pound = 0.4536 kilograms
1 short ton = 0.90718 metric ton
1 short ton = 2,000 pounds
1 long ton = 1.016 metric tons
1 long ton = 2,240 pounds
1 metric ton = 1,000 kilograms
1 quart = 0.94635 liters
1 US gallon = 3.7854 liters
1 Imperial gallon = 4.5459 liters
1 nautical mile = 1.852 km

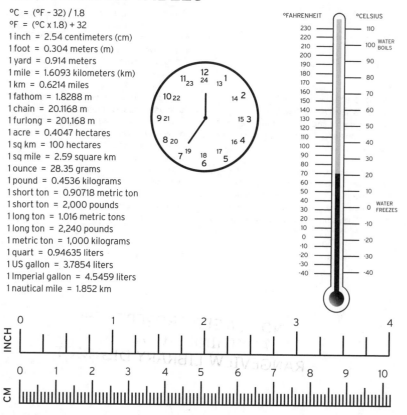

MOON SANTA FE, TAOS & ALBUQUERQUE

Avalon Travel
Hachette Book Group
1700 Fourth Street
Berkeley, CA 94710, USA
www.moon.com

Editor and Series Manager: Kathryn Ettinger
Copy Editor: Rosemarie Leenerts
Graphics Coordinator: Suzanne Albertson
Production Coordinator: Suzanne Albertson
Cover Design: Faceout Studios, Charles Brock
Interior Design: Domini Dragoone
Moon Logo: Tim McGrath
Map Editor: Kat Bennett
Cartographers: Brian Shotwell, Stephanie Poulain, Larissa Gatt
Indexer: Greg Jewett

ISBN-13: 978-1-63121-889-7

Printing History
1st Edition — 2006
5th Edition — June 2018
5 4 3 2 1

Front cover photo: traditional *farolitos* lighting up adobe structures in Santa Fe © Julien McRoberts / Danita Delimont / Alamy
Back cover photo: Albuquerque International Balloon Fiesta © Steven Horak

Printed in Canada by Friesens

Avalon Travel is a division of Hachette Book Group, Inc. Moon and the Moon logo are trademarks of Hachette Book Group, Inc. All other marks and logos depicted are the property of the original owners.